MECHANICS' INSTITUTE
ᛚ MECHANICS' ᛌ
MERCANTILE LIBRARY

PREACHERS OF HATE

ALSO BY **KENNETH R. TIMMERMAN**

SHAKEDOWN
Exposing the Real Jesse Jackson

SELLING OUT AMERICA
The American Spectator Investigations

THE DEATH LOBBY
How the West Armed Iraq

WEAPONS OF MASS DESTRUCTION
The Cases of Iran, Syria & Libya

POISON GAS CONNECTION
*Western Suppliers of Unconventional Weapons
and Technologies to Iraq and Libya*

ISLAM AND THE WAR ON AMERICA

PREACHERS OF
HATE

KENNETH R. TIMMERMAN

CROWN
FORUM
NEW YORK

Published by Crown Forum, New York, New York.
Member of the Crown Publishing Group, a division of Random House, Inc.
www.crownpublishing.com

CROWN FORUM and the Crown Forum colophon are registered trademarks of
Random House, Inc.

Printed in the United States of America

Design by Barbara Sturman

Library of Congress Cataloging-in-Publication Data
   Timmerman, Kenneth R.
     Preachers of hate : Islam and the war on America / Kenneth R. Timmerman.—
1st ed.
     Includes bibliographical references and index.
     1. Arab-Israeli conflict. 2. Religion and politics—Middle East. I. Title.
DS119.7.T53 2003
956.9405'4—dc21   2003011455

ISBN 1-4000-4901-6

10 9 8 7 6 5 4 3 2 1

First Edition

For Ayatollah Mehdi Rouhani (1932–2000),

whose vision of tolerance is sorely needed today.

CONTENTS

For happily the Government of the United States, which gives to bigotry no sanction, to persecution no assistance, requires only that they who live under its protection, should demean themselves as good citizens. . . . May the Children of the Stock of Abraham, who dwell in this land, continue to merit and enjoy the good will of the other Inhabitants; while every one shall sit under his own vine and fig tree, and there shall be none to make him afraid.

GEORGE WASHINGTON
"Letter to the Jews of Newport, Rhode Island," 1790

PREACHERS OF HATE

INTRODUCTION

WHY THE "NEW" ANTI-SEMITISM IS
AN ATTACK ON AMERICA

A few years ago, Rabbi Abraham Cooper of
the Simon Wiesenthal Center in Los Angeles asked me to interview radical
Islamic clerics during a reporting trip I was making through Syria, Jordan,
and Gaza. He suggested I ask them about *The Protocols of the Elders of
Zion,* a notorious anti-Semitic forgery invented by the intelligence service
of the Russian czar in 1895, and whether they believed that Jews had a plan
to conquer the world, as it asserted. I thought he was joking. "Just ask the
question," Rabbi Cooper insisted. "See what they say."

The results, which I published in a monograph with the Simon Wiesenthal Center, were stunning.[1] Not only did every one of the people I asked
believe in the anti-Semitic lies put forward in the *Protocols;* some offered
to pull out their own copy just to show me that it was real. None questioned the authenticity of the *Protocols,* which claimed to be the actual

minutes of conspiratorial meetings of Jewish leaders. Most offered up their own anecdotes as proof that "world Jewry" had a plot to dominate the world and destroy Islam.

Americans will be stunned to discover the depth and extent of anti-Semitic hatred in today's Middle East and that Arab leaders from Saudi Arabia to Egypt are not just encouraging it, but spending a great deal of money to spread the kinds of lies inherent in the *Protocols* and other anti-Semitic tracts, even as they declare their support for peace in the Middle East. They will be even more shocked to learn that anti-Semitic attacks are reemerging in Europe less than sixty years after the Holocaust and that hatred of the Jews is spreading with incredible speed on college campuses and among left-wing politicians and intellectuals in America, a land that provided one of the first sanctuaries from oppression to European Jews.

It is vitally important that Americans of all backgrounds understand that much of today's anti-Semitism, while aimed at Jews, stems from a belief system that equally rejects America and indeed Western civilization as a whole. When Jews are killed in Jerusalem, or synagogues are attacked in Britain and France, Americans in New York, Philadelphia, and Chicago become more vulnerable. When Arab leaders invent new versions of the old blood libels, blaming the Israeli Mossad for the September 11 attacks and claiming that Jewish law requires that Passover matzah be made from the blood of gentile children, the Arab street sees more justifications for attacking America. Jews are like the canary that miners take down into the pits to warn them when they are about to die. Jews get attacked first, when the enemies of America can't attack Americans. But make no mistake: we're next. It begins with the Jews, but it never ends with the Jews.

Just as the Jews throughout history, Americans see themselves as "special," a chosen people, with a mission for the world. Just as the Jews, America believes it embodies eternal values of absolute good that we seek to spread to others. The same cultural, religious, and national identity that has maintained the Jews as a separate people for thousands of years is now being championed by America as the world moves hesitantly toward global values and global rules. We use different terms—the rule of law, not Torah; freedom, not God; republic, not nation—but the absolute and transcendent nature of the concepts underpinning the American way of life are obvious and present a constant challenge to other peoples with competing (and less successful) ideologies.[2] If you hate the Jews, you must also hate America. Such is the simple logic of the anti-Semite when facing a complex world. Such, increasingly, is the logic of the Middle East. It is a message that is reinforced day in and day out by the official Arab media.

In an infamous fatwa issued in February 1998, Osama bin Laden called on Muslims to kill Christians and Jews throughout the world—not just military personnel, but civilians—because we have seized and occupied Arab land. Our treachery, bin Laden claims, started with the Christian conquest of Andalusia from the Muslim caliphs in the thirteenth century! On state-sponsored Al-Jazeera television, portrayed complacently as the "CNN of the Arab world" by mainstream media organizations in the United States and Europe, bin Laden and Muslim preachers who openly sympathize with him spread their message to the Arab masses and intellectual elites. Murdered Americans are not victims but oppressors who are the legitimate targets of holy war, they argue. Those who die while killing us are blessed of Allah. For as long as they are physically capable, bin Laden and his followers will strike at America. To their mind, September 11 was just an opening act.

Today's hatred of America and of Western values is an ancient story that is little different from the virus that has erupted periodically into anti-Semitic pogroms in Europe and resulted in the Holocaust. In one sense, the terrorists and their enablers in government and in the mosque are looking for someone to blame, a scapegoat. The Arab world shines for its lack of democracy, its political systems based on arbitrary rule, and the abject corruption of its leaders. Many young Arabs see nothing in their societies that appeals to their sense of pride other than the dreams of a glorious past. Increasingly, that past is being rewritten by the leaders and their proxies to openly anti-Semitic themes—including revisionist interpretations of the Koran and allegations of Jewish plots—to focus the attention of their people elsewhere than on their own failure. Arab leaders have failed to transform their fabulous oil wealth into real power or build any lasting monument to civilization, but when they look around to ascribe blame, they can find only the Jews.

But there is much more at the heart of this than just scapegoating. If the Muslim world were just seeking a scapegoat, then economic development and education should be sufficient to conquer hate. Yet in many

Arab societies and in Iran, it was precisely when they were awash in petrodollars and their societies yearning Westward that the anti-American and anti-Jewish virus erupted in full force. It was precisely to prevent that Westward yearning (for which the Iranians invented a special term—*gharb-azadeghi,* meaning "besotted by the West")[3] that Ayatollah Khomeini and his acolytes exhorted young Iranians to hate, identifying America as the "Great Satan" and Israel as the "Little Satan." Similarly, to prevent young Saudis, who had grown up spoiled on oil from turning Westward, the Saudi government poured billions of dollars into the anti-Soviet crusade in Afghanistan in the 1980s and shipped radical mullahs to Pakistan, where they built a vast network of religious schools, steeped in anti-Semitic beliefs, that have spawned the anti-American, anti-Western jihadis who are faithful to bin Laden and his cause.

Scapegoating, ignorance, underdevelopment, poverty: all have been used as excuses for the visceral hatred of Jews and America now rampant throughout the Arab and Muslim world. Yet just as with Nazi Germany, these explanations fall wide of the mark. "It was not because of racism that Nazis hated Jews but because of their hatred of Jews that the Nazis utilized racist arguments. The Jew-hatred came first. . . . It was, like all other forms of anti-Semitism, hatred of the challenges posed by Jews and Jewish values."[4] With today's anti-Semites and anti-American fanatics, nothing has changed. The hatred and the rejection of others come first; the rationale can always be invented later.

In November 1997 I made one of my periodic trips to Gaza. It had already been four years since the signing of the Oslo Accords, which granted Palestinian autonomy and brought Yasser Arafat and his PLO clique to Gaza to assume control; yet during that time little had changed. Despite hundreds of millions of dollars in foreign aid and international development assistance, the city's streets still turned into rivers of mud whenever it rained, the beachfront was awash with sewage and trash, and the only new buildings that had gone up were government offices and villas owned by Palestinian Authority (PA) officials. When I asked the owner of the hotel where I was staying why no one had ever thought to clean up the beach, he said, "There is no money. The PA is broke. We can do nothing because of the Israeli occupation." When I pointed out that the occupation had ended in Gaza four years ago he just kept repeating that their lives were a misery because of the Jews.

† † †

Preachers of Hate is not intended to replace the numerous works of scholarship or analysis on anti-Semitism; it is a layman's guide to the wave of anti-Jewish and anti-American hatred sweeping across the Arab world, Europe, and even America. But this book is also a journey of discovery by a reporter who thought he knew the Middle East well, as he comes to grips with hatred and bigotry masquerading as the will of God. I felt it was essential to include my own impressions of the Arabs, Iranians, and Europeans I encountered and interviewed, to give a personal flavor to what otherwise could appear as a mind-numbing litany of racism, irrationality, and hate. From afar, the demented rhetoric that spews from the anti-Semitic mind appears almost surrealistic. Sixty years after the Holocaust, such thinking is inconceivable to most of us in the West. But from up close, where the intended victims are just around the corner, the words of many of the people quoted in this book are nothing less than an incitation to murder. *Preachers of Hate* is aimed at helping Americans to understand why they, too, have become targets of hate, just as Jews have been for centuries. This is the very essence of the war on terror.

September 11 should have shown us that we can no longer ignore the preachers of hate and their rhetoric, nor can we continue to make excuses for their behavior based on supposed "cultural differences," "oppression," or "hopelessness." We are not faced with a social problem, which liberal policies and public money can solve; we are facing dedicated murderers. If we are to craft serious and effective policies to combat them, we must begin by recognizing the uncompromising depths of their hatred. The first step is to open our eyes, open our ears, and open our minds to understand what they are saying about us and about themselves. We have not a moment to lose.

"THE JEWS DID IT!" 1

Foreigners often call us naive, because as Americans we are brought up to revere the truth. Obvious falsehoods seem to us . . . well, obvious falsehoods. That is why it is going to be difficult for many readers in America to comprehend the lies that are told and believed around the world about America and about the Jews. You want to shake your head in disbelief, just as I did when Rabbi Abraham Cooper suggested that I ask Arab Muslim clerics about *The Protocols of the Elders of Zion*. Is it truly possible that educated individuals, people who have access to the international media, television, and the Internet can believe such outright lies? If they can, what will ever convince them to recognize the truth when they see it?

Within days of September 11 a myth was born that spread so quickly, and tapped sources of belief so deeply rooted into the consciousness of ordinary citizens, that today it has become an established fact throughout the Muslim world. There were no Arabs on board the four aircraft that were hijacked and crashed as weapons, killing more than three thousand people on September 11. Nor was Osama bin Laden and his al-Qaeda network even remotely involved. The entire attack was planned, orchestrated, and carried out by the Jews as part of their ongoing conspiracy to dominate the world.

More than one year later, Egyptian strategist Abdel Moneim Said, the head of Egypt's leading think tank, marveled at the "complete state of denial" that had gripped the Arab world in the face of massive and compelling evidence about the perpetrators of September 11. The flights of fancy, the accusations against the Jews, were "indicative . . . of faces that cannot look themselves in the mirror, of minds that are aloof to logic, of hearts incapable of confronting the facts," he wrote. "But this is not all that 11 September exposed."[1]

† † †

In the West Bank town of Nablus, on September 11, 2001, several thousand people poured into the streets shortly after news of the attacks on America was broadcast on Palestinian state radio. "Demonstrators distributed candy in a traditional gesture of celebration," Associated Press reporter Mohammed Daraghmeh noted.

Daraghmeh captured a poignant moment in what appeared to be a spontaneous outpouring of anti-American hate. "Nawal Abdel Fatah, 48, wearing a long, black dress, threw sweets in the air, saying she was happy because 'America is the head of the snake, America always stands by Israel in its war against us.' Her daughter Maysoon, 22, said she hoped the next attack would be launched against Tel Aviv."[2]

Smaller demonstrations took place later that afternoon and early evening in the Arab quarters of Jerusalem, where young children were led in chanting anti-American slogans by adults. "Some drivers passing the scene honked their horns and flashed victory signs from their windows."[3] At the Ein el-Hilweh refugee camp in the southern Lebanese port city of Sidon, an Associated Press photographer snapped pictures of Palestine Liberation Organization (PLO) fighters celebrating by firing assault rifles into the air when news of the attacks on America was broadcast.[4]

In one sense, the attacks were "not good because innocent people suffered," said Ahmed Ali, forty, a Palestinian cook who worked in a restaurant in East Jerusalem. "But it's good because America is the only country that supports the Israeli oppression. They are right now suffering as we are suffering. . . . I tell you on behalf of the Palestinian people that we are really happy at what happened."[5]

Arabs living in the West expressed similar "comprehension" of the attacks and the motives of the attackers. In the Washington, D.C., suburb of Fairfax, Virginia, public school officials ordered high school students to return home by noontime on the day of the attacks. "They closed the schools not out of fear of a terrorist attack, but because Muslim students were shouting for joy," said David Keene, president of the American Conservative Union. Keene told the story at a highly charged session of conservative activist Grover Norquist's weekly "coalitions" meeting in Washington the next day.[6] Norquist, whose Islamic Institute had hired as executive director a former lobbyist for the pro-Hamas American Muslim Council (AMC), sat stony faced as friends of Barbara Olson, the wife of U.S. solicitor general Ted Olson, told the story of Barbara's final moments on board American Airlines Flight 77 before terrorist Hani Hanjour crashed it into the Pentagon. "We sympathize with you, but you've got to understand," pleaded one of Norquist's associates from the Islamic Institute, in an effort to explain why some American Muslim groups weren't cooperating with the FBI. "Our people are afraid of getting scapegoated."

"No, *you've* got to understand," thundered the normally soft-spoken Keene. "Thousands of Americans have just been murdered, and 'your people' were cheering when they heard the news."

Rasha Abu Ramadan, an executive member of the Palestinian Student Committee at the University of Ottawa told a reporter that Palestinians in Canada welcomed the attacks because it helped make people realize what Palestinians were suffering at the hands of the Israelis. "So many of our children die every day and it is the [United] States, it is Israel, that are the ones implementing all these bombings and all these things that happen to us," she said."[7] In Cairo, grocery store owner Izzat Hassan Ali told a reporter he felt pleasure at the thought of Americans dying. "As they did to other people, [it] is happening to them now. They hit innocent people in Afghanistan and Iraq, and now it backfired on them."[8]

State-controlled television in Saddam Hussein's Iraq played a patriotic song, "Down with America!," as it broadcast footage of the collapse of the World Trade Center (WTC) towers.[9] The Iraqi dictator gloated that

America deserved what it got. "Those who do not want to reap evil should not sow evil," he said. The question now, he added, was whether the United States "would deliver itself and the world from the evils and terrorist crimes of its rulers against the world, or whether those rulers who have become a dummy in the hands of international Zionism . . . will divert the feelings of the Americans into new terrorist designs against the world that satiate the Jewish Zionist greed for evil money and innocent blood."[10]

In Gaza, Palestinian leader Yasser Arafat viewed television footage of the attacks—and of the outpouring of joy on the Palestinian streets—with trepidation. "We are completely shocked. It's unbelievable," he said. "We completely condemn this very dangerous attack, and I convey my condolences to the American people, to the American president, and to the American administration, not only in my name but on behalf of the Palestinian people."[11] Expressions of condolence flooded in from leaders throughout the Arab World who universally condemned the bombings, while invariably adding a qualifying "but . . .". The "but" most frequently referred to the sufferings of the Palestinian people at the hands of "the Jews" and America's role in supporting Israel.

Leaders of the Islamic Republic of Iran were worried—just as Arafat was—that the United States would connect them to the terrorist attacks and strike in retaliation. Within three hours of the attacks, a top Iranian official was on the phone with a relative in Los Angeles, seeking to send his wife and children to what he called a "safe haven" in the United States. He feared the attacks—and the inevitable American response—would plunge Iran into war.

The official has long commanded Iranian military forces and is a member of the innermost circle of power in Tehran. I learned of his near panic from the relative, who spoke with me several times that afternoon and the next day, asking me what he should do. "More attacks will come," the official warned his relative. "Watch out for your own safety."[12]

In Iran at 9 A.M. Pacific time on September 11, a television station had just reported that a Japanese group with ties to Osama bin Laden was responsible for the attacks, the official said. He was curious if the report had been picked up in the United States. The relative switched on his television but couldn't find it. I tracked the report the next day, with the help of a U.S. official who was monitoring foreign coverage of the attacks. It had aired on Al-Manar television in Lebanon at 9:20 A.M. Pacific time, twenty minutes *after* the official called his relative in California.[13]

Al-Manar TV is owned and operated by Lebanon's Hezbollah Party, a group identified on the State Department's "List of State-Sponsored Terrorist Groups" as financed by the government of the Islamic Republic of Iran. Al-Manar was interviewing Fakhri Qa'war, chief editor of the Jordanian *Al-Wahda* newspaper, who said he had received a call at his office from someone speaking in Arabic "with a foreign accent" claiming responsibility for the attacks in the name of the Japanese Red Army. "He said that the [Red] army is avenging the Japanese people, who were attacked by a nuclear bomb in Nagasaki and Hiroshima 56 years ago."[14]

The Japanese "Red Army" story was clearly a hoax. But the fact that a top Iranian government official quoted the report *before* it actually aired and provided a detail—a suspected tie between the Japanese terrorist group and Osama bin Laden—that did not appear in the report as it was broadcast, suggests it also may have been a plant. This crude, initial attempt to divert attention from the true identity of the September 11 hijackers was repeated once more—in the Syrian government daily *Teshreen* two days later[15]—but vanished as a more vicious conspiracy theory swept across the region.[16]

†††

On September 12, 2001, once television footage of celebrating Palestinians was broadcast around the world, Palestinian leader Yasser Arafat realized he needed to act more forcefully to distance himself from the attackers, at least in the eyes of the American media. After symbolically giving blood, which he said was intended for American victims, he angrily rejected suggestions that Palestinians had rejoiced over the attacks. "For your information," Arafat told *The New York Times,* "it is clear and obvious that it was less than 10 children in East Jerusalem, and we punished them." The *Times* reporter then commented: "It was unclear how this assertion could be squared with photographs suggesting that there were more people."[17]

Arafat went on to suggest that the "Israelis were taking advantage of the world's focus on the horror in the United States, and perhaps exploiting its anger over Tuesday's images, to tighten restrictions on Palestinians and to assault the West Bank town of Jenin, where seven Palestinians were killed today."[18]

Arafat's hint that Israel was exploiting September 11 was soon picked up and amplified throughout the Muslim Middle East. Within twenty-four hours of the attacks, as information on lead hijacker Mohammed Atta and his accomplices began to appear in the U.S. press,[19] a new myth was born in the Muslim world. It began on the Internet and was repeated within hours on radio, television, and newspapers from Islamabad to Cairo: September 11 was a plot planned and carried out by the Jews!

The story spread like a wildfire. First to allege the "Jewish conspiracy" was Dr. Anwar Ul Haque, a self-styled Koranic scholar who claimed in an article distributed by the Islamic News and Information Network that the "attacks on New York and Washington are carried out by Mossad (Israeli secret agency) with full backing of Zionist elements in the FBI and CIA."[20] In the same breath, Haque reminded readers "that President Clinton (whose mother and wife were most probably of Zionist lineage) had appointed an Israeli agent as USA ambassador to Israel!"[21]

Dr. Haque is not some anonymous Internet warrior to be easily written off, but a prominent Pakistani surgeon who is chief pathologist at the Pakistan government's prestigious Institute of Medical Sciences.[22] His point of view is not that of an extremist, but is shared by millions of Muslims who consider themselves to be part of the Muslim mainstream. The main motive behind the attacks, he argued, was "to defame Muslims and Islam so that Americans and Europeans may not enter in the folds of Islam. . . ."[23]

"If the terrorists were Arabs or Palestinians, then they would have taken the planes to Israel and dropped it [*sic*] at the head of the mass killer Sharon," Dr. Haque explained matter-of-factly.[24] His views were never challenged in the media of any Muslim country, including his native Pakistan.[25]

When I caught up with him nearly nine months later, Dr. Haque confirmed that he had written the September 12, 2001, article and expanded on his beliefs that Israel and the Mossad were behind the attacks. "[The]

World Trade Center was twice attacked by the Zionists," he told me. In 1993, he said, "an Israeli agent" had tricked a "poor Palestinian" named Salameh, the driver of the Ryder truck that exploded in the parking garage beneath the World Trade Center. The aim was to spread the blame for the attack "through Salameh to Islam and Muslims. . . . Later on, on 11th September, WTC was attacked again. . . . At least two Israeli secret agencies were directly involved in this attack."[26]

Then he summarized many of the beliefs that have now become an integral part of the September 11 myth circulating in the Muslim world:

"The drama of 11th September included remote control of the planes and demolishing the buildings through previously implanted dynamites in it. Simple hitting of the building by a plane would have not melted the strong steel frame and skeleton of the buildings. This time hardly any Jew was killed despite the fact that the Jews owned many big offices in the building. So far two Israelis (not necessary Jews) are known to have died in the entire game: one in the WTC and one in [the] plane. Mr. Bush's claim that 129 Israelis died turned out to be a white lie."[27]

Dr. Haque's allegations were only the beginning. The Simon Wiesenthal Center in Los Angeles and the Middle East Media Research Institute (MEMRI) in Washington, D.C., have compiled several detailed accounts of Arab and Persian media reporting on September 11, which show clearly that his beliefs are not isolated, unusual, or the product of one group or even one country. Indeed, a rash of comments, "investigations," and "revelations" soon followed in the official media from Cairo to Tehran, claiming Mossad had carried out the September 11 attacks.[28]

To virtually all these commentators it was clear that Mossad was seeking to "incite the American administration" against the Islamic world by falsely claiming that Arabs had carried out the attacks. "Using these charges, they want to deflect the suspicion that Mossad elements and their collaborators carried out such crimes in order to spoil relations between Muslims/Arabs and America," wrote the editor in chief of the Egyptian government daily *Al-Akhbar,* one of the most prestigious newspapers in the Arab world.[29] The official Palestinian Authority Web site spread a similar warning, noting that Mossad agents "posing as 'Muslim leaders' were spreading disinformation about Islam and praising the terrorist acts in the U.S."[30] As details from the criminal investigation began appearing in the press, denials of Arab involvement became increasingly strident. On September 13, the Jordanian government daily *Al-Dostour* spelled out the allegations that the attack on America was in reality a vile Jewish plot, and this in a country reputed to be the most moderate and pro-Western in the Arab world.

Columnist Ahmad al-Musallah proclaimed: "What happened is the work of Jewish-Israeli-American Zionism, and the act of the large Zionist Jewish mind controlling the world economically, politically, and through the media."[31] His fellow columnist Rakan al-Majali used the traditional reverse logic of the Arab street, arguing that he who allegedly "benefitted" from the crime must therefore be the criminal. "It is obvious that Israel is the one to gain greatly from this bloody, loathsome, and terrible terror operation, and it seeks to gain further by accusing the Arabs and Muslims of carrying it out. . . . Only Israel does not fear that the Jews will be discovered to be behind this operation—who inside or outside the U.S. would dare to accuse them, as any harm to them means talk of a new Holocaust? They, more than anyone, are capable of hiding a crime they carry out, and they can be certain that no one will ask them what they have done."[32] In another Jordanian government daily, columnist Jihad Jbara arrived at the same miraculous conclusion: "I personally eliminate the possibility that Arab and Islamic organizations stood behind these acts. . . . Why [not assume] that Zionist organizations perpetrated it, so that Israel could destroy the Al-Aqsa Mosque while the world was preoccupied with what happened in America . . . ?"[33]

Similar conspiracy theories erupted elsewhere. The English-language *Tehran Times,* which is published by the Iranian government, also used reverse logic to ascribe motive to Israel. "The only ones to benefit from any action that would serve to discredit and demonize the Islamic movement are the Zionists and certain anti-Islamic elements in the West," the paper stated.[34] In more flamboyant style, as was his manner, Lebanese Druze leader Walid Jumblatt told Palestinian Authority daily *Al-Ayyam* that September 11 "was a large intelligence operation, behind which might be the Mossad and American intelligence, with the aim of [bringing about] a new war in the region so as to impoverish and conquer it."[35] None of these newspapers is published by a fringe group or by radical

Islamic fundamentalists. They are all government organs, officially sanctioned and vetted, that rarely stray from the official government line in their own countries.

So far, no "facts" had emerged to buttress the suspicion that Israel was behind September 11. But anti-Semitism is a potent toxin. As more details about the identity and final movements of the September 11 hijackers became public, commentators resorted to outright invention to make their case. Raed Salah, the head of the Islamic Movement in Israel, wrote in the movement's official mouthpiece that "the manifests of the two airlines, American Airlines and United Airlines, whose planes crashed into the Pentagon and the World Trade Center, included not a single Arab." Because of this, it was all the more puzzling, he wrote, that "three days later the FBI released the names of 19 Arab passengers, claiming that they were the hijackers of the four planes."[36]

Similarly, Palestinian columnist Khalil al-Sawahri, writing in *Al-Ayyam,* simply declared that the letter left behind by Mohammed Atta in the rental car he had abandoned at Boston's Logan Airport was a forgery. "Its disseminators are the circles of Orientalists who are making efforts to tarnish the image of the Arab Muslim. [They] began by falsifying history, deceitfully falsifying and attributing to themselves the stories of prophecy [and later Islamic history] and [continued with] modern films, particularly American, in which Hollywood made an effort to present [Arabs] as thieves, terrorists, bandits, base, dirty, and so on."[37] By "Orientalist circles," this columnist clearly meant the stereotyped "Jew" of *The Protocols of the Elders of Zion.* The theme of denial—whether it's the Holocaust or September 11—is central to the anti-Semitic mind-set.

Soon the allegations of a Jewish conspiracy would get much more specific with the addition of a striking new detail: the missing four thousand Jews who worked at the World Trade Center but, supposedly, had not come in the day of the attack. "When it became known that there had been an attack on the WTC in New York, the international media, particularly the Israeli media, exploited the incident and began to mourn the 4,000 Israelis who had worked in the two towers. Then there was no more mention of these Israelis, as it became clear that they hadn't even arrived for work that day," the Al-Manar television network broadcast from

Lebanon.[38] This is the same Iranian-controlled network that initially had tried to pin the blame on an obscure cooperation between the Japanese Red Army and renegade Saudi financier Osama bin Laden.[39]

The myth of the "missing" four thousand Jews soon became the cornerstone of the Muslim "case" against Israel and quickly spread over the Internet and the traditional media.[40] Next, it was picked up by a weekly published by the Palestinian Authority. "The investigation of these attacks did not begin from the proper starting point; rather, it was swept away by public opinion, shaped by the American media which is controlled by the Jews. . . . Why did they inform the Jews that there was no further need for their services only three days before the attacks? Why did they announce huge losses in the technology sector, in which most of the employees are Jews, with offices in the trade building [WTC]—which made the Jews leave the place? Why did rumors spread among the Jews that the 'appointed time for the execution of the attack' was a day off work?"[41]

The rumor became a "fact" in the eyes of the hard-line Tehran daily *Kayhan.* "It is known that 4,000 Jews worked at the WTC in New York and that these people did not come to work that day," the paper reported on October 2.[42] Raed Salah, writing in a pro-Hamas daily three days later, provided imaginary details: "A suitable way was found to warn the 4,000 Jews who work every day at the Twin Towers to be absent from their work on September 11, 2001, and this is really what happened! Were 4,000 Jewish clerks absent [from their jobs] by chance, or was there another reason? At the same time, no such warning reached the 2,000 Muslims who worked every day in the Twin Towers, and therefore there were hundreds of Muslim victims."[43]

Dr. Gamal 'Ali Zahran, head of the political science faculty at Suez Canal University in Egypt, wrote in the Egyptian government daily *Al-Ahram:* "At the WTC, thousands of Jews worked in finance and the stock market, but none of them were there on the day of the incident. Out of 6,000 killed, of 65 nationalities from 60 countries, not one was a Jew!!"[44] The myth of the missing Jews was also presented as "fact" in the Saudi-sponsored daily *Al-Hayat* in London.[45]

Speaking in Tehran on October 24, Syria's ambassador to Iran, Turky Muhammad Saqr, suggested that his government was building a dossier

that would establish all the facts of Israel's responsibility for September 11 for release to the public or to some international organization (it never did). "Syria has documented proof of the Zionist regime's involvement in the September 11 terror attacks on the U.S.," he said. The fact that "4,000 Jews employed at the WTC did not show up for work before the attack clearly attests to Zionist involvement in these attacks."[46]

Many more pieces of spurious evidence were invented, combined with a string of otherwise unrelated coincidences. Al-Manar television, in one such report, claimed that Israel's General Security Services had "stopped Prime Minister Ariel Sharon from going to New York" on the eve of the attacks.[47] Syrian columnist Mu'taz al-Khatib noted that former prime minister Ehud Barak had been invited well ahead of the attacks for a live television show by the BBC. "Barak's presence in the BBC's head office minutes after the explosion, at a meeting set in advance, to speak for 30 minutes of the danger of terrorism and chastise the 'rogue states,' particularly the Arabs," was yet another proof of Israel's involvement, he wrote.[48]

Egyptian cleric Sheikh Mohammad Gamei'a, the Muslim world's most respected authority on questions of religion and ethics, had just returned from New York to Al-Azhar University in Cairo. His views are all the more significant because for several years he was the prayer leader at Manhattan's biggest and most influential mosque. He summed up the Israeli conspiracy in an October 5, 2001, interview:

Jews "are the only ones capable of planning such acts," he claimed, laying out a series of "facts" that any serious publication would have dismissed as pure fantasy. "First of all, it was found that the automatic pilot was neutralized a few minutes before the flight, and the automatic pilot cannot be neutralized if you don't have command of the control tower. Second, the black boxes were found to contain no information; you cannot erase the information from these boxes if you do not plan it ahead of time on the plane. Third, America has the most powerful intelligence apparatuses, the FBI and the CIA. . . . How did [the perpetrators] manage to infiltrate America without their knowledge? Fourth, Jews control decision-making in the airports and in the sensitive centers in the White House and the Pentagon. Fifth, to date, America has presented no proof incriminating Osama bin Laden and al-Qaida. If we take these things into account and look closely at the incident, we will find that only the Jews are capable of planning such an incident, because it was planned with great precision of which Osama bin Laden or any other Islamic organization or intelligence apparatus is incapable. . . ."[49]

Contemporary conspiracy theories get additional fuel from rumors of mysterious technologies exploited by a small circle of intimates. Thus, one popular explanation for how Jews employed at the World Trade Center towers were warned not to come to work on the morning of September 11 revolved around a warning allegedly sent to four thousand cell phones simultaneously at 7 A.M. that morning by the Israeli communications firm Odigo, which manages several instant messaging service (IMS) networks. The rumor began when Odigo's CEO, Micha Macover, told an Israeli newspaper reporter that two of his workers received unexplained messages over the network two hours before the attack, predicting that some kind of attack would occur that day. When he learned about the message, Macover said he turned over the information to the Israeli security services and to the FBI. "I have no idea why the message was sent to these two workers, who don't know the sender. It may just have been someone who was joking and turned out they accidentally got it right. And I don't know if our information was useful in any of the arrests the FBI has made," Macover said.[50] The Odigo story was soon picked up by *The Washington Post*'s on-line "Newsbytes" column written by Brian McWilliams.[51] The only problem was that both stories appeared well *after* the original reports in the Arab media about Mossad warnings and missing Jews. The Odigo story was eventually discounted as a tantalizing coincidence involving two individuals, not four thousand. But to the conspiracy minded there is no such thing as a coincidence.

Other mysterious technology "accessible only to the Jews" was used to explain how the Israelis carried out the September 11 attacks and managed to pin them on the Arabs. According to one report that appeared in a Palestinian newspaper in Israel in December 2001, the planes had not been hijacked but were remotely guided to their targets using a system developed by a Jewish-owned company: "Airplanes can be remotely controlled using a modern system called 'GPLS' [*sic*—an apparent reference to the global positioning system]. The U.S. invested some $3.2 billion in developing this system. Additionally, the Department of Defense collaborated with a group of companies [called] Raytheon that specialize in developing aerial missile defense and air traffic control systems. The air traffic control system can be activated remotely by satellite. The moment an airplane, civilian or military, enters the system's range, the operator can decode the signals and signs of the plane's flight system, completely controlling it and directing it toward whatever target he wishes. Also, all the plane's communications apparatus can be silenced. According to the unfolding of the attacks on New York and Washington, and according to the evidence . . . the planes were not hijacked; they were remotely controlled and forced to fly toward the targets fed into [the system] by the planners. Therefore, the FBI will investigate the president of this group of companies, whose name is Daniel Burnham, and the head of the engineers responsible for the GPLS system whose name, Bruce Solomon, attests that he is Jewish."[52] I heard these claims repeated without question more than one year later in Cairo from the mouth of Egyptian journalist Magdi Sarhan, managing editor of the liberal opposition daily *Al-Wafd*.[53]

Pouring additional fuel on the fire was none other than Saudi interior minister Prince Nayef bin Abdul Aziz, third in line to succeed the ailing King Fahd and the Saudi official who personally handled the U.S. requests for information on the hijackers. For well over a month, Prince Nayef in the name of his government denied that any Saudi national had been involved in the attacks. "It is strange that no other nationality, apart from Arabs, has been accused of carrying out this action," he told an interviewer on October 16. "Washington has failed to supply any evidence about the involvement of Saudi nationals in the September 11 attacks. . . . I don't believe this is clear. There were more than 600 passengers on board the four [hijacked] planes. We are surprised why Arabs, particularly the Saudis, have been singled out [for blame]."[54] It took until February 6, 2002—nearly five full months—for the Saudi government to acknowledge that fifteen Saudis had been among the hijackers.[55] Despite all of this, a well-respected researcher at Cairo's state-run Al-Ahram Center for Political and Strategic Studies, Diaa Rashwan, told me one year later that the Arab world was still waiting to see the evidence of bin Laden's involvement. "Why has the U.S. Justice Department never issued an indictment?" he said. "This is a joke, and it raises serious doubts about the version given us of what happened on 9/11." It was "impossible" that the nineteen hijackers were Islamic radicals, because they didn't fit the recruitment profile he had studied in Egypt. "The U.S. story is full of holes and contradictions; it is the biggest conspiracy in history," he said.[56]

†††

Most Americans and Europeans believe that a fairly accurate picture of the events of September 11 began to emerge in the days and weeks following the attacks. From Boston, video surveillance footage was retrieved showing lead hijacker Mohammed Atta passing through an airport metal detector, composed, well dressed, boarding pass in hand. In New Jersey, the 2001 Mitsubishi Galant used by accomplice Ziad Jarrah was found in the airport parking lot. In the car, investigators found a speeding ticket Jarrah received in Maryland just two days before the hijackings.[57] In Boston, a five-page handwritten document subsequently called a "suicide letter" was retrieved, penned by Atta, in which he commended his fellow hijackers to pray as they boarded the airplanes. "Everybody hates death, fears death, but only those, the believers who know the life after death and the reward after death, would be the ones who would be seeking death," he exorted his fellow murderers. "Keep a very open mind, keep a very open heart of what you are to face. You will be entering paradise. You will be entering the happiest life, everlasting life." In a section entitled "The Last Night," he wrote: "You should pray, you should fast. You should ask God for guidance, you should ask God for help. . . . Continue to pray throughout this night. Continue to recite the Koran." When the hijackers entered the plane, he instructed them to pray as follows: "Oh God, open all doors for me, Oh God, who answers prayers and answers those who ask you, I am asking for your help. I am asking for your forgiveness. I am asking you to lighten my way. I am asking you to lift the burden I feel."[58]

Within four days, the Federal Bureau of Investigation released the names of the nineteen hijackers.[59] Fifteen were Saudi nationals, two were from the United Arab Emirates, one was Lebanese, and one was Egyptian.[60] Before the week was out, the FBI released photographs of the suspects and stated unequivocally that all had emerged from Osama bin Laden's al-Qaeda training camps in Afghanistan. In case any doubt remained, three months later, on December 13, Osama bin Laden himself appeared in a videotaped message broadcast in Arabic on the Qatar government–backed Al-Jazeera satellite television network, gloating to followers that he had managed to keep even his trusted spokesman, Sulaiman Abu Ghaith, in the dark as he finalized preparations for the attacks.[61]

So how could responsible media organizations in the Muslim world report such an extraordinary and counterintuitive story with such alacrity? How could educated people in a region of the world that invented the alphabet and mathematics, and preserved Aristotelian logic while Europe was plunged in the Dark Ages for more than a millennium, believe such obvious lies?

One answer comes from Saudi Arabia, where Interior Minister Prince Nayef continued to fuel conspiracy theories in order to cover up his own government's involvement. In November 2002, at the same time his government had launched an expensive public relations campaign in America to highlight the Saudi kingdom's cooperation with America in the war on terror, Prince Nayef once again blamed the Jews. "We know that the Jews have manipulated the September 11 incidents and turned American public opinion against Arabs and Muslims," he told the Kuwaiti daily *Al-Siyassa* in an interview. "We still ask ourselves: Who has benefited from September 11 attacks? I think they [the Jews] were the protagonists of these attacks."[62]

How many Jews actually died in the World Trade Center attacks is not known with any precision. The official New York City "Missing Persons List" does not categorize victims by their religion or nationality. But ask families with names like Adler, Aron, Berger, Bernstein, Cohen, Eichler, Eisenberg, Feinberg, Friedlander, Goldstein, Greenstein, Horwitz, Jablonski, Kestenbaum, Kirchbaum, Kleinberg, Levi, Levine, Mayer, Rosenberg, Rosenblum, Rosenthal, Sachs, Safronoff, Schwartz, Shulman, Shwartzstein, Silverstein, Solomon, Steinman, Temple, Weil, Weinberg, Weingard, Weinstein, Weiss, and Zukelman what they wouldn't give to see their loved ones again. Why didn't *they* get a conspiratorial cell phone message warning them to stay home? By all appearances, the 9/11 hijackers were equal opportunity murderers.[63]

The widespread denial of the events of September 11 in the Arab and Muslim world (and in some circles in Europe, as we will see later) did not emerge from a vacuum. The 9/11 myths were neither unusual nor isolated. They spewed forth naturally from a deep underground sea of hate that has been bubbling under the surface for many years. For centuries, it has been known as hatred of the Jew. For many Americans, brought up in a society that has banned hate speech and vigorously combated racism and prejudice, it is hard to comprehend that other nations not only tolerate such barbarity, but openly encourage it as state policy. The events of September 11, and the reactions from the Arab world that followed, show how thoroughly America has become identified with the Jew of anti-Semitic tradition. It's a complex story, but one that needs to be told.

✝ ✝ ✝

The "ideological prologue"[64] to September 11 was a raucous, hate-filled event that played itself out half a world away in Durban, South Africa, a normally stately coastal city along the Indian Ocean. The third United Nations World Conference Against Racism was intended to counterbalance the G-8 summits so the "forgotten peoples" of the world could make their voices heard amid the clamor of globalization and international capitalism. Jesse Jackson was there, demanding that America pay trillions of dollars in reparations for slavery, an institution America led the world in abolishing more than 140 years ago. Fidel Castro and Yasser Arafat were there, as were AIDS activists, homosexual groups, women's rights organizations, former Communists, Maoists, environmentalists, and animal rights and global-warming activists.

In the end, neither Jesse Jackson nor anyone else said one word about actual slavery—the real kind, still going on today in Sudan. Nor was racism—the real kind, that led to the slaughter of hundreds of thousands of Tsutsis in Rwanda—on the agenda. Anti-Semitic violence was not on the table, despite the continuing murder of Israeli civilians and foreign tourists in cafés, restaurants, and street markets and the desecration of Jewish synagogues across Europe. The nations of the world and some six thousand nongovernmental organizations (NGOs) had come together for a different purpose. It was so overwhelming that it united such otherwise opposing groups as radical Islamic fundamentalists from Saudi Arabia, Iran, and Malaysia and sexual libertarians and abortion-on-demand activists from Europe. It united Yasser Arafat, Jesse Jackson, and the six-teen governmental delegations of the European Union, whose representa-tive, Swedish ambassador to Switzerland Johan Molander, helped prepare the documents and resolutions that were to be adopted in Durban. That purpose was a deep-rooted, unquenchable hatred of America and of the only successful democracy in the Middle East, Israel.

The single-minded focus and vehemence of the hatred was breath-taking, even for such a seasoned veteran of the United Nations as Shimon Samuels, who heads the Simon Wiesenthal Center's European office. One of Dr. Samuels's missions in recent years has been to monitor and attempt to influence the official anti-Semitism emanating from international orga-nizations such as the United Nations. He was the only representative of a Jewish organization elected to the NGO Forum's Coordinating Commit-tee; and from there he was voted an alternate member of its twenty-member International Steering Committee, which supervised the drafting of conference documents.

In February 2001, the last of four preparatory conferences was con-vened in Tehran, capital of the Islamic Republic of Iran. That the Islamic Republic of Iran should have a seat at a forum ostensibly devoted to human rights was a travesty in itself, given its systematic repression of ethnic minorities and wholesale massacre of political opponents. "I was curious to see if the Iranians would actually ban me because I was a Jew," Samuels told me. They did, but with a delicacy that even today brings a wry smile to his face. "I kept on calling the Iranian embassy to ask them when my visa would arrive. Finally, they called back a few hours after the last flight to Tehran had left. I could have my visa, they said, but I'd have to rebook another flight and arrive once the conference was over. They made their point."[65]

The Tehran conference was significant because that is where some twenty-two paragraphs of rabid anti-Semitic prose was added to the offi-cial conference documents, under the watchful eye and guidance of Johan Molander, who was the European Union representative at the meeting. Conveniently, not only were Jewish NGOs excluded from attending the Tehran preparatory conference, but so were NGOs representing the Baha'is, a dissident Shiite sect brutally persecuted by the Islamic regime in Iran, as well as government delegations from the United States and Israel.[66] "It's much easier to have a debate on the Middle East if the United States is not involved," Molander commented smugly to former Swedish Liberal Party leader Per Ahlmark, who was attending the conference as an NGO delegate.[67] The same groups and the same governments who gang-banged America and Israel at the Durban conference were later reborn as an international "antiwar" movement, united to oppose the U.S.-led coalition to liberate Iraq.

Shortly before flying down to Durban in late August, Samuels had a bad feeling about what was about to happen. Over the past two years throughout Europe he had witnessed an "incremental process of semantic theft," where terms like "holocaust" and "genocide" were used loosely to describe not the murder of six million Jews by the Nazis, but virtually any action by Israeli soldiers against Palestinians. "Left-wing movements in Europe marked 'Kristallnacht 1938' in November 2000, while ignoring more than 100 anti-Semitic attacks on synagogues worldwide in the same month," he wrote.[68] Even a ceremony to honor the Righteous Gentiles of France was marred when the Paris city government attempted to bar the Israeli ambassador from attending. The effort to delegitimize Israel and to demonize Jews—the live kind, not the victims of the Nazi death camps—was in full swing throughout Europe and at the United Nations. Despite his premonitions, Durban was uglier than anything he could have imagined.

In the documentation packets handed out at the official registration desk, the tens of thousands of delegates who attended the conference received a pamphlet distributed by the Arab Lawyers Union, which contained caricatures of hook-nosed Jews worthy of the Nazi propaganda newspaper *Der Stürmer*. On the cover, the booklet bore the title "That Is the Fact . . . Racism of Zionism & 'Israel' " over a huge swastika that was intertwined with the Israeli Star of David. On the back cover, the booklet reproduced the official logo of the United Nations conference. "It was clearly designed to look to a casual observer like an official conference document, which it definitely was not," Samuels recalls. "I gave it to Mary Robinson just before she rose to give her speech at the opening dinner for the NGOs." Robinson, a former president of Ireland, was the United Nations commissioner for human rights and secretary-general of the conference.

What happened next shocked nearly everyone at the dinner, especially Samuels, who had seen Mrs. Robinson bow and scrape to every demand from the Arab and Islamic groups.[69] "She stood up at the podium and waved the book, and said it had no place at a conference dedicated to human dignity. 'When it comes to this,' she said, 'I am a Jew.' She repeated it three times: 'I am a Jew.' "[70]

The reaction to her speech was so childish, it would have been amusing if it weren't indicative of the rabid anti-Semitism swelling the Durban conference halls. The next day, Samuels says, he "received a call from a puzzled reporter from the German Press Agency, asking me, 'Is it true? Is she really a Jew?' That evening, Hamas sent out an e-mail saying, 'We knew it all along. Now she's going to get it.' "

Beyond the words, violence was never very far away. When the handful of Jewish groups who attended the conference sought to present evidence of how they had been "harassed and discriminated against" during the pre-Durban meetings, Arab activists stormed the hall and "began shouting, singing and pushing in front of the speakers" until they had to cut short the press conference.[71] "This is typical of how we have been treated during this conference," said Rabbi Abraham Cooper, the associate dean of the Simon Wiesenthal Center, who had joined Samuels in Durban. For Anne Bayefsky, a visiting professor at New York's Columbia University Law School, "it couldn't get much worse. Some of the Jewish delegates are hiding their accreditation badge because it identifies them as from Israel or as Jewish."[72]

Fierce anti-Israeli demonstrations on the streets of Durban became "a venomous carnival of incitement," with demonstrators handing out flyers "portraying Jews with fangs dripping blood and wearing helmets inscribed with Nazi swastikas."[73] One flyer showed a picture of Hitler saying: "What if I had won?" Underneath were two possibilities. "The good things—there would be NO Israel and NO Palestinian's blood shed. The bad thing—I wouldn't have allowed the making of the new Beetle."[74] Full-size posters of Hitler were on display at the stand of the Arab Lawyers Union in the conference documentation center.[75]

Lord Greville Janner, a member of the British Parliament and longtime pro-democracy activist, called Durban "the worst example of anti-Semitism that I have ever seen." The *Jerusalem Post* titled one of many articles on the conference "Festival of Hate."[76] At issue were two sets of declarations—one from the government conference, the second from the NGO forum—that sought to establish Israel as an outlaw state. They also reintroduced the "Zionism is racism" resolution that had been passed annually since 1975 by the United Nations General Assembly at the request of the Soviet Union and Cuba until the first Bush administration succeeded in repealing it in 1991.[77] It was the threat of reintroducing that resolution that ultimately convinced the United States and Israel to walk out of the conference on September 3 in protest.

The government declaration, originally drafted in Tehran, referred to Israeli "ethnic cleansing of the Arab population of historic Palestine" and called Israel's policies "a crime against humanity."[78] Intended to be adopted by the entire conference as an official United Nations statement that would shape future policy discussions and international law, the document accused Israel of "genocide" against the Palestinian people and labeled Israel as a "racist apartheid state." It referred to the creation of the state of Israel as "the Catastrophe" ("al-Nakbaa"), a term used regularly by Arab leaders and polemicists, and called it a "third holocaust." Per Ahlmark says he was outraged by the open support the Swedish government gave to such statements. "The Durban conference amounted to a United Nations intellectual and propaganda pogrom," Ahlmark says. Shimon Samuels called the resolutions "the UN's *Mein Kampf*."[79]

Arch Puddington, vice president of the New York–based human rights organization Freedom House, observed that the drafters of the official declaration "left open for further decision the question of whether to spell the word *Holocaust* with an upper- or lowercase 'h,' with some countries arguing that Hitler's genocide had been a Jewish fabrication and others denying that Jews had been the focus of mass murder.

"A delegate from Iran called Zionism 'the greatest manifestation of racism,'" Puddington wrote, "and demanded that anti-Semitism (in its proper sense of discrimination against Jews) be struck from the conference's official register of bigotries because it is not a 'contemporary form of racism.' Syria weighed in with the claim that the Holocaust is a 'Jewish lie'; Egypt insisted that it would not accept a conference declaration that did not explicitly identify Israel as a racist state."[80]

The NGO statement in Durban went even further, calling for the convening of an international war crimes tribunal to try Israel for alleged crimes against the Palestinian people. And while Mary Robinson condemned it, she ultimately couldn't prevent it from being adopted at the NGO forum. "It is perhaps the most horrific document ever presented and finalized under the overall tent of the United Nations," Rabbi Cooper told reporters in Durban on September 1.[81]

Until the American delegation walked out with the Israelis, U.S. diplomats worked with a handful of Europeans behind the scenes to eliminate some of the worst excesses from the conference documents, which the Americans feared could lay the legal groundwork for a war crimes tribunal against Israel and possibly the United States. Those were legitimate fears. But Shimon Samuels saw a far deeper harm in the works at Durban: the banalization of intolerance and hate. "Durban set a new baseline for institutionalized anti-Semitism at the UN," he said.

Alan Baker is a human rights lawyer who served as a legal adviser to the Israeli negotiating team in Durban. He expressed concern that the NGO document "calls upon the UN to create educational packets for schools and universities explaining the 'racist' nature of Israel, and how it is 'an apartheid state.'" The problem goes way beyond Durban or even the Durban generation, because "this filters down, seeps into people's consciousness. Think Palestinians, think victims; think Israel, think apartheid. In Africa, South America, in Third World countries, this will be what is taught, it will be part of the curriculum," Baker said. "If Israel and Zionism are absolute evils, then anything you do against these evils is not only legitimate, but even a mitzva." The net effect of the hate language "is to give a sheen of legitimacy to the worst form of Palestinian violence," he added. "For how can you condemn blowing up Israeli children, women and men, if they are racist and perpetrators of apartheid."[82]

Haim Avraham, the distraught father of a kidnapped Israeli soldier named Binyamin Avraham, expressed what many Jewish observers at Durban were already thinking when he blurted out in the conference foyer: "They are paving the way here for another Holocaust." His message was clear. "The Holocaust did not befall the Jewish people overnight, but came about after centuries of systematic delegitimization. It was easy to

kill Jews en masse, for the ground had been prepared by years of view-
ing the Jews as subhuman. In Durban, a new process of delegitimization
picked up steam."[83]

As the Americans were packing their bags, ordered home by Secretary
of State Colin Powell, the Israelis made one last effort to stand up to the
assembled world powers in an address delivered in halting English by a
low level Foreign Ministry official named Mordechai Yedid. He took
direct aim at the central contention of many European governments and
left-wing organizations that have become the fellow travelers of prejudice—namely, that the criticism of Israel expressed at the conference was
not anti-Semitism—that is, hatred of the Jew—but anti-Zionism, an
acceptable form of political opposition to Israeli government policies.
"Anti-Zionism, the denial of Jews the basic right to a home, is nothing but
anti-Semitism, pure and simple," he declared. "The venal hatred of Jews
that has taken the form of anti-Zionism, and which has surfaced at this
conference, is different in one crucial way from the anti-Semitism of the
past. Today, it is being deliberately propagated and manipulated for political ends."[84]

What begins with the Jews doesn't end with Jews. That is a lesson
that should have been clear after Hitler and the Holocaust. The German
Protestant theologian Martin Niemoeller put it eloquently in a since
famous comment made to a student who asked why no one in Germany
stood up for the Jews against Nazi persecution. "First they came for the
Communists, and I didn't speak up because I wasn't a Communist. Then
they came for the Jews, and I didn't speak up because I wasn't a Jew. Then
they came for the trade-unionists, and I didn't speak up because I wasn't a
trade-unionist. Then they came for the Catholics, and I didn't speak up
because I was a Protestant. Then they came for me, and by that time no
one was left to speak up." Niemoeller was arrested by Hitler on July 1,
1937, and jailed for seven months, then rearrested and sent to a concentration camp for the duration of the war. He was liberated in 1945 and became
a pacifist and ultimately president of the World Council of Churches in
the 1960s, an institution that—supreme irony—subsequently became a
fierce opponent of the right of the Jews to a national homeland.[85]

Three days after the Durban conference came to a close, terrorists
descended on New York, Washington, D.C., and a lonely field in Pennsyl-

vania. Americans all across the country saw firsthand on their television screens the horror that Israelis know virtually day in and day out. But the real forces at work were ancient, well oiled, proven, and deadly.

Albert Speer was not only the top Nazi official in charge of making Hitler's war industry operate with deadly efficiency: he was Hitler's close confidant. Jailed in Spandau for war crimes and crimes against humanity following his trial in Nuremberg in 1945, Speer kept a diary that was subsequently published in English translation. Just two years after Hitler's suicide in his Berlin bunker, in an entry dated November 18, 1947, Speer recalled the crazed Wagnerian fantasies of the man who had just destroyed Europe and caused the death of sixty million people:

"I recall how [Hitler] would have films shown in the Reich Chancellery about London burning, about the sea of fire over Warsaw, about exploding convoys, and the kind of ravenous joy that would then seize him every time. But I never saw him so beside himself as when, in a delirium, he pictured New York going down in flames. He described how the skyscrapers would be transformed into gigantic burning torches, how they would collapse in confusion, how the bursting city's reflection would stand against the dark sky."[86]

It all came full circle on September 11 when Hitler's fantasies met Osama bin Laden. As Jews have known for centuries and Americans are just learning: Marry hatred to deadly capabilities and you get murder.

HORROR AT PASSOVER 2

It was raining on the evening of March 27, 2002, just cold enough that Arab men in his village donned the cheap leather jackets and old overcoats they reserved for the winter months. Abd al-Basat Odeh knew the weather would be his blessing, because everyone would be wearing long overcoats similar to the one his handlers had given him. Although the coats of the Jews would be newer and of finer cloth because it was Passover, he was a Jewish woman, and no one would think to question a woman. The wig of long straight hair and the large tinted glasses would hide the fact that he had just shaved off his beard. Only Allah would know the truth, or so he thought.

At twenty-five, he was old enough to remember how Netanya used to be: packed with tourists from Europe and America who came to enjoy a Mediterranean idyll in the summer, but sleepy and dusty in winter when the tourists left and the cafés and beaches lay empty. The quiet times were long gone, and in recent years Netanya had swollen to 185,000 people to become the sixth largest city in Israel, thanks to the influx of nearly 50,000 Jews from the former Soviet Union and Ethiopia.[1]

Odeh knew Netanya well, and he knew the Jews, and that was why Mohaned, the Engineer, had chosen him for this mission. Odeh would do anything just to win a smile from the Engineer, to feel his brotherly arm grasp his shoulder, to get him to ruffle his short curly hair. Everyone knew his name, but few had ever been graced to actually meet him.

For nearly three years, Odeh had taken a bus almost daily from the family compound in the West Bank town of Tulkarm, where he lived with his parents, eight siblings, and nearly thirty other relatives. Perched on the Samarian hills, Tulkarm overlooked the Plain of Sharon, the narrow waist of Israel, where a scant eight miles separated the Jews on the coast from the Palestinian settlements on the West Bank plateau. "In Texas, some of our driveways are longer than that," George W. Bush had said when he'd toured the area two years before he was elected president.[2]

They were so close to the Jews that Palestinian children in Tulkarm grew up playing soldier, lobbing mortars from the edges of the twisting village streets, hoping to hit enemy vehicles traveling on the valley road down below. The stones clattered harmlessly down the steep rocky hillside, but when Abd al-Basat got older and met Mohaned Taher and the secretive men of the Izz al-Din al-Qassem brigades, the underground military wing of the radical Islamic group Hamas, the play became serious.

For four months he donned a white linen jacket and worked in one of Netanya's bustling seaside hotels, waiting tables in the restaurant, learning the routines, just as Mohaned had taught him. He watched the young men and women sitting together, smoking, drinking, and talking, and steeled himself to betray nothing as he brought them grilled fish and wine. But tonight Abd al-Basat Odeh was not going to serve the Jews: he was going to kill them.

His childhood friend Nasir Yatimah helped him prepare. It was Nasir who fetched the martyr's belt Mohaned had prepared for him from its secret hiding place above the squat toilet in the mosque. It was Nasir who brought the stylish black leather jacket, the yellow glasses, the Italian boots with their high heels, and the wig. It was Nasir who drove down to Tel Aviv and rented the videocamera and tried to coach him on what to say. But Abd al-Basat Odeh didn't need any coaching. Holding an M-16 rifle, he looked straight into the camera and said he was proud to become a martyr. He was proud to kill the Jews because they were the sons of monkeys and pigs. He was going to transform the homes of the Jews into houses of mourning. Every Muslim should feel joy in his heart, because he was going directly to the Garden of Eden, where seventy-two beautiful virgins were waiting to marry him.[3]

After they made the tape, Abd al-Basat Odeh put down the M-16 rifle and shaved his beard carefully, lathering twice so as not to nick himself.

†††

The Park Hotel had hosted a Passover seder for many years. It was a family time, when grandparents and children and grandchildren gathered to celebrate the deliverance of the Jews from the Angel of Death and their survival as a nation. It began with the reading of the Haggadah, the story of the liberation from Egypt. Despite the return to Israel after two thousand years of exile, it was still a rushed meal. The bread, which had no time to rise in their haste to leave, was left unleavened. They ate it in haste along with parsley dipped in salt water, a bowl of tears, and with bitter herbs to remind them of the harshness of their life as slaves. But once food was devoured, the talk flowed. It was the one evening of the year when families across Israel got together in all their living generations. Many celebrated in restaurants such as the Park Hotel. Odeh knew where to find them.

For Israelis and Jews the world over, the opening feast of Passover always includes a ritual question and answer between parents and children: Why is this night different from all other nights? Abd al-Basat Odeh quietly placed his hands on the martyr's belt around his waist, snug and heavy, and knew why this night was different. It was because the Angel of Death was not going to pass over the houses of the Jews. He was the Angel of Death. And he was coming.

After strapping Mohaned's green khaki explosive belt around his waist and donning the wig and yellow glasses, he left Tulkarm with his driver, Fathi Khatib. Shortly after 2 P.M., they set off to find Jews. Fathi knew all the back roads into Israel but didn't worry if the Israelis stopped them. Their old Peugeot 305 had Israeli plates, and his fake Israeli identity papers had already fooled more than one Jewish policeman.

Once they reached the coastal plain, they drove into the suburb of Herzliya, but no crowds were on the streets and all the restaurants were empty. So Fathi headed farther south to Tel Aviv itself. It was already dark when they drove past the deserted United States embassy along the beach-front. Except for the Yamit, just across from the embassy, the big seaside hotels were far up off the street. Nowhere did they see large numbers of Jews congregating, so they drove on. Mohaned had told them to pick a target where they could kill many Jews. It was not here.

Then Odeh remembered Netanya. He told Fathi he had stolen cars in Netanya, not that he had served the Jews. The Netanya hotels were much smaller, right off the road, and you could see directly into the lobbies through the plate-glass windows. After driving around once, they would pick the hotel with the most Jews. Fathi would park the car nearby and report back to Mohaned by cell phone once the operation took place.

They drove slowly up the hill to the Sharon Mall, already deserted as Jews were preparing for the seder. Odeh quietly said a prayer. It was here that martyr Mahmoud Marmash dispatched five Jews to their death ten months earlier, right on the main road into Netanya. The Jews were so stupid, they had no guards in front of the mall entrance on that Sunday morning. But there were guards there now, and they drove on.

He remembered how Mohaned had gone quiet and the cold glaze came over his eyes when Abd al-Basat first told him about the Passover seder. It was perfect, he had said. The Angel of Death would have a special surprise for his victims that night: small pellets of dried cyanide that would release a deadly poison gas when the bomb went off.[4] It would remind the Jews of what Hitler had nearly done. It would remind them that the great German lived on. We are going to finish off the task.[5]

When the security guard stationed at the entrance of the Park Hotel saw the young woman in her stylish jeans, dark overcoat, and tinted glasses give him a shy smile, he simply waved her through. Perhaps he didn't notice the slight bulge of her midriff, where she was carrying twenty pounds of explosives in one-inch cylinders, packed around thousands of tiny steel pellets. After all, it was rainy and cold, everyone was wearing overcoats, and she opened her bag voluntarily. According to another version of the story, the guard never actually saw Odeh enter the hotel because he had gone to check the hotel grounds just moments beforehand, to make sure the entrances from the pool deck and the sea were still locked. Yet other survivors claim the guard kept his hands in his pockets and never patted anyone down. They all agreed that it was shortly after 7:15 P.M. when Odeh entered the lobby, still noisy with holiday guests who had not yet taken their seats.

Odeh hesitated just long enough as he considered blowing himself up in the lobby that he attracted the attention of the reception clerk. She called out to him and asked him if he needed help. When she did, he walked quickly through the glass doors into the main ballroom, where 180 people were gradually taking their seats to begin the seder.

Hotel manager Amiram Hamami, forty-four, was posted at the door of the ballroom, checking everyone's tickets and pointing them in the direction of their assigned seats. "We didn't just let anyone come in," his mother-in-law, Paulette Cohen, a part owner of the hotel, told me. "After all, this was the Passover seder. Tickets cost four hundred shekels each— $100!" Hamami was a trained member of the police auxiliary, and under his suit jacket he was armed. Just before Odeh entered, Hamami was called into the ballroom to help a waitress with a guest who wanted to change her seat. She was an older woman with a walker, seated at table one, at the left-hand side of the center of the ballroom. "She wanted to be moved to table two, just a few meters away," Mrs. Cohen recalls.

As Hamami left his post at the door to speak to the woman, Odeh followed just a few steps behind. It was an oval-shaped dance floor, recessed from the rest of the room, where five large tables set for the seder were already packed with guests. Surrounding them, some two feet higher in a semicircle all the way around the room, were nine more tables, most of them full as well. Another eight tables were set along the huge wall of windows facing the sea. At the head of the room, in front of Hamami, was a small stage where a rabbi would read the prayer ritual in a few minutes. It was noisy as family members greeted one another, calling across the room to friends they hadn't seen since last year's seder. There, in the very center of the ballroom, packed so close with Jews that he could smell the steam from their wet clothes, Odeh reached his right hand inside his coat and pressed the button that detonated the bomb.

If it had been warmer that evening and the windows had been open, the bomb wouldn't have wreaked such carnage, police say. Open windows offer an instant escape route to the intense pressure caused by an explosive blast. But it was wet and rainy, and all the windows in the hotel were sealed against the cold.

Amiram Hamami was the first victim. He took the blast full in the back, shielding the older woman with the walker he had been trying to help.

Just to the bomber's left, Anna Vaishlaine, a young curly-haired waitress from Simferopol, Ukraine was bending over an elderly man having trouble reading the menu. It was her first night on a new job, and the twenty-five-year-old immigrant wanted to be as helpful as she could. Later, she told a reporter that she could not remember the blast, the blinding light, the hot searing metal of the bomb itself or the wet sticky mass of body parts flying through the air. The first thing she remembered when she woke up was being partly covered by an overturned table and feeling a cold spray coming down on her from the burst sprinkler system. It hurt when she tried to call out for help because a piece of metal had pierced her lungs. That was when she realized she couldn't feel her legs.[6]

"My friend said, 'Look at this strange man at the entrance. He looks like a suicide bomber.' And I told her you're crazy, it couldn't be," Vaishlaine recalls. "Now when I think about it . . . he was looking to see where the best place would be to stand in order to cause the most damage." Doctors later speculated that her "simple, helpful gesture" in helping the elderly man read the menu had "positioned her in just such a way that shrapnel would pierce her spine and leave her legs paralyzed."[7] Anna survived, but her eighteen-month-old son, Yonatan, will probably never see her walk.

Paulette Cohen, the sixty-seven-year-old part owner of the Park Hotel, was fetching cola from a storage room out back when the bomb went off. At first, she told me, she thought it was thunder. "I've heard thunder like that before. I didn't think it was a bomb. The blast threw me backward several feet, knocking my keys out of my hands." It was only when she dashed back into the dining room that she understood. "It was dark and people were moaning. From somewhere, there was white smoke. It took me a few seconds to realize that the sprinklers had gone off and were putting out a fire."

Joel Leyden, forty-eight, was driving toward Netanya with his wife and eighteen-month-old baby for the Passover seder when the explosion shook the windows of his car. Within minutes, he reached the Park Hotel. He passed five bodies laid out on the pavement outside and rushed into the dining room, where the force of the explosion had blown tables, chairs, and bodies against the walls and through the windows. Tiles and wires were hanging from the ceiling, and water was everywhere, running red with blood. To his surprise, in the midst of the devastation, he found a single table still standing, set with a white tablecloth and arrayed with fancy seder silverware. But everyone still inside the dining room by the time Leyden arrived was dead. "This was a battlefield where only one side was carrying weapons," he said. It reminded him of the smoking ruins of the World Trade Center, which he had visited while on holiday in New York.[8]

Outside the hotel, people were being bustled, bleeding and hastily bandaged, into the ambulances that kept rushing onto the scene. "I saw the body of an old woman in an elegant black dress," Leyden said. "Her foot had been blown off. A man in his mid-sixties, dressed in a smart blue suit, was walking around in a daze, blood pouring out of his head. Like him, most people were in shock, even many of the emergency workers. How can anyone act like this?"[9]

One of the victims was a nameless ten- or twelve-year-old girl, lying dead on the ground, her eyes wide open as if in surprise. Another girl, the same age, was so badly wounded that doctors couldn't identify her. For two days, rescue workers told me, two sets of parents stayed at the hospital, hoping and praying that the wounded girl was their daughter.[10]

Ernest and Eva Weiss were concentration camp survivors. They had taken their seats at table four along with George Yakobovits and his wife when Odeh detonated his bomb just a few feet to their right. None of them survived this time.

Their daughter, Edit Frid, was a nurse at a Netanya hospital, and that's where her two children raced as soon as word of the bombing hit the airwaves. Her husband was a dentist. The children had been heading for the Park Hotel for the seder but had been running late. Only their tardiness saved them from the same fate that struck down their parents, who were sitting next to the Weisses at table four and took the full brunt of the bomber's blast.[11]

Sitting at table seven with her back to the bomber was Frieda Britvits, who had been deported by the Nazis. She had survived Auschwitz, but not this. She perished along with her husband, Alter, and two others.

Dvora Karim, originally from Iran like several other victims, died sitting next to her husband Michael at table three. She had escaped the murderous rampages of the Ayatollah Khomeini in the early 1980s, one of some fifty thousand Jews saved during a daring, secret operation orchestrated by a little-known rabbi in Brooklyn, who told me his story years later. They took the bomber's blast straight in the back.

Rami Governik is a former paratrooper, who at age fifty has fought in two wars and has seen his share of battlefield agony. He didn't go inside the hotel the first night. As the representative of Netanya mayor Miriam Fierberg, he told me, he felt his job was to help the living, not the dead. But the next day he did, and it still made him pause, months after the fact. "I've seen scenes of devastation before," he said. "But when it happens in the middle of a town, you're not ready for it. In war you expect death, but when you send your boy to school you don't expect to get him back in a box."

† † †

Within minutes of the bomb blast, pagers all over Israel were going off, summoning government ministers, police, and hospital workers to the scene.

At around 7:30 P.M., Bar-Yochai Shimon's beeper went off just as he was finishing his seder with his family. As commander of the local chapter of Zaka—the police auxiliary victim identification unit, organized by Orthodox Jews—he recognized the number that had paged him. It was the police hot line in Netanya. When he learned there had been a bomb blast at the Park Hotel, he phoned the other members of his unit. Still wearing his strummel, the large, round fur hat worn by Hasidim, and his best long silk jacket, which he reserved specially for Passover, he arrived at the Park Hotel shortly before 8 P.M. and assembled his team.

"Our job is to go in after the Magen David [Red Cross] have evacuated the wounded," he told me. "We must collect every bit of flesh and wipe up blood, so the victims can be given a proper burial according to Jewish law."

The Zaka units operate as two-man teams. "One man carries a plastic bag for the body parts, the other man has the towels," he said. The devastation this night was so great, they sent twelve men to the hotel and another ten to the Sanz Medical Center at Laniado Hospital, to help tend the more than one hundred wounded.

Bar-Yochai has been on scene where all eleven bombs that have gone off in Netanya since the second *intifada* broke out on September 28, 2000, but this one was by far the worst. "The sprinklers had burst, so there was water all over the floor, mixed with blood. In the central area, where the bomb went off, it was nearly up to our knees because there was a wall surrounding the dance floor. When we first went in, we saw fingers, hands, eyeballs, and smaller bits of flesh floating in the water like fish."

Rabbi Aaron Friedman, who ministers to the Kiryat Sanz Hasidic community where the Netanya Zaka unit is based, says the Park Hotel bombing presented an unusual problem. "Our men couldn't figure out to whom many of the body parts belonged," he said, "because of a new technique used by the bomber which ripped apart the bodies in a way none of our people had seen before."

Mohaned Taher, the Hamas bomb maker, had packed thousands of steel balls—each slightly larger than a BB—around the explosives; they tore off limbs and propelled them far across the room. In some cases, as senior surgeon Dr. Yakov Yulano discovered later that evening, they had entered and left the victims without a trace.

"I went up to the emergency room at Laniado Hospital," says American-born Sanz president Chaim Jacov Deutsch. "Dr. Yulano took me to a girl who had no apparent injury. She wasn't bleeding, but clearly she was in shock. He set her aside and made sure nobody moved her. When he X-rayed her, he found two steel pebbles lodged in her brain."

Bar-Yochai and his team started their gruesome task at 10 P.M., after the ambulances had left and family members had gone to the hospital, hoping to find their loved ones among the wounded and not the dead. "When you go onto a scene like this you don't think," he said. "You go in to do a job. It's only later that it hits you." By 4 A.M., the Zaka team had reconstituted eighteen bodies, ten of them from pieces, but there were bags and bags of body parts that didn't fit any of the dead. When he got home, his wife and his five children were sleeping, and he found the remains of the seder meal. "I tried to take a drink of water, and choked. That's when it hit me," he says.

The Zaka team went back the next morning to finish up by the light of day. "We saw pieces of flesh hanging from the broken windows, fingers, hands," Bar-Yochai said. After another five hours, they declared the site cleaned, but there was so much unidentified flesh, they sought rabbinical approval to bury the remains in *kever achem,* a brotherly (common) grave. "We had to bring the remains to the cemetery in a garbage truck," Rabbi Freidman recalls.

✝ ✝ ✝

Altogether, some 29 people died, and more than 159 were injured, some of them, like Anna Vaishlaine, for life. But miracles also happened that night.

Sigurit Samra, a thirty-five-year-old English teacher, counts herself among the lucky. She and her husband and all four of their children were standing along the wall to the right of the bomber, and only one of them got seriously hurt. It was their four-and-a-half-year-old son, Gabriel. The bomb blast severed his windpipe and broke two bones in his neck. When they picked him up off the floor, he was bleeding all over from flying glass. Rescue workers transported him to the hospital, where he was operated on twice that night. But after the operations, he didn't wake up.

"We were praying, calling rabbis, calling friends," she told me. "All Israel was reading about the boy in the hospital in a coma and praying. And then, five days later, he woke up and began to move his legs."

Not far from Gabriel were her twins, still in their double stroller. Although people on all sides of them were killed and wounded, they didn't receive so much as a single cut from flying glass. "Their stroller was full of holes, it's stained with so much blood that we can never use it again, but we keep it because it saved my children. Truly, an angel kept them!"

It takes courage on Sigurit's part to tell me her story, and it is difficult for me as a parent to hear it. "I wasn't hurt, but I carry this in my heart," she says. "It has changed my life, changed my ideals. It's even changed my relationship with my husband. Now I have to consider every word I speak, because one moment can change everything. Before it was always new car, new cell phone—always things. Now . . . every moment I see my children alive, I thank God."

At the next table, her brother-in-law, Arieh Ben Aroya, forty-two, was struck down, his twenty-year-old daughter, Sheri, paralyzed. "She was an officer," Sigurit says. "She was a good student. She was tall. Beautiful. Responsible. Everything a mother wants. Now she's paralyzed and in a wheelchair and can't do anything for herself. My father lost an eye; my mother had surgery—but they are alive! But Sheri. . . . She's young and she can't speak or write or even feed herself."

Perhaps the worst of it for Sigurit Samra was actually seeing the bomber's face as he came into the ballroom. From the way he was dressed—the long hair, the yellow glasses, the fashionable jeans and boots—she remembers thinking he was a transvestite. "I thought, perhaps he has come to the seder to show respect for his parents. Maybe he is going through some kind of psychic turmoil, wanting to change his sex. My husband thought he was French, since everyone knew there were a lot of French guests at the hotel."

Some of the eyewitnesses who had seen Odeh's long hair and his fancy high-heeled boots mistook him for a woman. But Sigurit says she could tell that he had just shaved. "He had a lovely face. I never thought he was a terrorist. He looked like a very nice man. I remember thinking later, I couldn't imagine someone very normal like you could do something so disgusting."

Several witnesses I spoke to still remember the police coming out with Odeh's head in a plastic bag, which is why they knew immediately he wasn't a woman. The place where he stood when he blew himself up was visible for many months, before workers filled the small gray triangular hole in the tile floor with cement. Seven months after the bombing, the Cohens were renovating the ballroom in preparation for an upcoming wedding. "We mustn't give the terrorists the joy of success," Paulette Cohen explained. "So we rebuild."

Palestinian politicians simply shrugged when asked about the mayhem and said Odeh's murder spree was a "reminder to Arab leaders then gathered in Beirut that the Palestinians remained capable of combating Israel and determined not to be sold out."[12] The PA later named a soccer team in Tulkarm after Odeh. A leading Saudi government-controlled daily gushed with praise for the bomber.

> May Allah have mercy upon you, oh Abd al-Basat Odeh, mujaheed and martyr. . . . Courageously, full of willingness to [wage] Jihad, and with faith filling your heart, you executed your assignment and sacrificed your pure soul for your religion and your homeland. . . . May Allah have mercy on you, oh beloved of the Arab nation, oh Abd al-Basat. You evoked hope that had begun to dissipate; you restored life that had begun to expire; you revived the Arab pride, valor, chivalry, and sacrifice that had begun to die, and you caused pain to [the people] who had begun to celebrate and sing atop the bodies of the children, youths, and mothers of your people.[13]

†††

There was one final victim from the Park Hotel, a hotel chef named Arkady Wieselman. When the bomb went off, Wieselman had been in the hotel freezer, where he had gone to get vegetables just moments before. Wieselman rushed from the kitchen and helped tend to the injured out on the sidewalk. Later, he adopted the family of dead hotel manager Amiran Hamami, cooking for them during the mourning period. A thirty-seven-year-old immigrant from Russia, Wieselman had worked at the Park Hotel for ten years and knew Ami Hamami and his wife, Rina, well. "He was upset about all these terror attacks in Netanya. He has two children and he was afraid that it could happen at their school, anywhere," Rina said.[14]

Seven weeks after the Passover massacre, Wieselman went to the central market in Netanya, which spreads out over an area covering several city blocks just one hundred meters down the hill from the police station. It was a Sunday, his day off, and going to the market was a reaffirmation that life went on as usual despite the terror. As he went up to a fruit and vegetable stall, just at the entry of the covered souk, a Palestinian dressed as an Israeli soldier pressed the button and blew them up. Wieselman and two other Jews were killed that day. "I thought it was impossible that something like this would happen again to the people at the Park Hotel," said Rina Hamami.[15] But in Israel, tiny country that it is, lightning can indeed strike twice.

✝✝✝

Israel's minister of public security, Uzi Landau, was beeped at home within minutes of the bombing and rushed to the scene after asking his brother to take his place leading the seder. When he saw the devastation inside the Park Hotel, and the bodies lined up on the pavement, he knew it was not terror but a massacre. "This was our 9/11," he told me. There was never any doubt that Israel would strike back hard. The only question was how hard and how far. "We knew we couldn't go after the mosquitoes any longer. It was time to dry out the swamp."[16]

That same evening, Hamas released Odeh's suicide tape, calling the devout Muslim "the Lion of the Holy Revenge." With that information, and the bomber's head for positive identification, it didn't take long for Israel's police and intelligence services to track Odeh to Tulkarm, a town under the control of Yasser Arafat. His name had appeared on a list of wanted terrorists the Israelis had given to the Palestinian Authority several weeks earlier. Instead of arresting Odeh, Arafat's security services did nothing.

Defense Minister Benjamin Ben-Eliazar asked his top military planners to prepare options for retaliatory attacks. The next evening, Prime Minister Ariel Sharon convened the full cabinet. "There were lots of debates of how we should respond to Palestinian terror *before* the Park Hotel," says Uzi Landau. "From one atrocity to the next we moved from total restraint to limited response, from limited response to focused interception." By the time the cabinet actually met to hear the military options, the die was cast. "The basic decision to go out to get them had already been made," Landau says. "All that remained was to talk about tactics. Should we mobilize all our forces and launch a simultaneous attack to bring down the entire terrorist infrastructure at once? Or should we mobilize some forces and do it bit by bit? It was that second option which we adopted. Although I would have preferred a more vigorous response, it was an important move in the right direction. By then, it had become crystal clear to everyone that the Oslo process was the reason for the problem, not the solution."

The response from reservists to the mobilization was stunning. Many more reservists than were actually called left their normal jobs and showed up at their units the next day, ready to fight. Some asked to raise their medical profile "so they could volunteer," said Israel Defense Forces (IDF) spokesman Brigadier General Ron Kitrey. Reservists even came from overseas "because they heard of the situation," he said.[17]

Operation Defensive Shield began immediately, with Israeli troops moving into Palestinian refugee camps and cities the intelligence services had identified as terrorist havens. Israeli officials vowed not only to smash the operational cells, but to track down every member of the team of murderers that had shattered the Passover, no matter how long it took, senior police officials told me. Just one week after the bombing, on April 5, a top leader of the Hamas military wing, Qais Adwan, was killed along with six others in a gun battle. At first, the Israelis thought he was the "Engineer" who had made the Park Hotel bomb. Then, on April 15, they had a stroke of luck. A young Palestinian who lived in Tulkarm, named Nasser Yatima, confessed to Israeli interrogators who had arrested him during a security sweep five days earlier that he had retrieved the explosive belt from its hiding place in the mosque and delivered it to Odeh on the day of the bombing. Yatima eventually led the Israelis to Fathi Khatib, who drove Odeh to Netanya, and to Mohaned Taher, the bomb maker.

Sometimes referred to as "Engineer 4," Taher was well-known to the Israelis. "They usually make these bombs in batches, so you see the same type of explosives, the same detonators, the same batteries," says Gal, a thirtyish bomb technician from Jerusalem who now teaches at the national police training school in Bet Shemesh, some twenty kilometers south of Jerusalem. "These explosive belts are not terribly sophisticated," he told me. The one used in Netanya consisted of nothing more than a series of one-by-ten-inch cartridges packed with homemade explosives and tiny steel balls, activated by a simple button. "It doesn't have to be sophisticated to kill people," he says. "Smart bombs, dumb bombs: when they are set off inside a crowded restaurant, it doesn't matter. They are equally deadly."

The Israelis arrested five members of the Hamas terror cell that had participated in the massacre, including Nasser Yatima and Fathi Khatib, and sentenced them to life plus twenty years. "They are not worthy of being among people," the military judges wrote in their verdict. "They will rot in jail for the rest of their lives and will not see the light of day."[18]

But the Israelis reserved a special fate for Mohaned Taher, who was responsible for a series of murderous attacks that had caused the deaths of 121 Jews. On June 30, a special Israeli counterterrorism unit found Mohaned holed up in a house in Nablus and made sure he would never murder Jews again.

"Morally, I have nothing against killing these people," the commander of Israel's Border Guards troops, Major General David Tsur, told me at his headquarters astride the spectacular ravine of Ein Kerem that winds down from Jerusalem to the coastal plane. "In the United States, you call this targeted killing. We call it interception. We're talking about ticking bombs." But wherever possible, Tsur added, he preferred capturing the terrorists alive, "because then we can learn how they were recruited, what kind of bomb they had, what kind of instructions they were carrying, and how they planned to penetrate Israel."[19]

The Passover bombing was the straw that broke the camel's back. "This completely changed the way ordinary Israelis looked at the relationship with the Palestinians," says Rami Gouvernik, the former paratrooper who now works for Miriam Fierberg and who until recently considered himself a member of the "peace" camp in Israel. "It went over every line. They killed old people, young people, all of them innocent. They attacked on Passover, when 97 percent of Israelis—religious and nonreligious Jews—are celebrating. The Park Hotel massacre put an end to the peace process once and for all. Until then, many of us still believed there was hope. All of a sudden we realized there was no one to talk to, and that we had to do what we had to do, to put an end to the terror once and for all."

It also should have effectively put an end to the myth that such bombings were about land and politics. Killing Jews, innocent Jews of all ages, on Passover, at a seder, sends the very clear message that the bombers and those who back them hate Jews for being Jews—just as the Nazis did.

Abd al-Basat Odeh believed he would go to heaven for killing Jews. And he was not alone. From October 2000 until the end of September 2002, a scant two-year period, Israel was hit with 156 suicide attacks. Some of them involved multiple bombers, who would wait until rescue squads had arrived on scene and then detonate a second bomb to kill more. In 2002 alone, more than 2,400 people were killed and wounded.

The carnage would have been much worse if the Israeli police bomb squad hadn't succeeded in dismantling another 392 bombs, some of them taken from would-be suicide bombers who wrestled with police robots after being shot.[20]

But such hate had a source.

"THEY HAVE A PLAN!"

3

In the fall of 1994, when hope had partially replaced despair in the Middle East and the phrase *peace process* was still relatively fresh, Yasser Arafat's duplicity and shameless corruption were excused as the necessary attributes of a wily guerrilla leader. Everyone then in power, from Bill Clinton to Shimon Peres and Yitzhak Rabin, expected the sixty-six-year-old Arafat to "mature" as he dealt with the day-to-day responsibilities of government. Few people at that time understood or wanted to understand what was going on under the surface.

I got a good taste of those undercurrents during a swing through Syria, Jordan, and Gaza in autumn 1994. I'd timed my trip to coincide with the Israeli-Jordanian peace treaty, which was signed at a specially erected tent in the desert on October 26, 1994, and witnessed with great fanfare by President Clinton. In addition to government officials, I planned to speak with radical Islamic fundamentalist leaders and Palestinian groups who had announced their rejection of talking with Israel.[1]

For many years, I had been meeting with Palestinians from a wide variety of backgrounds—guerrilla leaders and propagandists in Beirut, farmers, shopkeepers, and politicians in the West Bank, and cosmopolitans such as the PLO's representative in France, Ibrahim Souss, a concert pianist who became a personal friend and dinner guest at our house outside of Paris. While they were all highly critical of Israel and blamed Israel for the conflict (and in some cases for their personal ills), most expressed willingness to live side by side with Israel with clear, recognized borders between the two states. I could not remember any of them uttering the type of crazed conspiracy theories that have made the *Protocols* the premier cookbook of anti-Semitic hate for over a century. Their hatred of Israel was political, not visceral—or so I thought.

Like most reporters, I had read so many "hate Israel" and "hate America" pieces in the Middle Eastern press over the years that I no longer paid them much attention. It simply wasn't news when an editorialist in Cairo or Damascus accused Israel of evil deeds or when an Iranian leader blamed America for his country's troubles. The Arabs were just playing to their "street," exploiting petty hatreds and envy for political purposes, while the Iranians were trying to divert attention from their own disastrous management of the economy, which was the direct result of having put village clerics with a grade-school education in charge of a major oil-producing nation of sixty million people. They weren't anti-Semites; they were just anti-Israel or anti-imperialist, as hatred of America's freedoms used to be called before the collapse of the Soviet empire.

The term *anti-Semitism* was invented in 1879 by an otherwise undistinguished German journalist named Wilhelm Marr, although "the special hatred of the Jews which it designated was very old, going back to the rise of Christianity."[2] Jew-hatred has prompted extraordinary crimes over many centuries. In the good times, Jews in Europe and the Ottoman empire were called upon to finance kingdoms and dynasties, all the while relegated to ghettos, where they were tolerated, if not loved. In bad times, they were rounded up and massacred in periodic pogroms. *The Protocols of the Elders of Zion* codified the fear of a Jewish world conspiracy and elevated it to an almost mythic level. The work made its first appearance in 1895, an invention of the Russian czar's secret service, which modeled it on an earlier tract purporting to expose the machinations of the French emperor Napoleon III. The czar's forgers "took this pamphlet, substituted world Jewry for the French emperor, and added a number of picturesque details borrowed from an obscure German novel," writes Middle East scholar Bernard Lewis.[3]

Ignored elsewhere at first, the *Protocols* entered widespread circulation during the Russian civil wars of 1918–1921, when "the leaders of the White Russians used the *Protocols* extensively to persuade the Russian people that the so-called revolution was no more than a Jewish plot to impose a Jewish government on Russia, as a step toward the ultimate aim of Jewish world domination." The notion of a Jewish world conspiracy, of course, dominated the warped ideology of Adolf Hitler and the Third Reich and was epitomized in the anti-Semitic rantings of the Nazi party broadsheet, *Der Stürmer.* By blaming Germany's ills on a Jewish "plot," Hitler had a scapegoat and an enemy ready-made. This has always been one of the staples of classic anti-Semitic beliefs.

Like most Americans of the postwar baby boom generation, I was brought up to dismiss this type of propaganda for the transparent bigotry that it was. The horror of the Holocaust has become even more distant for my children, brought up by teachers and university faculty to believe that only "right-wing nuts" could be capable of racism and intolerance. But Jew-hatred runs like a silent river deep in the human psyche. In some places it hides in subterranean reservoirs that can be tapped only through a massive, conscious effort, as was done by Hitler and Joseph Goebbels. In others, it lies just beneath the surface and gushes forth in all its ugliness from the slightest pinprick. As I was about to find out to my surprise, nowhere does it simply disappear, wished away by the politically correct.

†††

Dr. Ahmad Bahar is widely recognized in Gaza and by Western diplomats as one of the main spokesmen of the political wing of Hamas. He heads the Islamic Society, a "charitable" institution that collects funds from the United States, Germany, Jordan, Saudi Arabia, and Arabs in the West Bank and Israel.[4] He also teaches Arabic language and literature at the Islamic University in Gaza. Dr. Bahar received a master's degree in Egypt and says he took a doctorate in Arabic language studies from Oum Durman University in Khartoum, Sudan.

I met him in his sparsely furnished office at the Islamic Society in

Gaza. With his thick gray beard, plain gray robe, and simple headdress, he could have been a village schoolteacher. During a taped interview, Dr. Bahar sketched out a system of beliefs derived extensively from *The Protocols of the Elders of Zion,* a work Dr. Bahar recommended to his university students to explain the behavior and ambitions of the Jews.

"We know from *The Protocols of Zion* that the Jews want to conquer the world," he told me matter-of-factly. "Why else do Jews come to Palestine from the United States, Russia, and elsewhere, when they have never seen Palestine before? They come because the Talmud exhorts them to do so. It says that any Jew who doesn't come to Palestine is an atheist and a criminal. In the *Protocols,* the Jews themselves explain that they want to control the whole world and that other people are servants and they, the Jews, are the masters. So it is written."[5]

I asked Dr. Bahar about the origin of this work that has become the defining text of anti-Semites the world over.

"The *Protocols* were written by those who call themselves the Wise Zionists," he said, "who met to plan how they would take over the world. They colored their plans with religion, in order to gather support from Jews from all over the world. They claim in the *Protocols* that they are the chosen people of God and try to implant this concept into the minds of the Jews as if it had come directly by the Torah and the Talmud."

His literal interpretation of the *Protocols* intrigued me. Here was an educated man who apparently accepted a known fabrication as gospel truth. For Ahmad Bahar and so many others, the "wise men of Zion" *actually held* a series of conspiratorial meetings to hammer out a plan for world domination, and the *Protocols* are the *actual written minutes* of those meetings.

The book was so well-known that he didn't even bother to assign it to his students. "It is in every student's personal library, so they can read it for themselves. But sometimes, if we want to bring an example to the students, we use a quotation from these protocols. It is scientific."

It was absolutely clear, he added, that the state of Israel was now implementing the *Protocols* in real life. According to Bahar, Israel's main goal through the peace process was to end the Arab economic boycott of Israel and force open trade with its neighbors, which Israel would of course dominate. "This shows that Israel wants to control the economy, as it is written in the *Protocols,*" he said. "If Israel fails to occupy those Arab countries militarily, Israel will now be able to occupy them economically and politically."

Aiding Israel in its goal of conquest, he believed, was the weakness and corruption of the Arab regimes, a theme that was already being picked up and amplified by Osama bin Laden, although few paid him much attention at the time. "Today, we do not have one leader, one army, one discipline, one regime," Bahar said. "If Muslims all over the world unite, they can implement the empire of Islam. The Islamic empire would have its leadership, say, in Egypt, and the rest of the Arab countries would be like states in this empire. We would have a central leadership, a central army, and a central policy." Jews and Christians would be welcome to live as subject peoples *(dhimmis)* in this Islamic republic as long as they did nothing to oppose Islamic domination. "We look forward to a day when Israel will cease to exist," he said simply.

†††

The Islamic "viewpoint" in Gaza and elsewhere is much less diverse than opinion in most democratic societies. Instead, there are a finite number of variations of a very small number of central themes. Holocaust denial is one of them.

Dr. Saud Shawa was a prominent political leader, associated with Hamas, who was on the board of trustees of the Islamic University in Gaza. A veterinarian by profession, Dr. Shawa received his doctorate from Cairo University in 1980 and is fluent in three languages in addition to Arabic (French, Hebrew, and English). Well-spoken, affluent, a member of Gaza's upper-middle class, Shawa represents a new power base for Hamas of wealthier Gazans who had traditionally supported the more conservative and less violent Muslim Brotherhood. Two of Shawa's brothers are also prominent political leaders in Gaza.

"Just as the Israelis today control the international economy, so they want to control us," he told me. "The superiority of Israeli businessmen will allow them to overcome Arab businessmen, primarily because of their superior organization. Jews for centuries have been better at business than others. And now, with new technology, they are getting even better. The Israelis are extremely professional at implanting Jewishness around the world. They are the supreme power in finance and in the media—the two most important elements of power in the world."[6]

Conspiratorial Jewish control of the media and of world financial institutions—twin pillars of the anti-Semitic belief, as laid out in *The Protocols of the Elders of Zion*—showed that Muslims and Christians "cannot trust the Jews," Shawa said. "It is written in the Holy Koran that the children of Israel will never respect their signature in any agreement with others. We have seen this in their relations with America—their ally. So why should we expect Israel to respect the Palestinian side, which is the weak side?"

Shawa, Bahar, and other Hamas spokesmen were anxious to take their case to the international media in the hopes, as Shawa put it, that they might find some media organization *not* controlled by the Jews. "Unfortunately, the Arabs, and especially the Islamists, have no chance yet to explain themselves to the international community as they should," Shawa said. "The Zionist movement, the Jewish media, claims that the Islamists are terrorists. But they are not. When anyone believes in Allah, they should respect the life of others, and try to help them, not kill. The Islamists hate no one—they kill no one—just because he is Jewish. It is only the Jews who kill, and most of those they kill are actually Christians."

I asked Shawa that if Islam believes in the supreme value of human life, how did he explain the terrorist attacks against Israeli civilians by Hamas and Islamic Jihad? His answer was another example of the type of twisted logic that can turn night into day, black into white, murder into righteousness.

"Those who believe in Allah must defend themselves against the attacks from any foreign country, any occupying power," he said. "The Israeli side has been occupying Palestine since 1948 until now. So according to the orders of Allah, the Islamists should defend themselves and try to end this foreign occupation. Before 1948, the Jews lived in Palestine and no one killed them, no one harmed them. And I have not heard that any Jew has been killed in Europe or America just because he is Jewish. The contrary is true. We have been killed by the Israeli side since 1948, just because we believed in Allah, and we are the owners of this land and are a peaceful people. I do not think that the Palestinians travel to Poland to kill the Jews there. But the Polish Jews came to Palestine to kill us. This is a mystery which the Zionist media all over the world has hidden, or tried to keep hidden, until now."

I expressed surprise and pointed out that six million Jews had been murdered during the Holocaust just because they were Jews.

"This is also a big illusion of the Jews," he shot back calmly. "A lot of Jews may have suffered in that war. Many people may have been killed. But they suffered like any other people who suffered in that war. French people have been killed, British people were killed, Americans, Norwegians, and so on. So to say that the Jews suffered especially is an illusion. Who could make photographs at that time? No one. But after that, the Jews made video films, movies, to convince the people that this was reality and that this actually happened. These were films produced by the Jews, but there are not any actual photographs from that period of history, which did not yet have film."

"So you're saying that the films about the Holocaust are fakes, because they had no real photographs?" I asked.

"Exactly, exactly."

"You believe there is no evidence that the death camps existed?"

"Even if they existed, it was only small, and the Jews are exaggerating the photos to generate emotion and sympathy, to make it appear as if the war was only against the Jews. That is not history."

"So if Jews suffered during World War Two, they suffered as French people, or as Norwegians, but no more?"

"Exactly, exactly," Shawa replied enthusiastically. "We also suffered, but the absence of Arab media means people in the world never hear about our suffering. During the Suez war, fifty-six Palestinians were killed in a village in northern Palestine. It happened on November 2—the anniversary of the Balfour Declaration—but no one remembers them. No Arabic film ever focused on their suffering. The Jews are much superior in this."

In our conversation so far, Dr. Shawa had volunteered his belief in several of the core elements of the world Jewish conspiracy. So I asked him if he had ever heard of *The Protocols of the Elders of Zion.*

"Of course. It explains the religious theories of the Jewish religion."

"Is this a book that people read here in Gaza?" I asked.

"Yes, it is easy to find in any bookstore for one dollar."

"Do you have a copy you could show me?"

"Of course."

He turned from his desk and took down a book called *Al-Dawa Islamiyya—The Islamic Call*—which contained a synopsis of *The Protocols of the Elders of Zion*. He showed me the Arabic text, then chose a passage and offered a rough translation. "They say here that the Jews should gain all the money of the whole world by establishing financial banks, insurance companies, nightclubs, circuses, theaters. They should gain more money from sexual affairs and industries that depend on sexual affairs such as cosmetics, hairdressers, and the like. They should build up the industries that depend on sex, and other industries where people will lose their money even faster such as gambling clubs and lotteries. All of these things are forbidden in Islam. This is a crime against society, because it breaks the family, the first cell of the community. So the Jews are trying to kill the social ethics of people all over the world.

"You also have international Jewish professors like Darwin, who falsely trace the origin of the human being to the monkey. But it is written in the Holy Koran that Allah created the human being as a human being, not as a monkey."

Perhaps the most astonishing thing about what Dr. Shawa was telling me was the utter coherence of his beliefs. There were no gaps, no flaws, no exceptions, no questions. It was all of a piece, so thoroughly ingrained to his thinking that it was second nature. He never had to search for an answer.

"Why do we never hear about these things outside the Arab world?" I wondered.

He shrugged. "Because we have no chance to explain ourselves. All I am telling you is the history of the Jews. It is based on hereditary factors of the Jews."

"Does everyone know about these Protocols?" I asked.

"It is well-known in the Arab countries. But the international media has no interest in this yet, because they don't want to oppose the Jewish ideas. The media should read the *Protocols* to understand that the Jews are also against the Christians, not just the Muslims. They have a plan. They want to control the whole world."

†††

Hamzi Mansour was the spokesman for the Islamic Action Front (IAF), the legal opposition in neighboring Jordan that serves as a front for Hamas and Islamic Jihad. He speaks an eloquent, literary Arabic. Well educated, he has frequently appeared on Jordanian television. He is no rabble-rousing populist or scruffy guerrilla leader. Like most opposition parliamentarians in Amman, Mansour feels most comfortable wearing a Western suit and tie, which he supplements with an Arab headdress. While he doesn't refer openly to the *Protocols,* the language he uses is almost identical to that used by Hamas leaders in Gaza. Mansour explained to me that the IAF was seeking the imposition of Islamic law (Sharia) and for Jordan's monarch to declare the country an Islamic state. Further down the line, he said, the IAF was seeking the unification of all Arab and Islamic states into one nation. "Islam starts with unity in Jordan first, then in the Arab and Islamic circles, then humanity at large."[7]

Mansour was categorical about Israel: "We believe that the situation in Palestine should go back to 1918—that is, before the Balfour Declaration, when there were just a small number of Jews living as citizens in Palestine. Today, there is no room in Palestine for seven million Palestinians and four million Jews. All the Palestinians should be able to return to their homes. Likewise, all the Jews should return to Poland and Russia and wherever they came from, too."

Like most of the Islamic groups, the IAF claims that Israel—all of Israel, from Galilee to Tel Aviv, from Jerusalem to Eilat—exists on occupied Arab land and that this occupation justifies violent resistance. "The Palestinian people have the right to resist the occupation, while Muslims and others are duty-bound to help them, even if this struggle continues for one hundred years," Mansour said. "It took that long to expel the Crusaders—even longer. And yet, in the end they were forced to return to their homes. The same will happen with the Jews."

Mansour and his followers are convinced there "can be no peaceful coexistence between innocent Muslims and so-called Israel. There is no way that a criminal can live side by side with the innocent."

†††

In early 1994, Amman was rocked by a series of bomb attacks that led to the arrest of several Afghan veterans affiliated to the IAF and to the Muslim Brotherhood. The head of Jordanian intelligence, Mustafa Kaisa, reportedly feared that the "Afghans" had established other clandestine terrorist cells and might be cooperating with Hamas, since many of the Afghan veterans were of Palestinian origin. As one of King Hussein's most trusted advisers explained to me in private, "Here you have pumped up this baby in an effort to fight the Soviets and later, to undermine the PLO. And now it has turned into a monster."[8] His prescient words were an eerie precursor of things to come. The core belief system of the Islamists justified war against all infidels, whether they were Soviets in Afghanistan, Jews in Israel, or Americans in New York, Paris, or Bombay. This was equal opportunity hate.

The leaders of the Muslim Brotherhood in Jordan are Islamic scholars, university professors, and members of Parliament—all of them highly educated and well aware of the world beyond Jordan's borders. Their spokesman in Amman, Yahya Shaqra, spent most of his adult life in the Gulf countries working as an engineer. Born in the British mandate of Palestine in 1946, he belonged to the first generation of Palestinian refugees and remains bitter about his exile. "There can be no real peace until everyone returns to their real homes—the Jews back to Europe, and the Palestinians back to their original homes in Palestine. Only then will everything be settled."[9] He also referred to the Crusades as his favorite history lesson. "We do not recognize Israel, and we never will. But we can wait. Look at the Crusades: it took four hundred years to expel the Crusaders, but we did. The same will happen to the Jews."

Dr. Abdallah Akailah, another member of the Muslim Brotherhood in Amman, was known in the Jordanian press for his "moderate" views. He studied at UCLA between 1978 and 1982, receiving both a master's degree and a Ph.D. We met in his office in the Jordanian Parliament building in Amman. He spoke in fluent, virtually unaccented English. "We believe that all Palestine is the land of Muslims and Arabs, and that nobody can claim the right to abdicate any part of it. Our conflict with the Jews is central. It was never a conflict just of three hundred kilometers of land, or over water rights," he said. "Through this so-called peace treaty [with Jordan], Israel has achieved what it could never achieve in forty-six years of war. Because of this, every Muslim in the world is with Hamas."[10]

Like Shaqra and Mansour, Dr. Akailah believes that all Jews should be thrown out of the former British mandate of Palestine. "We think Israel is an illegitimate state, which came and occupied Arab land. Everybody should go back to where they came from. The Jews should return to Russia, Poland, and Germany. . . . We see no role for Israel in the region."

I encountered the same public identification with Hamas in Damascus among secular Palestinian groups such as the dissident Fatah wing led by Sa'id Musa Muragha (Abu Musa).[11] With Arafat committed (temporarily, as it turned out) to peaceful coexistence with Israel, many of his secular opponents threw in their lot with the Islamist groups and joined their call to establish an Islamic republic in "all of Palestine."[12] This marriage between the secularists and the Islamists was a new development in 1994. Slowly it was becoming clear that there was no real difference between the so-called secular drive to push the Israelis into the sea because they were an occupying power and the Islamist desire to kill Jews because they were rejected by Allah. It all came down to one simple, shared belief: a hatred of the Jews.

Commenting on the statements I had gathered from these Hamas leaders and their sympathizers, Rabbi Marvin Hier of the Simon Wiesenthal Center said they showed "that despite the passage of time, the old lies used by Hitler, Goebbels, and Streicher still have currency in our world and are not only mouthed by the uninformed and uneducated but have the solid support of important segments of the intelligentsia in the Islamic world. Lecturers at universities, doctors, businessmen, engineers, have come to regard the infamous *Protocols of the Elders of Zion* as a holy work of truth, rather than as a slanderous fiction used historically to malign Jewish integrity and threaten Jewish lives."[13]

Dr. Abdul Aziz Rantissi is a pediatrician and one of the main Hamas spokesmen in Gaza. He receives journalists in a bare office off his medical practice on Orabi Street not far from the United Nations beach camp, a sprawling compound of air-conditioned Quonset huts where foreign soldiers can drink beer and watch forbidden videos protected by sentries and barbed wire. By the time I met Rantissi in 1997, not long after his release from an Israeli jail, Palestinian suicide bombers had murdered hundreds of innocent Israeli civilians, and I had met two of them in person. One, a young man introduced to me by Islamic Jihad militants in Gaza, spoke of yearning for death and Jewish blood. We met in an abandoned garage heated only by a twig fire, while outside the activists chanted slogans that became eerily familiar to me years later, when I heard them repeated by the grand mufti of Jerusalem, Ikrima Sabri. "Our dead are in heaven, while their dead are in hell," one of the banners they chanted read. "We are seeking death, while the Jews seek life and its joys." Six days after our encounter, the young man—whose name was Hisham Ismail Hamed—strapped explosives around his waist and rode his bicycle into an Israeli army checkpoint near Gaza, obliterating himself and three Israeli soldiers. The second bomber had been captured by Arafat's security forces in Gaza after a failed suicide attack by a member of his terror cell. Treated gently and with respect by his Palestinian Authority jailors, he vowed to me that he was ready to carry out a suicide attack just as soon as he was released, if "all" of Palestine had not been liberated. I asked him what could possibly motivate young men to carry out such attacks. He launched into a long, familiar tirade about the Israeli "occupation," but I knew that something was missing. Palestinian leaders had been complaining about Israeli actions for fifty years, but only recently had young people taken the dramatic step of blowing themselves up just to kill Jews. What was it that had changed? I wondered. "They know that these bombings are the same as fasting and observing Ramadan," Rantissi said. "They increase their blessings with God."[14]

Rantissi's words might seem odd to Americans or Europeans, but they make perfect sense to Palestinians and other Muslim Arabs who have been fed the steady diet of anti-Semitic filth that state-sponsored preachers throughout the Middle East have been doling out to the faithful for the past two decades. Fasting and observing Ramadan are two of the Five Pillars of Islam, which the Prophet Mohammad exhorted his followers to observe. In the hierarchy of traditional Islam, prayers performed during Ramadan are believed to have a greater intercessionary value, as do prayers uttered in one of the Two Holy Mosques in the Arabian peninsula.

What Rantissi was saying was that carrying out suicide attacks will have the same effect, in effect elevating murder into a sixth pillar of Islam.

With each new suicide bombing, the Clinton administration was pressing the Israelis to make fresh concessions to the Palestinians, on the assumption that an improvement in Palestinian living conditions, more money, more jobs, fewer roadblocks, and fewer reprisals by Israel some- how would decrease the tension. A similar dynamic was set in motion after the June 4, 2003, Red Sea summit, when Palestinian Prime Minister Mahmoud Abbas (aka Abu Mazen) pledged to crack down on terror if only the Israelis would improve living conditions for Palestinians and dis- mantle "illegal" settlements. I asked Rantissi how much he felt the Israelis had to give before Hamas and Islamic Jihad would call off the sui- cide bombers.

"The Jews should go to America and make their state there. It's a big land, and millions of Jews are already there. This is the only solution: Establish Israel in America. . . . There is no room for Jews and Palestinians to live together." He has not changed that view today.[15]

Rantissi also believed the Holocaust was a Jewish invention. "Any massacre that may have occurred in Europe was because of the corrup- tion of the Jews. We believe the Jews will spread corruption until the end of time. The Koran says this in *Al-Isra'a*. The Jews also believe this," he added. "The Torah says the Jews would spread corruption around the world, and that Jews would establish a strong state at a time when Muslims were very numerous but weak. The Prophet Muhammad (Peace be upon him) said that when this happens, the Muslims would be like froth on the river, without any value. But then the Muslims will return to their religion and their strength, and the Jews will be destroyed in Pales- tine. This is all in the Koran and the hadith. If I do not believe in this, then I will go to hell. All Muslims believe this."[16]

The deep anti-Semitism that pervades the mind-set of these leaders went mostly unreported in the Western media until just recently. Until September 11, it was politically incorrect to suggest that Muslim leaders such as these might actually *hate* Jews. Yet the evidence had been out in the open for some time. In the forty-page Hamas charter, dated August 18, 1988, and leaked to the press a few weeks later (see Appendix B), Hamas leaders cite the *Protocols* repeatedly. They allege "the Zionist invasion" relies "upon the secret organizations which grew out of it such as the Free Masons, Rotary and Lions Club. All these organizations, both secret and public, work for the sake of Zionism."[17]

In Article 32 of the Charter, the Hamas founders spell out these beliefs in more detail, making clear that Israel and America are engaged side by side in a struggle against the Muslim world. "World Zionism and the imperialist powers are trying through wise movement and careful planning to get Arab countries one by one out of the circle of struggle with Zionism so that finally they will face only the Palestinian people . . . today it will be Palestine, but tomorrow it will be some other country since the Zionist plan has no limits. After Palestine, they aspire the destruction of the areas they reach, they will still aspire to further expansion. Their plan is *The Protocols of the Elders of Zion,* and their present [conduct] testifies to the truth of what we say."

But the most sweeping statement of belief in a world Jewish conspiracy found in the Hamas Charter could have been copied directly from *Mein Kampf:*

Our enemies have planned from time immemorial in order to reach the position they've obtained now. They strive to collect enormous material riches to be used in the realization of their dream. With money, they've gained control of the international media beginning with news agencies, newspapers and publishing houses, broadcasting stations . . . with their money, they have detonated revolutions in different parts of the world to obtain their interests and reap their fruits. They were behind the French Revolution and the Communist Revolution and were also responsible for most of the revolutions we've heard about elsewhere. With their money, they have created secret organizations which spread through the world in order to destroy societies, and to achieve the Zionist interest such as the Free Masons, the Rotary and the Lions Club. All these are destructive espionage organizations. With their money, they've been able to take control over the imperialist countries and push them to occupy many states in order to suck the riches of these countries and spread corruption there. The same goes for international and local wars. They were behind World

War I in order to destroy the Islamic Caliphate [Turkey] and make
material profit. Then they obtained the Balfour Declaration and established the League of Nations in order to rule the world through this
organization.

They were also behind World War II where they made enormous profits from speculation in war material; paved the way for the creation of
their state and inspired the establishment of the United Nations and Security Council to replace the League of Nations in order to rule the world
through them. There is no war anywhere in which their fingers do not
play. . . . The Imperialist powers in the capitalist West and the Communist East support the enemy with everything they can. And they switch
roles. . . . In the day that Islam will appear, the powers of heresy will unite
to confront it because the nation of heresy is one.[18]

Looking at the conflict, former Lebanese president Charles Helou
called it a "war of religion" between Jews and Muslims. "This is why a
territorial solution is not enough," he told me when we met in Beirut at a
conference on the Arab-Israeli conflict. "The enemies have to learn to love
each other, to grant each other a place in paradise." To Helou, a Maronite
Christian, the conflict was reminiscent of sixteenth-century France, when
Catholics and Protestants fought long wars over the French throne. When
a Protestant, Henri IV, signed the Edict of Nantes in 1598, granting full
political and religious freedom to French Protestants, his Catholic successors reversed him and under Louis XIV and Cardinal Richelieu began per-
secuting Protestants again. "Remember, it took a full century to revoke the
Edict of Nantes. A conflict among prophets is always a major event in the
history of the world."[19]

THE ELEMENTS OF HATE

4

What I saw in Gaza and Amman were all the classic elements of Muslim anti-Semitism, so thoroughly engrained into the consciousness of leaders and ordinary citizens of the Arab world that they spouted them as received truths, irrefutable, immutable, and beyond question, as if they had been handed down directly from God. This is not a simple political dispute over territory, boundaries, and national sovereignty. It is a deep-seated hatred and denial of the other that has clear historic precedents and has found fertile ground in a Muslim world that has been in steady decline since the collapse of the Ottoman empire after World War I. Understanding this hate is of paramount importance for Americans, since we are seen as co-responsible with the Jews for the decline and fall of the empire of Islam.

Clearly the most widespread expression of Muslim anti-Semitism today is the notion of a Jewish world conspiracy, as typified in *The Protocols of the Elders of Zion* and similar works that pretend to set out the dreams and designs of "world Jewry." When this hateful fantasy is turned against America, "world Jewry" is replaced by "imperialism" and "globalization" as the malign forces threatening a society that is profoundly insecure and feels under siege because it is incapable of adapting to the modern world. Conspiracy theories are effective tools for controlling populations taught to feel powerless in the face of momentous events their leaders are unable to control or derail.

Apologists of Islam and the political Left in Europe dismiss claims of anti-Semitism by saying they are opposed to the Jewish state, not to Jews. But since the first days of Israel's existence as a modern nation-state, anti-Zionism and anti-Semitism have been irrevocably intertwined in the popular mind and press. The official Syrian, Egyptian, and Saudi media have feasted on a steady diet of Jew-hatred since the early 1950s. One seminal text, published in Alexandria in 1950, claims that Jews remain Jews even if they embrace Christianity or Islam. It concludes: "The Jews and Zionism are like an evil tree. Its root is in New York, its branches are all over the world, its leaves the Jews—all of them, old and young, male and female, without exception, are its thorny leaves and poisoned thorns, and the poison is swift and deadly."[1]

Arab leaders such as Gamal Abdel Nasser and Anwar Sadat of Egypt and King Faisal of Saudi Arabia have been giving away copies of *The Protocols of the Elders of Zion* to visiting dignitaries and journalists since the 1950s.[2] Nasser's brother Shawqi edited and wrote a preface to one Arabic-language edition, published in Cairo in 1968.[3]

For fifty years, Arab leaders have actively encouraged the official media in their countries to spread hatred of the Jews themselves, not just Israel, but this practice has accelerated dramatically today. The depth of Jew-hatred spread liberally from Rabat to Riyadh and Tehran ranges from the classic accusation of medieval Christiandom that the Jews murdered Christ to the blood libel that Jews murder non-Jews in order to obtain blood to make Passover matzah or Purim pastries. It includes an extraordinary panoply of beliefs, fabrications, and hallucinations that defy the rational mind, from denial of the Holocaust to lies that Israel has used chemical weapons against Palestinian civilians or has laced chewing gum sent into the territories with aphrodisiacs to pervert the morals of Muslim men. Along the way, it highlights Koranic verses that portray Jews as the sons of "monkeys and pigs" and that accuse Jews of betraying the Prophet

Muhammad. This pseudoreligious aspect of Muslim anti-Semitism fuels popular imams and prayer leaders who enthusiastically provide their followers with religious justifications for murdering Jews. "The aim is not simply to morally delegitimize Israel as a Jewish state and a national entity in the Middle East, but to dehumanize Judaism and the Jewish people as such," writes historian Robert Wistrich.[4]

While the bulk of this hate literature has been examined by scholars over the years, it has remained inaccessible to Western journalists who were not fluent in Arabic or Persian, and even less so to the general public. The U.S. government's Foreign Broadcast Information Service (FBIS), which published daily compilations of the Arabic-, Persian-, and Hebrew-language broadcast media (along with a smattering of articles from the written press), had tended to focus on diplomatic traffic. Although it was funded by the Central Intelligence Agency, many FBIS translations were filed by Foreign Service officers on post in the region, who dismissed the outrageous outbursts by Muslim clerics and the anti-Semitic statements of political leaders as so much huffing and puffing. In the late 1980s, the Middle East FBIS publications focused on the so-called rogue states, Iran, Iraq, and Libya, with emphasis on Saddam Hussein's growing military power, Libya's chemical weapons program, and Iran's support for international terror. FBIS regularly published the rantings of Colonel Muammar al-Qaddafi and radical anti-American sermons by Iranian clerics as examples of the irrationality of these regimes. They translated the entire annual budget debate in the Iranian Majlis (Parliament), so voluminous it took up a separate booklet. As a daily reader of FBIS for nearly a decade (1985–1994), however, I cannot recall a single instance where the type of hate speech you'll see here was translated by FBIS from the official Saudi, Egyptian, United Arab Emirates (UAE), or Kuwaiti press. It is quite possible that the State Department diplomats shied away from translating Friday prayer sermons from Mecca because they knew it would outrage the U.S. Congress. These countries were U.S. allies—at least, so Congress and the public were told. To hear sentiments such as these would severely challenge that assertion.

††††

Within months of Arafat's entry to Gaza in July 1994, Israeli journalists and scholars such as David Bedein, Michael Widlanski, and Itamar Marcus began picking up disturbing trends. "Arafat would be talking about peace in English," says Bedein, who runs the Israel Resource News Agency in Jerusalem. "But in Arabic, he was going from village to village, preaching jihad." Bedein hired an Arab film crew to cover Arafat's appearances and by 1995 pulled together the footage into a video with English-language subtitles that he distributed to the U.S. and Israeli governments and the press. But no one wanted to know what was going on.[5]

Yigal Carmon, a former counterterrorism adviser to Israel's Likud and Labor prime ministers, is a master linguist and worked with Bedein on the project. He remembers well what happened next. "We handed out the video just before Prime Minister Peres met with Arafat in Taba in December 1995. A journalist asked Peres what he thought of Arafat's latest speech, calling for jihad. So Peres turned to Arafat, addressing him as 'Mr. President'—the first time an Israeli prime minister had ever done so in front of television cameras—and asked him to dispel the rumors about 'forged videos' circulating in the media. Arafat said, 'No, they are not forged. Those were my words.' But then he claimed that in Arabic 'jihad' does not mean war." And, incredibly, that was the end of it. Hard-documented evidence of Arafat's duplicity was not considered newsworthy by the press or of concern to the U.S. or Israeli governments.

Carmon is something of a legend within the intelligence community. On his last day in office as Prime Minister Rabin's counterterrorism adviser, he was giving a briefing at the Pentagon. It was February 26, 1993, and his subject was Islamic fundamentalism. "I gave them quotes, sources, and ended up an hour-long presentation by telling them that Islamic fundamentalism was an imminent threat to the United States," Carmon recalls. "It was a around 10 A.M. when I had finished. They said thank you very much, very polite, but you could see in their eyes that they thought I was nuts. As I was getting ready to return to Israel, at twelve twenty-four, boom—it was the first World Trade Center attack." All of a sudden Carmon's "wild" predictions bore down with all the ominous weight of tragedy.

Israeli scholars and journalists continued to monitor Arafat's statements in Arabic. Itamar Marcus, who had been working as an assistant to the Labor Party minister of religious affairs, left government and in 1996 founded Palestinian Media Watch, a nonprofit organization that has monitored and translated excerpts from official Palestinian Authority television, newspapers, schoolbooks, and government statements. But still no one was looking at the wider situation elsewhere in the Arab world and Iran.

Not long after the Arafat tape, Carmon was chatting at the water cooler in a video studio with friends, and it dawned on him. "I realized that access to primary sources in the Middle East is very limited. People are just not getting them. So I decided to work on this niche." In Washington, the owlish Carmon teamed up with a young scholar named Meyrav Wurmser, whose articulate speech and cover girl looks made her a natural choice for U.S. television bookers. Together they recruited a team of volunteer Arabic- and Persian-language linguists with the aim of scouring the official and semiofficial press in the region and began to raise money from private donors. "We didn't focus on the Arab-Israeli conflict, as others were doing," Carmon says. "Our idea was to bridge the gap between the Middle East and the United States. I wanted to give legislators, the media, government, and academia access to full-source material, not just summaries. They needed to hear the full music, not just thirty-second sound bites. I wanted everyone in America to be able to read an editorial from Al-Ahram [the leading government-owned daily in Egypt] with their morning coffee, just as they would read The New York Times." Since then, the Middle East Media Research Institute has brought the cultures of the Middle East to Congress, journalists, and the public in unadulterated translations, without comment, much to the displeasure of the radical Islamists and their apologists in America. "It's a free country and they can print what they like," groused Ibrahim Hooper of the Saudi-backed Council on American Islamic Relations (CAIR).[6]

But no one has challenged the scrupulous accuracy of MEMRI's translations, which are drawn from the mainstream print and broadcast media in the Middle East. "Anti-Semitism is definitely part of it," Carmon says, "but it's not the whole picture. It's maybe 10 percent of what we do. We also work on Iran. We have an economic project. And we have a reform project that publishes in English the work of Muslim reformers who normally get shut out of the media by the Saudi-financed news media."

Four years after MEMRI began work, other groups caught on and launched their own translation services. One of these, the opposition Saudi Institute in Washington, D.C., has begun exploring the extensive anti-Semitic and anti-American propaganda directly funded by the royal embassy of Saudi Arabia and by surrogates such as the World Muslim League and ostensibly private foundations, which have placed Saudi-trained clerics in the overwhelming majority of the 1,400 registered mosques in the United States.[7]

What emerges most strongly from MEMRI's work is the stark difference between the reality of the Middle East and the way it has generally been portrayed in the Western press, which has adopted the political filters of Western governments in its quest to make the region appear hospitable to trade and commerce. Yet even Anwar Sadat, the Egyptian president hailed as a "moderate" and a "peacemaker" in the West because he became the first Arab leader to make peace with Israel, expressed rabidly anti-Semitic views at the very moment he was shaking hands with Israeli prime minister Menachem Begin in Jerusalem in 1977. As a young officer, Sadat had been a keen admirer of Adolf Hitler, an affection he never abandoned over the years. In 1953, rumors spread that Hitler was still alive and living in Brazil. This prompted the Egyptian weekly *Al-Musawwar* to ask public figures what they would say to the führer if they could write to him. Sadat was one of those who replied: "I congratulate you with all my heart, because, though you appear to have been defeated, you were the real victor. You were able to sow dissension between Churchill, the old man, and his allies on the one hand and their ally, the devil, on the other. . . . That you should become immortal in Germany is reason enough for pride. And we should not be surprised to see you again in Germany, or a new Hitler in your place."[8]

Twenty-four years later, Sadat made his historic trip to Jerusalem as president of Egypt, becoming the first Arab leader in history to address the Israeli Parliament, the Knesset. Even as he stood before the television cameras and history, with the full Israeli government looking on in approval, Sadat displayed his favorite tie, an eye-dazzling pastiche of large unmistakable Nazi swastikas plastered up and down his chest.[9] Today, a whole generation of Egyptians, such as Hitler Tantawi—director of the Administrative Monitoring Authority, which audits government agencies—bears witness to the admiration many people felt for the German führer.

I had gotten a first glimpse of the disconnect between the official discourse and what Arab and Muslim leaders were saying among themselves in 1994, when my verbatim interviews with Islamic leaders were published as a monograph by the Simon Wiesenthal Center in Los Angeles. Their explicit, unapologetic anti-Semitism was so different from what one could read in *The New York Times* or *The Washington Post* that I felt it merited being read in full. But I had no idea just how important reading such transcripts would become in exposing a deep underlying system of beliefs that has become the mainstream throughout the Muslim Middle East. MEMRI changed all that.

"To understand any conflict, you have to see the whole picture," says Carmon. "Media represents the present, what is happening today. Schoolbooks are the future, because they shape the leaders and citizens of tomorrow. Religious institutions are the soul. You need to examine all three to see whether a problem is just froth on the waves, or whether it goes much deeper."

† † †

Employing the invaluable MEMRI translations, one can start to understand the "what" of contemporary Muslim anti-Semitism.

"What exactly do the Jews want?" asks an editorialist writing in the leading Egyptian government daily, *Al-Ahram,* on June 23, 2001. To find out, he suggests readers look at the Ninth Protocol of the elders of Zion.

We have limitless ambitions, inexhaustible greed, merciless vengeance, and hatred beyond imagination. We are a secret army whose plans are impossible to understand by using honest methods. Cunning is our approach, mystery is our way. [The way] of the "Free Masons," in which we believe, can not be understood by those among the gentiles who are stupid pigs. . . .

In order to destroy the gentiles' industry, we create scalping and raise the prices of basic commodities and industries' raw materials. We control the stock market, distribute drugs, and create chaos among the blue-collar workers. We persecute any wisdom amongst gentiles. We spread out disputes, conflicts, and hatred between peoples by using harmless organizations such as: "The Rotary Lyons Clubs" and "The Jehovah Witnesses." We seek out and feel what is going on inside people's minds and hearts. . . ."[10]

The Free Masons are seen as the leading edge of world Jewry in their goal "to destroy the world and build it anew according to the Zionist policy so that the Jews can control the world and destroy the [world's] religions," the same article goes on. "Their goal is that there won't be any other religion but the religion of Moses, no other law but that of Moses, and no other book except for the Torah."

In case his readers had been wondering about momentous events that have changed world history over the past several hundred years, this writer and hundreds others like him has an answer: They were all caused by the Jews as part of their grand scheme of conquest. Thus, according to the *Al-Ahram* editorialist, "Jewish Karl Marx using his Communism and Marxism . . . actually destroyed the Church in Eastern Europe" as part of the Jewish scheme.[11] If Mikhail Gorbachev ultimately dismantled the Soviet Union, that, too, was part of a larger Jewish plan of world domination, since it put Russia into the hands of a coterie of Jewish bankers and tycoons who controlled President Boris Yeltsin.[12]

In December 2001, during the second half of the holy month Ramadan, well-known Egyptian actor Muhammad Subhi announced he was producing a thirty-part extravaganza with a cast of four hundred, which purported to be a dramatic presentation of the twenty-four Protocols of the elders of Zion. Entitled *Horseman Without a Horse,* the series, ultimately translated by MEMRI, traced the history of the modern Middle East from the 1948 war back to the early days of the Zionist movement in Basel, Switzerland, and London. The main thrust of the series, actor-producer Subhi told the weekly *Roz al-Youssuf,* was to examine whether the Protocols "are an invention—as [the Jews] claim," or whether they accurately document a Jewish world conspiracy. "All we have to do is to trace the [implementation of the] twenty-four Protocols; if we find that some of them have come to pass, we must expect that the rest also will." Subhi said he "found that nineteen of the twenty-four Protocols had [already] been put into practice." His film would expose those Protocols "in a dramatic, comic, historic, national, tragic, and romantic manner."[13] The series was expanded to forty-one episodes during production.

The Egyptian government was stung by international criticism for its eagerness to broadcast the series on state-run television. "We pointed out the damage such a film would do to their image, and that in our view there is no acceptable level of anti-Semitic content," U.S. ambassador David Welch told me in Cairo. After Welch's repeated protests, Information Minister Safwat el-Sherif convened a special committee to review the script. Not to worry, he concluded: the committee decided it was not anti-Semitic and allowed the series to be broadcast during Ramadan in 2002.[14]

In response to concerns expressed by Congressmen Benjamin Gilman (R-N.Y.) and Henry Waxman (D-Calif.) just before the series aired in November 2002, Egyptian president Hosni Mubarak urged the congressmen to "hold your judgment of this series till you have a chance to see it." Not only was it *not* anti-Semitic, Mubarak said, but the series "is in no way based on *The Protocols of Elders of Zion* and does not try to prove or disprove them." Such accusations were nothing but an anti-Egyptian "campaign," he insisted.[15]

Those who say that the anti-Semitism in the Egyptian media is evidence of a free press should think again. While the government doesn't control every line of every story, it still maintains a censorship office that vets major stories. Even more important, the government owns all the major dailies, and radio and television stations. The top editors of the Egyptian press are not only appointed and paid by the government, they are close confidants of the president and are considered his quasi-official mouthpieces, whenever he chooses to use them. When the United States complained in April 2001, five months before September 11, of a "drumbeat" of criticism against the United States and Israel, the Egyptian government intervened. "The Ministry of Information called editors and said tone it down, and they did," a U.S. official in the region told me.

At times, the censor's scissors reach even beyond Egypt's borders. When Egyptian American intellectual Saad Eddin Ibrahim wrote a humorous article about Mr. Mubarak's son in an Arabic-language weekly published in London in 1999, the Egyptian government sentenced him to seven years in prison on charges of sedition. After intense pressure from the U.S.

government, Professor Ibrahim was ultimately released in December 2002, pending an appeal.[16]

After watching excerpts of the film, which Carmon played to a packed House Foreign Affairs Committee hearing in early February 2003, Congressman Tom Lantos (D-Calif.) expressed disappointment with Mubarak. "Each time I meet with President Mubarak," he said, "I present him a series of anti-Semitic cartoons that have appeared in the Egyptian press. His response is invariably that the media is free and not controlled by the government." This was "palpably untrue," Lantos added, noting that the most vicious anti-Semitic cartoons and articles actually appeared in media directly owned and managed by the government.

Sheikh Muhammad Sayyid Tantawi, rector of al-Azhar Islamic University in Cairo, dismissed the criticism in an interview with an Egyptian newspaper. "The charge of anti-Semitism was invented by the Jews, as a means of pressuring the Arabs and Muslims and with the aim of implementing their conspiracies in the Arab and Muslim countries. It should be disregarded," he said.[17]

†††

Field Marshal Mustafa Tlass understands power. For the past thirty years, despite all the ups and downs of Syria's domestic political situation, he has presided over his nation's Defense Ministry. During that time, Syria has fought two wars with Israel and occupied neighboring Lebanon, where it helped to establish an aggressive terrorist organization—Hezbollah—that has murdered Jews around the world. When Islamic fundamentalists rose up against the Baathist regime in the town of Hama in February 1982, General Tlass and the Syrian high command ordered government troops to raze the city, murdering twenty thousand of their fellow citizens. The neighborhood around the main mosque that had been the stronghold of the fundamentalists was paved with asphalt and turned into a parking lot.

Mustafa Tlass has long fancied himself a poet and a scholar, not just an army general. In 1984, Tlass published a work entitled *The Matzah of Zion,* which purports to tell the true story of how Damascene Jews murdered a Christian priest in 1840 to obtain his blood for their Passover matzah. In Tlass's preface to this purportedly historical work, he warns: "The Jew can . . . kill you and take your blood in order to make his Zionist bread. . . . I hope that I will have done my duty in presenting the practices of the enemy of our historic nation. Allah aid this project."[18]

Tlass explained that his account of the so-called Damascus Affair was based on "classified" investigative reports from the French Foreign Ministry he had unearthed in Paris, Vienna, and in the archives of the American University in Beirut. "Damascus was shaken by a heinous crime [in 1840]," he wrote. "Father Thomas al-Kabushi fell victim to the Jewish community, who wanted to extract his blood for the manufacture of festival unleavened bread for the Festival of Kippur (Day of Atonement) [sic— should be Festival of Passover]. Here opens before us a page even more ugly than the crime itself: the religious beliefs of the Jews and the destructive perversions they contain, which draw their orientation from a dark hate toward all humankind and all religions."[19]

What actually happened in Damascus in 1840 is well-known to historians and involved a plot by a pair of French consuls in Damascus, not a conspiracy by local Jews. "In Damascus, a partially-Christian city, a Capucin monk, Father Thomas, mysteriously disappeared in February 1840," writes Léon Poliakov, a French historian of anti-Semitism. "French consuls Ratti-Menton and Cochelet imputed his disappearance to the Jewish community, and leveled accusations against them of ritual murder. After severe torture some died, some renounced their faith, while others made false confessions."[20] Inspired by the French and their own clerics, crowds of Christians and Muslims went on a killing spree to avenge the missing priest, murdering Jews and plundering their possessions. To this day, despite the repudiation of the blood libel by Vatican II in 1965, a plaque commemorating the "Damascus Affair" can still be found in the Terra Sancta Church in Damascus. Inscribed in Italian and Arabic, it reads: "Here rest the bones of Father Thomas of Sardinia, a Capuchin missionary, murdered by the Hebrews on the 5th February 1840."[21] In fact, the remains of Father Thomas were never found.

When David Littman, representing a progressive Jewish organization, read passages from General Tlass's preface at the annual meeting of the United Nations Commission on Human Rights in Geneva in 1991, he was astonished by the response from the Syrian delegate, Ms. Nabila Chaalan.

Clutching a copy of *The Matzah of Zion,* with a vivid color illustration of three knife-wielding Jews wearing skullcaps drawing blood from the horrified Christian priest on its cover, Ms. Chaalan repeated Tlass's claim that the book was solidly grounded in "the historical realities recorded in the legal investigative files of France." In the name of the Syrian government, she said, "We should like to urge all members of the Commission to read this very important work that demonstrates unequivocally the historical reality of Zionist racism."[22]

Since it was revived by General Tlass in 1984, the blood libel has become a staple of anti-Semitic hate throughout the Middle East. At the beginning of the second *intifada* in October 2000, the Palestinian Liberation Army mufti, Sheikh Colonel Nader al-Tamimi, took part in a debate on the Qatar-based television news station Al-Jazeera and claimed, "There can be no peace with the Jews because they use and suck the blood of Arabs on the holidays of Passover and Purim."[23] Just four days later, *Al-Ahram* daily in Cairo published a full-page article by columnist 'Adel Hamooda entitled "A Jewish Matzah Made from Arab Blood." Recalling a story he had heard from his grandfather that he had always thought "was a fairy tale," Hamooda recounts how he discovered "the truth" in a book published in Cairo in 1898, which purports to be based on interrogation files of Jews who confessed to the murder of Father Tomas.[24] In it, Hamooda writes, the "murderers" vividly describe how they handcuffed the priest, "put his neck on a basin and slaughtered him . . . very careful to make sure that not a single drop [of blood] was spilled."

> The blood is put into Matzah, which is not given to everyone, only to the most Orthodox Jews. They send flour to the Chief Rabbi Yakov Antebi who kneads the dough himself and puts the blood into it secretly without anyone knowing it. He sends Matzah to whoever sends him flour.

Hamooda's description of the alleged ritual murder goes on for pages. "The amazing thing is that none of the Rabbis who committed this terrible crime repented or felt that they committed a crime. The explanation for this is found in the Talmud. . . . According to the Talmud, Jewish souls are more precious to God than other souls, because the souls of non-Jews are devilish and resemble animal souls. They believe the non-Jews are like dogs, donkeys, and bulls and that their homes are mangers and that they are profane souls whose lives are worthless which is why it is permitted to murder, slaughter, cheat, deceive, steal from, and beat them, rape their wives and mock them."

> These [Jewish] convictions justify in their eyes the murder of Father Tomas and his servant Ibrahim Amara. This also explains what we see on TV screens where Israeli occupation armies kill children mercilessly while chewing gum as if they are on a trip or at a ball . . . not as if they kill human beings, rather as if they were killing stray animals in accordance with the religious law set forth in the Talmud.

After presenting the blood libel as fact, the *Al-Ahram* commentator completed this amazing piece of invective with a conclusion that could have been written by the propagandists of the Third Reich:

> The bestial drive to knead Passover Matzahs with the blood of non-Jews is [confirmed] in the records of the Palestinian police where there are many recorded cases of the bodies of Arab children who had disappeared being found torn to pieces without a single drop of blood. The most reasonable explanation is that the blood was taken to be kneaded into the dough of extremist Jews to be used in Matzahs to be devoured during Passover.[25]

Thanks to MEMRI, readers and policy makers in America and Europe can read the type of filth that the Egyptian government's flagship newspaper puts out every day to millions of Egyptian citizens. Hamooda's slanders were not condemned by anyone in a position of authority in Egypt or elsewhere in the Arab world. On the contrary: when a French group filed a complaint for hate speech against Hamooda and the government-owned newspaper that published his article, Egyptian foreign minister Ahmed Maher personally intervened with the French government to get the case transferred to an Egyptian court, where it has gone nowhere.[26] But the article attracted the attention of an Egyptian film producer named Munir Radhi, who told the Egyptian weekly *Roz al-Youssuf* four months later that he had signed a contract with General Tlass to make a film adaptation of *The Matzah of Zion*, tentatively titled *Hariri's List*, after the rabbi accused of the ritual murder. The reason for changing the name of Tlass's famous work, Radhi explained, was to respond to "*Schindler's List,* which supports the idea of the Jews' right to the land of Palestine." The heroes of his movie "will expose much more horrible things than this loathsome crime," he said, such as "the connection between Western colonialism and the Zionist movement."[27] The Tlass Publishing House announced the eighth reprint of his work at the Damascus Book Fair in October 2002, citing its tremendous popularity and "the will of the next generation to know about the Jews, how they harmed Arabs and others, and their motives to murder other human beings."[28]

These are not isolated examples, nor are Syria and Egypt alone in spreading such lies, whose aim is to portray Jews as monsters devoid of all humanity. In an article published in *Al-Riyadh,* a government-controlled daily in Saudi Arabia, Dr. Umayma Ahmad al-Jalahma of King Faisal University in Al-Dammam wrote her own version of how Jews are obliged by their holy books to slaughter innocents in order to use their blood in Purim pastries.

"I chose to speak about the Jewish holiday of Purim," this scholar begins, "because it is connected to the month of March. This holiday has some dangerous customs that will, no doubt, horrify you, and I apologize if any reader is harmed because of this."[29] Then, in the best parodic style of Jonathan Swift, who famously argued that the most rational solution to Irish poverty was for Irish parents to eat their babies, she explained in great detail the special preparations the Jews make for Purim. Only, as opposed to Swift's "modest proposal," she was serious.

During this holiday, the Jews must prepare very special pastries, the filling of which is not only costly and rare—it cannot be found at all on the local and international markets. Unfortunately, this filling cannot be left out, or substituted with any alternative serving the same purpose. For this holiday, the Jewish people must obtain human blood so that their clerics can prepare the holiday pastries. In other words, the practice cannot be carried out as required if human blood is not spilled.

For this holiday, the victim must be a mature adolescent who is, of course, a non-Jew—that is, a Christian or a Muslim. His blood is taken and dried into granules. The cleric blends these granules into the pastry dough;

they can also be saved for the next holiday. In contrast, for the Passover slaughtering, about which I intend to write one of these days, the blood of Christian and Muslim children under the age of 10 must be used, and the cleric can mix the blood [into the dough] before or after dehydration.

Let us now examine how the victims' blood is spilled. For this, a needle-studded barrel is used; this is a kind of barrel, about the size of the human body, with extremely sharp needles set in it on all sides [into which the victim is placed]. . . . These needles do the job, and the victim's blood drips from him very slowly. Thus, the victim suffers dreadful torment—torment that affords the Jewish vampires great delight as they carefully monitor every detail of the blood-shedding with pleasure and love that are difficult to comprehend.

After this barbaric display, the Jews take the spilled blood, in the bottle set in the bottom [of the needle-studded barrel], and the Jewish cleric makes his coreligionists completely happy on their holiday when he serves them the pastries in which human blood is mixed.

When MEMRI published an English-language translation of this extraordinary piece of hate literature in the United States, it caused a furor. Outraged commentary appeared in the *National Review* and in other publications, ultimately prompting the Voice of America (VOA) to broadcast an editorial on March 19 calling upon Saudi Arabia and other Arab nations to "stop newspapers and radio and television stations . . . from inciting hatred and violence against Jews." Editorials expressing official U.S. government policy are rare on VOA. Rarer still are comments that criticize governments considered friends or allies of the United States. They are broadcast only after extensive consultation with the Department of State and sometimes the White House.

The VOA editorial appeared to get the attention of the Saudi government. Within hours, the editor in chief of *Al-Riyadh,* Turki al-Sudairi, sent a curiously worded reply to MEMRI in Washington, explaining that he was out of the country when the article appeared, but that on examination, he found it "not fit for publication because it was not based on scientific or historical facts, and it even contradicted the rituals of all the known religions in the world, including Hinduism and Buddhism."[30]

Perhaps unconsciously, Mr. al-Sudairi adopted in his reply the same tones that Dr. al-Jalahma had used in her article. What had really concerned him, he began, was an article by an American journalist in the *National Review* "that proposed dropping nuclear bombs on the city of Mecca, sacred to Muslims." One of his deputies had asked whether they should report on it. "I asked him whether other agencies had picked up the same item, or [expressed] similar opinions, and he answered no. I was amazed that the next day all the Arab papers published this item, with no clarification that this was a private opinion." The "article" in question was a series of e-mail exchanges on the *National Review* Internet "blog" between editor Richard Lowry and several readers that began on March 7, 2002—well before Dr. al-Jalahma's article appeared.[31]

When Mr. al-Sudairi finally discussed the blood libel his paper had published, he failed to mention that Dr. al-Jalahma was well-known to his newspaper and had written earlier anti-Semitic tracts that had been published without notice. MEMRI included excerpts from one of these when it published Mr. al-Sudairi's disculpatory reply. Called "The U.S. Should Expel the Jews," it included long fictitious quotes attributed to George Washington and to Benjamin Franklin warning Americans of the "Jewish peril." Well-known to students of anti-Semitism, the purported quotes had actually been invented by the Nazi propaganda machine. The same fake quotes had resurfaced in an Egyptian government weekly in an article entitled "The Jews Are Bloodsuckers and Will Yet Conquer America." The author of that piece included a photocopy of a forged document that he claimed was kept at the Franklin Institute in Philadelphia. MEMRI phoned the chief librarian of the Franklin Institute, who flatly refuted the claim "and stated the Institute does not possess any such document." In fact, the forged document as well as the quotes were lifted directly from a 1935 Nazi publication entitled *A Handbook on the Jewish Question*.[32]

The Voice of America editorial did not put an end to anti-Semitic hate speech in the official Saudi media—far from it. The blood libel reappeared in full force in an article published in the government-controlled daily *Al-Jazeera* on September 6, 2002. The author was a respected Islamic scholar, Dr. Muhammad bin Sʾad al-Shweyʾir, who was editor in chief of *Islamic Research* magazine published by the Islamic Clerics Association of

Saudi Arabia and a past adviser to the former chief state mufti in Saudi Arabia, Sheikh Abdul Aziz bin Abdallah bin Baz. In his article, Dr. al-Shwey'ir repeated the blood libel that Jews use human blood for religious rituals. He also quoted extensively from *The Protocols of the Elders of Zion*, specifically citing the version prefaced by Shawqi Nasser, brother of the former Egyptian president.

> In the book . . . the 24th protocol appears: it represents the goal toward which the Jews strive with their tactics, their false media, and their treachery. The free world must take notice—primarily the West and America, where the intentions of the Jews have been revealed—as they gnaw away at the societies like the worm gnaws away at the wood until it is entirely consumed before signs [of the damage] are [visible]. [The West and America] must awaken, and must support the Muslims against them [the Jews] before it is too late. The 24th protocol is signed by representatives of Zion of the 33rd rank—that is, the most loyal rank of the Jewish Masons. They are the senior leaders of the Masons in the world.[33]

† † †

Bashar al-Assad never thought he would become president of Syria. An ophthalmologist by training, educated in Britain, the second son of dictator Hafez al-Assad was more accustomed to drawing-room discussions in European languages than to the rough talk of soldiers and intelligence officers who enforced the iron rule of Syria's Baath Party dictatorship. His father was head of the Syrian air force when he seized power in a military coup in 1970. Throughout the late 1980s and the 1990s, al-Assad groomed Bashar's older brother, Basel, as his chosen successor, sending the shy, more studious Bashar off to London to pursue a medical degree. Basel was given a junior officer's commission and made to work his way up through the ranks, where he was lionized by his peers. Basel was killed at the age of thirty-two in an automobile accident on January 21, 1994. He was believed to have incurred the wrath of the powerful "clan of the Alis," a forceful clique that included the head of Syrian intelligence, Ali Douba, and the Special Forces commander, General Ali Haidar. Analysts I spoke with in Beirut and Damascus at the time speculated that Basel had been killed because of an ostentatious campaign, at the behest of the United States, to eradicate opium and hashish in Lebanon's Bekaa Valley. The illicit drug trade generated more than $1 billion per year for the Syrian power elite and was considered too high a price to pay for American goodwill, these analysts believed.[34]

When Bashar succeeded his father as Syria's president in June 2000, he was initially greeted as a breath of fresh air. The Arab and Western press speculated that because of his Western education he would loosen his father's iron grip on Syria's economy and domestic politics. They also suggested that he would be more prone to make peace with Israel. Bashar quickly dashed those hopes; and on May 5, 2001, greeting Pope John Paul II on a historic trip to Damascus, he showed the world that he had been infected by the same anti-Semitic virus that had so obsessed his father throughout his long political career.

"All of us know much about the sufferings of the Christ at the hand of those who stood against divine and humanitarian principles and the values advocated by the Christ," he began, according to the official Syrian Arab News Agency, SANA.[35]

As the Head of the Holy See in Rome, Your Holiness embodies the summit of responsibility for maintaining those values, especially since there are people who invariably attempt to subject the peoples of the world to suffering and torments [ailments and agony]. This is why our brothers in Palestine are being assassinated and tortured, justice is violated, and the territories of Lebanon, the Golan and Palestine have been occupied by those who killed the very principle of equality when they pretended that God created a people chosen [distinguished] above all other peoples. We notice them aggressing Muslim and Christian Holy places in Palestine, violating the sanctity of the Holy Mosque (Al-Aqsa), of the Church of the Holy Sepulchre in Jerusalem and of the Church of the Nativity in Bethlehem. They try to kill all the principles of divine faiths with the same mentality that made them betray and torture Jesus Christ, and in the same way that they tried to commit treachery against the Prophet Mohammad (Peace Be Upon Him). The application of divine commandments [tenets] requires taking a stand against those who oppose them. . . .

Your Holiness, we feel that in your prayers, when you recall the agony of Jesus Christ you will remember the peoples of Lebanon, the Golan and Palestine who suffer oppression [suppression] and persecution. We expect Your Holiness to be on their side in their endeavor to regain what was unjustly taken [usurped] from them.

Al-Assad's remarks were greeted with dismay in the West. *The New York Times* lamented that al-Assad had reinforced his own "growing reputation for irresponsible leadership."[36] In Israel, commentators roasted the young president and cynically dismissed him as yet another failed Arab leader whose regime depended on repression and anti-Semitic lies to remain in power.

"Surely, there is little new in the kind of antisemitic vitriol spewed last week by the Syrian leader in the presence of a conspicuously silent Pope John Paul II," wrote Amotz Asa-El in the *Jerusalem Post*. "In portraying our forefathers and us as shameless traitors who betrayed anyone and everything, from Jesus and Muhammad to monotheism and Palestine, the young Assad's display of blind hatred and uncontrollable envy is but one more instance of vintage theological antisemitism custom-tailored to suit the momentary needs of a very secularist cause." After running through al-Assad's failures to stand up to "the generals and bureaucrats who thrive on the backs of the 17 million Syrians they have impoverished," he concluded: "And so, faced with his own cowardice and ineffectiveness, Bashar did the only admirable thing a self-respecting antisemite could do: bash the Jews."[37]

Taken aback by the criticism, al-Assad tried to explain away his remarks to the pope in an interview with a German reporter two days later and had the official news agency withdraw the full version of his remarks and in its place issue a heavily censored text that omitted all reference to Jews as the killers of Christ. "What I said in my address before the Pope is that the Palestinian sufferings in Palestine is similar to the suffering of Jesus Christ. . . . But the result was a campaign by the Israeli officials against the address alleging that it was an attack against the Jews," he told the German newsmagazine *Der Spiegel*.[38] When al-Assad flew to Paris for an inaugural visit with French leaders shortly afterward, he was greeted with jeers. Standing outside city hall in Paris, city council members held up signs that read "Assad=Antisemite." Paris mayor Bertrand Delanoe went so far as to condemn al-Assad's anti-Semitic remarks in his toast to the Syrian leader at a formal state banquet.[39]

It is entirely possible that the young Syrian leader never gave a second thought to his remarks and, indeed, was not intending to express hate but felt that in the presence of the holy father of Christiandom it was only natural to express his solidarity as a Muslim for the suffering of Christ "at the hands of the Jews," since Muslims had suffered the same. Such instincts, deeply ingrained, passed on from father to son, form the core of the anti-Semitic mind-set. Throughout the Arab and Muslim world, hate is becoming second nature.[40]

†††

One sure way of deepening Muslim hatred of Jews is to accuse them of falsifying the Koran. This is seen as a natural expression of the "perfidious nature" of the Jews. If you believe in a Jewish conspiracy to destroy Islam, then it follows "naturally" that the Jews would try to undermine the basic beliefs and values of Islam.

Samir Ragab is editor in chief of the government-sponsored *Al-Gumhuriya* daily in Egypt and a powerful propagandist who boasts of his close ties to President Mubarak. Government ministers sit on the executive board of *Al-Gumhuriya* publications that Ragab edits, such as the Egyptian science magazine *Al-'Ilm,* which has published articles by scientists who claim Israel is spreading the AIDS virus and using biological warfare against Arabs.[41] In one article that appeared under Ragab's pen in *Al-Gumhuriya* on April 16, 2001, he accuses an unnamed Israeli editor of publishing a Hebrew translation of the Koran "where certain chapters have been falsified by suppressing all references to cases where the Jews betrayed their promises, broke divine commandments, and betrayed the Prophet Moses." This was the ultimate affront to Muslims everywhere, he wrote. Denouncing such perfidy in editorial columns was not enough, he wrote. It was time for the Muslim masses to act.

We don't want to hear justifications, excuses or indefensible arguments. Instead, all Muslims should make the earth tremble under the feet of that nation of unbelievers and falsifiers. . . . Where are you, Muslims? You are so numerous, why do you remain silent? The Koran is in danger. Your Prophet is being humiliated. The Israelis are trying to throw doubt on your precious faith and to make it the subject of a debate after 1,400 years.[42]

Ragab's claims stem from a much deeper belief that Islam is locked in an ancient struggle with Judaism that was described by the Prophet Muhammad himself. Koranic verses singling out Jews for special vilification by the faithful have become extremely popular in recent years with Muslim clerics from Riyadh to Richardson, Texas. In sura 2, Jews are said to be "laden with God's anger" (verse 61) for failing to accept Muhammad's vision of a submissive faith. God rejected the Jews and ordered Muslims to humiliate them "because they had disbelieved the signs of God and slain the prophets unrightfully" (verse 58). In other verses (5:78–82), "the unbelievers of the children of Israel" were cursed by David and Jesus and in punishment were transformed into monkeys and pigs (5:60–65). Says scholar Robert Wistrich, "The Koran particularly emphasizes that the Jews rejected Muhammad, even though (according to Muslim sources) they knew him to be a prophet—supposedly out of pure jealousy for the Arabs and resentment because he was not a Jew."[43]

According to this logic, the Jews have falsified their own holy texts, to obscure the final truth as revealed by God to Muhammad. French scholar Meir Waintrater explains: "The logic of the accusation holds that Islam proclaims Muhammad as the last of the prophets, whose teachings incorporate and complete those of his predecessors. Abraham, Jacob and Moses are integrated into Islam, but only in the version given in the Koran and the hadiths. Therefore, anything in Biblical texts that does not conform with this version is the result of a falsification made up by the Jews."[44]

As we have seen, Muslim leaders often stress that their argument with the Jews has nothing to do with land, territory, or national sovereignty. This is a message we need to pay close attention to, since it demonstrates the speciousness of the favorite argument of the Left that blames all the violence in the Middle East on Israel and claims that if only Israel would recognize "legitimate Palestinian aspirations," the violence would cease and the whole problem would go away. On the contrary: the violence has little to do with Israel. Instead, it is directed against the enemies of Islam, those powerful forces—primary among them the United States—who are seen as trying to undermine Islamic values and Muslim culture.

A prominent Saudi cleric made this clear during Friday prayers in Mecca on October 27, 2000:

> All of these elements indicate clearly that our conflict with the Jews is not a conflict relating to an event, to a land, or to borders, but is indeed a conflict of faith, identity, and existence. Haven't we read what the Holy Koran says about this, "the worst enemies of the faithful are the Jews and the sinners"?[45]

This cleric, preaching from one of Islam's two holiest mosques, went on to remind his audience of the "bad heritage" of the Jews, who are "ungrateful toward their benefactors, cow-worshippers, prophet-killers, deformers of words, contradictors of the divine word. . . . They are hated and banished by God who turned them into monkeys, pigs and idol-worshippers who have strayed from the true path. Such are the Jews. . . ." He cited a famous passage in the hadith (the sayings of the Prophet Muhammad), which has become a staple of anti-Semitic clerics throughout the Muslim world. In this passage, the Prophet tells his companions:

> The time is near when the Muslims will fight the Jews and will kill them, where the Jew will have to hide behind a stone or a tree, and the stone or the tree would say to the Muslim: O Muslim, O Servant of Allah, a Jew is hiding behind me. Approach and kill him.[46]

The mufti of Jerusalem, Sheikh Ikrima Sabri, added a new twist to the theme that God had turned the Jews into "monkeys and pigs" when I met with him in his office in the Old City of Jerusalem, just on the other side of the Western Wall. It was not just because the Jews had "disobeyed God," he said, but because they had "killed Christ." Sabri pointed out that this anathema is contained in the Koran: "The Holy Koran informs us about the Jews, that they were punished. God Almighty was angry with them and punished them for what they had done to Jesus Christ. This is a relation between God Almighty and the Jews. We have nothing to do with it. This is in accordance with Islam. God Almighty gave the Jews a lot of things: science, prophets, and they disobeyed, and he punished them for this."[47]

† † †

The medieval Christian theme of Jews as poisoners of wells reappears in today's Muslim world with astonishing variety. In 1999, Libyan leader Colonel Muammar al-Qaddafi "revealed" that Libyan children in the city of Benghazi had been infected by the AIDS virus when foreign nurses— paid by the CIA and the Israeli Mossad—gave them poisoned injections during an immunization campaign sponsored by the World Health Organization. This particular slander was picked up two years later and replayed in great detail by the Egyptian government daily al-Ahram, which claimed that Qaddafi was now promising to hand over all information on this "vile crime . . . so the world will know of the plot." After accusing the CIA and Mossad, "Qaddafi added that this act, which is a malicious sex crime, reveals the ugly face of those who introduced the AIDS virus to Africa in order to exhaust its strength and deplete its resources with the intention of gaining control over Africa," Al-Ahram reported. Qaddafi went on to claim that "international monopolies strive to continue disseminating the AIDS virus as long as possible in order to double their profits from sales of pharmaceutical products which inhibit the effects of the disease."[48]

Zbeir Sultan, writing in the weekly magazine of the Syrian Writers Association on January 1, 2000, pointed out that Egypt had suffered mightily from such practices as a result of signing a peace treaty with Israel. His exposé was intended as a warning to other Arab states contemplating a similar "Peace of Zion." The Israeli embassy was a "den of spies," Sultan reported. "This dirty embassy" was sponsoring academic research "aimed at destroying the fabric of Egyptian society," he declared.

Surely, any reader remembers some of these methods, including the spreading of AIDS in Egypt through pretty, HIV-positive Jewish girls who came from Israel in order to sell themselves to Egyptian youngsters seeking pleasure. The Egyptian police caught many of them and their stories were published in the Egyptian press. Egyptian authorities also discovered Zionist

gifts for children made of animal-shaped chewing gum. An examination of
this [gum] discovered that it causes . . . sterility. For university students
[the Zionists] dispensed chewing gum that arouses sexual lust. . . .[49]

AIDS and spiked chewing gum were not all, he claimed. "Even the
Egyptian soil is not safe from the Satanic war waged by Zionism [against
the Arabs]. Tens of thousands of tons of seeds were sent [to Egypt] through
agricultural deals with the Zionist Entity. These seeds destroyed the
Egyptian soil, rendering part of it infertile." Two teams of Israeli agricultural experts in fact were working in Egypt, but they had come at
the request of the Egyptian government to develop desert agriculture.
Although they had produced "amazing results" of great benefit to Egypt,
which for two thousand years has suffered from the inability to grow crops
beyond the narrow Nile valley, they were accused in the Egyptian media
of "poisoning the land and destroying Egyptian agriculture."[50]

Similar slanders are spread regularly by top officials and government
media of the Palestinian Authority. Tayeb Abdel Rahim is the secretary of
the PA and works directly with Yasser Arafat. In June 2001, he told the PA
mouthpiece *Al-Hayat al-Jadida* that Israeli military jets were dropping
poisoned chocolates on the Gaza Strip, in an effort to commit genocide
against Palestinian children. To give his fantasy a realistic air, he provided
a wealth of seemingly factual detail: The chocolate candies had different-
colored wrappers; some of them smelled of coconut; the Israelis had
dropped them in school courtyards; eight children had been hospitalized
and were receiving treatment. The official Hamas Web site added that poisoned chocolates had also been dropped by Israeli aircraft and helicopters
in the West Bank cities of Nablus, Ramallah, and Hebron.

Al-Hayat al-Jadida went on to quote Palestinian police intelligence
official Abdel Rahman Barkat, who issued a warning to the population not
to buy leather belts made in Israel. The reason, he said, was that the buck-
les included a mysterious magnetic material that produced "extremely
painful illnesses." The belts were being sold at very cheap prices as part of
a $10 million program orchestrated by the Israeli army to spread debilitat-
ing illnesses throughout the Arab world, the official said.[51]

To gain international attention, Palestinian officials have never hesitated to spread false rumors to international institutions. On March 17, 1997, Palestinian delegate Nabil Ramlawi stunned the United Nations Commission on Human Rights in Geneva by claiming that "Israeli authorities . . . infected by injection 300 Palestinian children with the HIV virus during the years of the *intifada.*" His charge was given additional weight when the commander of the Palestinian General Security Service in Gaza (quoted in the semiofficial Palestinian press as an independent source) blamed Israel for sending out "Russian Jewish girls with AIDS to spread the disease among Palestinian youth." After these slanders appeared, a PA minister, Abdel Hamid al-Quds, told the Israeli newspaper *Yediot Aharonot* that Israel was "distributing food containing material that causes cancer and hormones that harm male virility and spoiled food products . . . in order to poison and harm the Palestinian population."[52]

The Washington Post reported in July 1997 that Palestinian Authority officials were accusing Israel of distributing "bubble gum spiked with sex hormones" in Palestinian areas in order to "arouse irresistible sexual appetites in women, undermining Islamic morals." Another goal was to "sterilize Arab women to suppress Arab population growth" and to "destroy the genetic system of young boys." When the gum was shown to the PA Health Ministry's director of public health, Abdel Jabbar Tibi, he said he long had "suspected there would be something related to hormones or sex. We are very open-eyed regarding things coming into our borders, especially from Israel. We expect many things."

A *Washington Post* reporter called PA Health Ministry spokesman Marwan Zaem for comment, after discovering that the gum in question had been imported directly from Spain. "These are agents of Israel," Zaem said dismissively. "I do not know if it is contaminated there or contaminated somewhere else." The *Post* then commissioned its own scientific analysis of the allegedly tainted gum and found no contamination whatsoever.[53]

A similar story had surfaced years earlier, in 1983, when a mass fainting epidemic among Palestinian girls in several West Bank towns led to claims that Israel was deliberately poisoning them as they approached childbearing age in a diabolical scheme to reduce the high Palestinian birth rate. Championed by the Arab League and the Islamic Conference, this specious claim was spread worldwide by journalists and editors—including those of the prestigious French dailies *Le Monde* and *Libération.* "Poisoned" girls were driven by the truckload to hospitals and paraded before reporters. When the reporters left, the girls would simply get out of bed and go home. At Israel's request, the International Red Cross sent a team to investigate and issued a weak statement that it had found "no evidence" to back the Palestinian allegations. If the girls had not actually been poisoned, the International Red Cross representative told reporters, then surely they were suffering from the "poison of occupation." The Centers for Disease Control in Atlanta ultimately sent a team of scientists to get to the bottom of the slander. After testing and interviewing many of the alleged victims, they concluded that the fainting was akin to mass hysteria "similar to teenage girls fainting at rock concerts."[54]

Yasser Arafat's wife, Suha, welcomed First Lady Hillary Clinton to Ramallah in November 1999 with a public speech dripping with Jew-hatred. With Mrs. Clinton smiling at her side, Suha Arafat accused Israel of crimes reminiscent of the blood libel. She claimed that the "intensive daily use of poison gas by Israeli forces in past years" was causing a high incidence of cancer among Palestinian women and children. She also claimed that Israel had contaminated 80 percent of the water sources used by Palestinians with "chemical materials" and that this "has caused widespread disease." Mrs. Clinton sat through this tirade without batting an eye and sat silently as Palestinian Authority health minister Riad Zanoun added to the lies by claiming the Israeli gas "has caused numerous miscarriages among Palestinian women." When Suha Arafat finished her speech, Mrs. Clinton applauded and planted a kiss on Mrs. Arafat's cheek.[55]

Arafat himself shocked an audience at the World Economic Forum in Davos, Switzerland, in 2001 by insisting that Israel was poisoning Palestinian territory for generations to come by using depleted uranium munitions and that Israeli troops were using nerve gas against Palestinian civilians. To illustrate his point, Arafat presented doctored film clips that had aired on official PA television showing "hapless victims racked with convulsions and vomiting."[56]

†††

These are not stories about "political" differences or differences of opinion: they are outright inventions, devoid of any basis in fact, created for the sole purpose of generating hatred of Jews. The goal is to depict Jews as hateful, bloodthirsty, child-devouring monsters, capable of the most malign plots. Killing Jews then becomes a moral act—a conclusion that is drummed into children and adults on a daily basis in mosques and on state-sponsored radio, television, and print media throughout the Muslim world today.

But hoaxes and lies were not enough. In order to build support for new violence against the Jews, it became vitally important to cast doubt on the founding "myth" of the state of Israel: the murder of six million Jews by the Nazis.

Arab leaders, radical Muslim clerics, and anti-Semites the world over have long been united in seeking to deny the existence of the Holocaust, on the theory that if they proclaimed loudly and repeatedly that Hitler's gas chambers had never existed, then there would be no justification for the existence of a Jewish state or, indeed, for Western societies to tolerate the presence of organized Jewry in their midst. When vocal Holocaust deniers first surfaced in the 1970s, under the guise of historical "revisionism," few in the West paid much attention, dismissing them as crackpots. Literally mountains of evidence from the Nazi death camps was on the historical record, from survivor accounts, deportation orders, Nazi newsreels, contemporary newspaper reports, postwar testimony at the Nuremberg war crimes tribunal, and of course Hitler's own speeches. Nazi archives document in great detail the incredible logistics of horror that sent several million Jews to their deaths during the final year of the war, diverting thousands of trains from carrying much needed troops and material to the front so they could carry Jews from Poland, Russia, and elsewhere to the extermination camps. Allied soldiers interviewed survivors, discovered mass graves, and documented the crematoria themselves. The attempt to "prove" the death camps never existed, under the guise of so-called historical research (conducted in the main by nonhistorians), smacks of Hitler's "big lie" technique. No one in his right mind could possibly believe such a monstrous fabrication; at least, such was the initial reaction in the West.

From the very start, however, this movement attracted widespread attention in the Muslim Middle East. The government of Saudi Arabia "financed the publication of a number of books accusing Jews of creating the Holocaust hoax in order to win support for Israel," notes author Deborah Lipstadt.[57] PLO publications followed suit. In editions dated December 23, 1989, and December 30, 1989, the Cyprus-based PLO journal *El Istiqlal* ran a two-part series that incorporated the Holocaust denial thesis under the headline BURNING OF THE JEWS IN THE NAZI CHAMBERS IS THE LIE OF THE 20TH CENTURY IN ORDER TO LEGITIMIZE THE NEW NAZISM. The articles claimed that "while Jews are complaining about their treatment by the Gestapo, the truth is that they were served healthy food. . . . Nazi camps were more civilized than Israeli prisons.[58]

Holocaust denial is arguably the most monstrous of all anti-Semitic lies. Denying the murder of six million Jews by Hitler's Third Reich not only denies Jews their basic humanity by wiping out the record of their existence and suffering, it simultaneously reaffirms all the allegations of a world Jewish conspiracy, since only a malign, powerful, conspiratorial people would be capable of tricking so many nations for so many years about what "actually" occurred during World War II. "By lying about the Holocaust, the Jew-haters try to destroy memory," says former Swedish deputy premier Per Ahlmark. "First the anti-Semites take Jewish lives; a few decades later they take their deaths from them, too."[59]

Although the logic the American and European "revisionist historians" employed was scarcely compelling, nevertheless their message has reached a wide audience. Most disturbing "is the success deniers have in convincing good-hearted people that Holocaust denial *is* an 'other side' of history—ugly, reprehensible, and extremist—but an other side nonetheless," writes Lipstadt, whose groundbreaking exposé of this movement was unsuccessfully challenged in a British court by Holocaust denier David Irving. (Irving lost his libel suit on April 11, 2000, and his appeal was denied December 18, 2000. Irving was forced to pay the costs of the trial, which the court estimated at £2 million.)

As other forms of anti-Semitism have become increasingly widespread in the Muslim world in recent years, so has Holocaust denial become an integral part of the litany of hate used to demonize Jews. The goal was obvious from the start. The July 1990 issue of *Balsam,* published by the

Palestinian Red Crescent Society, stated baldly that "the lie concerning the gas chambers enabled the Jews to establish the State of Israel."[60] Debunk the "lie," and Israel's legitimate claim to nation-status becomes moot.

Mahmoud Abbas (Abu Mazen) has long been considered Arafat's next in command. An urbane, sophisticated politician, with a love of fine food, Abbas was a premier architect of the 1993 Oslo Accords that put the PLO in control of Gaza and most of the West Bank. Intended as the first step toward a comprehensive peace settlement between a Palestinian state and Israel, the Oslo Accords explicitly prohibited "hostile propaganda" by either party against the other, including anti-Semitic hate speech.[61] In 1995, Abbas was questioned about a book he had authored in 1983 that claimed the Zionist movement "was a partner in the slaughter of the Jews" during the Third Reich. The book, entitled *The Other Side: The Secret Relationship Between Nazism and the Zionist Movement*, claims that the Nazis killed "only a few hundred thousand" Jews, not six million, but that "the interest of the Zionist movement is to inflate this figure so that their gains will be greater." While Abbas refused to retract those claims, in an interview with the Israeli daily *Maariv* he explained his position in terms of realpolitik. "When I wrote *The Other Side* . . . we were at war with Israel," Abbas said. "Today I would not have made such remarks. . . . Today there is peace and what I write from now on must help advance the peace process."[62] Abbas is considered a Palestinian "moderate" and was appointed by Arafat as his first prime minister in March 2003 as a sop to foreign donor governments, who sought to "democratize" Arafat's regime. He reasserted his views on the number of Holocaust victims in a May 28, 2003, interview with journalists from the Israeli daily *Yediot Aharonot*. "What do you expect of me, as a historian? To accept the numbers as they were written in the books?" But he added: "It is not a matter of numbers. Any murder is a heinous crime."[63]

No one else in the Palestinian Authority has followed even this timid lead. Holocaust denial, as other forms of anti-Semitism, has become a staple of the official PA media, even as Arafat and Abbas have pledged to eradicate hostile propaganda and hate speech from the official discourse. In an August 25, 1997, cultural affairs program on PA television that evoked Israel's annual commemoration of the Holocaust, the moderator informed his audience: "It is well-known that every year the Jews exaggerate what the Nazis did to them. They claim there were six million killed, but precise scientific research demonstrates that there were no more than four hundred thousand."[64]

In July 1998, an essay entitled "Jewish Control of the World Media" appeared in the Palestinian Authority daily *Al-Hayat al-Jadida* that sought to explain how the Jews got away with falsifying the history of World War II. "What Hitler did to the Jews actually exposed the Jewish plot" to seize control of the world media and the world economy, author Seif Ali al-Jarwan argued. "World public opinion, manipulated by the Jews, took advantage of these [persecutions], disseminating stories about a collective massacre. They concocted horrible stories of gas chambers which Hitler, they claimed, used to burn them alive." Al-Jarwan goes on to claim that the Holocaust was a total fabrication of the world Jewish conspiracy.

> The truth is that such persecution was a malicious fabrication by the Jews. It is a myth which they named "The Holocaust" in order to rouse empathy. Credible historians challenge this Jewish [myth], calling for [more] persuasive evidence to be presented. The Los Angeles Historical Society declared that it would grant US $50,000 to anyone who could prove Jews had been gassed to death.[65] Jews exerted intense pressure and cast accusations of anti-Semitism everywhere in order to silence this challenge. Even if Hitler's onslaught facilitated the persecution of Jews to some degree, Jews certainly benefited from its aftermath. . . ."[66]

Al-Jarwan's thesis was virtually identical to the themes put forward by Palestinian Prime Minister Abbas in his 1983 book of Holocaust denial. Official Palestinian Authority TV repeated those same themes just days before Abbas was to meet President George W. Bush in Aqaba in a May 27, 2003, broadcast dedicated to telling "truths" about World War II. Among those "truths" were these: The Nazis did not specifically plan the killing of Jews; the term "Holocaust" should refer equally to what has happened to Jews, Gypsies, and Palestinians; and Jews have "turned this truly tragic historical event into an industrial enterprise, an enterprise that will bring them a lot of capital and wealth."[67]

Official and semigovernmental media in Egypt, Syria, and Iran also sound these themes on a regular basis. In the Egyptian government daily *Al-Akhbar,* the following appeared in 1998:

The Jews invented the myth of mass extermination and the fabrication that 6 million Jews were put to death in Nazi ovens. This was done with the aim of motivating the Jews to emigrate to Israel and to blackmail the Germans for money as well as to achieve world support for the Jews. Similarly, Zionism based itself on this myth to establish the State of Israel. . . . I continue to believe that the Holocaust is an Israeli myth which was invented to blackmail the world.[68]

The Egyptian government daily *Al-Gumhuriya* added the monstrous claim that the Zionist movement had actually cooperated with Hitler's SS in exterminating European Jews. "Zionist propaganda continues, even today, to raise the issue of the Nazi crematoriums for Jews, although the historical evidence, revealed by renowned German, British, and French historians, proved that claims that such crematoriums existed in the Nazi detention camps are jokes." The real concern of Zionist leaders during World War II was to motivate more Jews to immigrate to Palestine, this author contends. When European Jews ignored these calls, "the Zionist movement cooperated with some Nazi leaders and especially the 'Hitlerist' SS in order to increase the terror against the Jews. This [phenomenon] reached the point where the Zionist movement cooperated with some Nazi military leaders in planning massacres against Jews in the detention camps."[69]

Columnist Muhammad ʿAbd al-ʿAzim wrote in the same Egyptian newspaper that six million Jews could not have been killed because "there were only three million Jews in Europe, as was determined by the great French intellectual Roger Garaudy."[70] The "great French intellectual" had been condemned two years earlier in a French court for hate speech because of persistent Holocaust denial. Needless to say, he was a frequent and warmly welcomed guest in the Arab world and Iran.

On May 27, 2001, a cleric from Egypt's renowned Al-Azhar University named Mahmoud Muhammad Khadhr penned an essay entitled "In

Defense of Hitler," which not only praised Hitler but again claimed the Holocaust was "exaggerated and blown completely out of proportion, thanks to the insistence of world Zionism to continue to stoke the fire." He went on:

It is hard to believe that the Europeans and Americans . . . cannot address the "Jewish Question," or more precisely, the false Holocaust, whose numbers and scope they have exaggerated until it has reached the level of the merciless destruction of six million Jews. . . . Anyone who knocks on this door encounters the most horrible accusations and is tried in all of the European countries and in the U.S. for anti-Semitism.[71]

The West reacted so negatively to the "truth" about the Holocaust for the simple reason that the "Zionist propaganda apparatus" ruled those countries and was terrified that their "lies" about the Holocaust would be exposed, he claimed. Dr. Khadhr explained his reasoning to his readers:

The first dubious fact is the number of six million Jews who were burnt in the gas chambers. Did they have families, children, who demanded compensation, or did Zionism see itself as their only heir? *If we assume* that every person had an average of five family members, this would bring the number of Jews affected to thirty million. It is certain that many Jews escaped before the ship sunk, that many of them therefore, survived, despite the so-called extermination and burning [in the gas chambers]. This would mean that the number of Jews in Germany was sixty million, although the total number of Germans has never reached this number. Even if we cross off one zero from the six million and are left with a tenth of this number, it would still seem exaggerated and would have to be investigated.

Just to cover all bases, Dr. Khadhr is careful to explain that whatever *did* happen to Jews in Germany was perfectly justified. "The Zionists were a fifth column in Germany, and they betrayed the country that hosted them, in order to realize their aspirations." Once Hitler discovered this, "he was enraged and took revenge on them for this great betrayal. Both the Zionist movement and the Allied Powers had an interest in keeping this matter a secret, so that people would not know that the Zionists were punished for helping the Allied Powers, for betraying [Germany], and for stabbing Hitler in the back."

Holocaust denial has become so commonplace in the Muslim Middle East that it now appears as a clue in Arabic-language crossword puzzles, such as this one from the official Palestinian Authority daily, *Al-Hayat al-Jadida,* in February 1999:

> *Clue:* Jewish center for eternalizing the Holocaust and the lies.
> *Answer:* Yad Vashem (the Israeli Holocaust memorial in
> Jerusalem).[72]

† † †

Both Syria and the Islamic Republic of Iran have become safe havens for Western Holocaust deniers such as Roger Garaudy and David Irving, promoting their work and hosting them at conferences and other government-sponsored events.

Teshreen is the official mouthpiece of the ruling Baath Party in Syria. In a January 31, 2000, article it claimed that Israel used "the legend of the Holocaust as a sword hanging over the necks of all those who oppose Zionism" and was seeking "to strangle any voice that reveals the truth." It named Garaudy and David scholars who "have already left their marks on European public opinion and media."[73] Similarly, the English-language *Tehran Times* claims that its "thorough research" has "proved that the issue of [the] Holocaust is nothing but a fraud" and a "plot of the Zionists."[74] Islamic Iran's supreme leader, Ayatollah Ali Khamenei, frequently sounds the same note in Friday prayers and other public speeches. "There is evidence which shows that Zionists had close relations with German Nazis and exaggerated statistics on Jewish killings" to promote Jewish immigration to Palestine. "The purpose was to install in the heart of the Islamic world an anti-Islamic state under the guise of supporting the victims of racism and to create a rift between the East and the West of the Islamic world."[75] It was one of the milder statements ever uttered about Israel or the Jews by Khamenei.

Another common theme in the anti-Semitic liturgy is to compare Israel to Nazi Germany, a notion that is frequently aired by the deacons of the

Left in Europe as well as by the Arab media. Often it takes the form of political cartoons dressing Israeli prime minister Ariel Sharon in a Nazi SS uniform and a U.S. president thinly disguised as Hitler. The Islamic opposition Labor Party in Egypt elaborated on this theme by alleging a pact between "the Crusaders' Nazism" and "Jewish Nazism" to implant "a base . . . in the land of the Muslims." As a solution, the writer urges his readers to take up the sword of jihad as "the ideal way to deter both kinds of Nazism, that of the Crusaders and that of the Jews."[76] Osama bin Laden has sounded similar themes in many of his speeches and anti-Western edicts, as has Saddam Hussein.

The current mufti of Jerusalem, the highest state-appointed cleric in the Palestinian Authority, likes to berate reporters for paying too much attention to the Holocaust and claims that the number of six million dead is exaggerated. "There are a lot of stories and we don't know which are true and which are false," Sheikh Ikrima Sabri told me in his Jerusalem office. "It happened. There is no doubt about that. But a lot of people are very suspicious about the number. Now Sharon is trying to make a new Holocaust of the Palestinian people!"[77] Sabri couldn't point to Israeli death camps and, when pressed, said that taking land was akin to murder. "Besides, Hitler did not kill all the Jews," he said. "That's why we still have Jews today!"

†††

The close ties between the Western Holocaust deniers and their allies and sponsors in the Arab world burst onto the public scene in December 2000, when the Los Angeles–based Institute for Historical Review announced it would hold its fourteenth revisionist conference in Beirut in April 2001. Every radical Islamic group in the Middle East was scheduled to attend, from Hezbollah, Hamas, and Islamic Jihad to al-Qaeda. The Syrian government, as the "supervisory" power over Lebanon, acted as the unofficial sponsor of the show. A government delegation from the Islamic Republic of Iran was scheduled to show up. Roger Garaudy and fellow Holocaust denier Robert Faurisson were guest speakers.

The Simon Wiesenthal Center urged the Lebanese government to intervene to stop the conference in the interests of peace. "There is a wide range of viewpoints as to how peace can be reached in your region," the Wiesenthal Center wrote to the Lebanese ambassador, "but certainly the introduction and acceptance of Holocaust denial into the mainstream of Lebanon and the Arab world is not one of them. It will only poison hearts and minds of the uninformed and further fan the flames of hate and mistrust in the region." Fourteen prominent Arab intellectuals, including Palestinian poet Mahmoud Darwish and Lebanese writer Elias Khoury, signed a petition denouncing the conference. In the end, Lebanese prime minister Rafik al-Hariri announced in March that his government would not allow the conference to take place. "Lebanon has more important things to do than holding conferences that hurt its international standing and smear its name," al-Hariri said. However, he never denounced the underlying thesis of the Holocaust deniers themselves.

The cancellation of the Beirut conference inspired the Jordanian Writers' Association to hold a similar one-day conference in Amman on May 13, 2001, despite attempts by the Jordanian authorities to block it. Two days later, the Al-Jazeera satellite television network in Qatar sponsored a heated debate on the subject between Dr. Hayat al-Hwayek ʿAtiya, the Arabic-language translator of Roger Garaudy, and Tunisian intellectual al-ʿAfif al-Akhdar, one of the fourteen Arab thinkers who had denounced the Beirut conference. Joining the show by telephone was Robert Faurisson, who called his theories the nuclear weapon of the poor. "We have proved and are still proving that there was no massacre or Holocaust of the Jews, and that there were no gas chambers for the Jews and that the figure of six million victims is exaggerated," Faurisson said. "If you want to protect Palestine, you cannot do so with guns and shells, but by saying the truth about the biggest lie of the twentieth and twenty-first centuries, the lie of the Holocaust."

When the debate got too heated, the Al-Jazeera moderator displayed on the screen an opinion posted by a viewer to the Al-Jazeera Web site: "Sons of Zion, whom our God described as the descendants of apes and pigs, will not be deterred unless there is a true Holocaust that will exterminate all of them at once, along with the traitors, the collaborators, the scum of the [Islamic] nation. . . ."

Picking up on that sentiment, Dr. ʿAtiya took out a large picture of a Palestinian baby named Iman Hiju who had allegedly been killed recently by Israeli soldiers. On the picture was a caption written in bloodred letters: "The murderers of the prophets are the murderers of the innocent." Pointing to the picture, she cried out: "This is the Holocaust! This is the Holocaust! There is no Jewish Holocaust. There is only a Palestinian Holocaust!"[78]

There was nothing extraordinary about this exchange. It was just another day of hate in the Muslim world, where scholars, journalists, editors, and government officials have been breeding falsehood for fifty years until truth has become a rare and suspect commodity.

Italian journalist Fiamma Nirenstein, writing from Israel, summed up the effect of this "relentless vilification" in an essay in *Commentary* that appeared just ten days before September 11.

> In the Arab world, where countervailing sources of information about Jews and the Jewish state are rare to non-existent, Israel has been transformed into little more than a diabolical abstraction, not a country at all but a malignant force embodying every possible negative attribute—aggressor, usurper, sinner, occupier, corrupter, infidel, murderer, barbarian. As for Israelis themselves, they are seen not as citizens, workers, students, or parents but as the uniformed foot soldiers of that same dark force. The uncomplicated sentiment produced by these caricatures is neatly captured by the latest hit song in Cairo, Damascus, and East Jerusalem. Its title: "I Hate Israel." From such hatred it is but a short step to incitement and acts of violence. Arab schools teach not just that Israel is evil, but that extirpating this evil is the noblest of callings.[79]

There is a good reason why the language, themes, and practices of anti-Semitism now common in the Arab world sound very familiar to many of us in the West. They were modeled almost directly on Hitler's Third Reich.

HITLER AND THE MUFTI   5

Many scholars of the Middle East see Muslim anti-Semitism as the political response to Jewish immigration to Palestine but see no history of anti-Semitism in Islam itself. "For most of the fourteen hundred years or so of the Arab Jewish encounter, the Arabs have not in fact been anti-Semitic as that word is used in the West— not because they themselves are Semites, a meaningless statement, but because for the most part they are not Christians," writes Bernard Lewis, America's preeminent scholar of the Middle East.[1]

Media-savvy leaders in the Middle East such as President Mohammad Khatami of Iran, who understand the language of the West, reinforce this view. In a much touted interview with CNN's Christiane Amanpour in January 1998, Khatami noted that "anti-Semitism is indeed a Western phenomenon. It has no precedents in Islam or in the East. Jews and Muslims have lived harmoniously together for centuries."[2] But Khatami's benign view was contradicted the next day by Supreme Leader Ayatollah Ali Khamenei, who told a leading government newspaper that the president was lying. "The history of the beginnings of Islam is full of Jewish plots against the Prophet Muhammad and of murderous attacks by the Jews . . . unequivocal verses in the Qur'an speak of the hatred and hostility of the Jewish people against the Muslims. One indeed must distinguish between the Jews [and] the Zionist regime, but to speak in the manner that we heard was exaggerated and there was no need for such a presentation."[3]

For Lewis, there was something premeditated and contrived in the rabid anti-Semitism of these leaders. "It still seems true that despite its vehemence and its ubiquity, Arab or Muslim anti-Semitism is still something that comes from above, from the leadership, rather than from below, from the society," Lewis wrote in 1986. He added—somewhat optimistically, as it turned out—that it was "a political and polemical weapon, to be discarded if and when it is no longer required."

But Lewis had his doubts even then that Jew-hatred can be turned on and off like water from a tap and gave multiple examples contradicting his own theory that it was a relatively recent phenomenon in the Muslim world. "It may be that the moment of choice has gone, and that the virus has already entered the bloodstream of Islam, to poison it for generations to come as Christiandom was poisoned for generations past," he concluded.[4]

In a two-part series that appeared in the popular Egyptian weekly *October,* Egyptian general Hassan Soueïlen summed up the type of hatred that has now become acceptable discourse in the Arab world.

"Historians, professors of racial theory, and sociologists all agree that humanity, throughout its long history, has never known a race such as the Jewish race where so many vile and contemptible traits are concentrated. . . . There is no difference, as some claim, between the Jew of yesterday and the Jew of today, or between the Jewish identity and the Israeli identity. In fact, Israel as a state is the receptacle for all the Jews of the world. Zionism is just the political and colonial aspect of the Jewish religion. . . . One characteristic that is deeply rooted in the Jewish identity can be seen in the rule: 'Lie, lie, lie again, until people believe you and until you believe yourself.' This characteristic appears in their lie concerning the Holocaust, that they claim was carried out by the German Nazis during the second world war against six million Jews. It is a huge lie, that they have succeeded in selling throughout the world."[5]

General Soueïlen goes out of his way to make sure his readers understand that his hatred of Jews is not merely "political." It is religious. It is racial. It is based on an "objective" understanding of the nature of Jews. Even the current object of hate—the state of Israel—is contemptible because it is an extension of Judaism, not because it is oppressing Arab Muslims. We would do well to listen and learn.

†††

Jews and Christians living under Islamic rule have historically been governed by the Pact of Umar, which dates from A.D. 720.[6] Under these rules, non-Muslims were *dhimmis* required to "always acknowledge their subservient position to Muslims." In A.D. 807, the caliph of Baghdad, Harun al-Rashid, codified that humiliation, following the Koranic prescription by Muhammad that urges Muslims to "fight against such of those who have been given the Scripture . . . and follow not the religion of truth, until they pay the tribute readily, being brought low" (9:29). He decreed that Jews must wear a yellow belt and a dunce cap, providing the model for the yellow star that later became the hallmark of Nazi Germany.[7] Failure to demonstrate the proper obsequiousness could result in death.

The fate reserved for Jews in an Islamic republic that was explained to me by Hamas spokesmen in Gaza is drummed into the faithful during Friday prayers. In a typical example, Sheikh Mohammad Ibrahim al-Mahdi told followers at the Sheikh Ijlin Mosque in Gaza they should blame themselves for the rise of the Jews, all the while they prepared their revenge. "Our [Muslim] nation has abandoned the leadership of the human race to the contemptible Jews and their auxiliaries, while we have remained in the back of the bus," he said in a sermon that was broadcast live on the official Palestinian Authority television network. "Today we welcome as we have always done in the past any Jew who wants to live in this county as a *dhimmi*—just as Jews have always lived in our countries as *dhimmis,* and were recognized to the point where some of them even attained the rank of state councillors and even ministers. We welcome the Jews as *dhimmis,* but power in this country and in all Muslim countries must be the power of Allah."[8]

Well before large-scale Jewish immigration to Palestine in the 1920s,

Jews were massacred periodically throughout the Muslim Middle East just as they were in Christian Europe. Muslims attacked Jews as "drinkers of Muslim blood" in Aleppo in 1853, Damascus in 1848 and 1890, Cairo in 1844 and 1901–1902, and Alexandria in 1870 and 1881. Murderous rampages against Jews also took place in the Moroccan cities of Casablanca (1907) and Fez (1912).[9]

Rachal Suissa, a Moroccan Jew who fled with her family during the exodus of 1963 as a six-year-old child, was a member of that thriving, if oppressed, Jewish community. Her father was a laborer. Her mother's family owned a large trucking company and made their fortune during the famine of 1938, when they brought food at their own expense to poor Muslim communities.

"Jews in Morocco were forced to live in ghettos," she told me at her home outside Oslo, Norway. "Jews depended on the goodwill of the police who controlled access to the ghetto. Even now, I can't sleep at night when I remember some of the stories my father told me as I got older."[10]

Friday evenings after mosque, Muslim mobs would regularly storm the ghetto in Casablanca. "Jews came to expect it," Rachal says. "How violent they were depended on the police. Often they would come seeking blood. One of my uncles was seized on the third-floor roof of his house and thrown to the street. He died a few weeks later. During one killing rampage, eight hundred Jews were murdered in the ghetto."

Whenever a Jew wanted to leave the country, he was required to register a family member with the police as a hostage. "If you didn't come back, they would arrest that person. Sometimes they killed them; sometimes they just let them go. It was all on the whim of the local police." Sometimes families would leave their oldest living relative behind as a hostage and secretly take the remaining family members to safety abroad.

Despite her family's prosperity, when the king of Morocco gave the Jews one month to leave the country in 1963, Rachal says few of her family or friends thought twice about leaving all their possessions behind—"even our bank accounts"—in order to leave.

"No one wants to talk about what it was really like living in Morocco as a Jew," she says. "People say it was fine, that Jews were treated well. But that's just a lie. There were regular murders, regular pogroms, daily harassment. It's like being raped: nobody wants to talk about it because you are too ashamed." More than 250,000 Jews—98 percent of the Jewish community at the time—took advantage of the king's offer and fled the country in 1963. Most went first to France, then found their way to Canada, the United States, and Israel.

†††

To understand how anti-Semitism became a driving political force in today's Middle East, mobilizing generations of youths and infecting military officers and political leaders, one has to return to the early days of the twentieth century, when the centuries-long decline of Muslim culture that culminated in the collapse of the Ottoman empire at the end of World War I coincided with the acceleration of Jewish immigration to Palestine.

In 1918, the de facto mayor of Jerusalem, Musa Kasim Pasha al-Husseini, mentioned to Zionist leader Chaim Weizmann that he had received a copy of *The Protocols of the Elders of Zion* from a British officer of the military administration in Palestine. Anti-Semitism in Europe was then in full bore. France was still recovering from the Dreyfus affair twenty years earlier, when a French officer was wrongly accused of spying on behalf of Germany simply because he was a Jew. Publications with titles such as *The Jewish Peril* and *The Talmudic Jew* abounded. In Russia, the White Russians spread the *Protocols* in an effort to stir up the notion that the Bolshevik revolution was part of a world Jewish conspiracy. And Britain, of course, was wrestling with the 1917 Balfour Declaration, when the British government declared its support for a Jewish national homeland in Palestine. "Innocently enough, al-Husseini asked Weizmann whether the Zionist leaders were also 'the elders of Zion,' and whether they shared the same program," recounts Middle East specialist Daniel Pipes.[11] Just three years later, in 1921, the first Arabic-language translation of the fabricated anti-Semitic playbook was published by Christian Palestinians.

The core anti-Semitic doctrine of a Jewish world conspiracy fell on willing ears among the Arabs of Palestine. It recalled Koranic lessons they had learned from childhood and "explained" the sense of helplessness they felt as Jews stepped up efforts to revive the ancient Jewish quarter of Jerusalem and bought abandoned tracts from willing Arab landowners to construct agricultural settlements where only desert had been before. The modern world was outstripping the backward farmers of rural Palestine, and leading this invasion of the unfamiliar were the Jews. Among the most receptive of the local Arab leaders to the conspiracy theories of the *Protocols* was another member of the al-Husseini clan.

Haj Mohammad Amin al-Husseini was a brilliant agitator and former Customs officer in the small Palestinian Arab town of Qalqilia who went on to become grand mufti of Jerusalem, the official "priest" and preeminent political leader of the Arabs. From his earliest years, Husseini was a ferocious opponent of Jewish immigration to Palestine. During the Muslim festival of Nebi Musa on April 4, 1920, Haj Mohammad Amin's followers went on a murderous rampage and, "inflamed by anti-Jewish diatribes, began attacking Jewish passers-by and looting Jewish stores."[12] He was subsequently convicted by a British military tribunal of inciting the violence, in which 5 Jews and 4 Arabs were killed and 211 Jews and 21 Arabs wounded. After skipping bail, Haj Mohammad Amin took refuge in western Palestine and was sentenced in absentia to ten years in prison. The leader of the hastily organized Jewish self-defense force, Vladimir Jabotinsky, received a fifteen-year jail sentence for halting the killing spree.

Referring to the disturbances in a white paper expressing the views of the British government in June 1922, Winston Churchill noted that the tension in Palestine "is mainly due to apprehensions, which are entertained both by sections of the Arab and by sections of the Jewish population. These apprehensions, so far as the Arabs are concerned, are partly based upon exaggerated interpretations of the meaning of the [Balfour] Declaration favouring the establishment of a Jewish national Home in Palestine. Unauthorized statements have been made to the effect that the purpose in view is to create a wholly Jewish Palestine . . . 'as Jewish as England is English.'" Churchill went on to quote the September 1921 resolution by the Zionist Congress, the supreme governing body of the Zionist Organization, stating "the determination of the Jewish people to live with the Arab people on terms of unity and mutual respect, and together with them to make the common home into a flourishing community, the upbuilding of which may assure to each of its peoples an undisturbed national development."[13]

But Haj Mohammad Amin was ferociously opposed to any form of cooperation between Jews and Arabs, which the fledgling Zionist movement was trying actively to promote. When young Arab and Jewish intellectuals established "an evening school for the teaching of Hebrew to the Arabs, Arabic to the Jews, and English to both," al-Husseini intervened to kill the project within a year.[14] His opposition to the Jews was unrelenting. "Remember, Abbady," he told a local official who came from an old Jewish family in Jerusalem, "this was and will remain an Arab land. We do not mind you [Jewish] natives of the country, but those alien invaders, the Zionists, will be massacred to the last man. We want no progress, no prosperity [deriving from Jewish immigration]. Nothing, but the sword will decide the future of this country."[15] That may be the single most telling statement any Arab leader has made to explain the deep, unacceptable challenge Arabs feel when faced by the success of the Jews.

Haj Mohammad Amin al-Husseini emerged from hiding not long after his trial. In recognition of his status among the Palestinian Arabs, the British mandatory authorities disregarded his record of incitement and appointed him grand mufti in 1922.[16] But instead of calming the population, as the British seemed to wish, he led a second massacre of Jews on August 23, 1929, in Hebron, where Jewish immigrants had established a thriving community on the site of Judaism's second most holy city. Given al-Husseini's new official status, the commission of inquiry appointed by the British Colonial Office treated him "with exceptional consideration," allowing him to testify behind closed doors at his own home. Al-Husseini is said to have "firmly asserted his belief in the authenticity of the notorious *Protocols of the Elders of Zion.*" He used the occasion to spread a libel— not the last of his career—that the Jews planned to "rebuild the Temple of Solomon at the seat of the Mosque of Omar,"[17] known more familiarly as the Dome of the Rock, a Muslim shrine on the Temple Mount.[18] Still in his capacity as grand mufti, he led a third massacre of Jewish settlers in 1936.

But al-Husseini owes his place in history to a meeting that took place on November 28, 1941, in Berlin, where he had gone to convince Adolf Hitler of his total dedication to the Nazi goal of exterminating the Jews, and offered to raise an Arab legion to carry out that task in the Middle East. For the mufti, the meeting with Hitler was the culmination of an eight-year effort to convince the Nazis to forge an alliance with the Palestine Arab Higher Committee he headed. Their once secret pact, which I shall describe, marks the beginning of Nazi-style anti-Semitism as a mass movement in the Arab world.

I asked Ruth Wisse, a Harvard professor of Yiddish literature who has long written and meditated on the implications of anti-Semitism, how important was the mufti's wartime visit to Berlin. "When I was asked to serve on the Holocaust Museum board in Washington, I said that this was the missing exhibit," she told me. "They wanted a complete story with a beginning, middle, and end. Hitler destroyed the Jews, and now Hitler was dead. It was almost a feel-good experience. Then you have the mufti spending the war with Hitler and urging him not to overlook any of these Jewish children in Palestine."[19] The mufti's close ties to Hitler, and his total embrace of Hitler's Final Solution, provides the common thread linking past to present. If today's Muslim anti-Semitism is like a tree with many branches, its roots feed directly off of Hitler's Third Reich.

The mufti first approached the Nazis through the German consul in Jerusalem in 1933, soon after Hitler seized power. "His objectives, as he explained on numerous occasions to German officials, were far-reaching. His immediate aim was to halt and terminate the Jewish settlement in Palestine. Beyond that, however, he aimed at much vaster purposes, conceived not so much in pan-Arab as in pan-Islamic terms, for a holy war of Islam in alliance with Germany against world Jewry, to accomplish the final solution of the Jewish problem everywhere."[20]

When the Nazis promulgated the Nuremberg laws to seize Jewish property and businesses in Germany the following year, "telegrams of congratulation were sent to the führer from all over the Arab and Islamic world," including Palestine.[21] But Hitler's government continued to express "a surprising lack of interest in the Arab world and its affairs."[22] One reason, historians agree, is that Hitler initially hoped the harsh Nazi policies would prompt German Jews to emigrate from Germany to Palestine, where he expected they would perish. "They will not take root there, their fortunes will be spent and the Arabs will liquidate them. . . . The Jews in Palestine are doomed, their end will be to leap from the frying pan into the fire," the editor of the Nazi Party newspaper *Angriff* wrote after a tour of Palestine in 1937.[23]

Captured Nazi documents published by the U.S. State Department in 1953 show that the mufti continued to petition the German Foreign Office for support. On July 21, 1937, a memorandum of conversation with German consul general Doehle in Jerusalem reveals the mufti once again pleading for Nazi support to fight the Jews. At that meeting, he agreed to dispatch a "confidential agent" to Berlin to maintain an open line of contact with the Axis powers.[24]

What changed the German attitude toward the mufti and his cause was the publication in July 1937 of a report by the British Royal Commission, headed by Lord Peel, which for the first time recommended the partition of Palestine into separate Jewish and Arab states. Once the conclusions of the report were known, the German minister of foreign affairs, Konstantin von Neurath, sent out instructions to German legations in Britain and the Middle East explaining the new directives of the Nazi leadership:

"Heretofore it was the primary goal of Germany's Jewish policy to promote the emigration of Jews from Germany as much as possible," because there was little expectation the Jews would prosper or gain political sovereignty in Palestine. "The formation of a Jewish state or a Jewish-led political structure under British mandate is not in Germany's interest," von Neurath went on, "since a Palestinian state would not absorb world Jewry, but would create an additional position of power under international law for international Jewry, somewhat like the Vatican state for political Catholicism or Moscow for the Comintern. Germany therefore has an interest in strengthening the Arab world as a counterweight against such a possible increase in power for world Jewry."[25]

Germany began broadcasting anti-Semitic propaganda in Arabic in the summer of 1938, fueling the passions of the mufti's followers throughout the region. They planted anti-Semitic lies in the Arabic and Persian press and bred espionage and sabotage networks from the Persian Gulf to Palestine. As Sami al-Jundi, an early leader of the Baath Party in Syria, wrote in his memoirs: "We were racists, admiring Nazism, reading its books and the source of its thought, particularly Nietzsche. . . . We were the first to think of translating *Mein Kampf.*"[26]

By 1939, when Hitler attacked Poland, and Britain and France declared war on Germany, the mufti realized his well-known pro-Nazi activities could land him in a British jail. Once again he packed his bags and fled Palestine, staying shortly in Lebanon (then under French control) before traveling onward to Iraq. Working with an old ally, Rashid Ali al-Gaylani, who became prime minister of Iraq in March 1940, the mufti "obtained promises of Axis support, and in April 1941 carried out an anti-British and pro-German coup" in Baghdad.[27] One of the coup plotters, a cashiered Iraqi officer named Khairallah Tulfah, later regaled a young nephew entrusted to his care named Saddam Hussein with tales of the mufti and their Nazi heroes.[28] In early June, al-Gaylani was overthrown, and his followers—tearing a page from the mufti's playbook—went on a murderous rampage against Baghdad's Jewish community. For two days, as a British force waited patiently outside the city gates to install their own government, troops and armed policemen loyal to al-Gaylani slaughtered 600 Jews, destroyed 911 houses, and ransacked 586 businesses belonging to Jews, according to official accounts.[29]

Once the British arrived in Baghdad, the mufti sought refuge in neighboring Persia. Shah Reza Pahlavi, a nationalist general who seized power in 1925, was such a fan of Hitler's theories of racial supremacy that he renamed his own country "Iran" shortly after Hitler's rise to power. (Iran means "Aryan" in Persian.)[30]

Soon Iran became unsafe as well. In October 1941, fearing the pro-Nazi shah would allow the Axis powers to disrupt the Allied supply line through Iran to Russia, the United States and Britain landed troops in Iran, arrested pro-Nazi government ministers, and replaced the shah with his young son, Mohammad Reza, a fearful and suspicious leader who ultimately attributed his own overthrow by Ayatollah Khomeini thirty-eight years later to yet another U.S.-British plot.

The coup in Iran meant that Haj Mohammad Amin al-Husseini had to flee once again. He sought refuge in the Italian embassy in Tehran, and on October 8, 1941, "with shaven beard, dyed hair, and an Italian service passport," he left for Italy with the rest of the Italian embassy staff now that the new shah had broken diplomatic relations with the Axis powers.[31]

But the expulsion from Tehran presented al-Husseini with a tremendous opportunity he had so far been lacking: direct contact with Axis leaders. During an initial meeting with Italian military intelligence after his arrival in Rome, the mufti said he was prepared to join the Axis war effort "on the sole condition that they recognize in principle the unity, independence, and sovereignty of an Arab state of a Fascist nature, including Iraq, Syria, Palestine, and Trans-Jordan."[32] His handlers offered him a modest stipend to fund his efforts (1 million lire, or around $40,000); but more important, they recommended that Mussolini receive him in person. Al-Husseini later described his meeting in Rome with Il Duce on October 27, 1941, as a total triumph. Mussolini, he wrote, expressed unremitting hostility to the Jews. "They are our enemies . . . and there will be no place for them in Europe, even in Italy where at most there are 45,000 of them out of a population of 45 million. They are few, but nevertheless only those who are deserving will remain. Not more than 2,500." (It is worth pointing out that Italian Jews never suffered the fate al-Husseini claims Mussolini had reserved for them.) Calling Mussolini "a veteran anti-Zionist," al-Husseini went on to quote him as uttering steadfast opposition to a Jewish state in Palestine. The Jews, Mussolini reportedly said, "have no historical, racial, or other reason to establish a state in Palestine. . . . If the Jews want it they should establish Tel Aviv in America."[33] It was an ominous foreshadowing of the comments Hamas leaders made to me more than five decades later in Gaza.

From Rome, the mufti traveled to Berlin, where he was greeted enthusiastically by the Islamische Zentralinstitut and the assembled Muslim leaders of Germany as the "Führer of the Arabic world." In a speech kicking off his visit, he called the Jews the "most fierce enemies of the Muslims" and an "ever corruptive element" in the world."[34]

The mufti also met with SS leader Heinrich Himmler and Foreign Minister Joachim von Ribbentrop, who were tasked with preparing the fateful interview with Hitler. The mufti had sent no fewer than fifteen drafts of a joint declaration he wanted Hitler and Mussolini to issue with him, announcing the intention to apply Hitler's Final Solution to the Jews of the Middle East. When the language had been scrubbed and the declaration sent to Hitler's staff, it was chillingly explicit: "Germany and Italy recognize the illegality of the Jewish National Home in Palestine. They recognize the right of Palestine and other Arab countries to solve the question of the Jewish elements in Palestine and in other Arab countries as required by national Arab interests, and *in the same way as the Jewish question in the Axis lands is being solved.*"[35] (Author's emphasis.)

The mufti found his soul mate in the German führer, who was prepared to accept him as an "honorary Aryan" because of the red beard and blue eyes he had inherited from his Circassian mother.[36] He began the meeting in Hitler's ornate reception room in the Reich Chancellery with a lengthy panegyric, dutifully shortened in the official Foreign Ministry "Record of Conversation," which nevertheless preserves the distinct Oriental flavor of the mufti's supplication.

> The Grand Mufti began by thanking the Führer for the great honor he had bestowed by receiving him. He wished to seize the opportunity to convey to the Führer of the Greater German Reich, admired by the entire Arab world, his thanks for the sympathy he had always shown for the Arab and especially the Palestinian cause. . . . The Arab countries were firmly convinced that Germany would win the war and that the Arab cause would then prosper. The Arabs were Germany's natural friends because they had the same enemies as had Germany, namely the English, the Jews, and the Communists. They were therefore prepared to cooperate with Germany with all their hearts and stood ready to participate in the war, not only negatively by the commission of acts of sabotage and the instigation of revolutions, but also positively by the formation of an Arab Legion. The Arabs could be more useful to Germany as allies than might be apparent at first glance, both for geographical reasons and because of the suffering inflicted upon them by the English and the Jews.[37]

Hitler was receptive to the spirit and ultimate goals of Haj Mohammad Amin al-Husseini, although he was unwilling for strategic reasons to commit troops as yet to liberate the Arab countries from the British. As World War II historian Bevin Alexander has argued, this was Hitler's fatal mistake.[38] But his total obsession with murdering the Jews had rendered him oblivious to military strategy and opportunities.[39] (The same could be said of the mufti and his followers in the Arab world, who invaded the new Israeli rump state in 1948 instead of accepting the partition of Palestine as proposed by the United Nations. More than fifty years and five wars later, the Arabs have less territory today than they would have had by accepting the original partition borders.)

> The Führer replied that Germany's fundamental attitude on these questions, as the Mufti himself had already stated, was clear. Germany stood

for uncompromising war against the Jews. That naturally included active opposition to the Jewish national home in Palestine, which was nothing other than a center, in the form of a state, for the exercise of destructive influence by Jewish interests. Germany was also aware that the assertion that the Jews were carrying out the function of economic pioneers in Palestine was a lie. The work there was done only by the Arabs, not by the Jews. Germany was resolved, step by step, to ask one European nation after the other to solve its Jewish problem, and at the proper time direct a similar appeal to non-European nations as well.

Germany was just then engaged "in a life and death struggle with two citadels of Jewish power," Hitler explained, "Great Britain and Soviet Russia." He didn't have the manpower of resources to deploy additional military forces in the Middle East. But once the war against Russia and Britain was won, he added, "Germany's objective would then be solely the destruction of the Jewish element residing in the Arab sphere under the protection of British power. In that hour the Mufti would be the most authoritative spokesman for the Arab world."

The deal was cut. Although the mufti was disappointed that help was not forthcoming immediately, he nevertheless was flattered by Hitler's unbending personal commitment to his cause and "thanked him profusely," according to the official account. He remained Hitler's guest for the remainder of the war.

During his years in Germany, the mufti appeared regularly on German propaganda broadcasts to the Middle East. In one Radio Berlin broadcast, on March 1, 1944, he urged Arabs to murder their Jewish neighbors: "Kill the Jews wherever you find them. This pleases God, history and religion. This saves your honor. God is with you."[40] Often he borrowed the themes and images of classic anti-Semitism. "The overwhelming egoism which lies in the character of Jews, their unworthy belief that they are God's chosen nation and their assertion that all was created for them and that other people are animals . . . [makes them] incapable of being trusted," he proclaimed on November 2, 1943. The mufti was also one of the first Arab leaders to make the claim that Jews were vilified in the Koran. "They cannot mix with any other nation but live as parasites among the nations, suck out their blood, embezzle their property, corrupt their morals," he went on. "The divine anger and curse that the Holy Qu'ran mentions with reference to the Jews is because of this unique character of the Jews."[41]

The mufti used the language of the Final Solution to describe how he planned to deal with the Jews of the Middle East, demonstrating how thoroughly he had understood and embraced Hitler's genocidal aims. "If, God forbid, England should be victorious, the Jews would dominate the world," he said in a November 11, 1942, broadcast. "But if, on the contrary, England loses and its allies are defeated, the Jewish question, which for us constitutes the greatest danger, would be finally resolved. . . ."[42] One year later, he praised Hitler for his results. "The Germans have never harmed any Muslim, and they are again fighting our common enemy," he explained. "But most of all they have definitely solved the Jewish problem."[43]

The mufti performed numerous other services for Hitler's murderous cause. At one point, he got wind that Adolf Eichmann, then a deputy to SS intelligence boss Reinhard Heydrich who is considered by most historians to be the architect of the Final Solution, was trying to cut a deal with the British government to exchange German POWs for five thousand Jewish children who also could have fled to Palestine. "The Mufti's protests with the SS were successful and the children were sent to death camps in Poland instead."[44] At another, he lobbied Hitler personally to block a plan to allow Jews to leave Hungary, again claiming they would settle in Palestine and reinforce a new center of world Jewish power. In 1942, with the personal approval of SS reichsführer Heinrich Himmler, he sent four of his aides to Saxenhaussen to visit the headquarters of Department D, the administration of the death camps.[45] According to one witness at the Nuremberg trials, the mufti personally visited Eichmann at Auschwitz, where he reportedly admonished the guards running the gas chambers to work more diligently.[46]

Nor were the mufti's efforts confined to propaganda and incitement. In 1943 he traveled to Bosnia, where he helped to raise a Bosnian Muslim Waffen SS company, the "Hanjar Troopers," who slaughtered 90 percent of the Jews in Bosnia and burned "countless Serbian churches and villages."[47] Other Bosnian Muslim units raised by the mufti were sent to Croatia and Hungary, where they participated in the killing of Jews. The

mufti's work in Bosnia earned him special favor with Himmler, who established a school in Dresden to train mullahs under his control. According
to Israeli scholar Yigal Carmon, a U.S. captain who seized the mufti's
wartime archives in Berlin in the days following the collapse of the Third
Reich in April 1945 found a photograph of Himmler and the mufti raising
wineglasses to each other in a chummy toast. The photograph was personally inscribed by Himmler "In remembrance to my good friend, Haj Amin
Husseini."

Hitler had courted many Arab leaders during the war, but they
deserted him one by one following the defeat at Stalingrad. As it became
increasingly apparent the Third Reich was doomed to collapse, they no
longer saw a benefit in being seen as allied with Hitler's regime. By war's
end, only the mufti remained. "The mufti stayed with Hitler until the very
end," says Carmon. "Why? Because the extermination of the Jews went on
until the very last day of the Third Reich. That was his benefit."

At one point, early during his stay in Berlin, the mufti received disturbing reports from confidants in the Middle East that Hitler planned to
exterminate the Arabs once he had finished the Jews, because they were
also Semites. (These reports appear to have been planted by British intelligence operatives, Carmon believes.) After sending a worried request for
clarification to the SS, the mufti received a reassuring letter in 1942 from
Professor Walter Gross, chief of the Department of Racial Policy at the SS,
confirming that the Arabs were a "noble race" in the eyes of the Nazis
because they were "racially pure" and not a "hybrid" like the Jews. Professor Gross restated these views publicly, in an article published in the
SS review *Weldkampf* entitled "Anti-Semitism or Anti-Judaism?" After
explaining his views, Professor Gross concluded: "We are not against all
Semites. The Arabs are a noble race. We are against the Jews."[48]

In 1945, liberated Yugoslavia under Marshal Tito sought to indict the
mufti as a war criminal for his activities in Bosnia, but with help from the
SS the mufti had already escaped Germany with other members of his
clan. "The SS gave him a plane and helped him fly to France three days
before Hitler's suicide, hoping that he could escape to North Africa, where
he had organized spy networks still in place," says Yigal Carmon. The
French caught him in Paris and placed him under house arrest, but they
eventually expelled him when they realized they couldn't recruit him as

an intelligence asset or agent of influence. He fled to Cairo, where he was welcomed and protected by successive regimes. The Jewish authorities in Palestine lodged a complaint against the mufti with the United Nations in 1947 and sought unsuccessfully to have him tried at Nuremberg as a war criminal.[49]

The mufti never attempted to disguise his Nazi beliefs or his wartime role as the mouthpiece for Hitler's genocide in the Arab world. His oft-proclaimed desire to exterminate the Jews worldwide, and his offer to Hitler to become his willing instrument in Palestine, cannot possibly be excused—as some apologists do today—as simple "anti-Zionism." The only Jews the mufti and his followers wanted to remain in Palestine were the descendants of the original inhabitants, who had lived as *dhimmis* under Muslim rule for the past 1,400 years. The rejection of a Jewish state very clearly signified to the mufti and his followers the extermination or forced emigration of every single Jew who had come to Israel from Europe or the Arab world since 1917, leaving those remaining to become subjects of Muslim rulers. The core beliefs of Arab anti-Zionism and Arab anti-Semitism are identical.

In 1961, when Adolf Eichmann's trial for war crimes began in Jerusalem, the mufti had left Egypt for Beirut, where he continued to infuse the next generation with his anti-Semitic beliefs.[50] Israeli prosecutors tried to get Eichmann to elaborate on his relations with the mufti, but he was uncooperative, claiming he vaguely recalled meeting the mufti at a Berlin cocktail party, but that was all. But the mufti's followers, writing in newspapers in Damascus, Beirut, Cairo, and Amman, wrote glowingly of Eichmann and expressed regret that he "had not finished the job."[51] In his memoirs, the mufti thanked Eichmann for his discretion and praised him as "gallant and noble."[52]

The mufti died in 1974, but the al-Husseini family continues to play a central role in Palestinian affairs. The mufti's nephew Faisal al-Husseini, was a leading PLO spokesman in the territories until his death on May 31, 2001, and regularly received journalists at Orient House, the de facto (and illegal) seat of Palestinian government in predominantly Arab East Jerusalem.[53] When the Israelis shut down Orient House in March 2002, they seized hundreds of thousands of documents that revealed that al-Husseini had been personally involved in coordinating and financing terrorist attacks against Jews.[54]

Haj Mohammad Amin's vicious anti-Semitic ideology formed a lasting impression on another young Arab nationalist, who became a close confidant and ardent disciple during his postwar exile in Cairo, when al-Husseini regaled his audiences with tales of Hitler's Germany. Born on August 24, 1929, Mohammed Abd al-Rahman Abd al-Raouf Arafat al-Qudwa al-Husseini enrolled at Cairo University in 1951. He came not to study, but because the university had become the hotbed of the Muslim Brotherhood and the Free Officers, unabashed Nazi sympathizers who, under Nasser's leadership, went on to stage a successful coup the following year. The coup was still far off, and the younger al-Husseini shortened his name in order to disguise his family ties. Ever since then, the world has known the mufti's most famous disciple as Yasser Arafat.

Arafat has always been coy in speaking to biographers about his family ties to the mufti, although in 1985 he paid homage to the mufti, saying he was "proud no end" to be walking in his footsteps.[55] Friendly biographer Alan Hart, who wrote with Arafat's approval and cooperation, claimed that Arafat's father, Abd-al Raouf Arafat al-Husseini, came from the "poor side" of the grand mufti's clan. The record was put straight by British journalists Andrew Gower and Tony Walker, who correctly state that Arafat's father belonged to the middle-class al-Qudwa clan in Gaza, "the Husseinis of Gaza," and was not directly related to the mufti.[56]

But Arafat's ties to the mufti were deep, personal, and long-lasting. As a young man in Cairo, he became the assistant of the mufti's top deputy, Sheikh Hassan Abu Saoud, who was Arafat's maternal uncle. The Abu Saoud were a prominent Jerusalem family, regarded as "minor aristocracy."[57] Palestinian biographer Said Aburish notes that Arafat became "a voluntary assistant to Sheikh Hassan [Abu Saoud]," the mufti's right-hand man, because he wanted to be close to the mufti, "a man whom Arafat came to adore and emulate, and whose name he later used as his own."[58] In an interview with the Palestinian daily *Al Quds* on August 2, 2002, Arafat called the grand mufti "our hero," and boasted that during the 1948 war with Israel, "I was one of his troops."[59]

Arafat continues to claim he is the sole heir to the mufti's legacy. In a

CNN interview in English in November 2002, he blasted Foreign Minister Benjamin Netanyahu for boasting that if elected prime minister, he would expel Arafat from the territories. Arafat countered: "[Netanyahu] has to remember that I am Yasser Arafat, and this land is my land and the land of my great-great-great-great grandfathers. He has to remember that I am a Husseini and I am a son of Abraham."[60] As so often with Arafat, he was a Husseini when it was convenient, but when it tied him to the grand mufti's Hitlerian past, he was not.

THE HOUSE OF WAR

6

Doaa ʿAmer is a professional TV anchor who hosts *Muslim Woman Magazine* on IQRAA-TV, a satellite channel broadcasting throughout the Arab world. As she tells it, her job is to educate the next generation of children to be "true Muslims." Readers accustomed to hearing Islam described as a "religion of peace" by pundits and apologists in the West will be surprised to learn what she means, but her view is neither extreme nor unusual in today's Islamic world—the real world of Islam, the day-to-day world of mosques and classrooms and tea shops and hubbly-bubblies and government-controlled news media that provide a daily diet of hate that until recently has rarely been translated into English.

Based in Jeddah, Saudi Arabia, IQRAA-TV has production facilities in the Middle East, North Africa, Europe, and North America and runs its satellite uplink through Avezzano, Italy. It claims to "bring the teachings of Islam into the homes and hearts of Arabs worldwide" by giving a "true picture of Islam." Its parent company, Arab Radio and Television (ART), calls itself "the leading producer of premium Arabic family programming and entertainment worldwide." ART and IQRAA-TV are no fly-by-night start-up ventures. They have been solidly financed by Prince al-Waleed bin Talal, the Saudi royal whose post–September 11 check for $10 million was refused by New York City mayor Rudolph Giuliani after al-Waleed made clear he considered it a bribe to change U.S. policy toward Israel. (Prince al-Waleed blamed Giuliani's rejection of his gift on "Jewish pressures.")[1] The Muslim family values his satellite television channel delivers to a mass audience would be censored in the West for bigotry, race hatred, and incitement to murder. They differ in no detail from the visions of murder and a world-conquering Islam proclaimed by Osama bin Laden. Yet they bear the approval of the Saudi government, America's ally in the war on terror.

Prince al-Waleed's business partner in this television venture is another Saudi billionaire named Saleh Abdallah Kamel, whose Dallah al-Baraka Group jointly controls ART and IQRAA-TV through a holding company called Arab Media Corporation (AMC).[2] Kamel was also an investor of the Al-Shamal Islamic Bank in Khartoum, which was identified in a 1996 State Department fact sheet as part of bin Laden's financial network of terror. Bin Laden pumped $50 million into Al-Shamal in 1991 shortly after moving to Sudan, the U.S. government claims, joining investors Tadamon Islamic Bank and the Faisal Islamic Bank, which were part owned and controlled by Saleh Kamel. Born in Mecca in 1941, Sheikh Saleh Abdallah Kamel became an adviser to the Saudi Ministry of Finance and a business partner of Prince Mohammad bin Faisal bin Abdul Aziz, son of former King Faisal and nephew of Saudi King Fahd, who gave his name to the Faisal Islamic Bank. Their far-reaching financial network crisscrosses the Muslim world, from Malaysia to Sudan, spreading its tentacles thanks to the anonymity of an obscure Swiss holding corporation based in the Geneva suburb of Cointrin known as the Dar al-Maal al-Islami (DMI SA), in which the two are partners.[3] Saleh Kamel has denied any involvement in terrorism, and six months after 9/11 he hired a top Washington, D.C., lobbying firm, Greenberg Traurig, to represent his interests in the United States.[4] In September 2002, Kamel was named in a multibillion-dollar lawsuit filed by relatives of victims of the 9/11 attacks, along with prominent members of the royal family and so-called charitable institutions.

IRQAA-TV was not Kamel's first venture into satellite broadcasting. In 1988, he helped create the first Arabic-language satellite broadcasting network, Middle East Broadcasting Corporation (MBC), which he sold in 1993 to Abdul Aziz and Walid al-Ibrahim, scions of another well-connected Saudi family, who subsequently bought United Press International (UPI). One of their goals in purchasing UPI, an Iranian-born intermediary who helped negotiate the deal told me, was to procure technology that would allow the Saudi royal family to prohibit antiregime satellite broadcasting from reaching the kingdom and to prevent Saudi citizens from accessing antiregime Internet sites, efforts that have had mixed success.[5] The al-Ibrahim brothers reportedly represent the business interests of Abdul Aziz bin Fahd, the king's youngest son, whose dedication to Islamic causes was revealed by a former CIA operations officer, Robert Baer.[6]

† † †

On May 7, 2002, wearing her customary body-length robe and a fashionable head scarf, Doaa ʿAmer announced to her viewers that she had a special guest. Broadcasting from Egypt, she begins in the soft-spoken, perky tones of a morning talk show host.

"Our report today will be a little different, because our guest is a girl, a Muslim girl, but a true Muslim." Exuding sincerity, the attractive young host addresses herself directly to the mothers in the audience, who like her could have a daughter the same age. "Allah willing, may our God give us the strength to educate our children the same way, so that the next generation will turn out to be true Muslims who understand that they are Muslims and know who their enemies are," she gurgles. "This girl will introduce herself immediately. She is the daughter of my sister in faith and of the artist Wagdi al-Arabi. Her name is Basmallah."

The camera pans slowly down and to the right as Ms. ʿAmer greets her guest, who turns out to be a small child.

"Peace be upon you," Ms. ʿAmer says, welcoming Basmallah onto her show.

"Allah's mercy and blessing upon you," the little girl replies.

> *ʿAmer:* Basmallah, how old are you?
> *Child:* Three and a half.

'Amer: Are you a Muslim?

Child: Yes.

'Amer: Basmallah, are you familiar with the Jews?

Child: Yes.

'Amer: Do you like them?

Child: No.

'Amer: Why don't you like them?

Child: Because . . .

'Amer (prompting): Because they are what?

Child: They're apes and pigs.

'Amer: Because they're apes and pigs? Who said they are so?

Child: Our God.

'Amer: Where did he say this?

Child: In the Koran.

'Amer: Right, he said that about them in the Koran. Okay,
Basmallah, what are the Jews doing?

Child: The Pepsi Company.

'Amer (approving laughter): You also know about the boycott,
Basmallah? Did they love our master Muhammad?

Child: No.

'Amer: No, what did the Jews do to him?

Child (Pauses, struggling for the right answer): The Prophet
Muhammad killed someone . . .

'Amer: Obviously, our master Muhammad was strong and could
have killed them. All right, you know the traditions about the
Jews and what they did to the Prophet Muhammad? Is there a
story you know?

Child: Yes, the story about the Jewish woman.

'Amer: The Jewish woman? What did she do to our master, the
Prophet Muhammad?

Child: The Jewish woman?

'Amer: Yes.

Child: There was a Jewish woman who invited the Prophet and
his friends. When he asked her, "Did you put poison [in my
food]?" she said to him, "Yes." He asked her, "Why did you do
this?" and she replied: "If you are a liar—you will die and

Allah will not protect you; if you speak the truth—Allah will
protect you."

'Amer: And our God protected the Prophet Muhammad, of
course.

Child: And he said to his friends: "I will kill this lady."

'Amer: Of course, because she put poison in his food, this Jewess.

Child: Oh.

'Amer (speaking directly into the camera): Basmallah, Allah be
praised, Basmallah, Allah be praised. May our God bless her.
No one could wish Allah could give him a more believing girl
than she. . . . May Allah bless her and her father and mother.
The next generation of children must be true Muslims. We
must educate them now while they are still children so that
they will be true Muslims.

Shortly before this program aired on IQRAA-TV, the station's part
owner, Prince al-Waleed bin Talal, contributed $27 million to a government-
organized telethon in Saudi Arabia that raised $109 million for the fami-
lies of Palestinian suicide bombers. Saudi King Fahd and Crown Prince
Abdallah each contributed $1 million, with their wives kicking in separate
checks of close to $1 million.[7] The official story was that the money was
intended for the families of Palestinian "martyrs" and to rebuild infrastructure in the West Bank and Gaza that had been destroyed by Israel's
antiterror campaign following the Passover bombing. But as documents
seized by the Israelis at numerous "charities" and government offices
throughout the West Bank during that campaign showed clearly, money
paid by Saudi Arabia and Iraq was considered as "blood money" and was
used by Hamas as an enticement to murder by providing a guaranteed
income to the families of the murderers.[8]

The telethon was hosted by a prominent Saudi government cleric
named Sheikh Saad al-Buraik, who took the opportunity of the live television coverage to harangue an audience at a Riyadh mosque against America, Christians, and Jews. "I am against America until this life ends, until
the Day of Judgment," he proclaimed on April 11, 2002. "I am against
America even if the stone liquefies. My hatred of America, if part of it
was contained in the universe, it would collapse. She is the root of all evils

and wickedness on Earth. . . . Oh Muslim Ummah, don't take the Jews
and Christians as allies. . . . Muslim Brothers in Palestine, do not have any
mercy, neither compassion on the Jews, their blood, their money, their
flesh. Their women are yours to take, legitimately. God made them yours.
Why don't you enslave their women? Why don't you wage jihad? Why
don't you pillage them?"[9]

Like the al-Ibrahim brothers, whose Middle East Broadcasting Network aired the telethon, Sheikh al-Buraik is closely tied to Prince Abdul
Aziz bin Fahd, the king's youngest son. The sheikh hosts a regular show
on MBC and the government's Channel One called *Religion and Life.* Just
days after this festival of anti-American and anti-Semitic hate aired in
Saudi Arabia, Prince Abdul Aziz bin Fahd traveled to Crawford, Texas,
with his uncle, Crown Prince Abdallah, as part of the official delegation
that met with President George W. Bush at his ranch.

† † †

If the pro-Nazi beliefs of Arafat's "uncle," the grand mufti of Jerusalem,
shaped two generations of Arab leaders after World War II, it fell to an
Egyptian scholar and onetime minister of education named Sayyid Qutb
(1906–1966) to set out the philosophical and religious underpinnings of
Jew-hatred that inflames today's neighborhood clerics and the Muslim
"street." Widely recognized throughout the Arab and Islamic world as the
most important scholar of his generation, Qutb is credited with having
spearheaded an Islamic revival that began in the late 1950s and that today
has replaced Arab nationalism as the predominant political force in the
region.

The Muslim Brotherhood that he invigorated and inspired attracted
Yasser Arafat to its ranks in the early 1950s in Cairo. Qutb's pupils assassinated Anwar Sadat in 1981, on the pretext that any leader making peace
with Israel was a traitor to Islam. They insisted on a version of Islam that
believed the Koran, as the Word of God, was the only legitimate source of
law. Other well-known disciples include Ayatollah Khomeini, the leaders
of Hezbollah, Hamas, and Islamic Jihad, and the spiritual leader of Sadat's
assassins, blind sheikh Omar Abdel Rahman, who now sits in a U.S. jail for
plotting to blow up the Lincoln and Holland Tunnels in 1994. So influential

was Qutb on Saudi terrorist leader Osama bin Laden that he has been called "the brains behind Osama."[10] While at King Abdul Aziz University in Jeddah in the late 1970s, bin Laden studied religion with Qutb's brother Mohammad.

Qutb's works combine a deep-rooted anti-Semitism with contempt of the West into a single ideology of Islamic superiority. Like many of the radical Islamic scholars I met in Gaza, Amman, Cairo, and London, he learned about the West during a sojourn in America, from 1948 to 1950. According to his English translator, Islamic scholar Hamid Algar, the Egyptian government sent Qutb to America on the mistaken notion that "direct acquaintance with America would incline him more favorably to official policies."[11] Instead, his years of study in Washington, D.C., California, and Colorado taught him to despise the West and declare that "the role of the white man has come to an end, whether he is Russian, American, English, French, Swedish, or anything else."[12]

Upon his return to Cairo in 1951, he joined the Muslim Brotherhood and became the editor of their official journal, *Al-Ikhwan al-Muslimum*. At first, Gamal Abdel Nasser, who seized power in Egypt in 1952, admired his works and offered him a cabinet position. But Qutb refused and criticized Nasser for putting national interests above the interests of Islam, a stance that landed him in jail and ultimately led to his execution by Nasser in 1966. It was from jail that he wrote his most influential works.

Among them was an essay entitled "The America That I Saw." While Qutb acknowledged the efficiency and technological achievements of America, he was shocked by its materialism and the sexual promiscuity of its women. Even the church, he noted, spent more time on bake sales than on prayer. America was "materially prosperous but morally rotten," he concluded. Americans were "people drowning in dirt and mud" and worthy of contempt because they had separated God from the state.[13]

According to Qutb and the school of Islamic thought he inspired, Islam is the doctrine governing man's entire life, not just a religion. Islam means "submission" to God's will as expressed in the Koran, not "peace." A true Islamic state therefore must base its law on the Koran. Every aspect of society, from rules governing the family, divorce, and child custody to economics and foreign policy, must be derived from Koranic principles. Today, governments in Pakistan and Saudi Arabia claim to have enacted

Qutb's doctrine of the Islamic state by proclaiming the Koran as their official Constitution. Unlike Christianity and Judaism, the view of Islam preached by Qutb and his followers knows no distinction between the secular and the divine. On the contrary, they claim that any attempt to separate them is the work of the devil. Their fundamentalist belief rejects all man-made laws and considers democracy as a lower form of atheism because it puts the will of the people over the will of the Divine.

Qutb combined his hatred and contempt of the West with profoundly anti-Semitic beliefs. In another work, "Our Struggle with the Jews," written in the mid-1950s, Qutb explains why the Jews represent an "eternal enemy" of Islam. "[The Jews] plotted against Islamic history, its events and its great men, and sought to bring confusion to them. . . . Anyone who leads this [Muslim] community away from its religion and its Qur'an can only be a Jewish agent," Qutb warns.[14] This theme is repeated frequently by Osama bin Laden and his disciplines in their calls to Muslims to rise up against "corrupt" Arab leaders from Riyadh to Rabat.

According to Qutb, Jews invented communism, psychoanalysis, and sociology with the specific intent of undermining Islam. "Behind the doctrine of atheistic materialism was a Jew; behind the doctrine of animalistic sexuality was a Jew; and behind the destruction of the family and the shattering of sacred relationships in society . . . was a Jew," he claims.[15]

The evil of the Jews is unlike anything in the history of the world, Qutb teaches. "The Qur'an spoke much about Jews and elucidated their evil psychology. Everywhere the Jews have been they have committed unprecedented abominations. From such creatures who kill, massacre, and defame prophets one can only expect the spilling of human blood and any dirty means which would further their machinations and evilness."[16]

Such was the river of hate from which Arafat, Sadat, and so many prominent Muslim leaders and scholars had drunk. In the writings of Qutb, as in the actions of his most notorious disciple, Osama bin Laden, the twin currents of Jew-hatred and a paranoid fear of the West commingled into a single poisonous brew. It was all-encompassing and without appeal. Qutb's writings continue to be taught throughout the Arab and Muslim world, and their message is clear. Islam is caught up in a monumental struggle with the forces of evil. For a good Muslim, there is only one path: Destroy the Jews and then the West.

✝✝✝

Organized, state-supported anti-Semitism got a tremendous kick in 1979 with two events that shook the Islamic world to its core. In both instances, hatred of the Jews was thoroughly intertwined with fear and hatred of America and the openness of the West.

The first milestone was the overthrow of Shah Mohammad Reza Pahlavi in Iran by revolutionaries loyal to Ayatollah Ruhollah Khomeini, a radical cleric who believed as did Qutb that a true Islamic state should govern every aspect of daily life. Under Khomeini's guidance, universities were closed, women were forced to adopt the veil and were excluded from society, at least temporarily, and Western businesses were tossed out of Iran. On November 4, 1979, Islamic "students" who called themselves the Followers of the Line of the Imam seized the U.S. embassy in Tehran and took fifty-four Americans hostage, beginning a dramatic power struggle between the Ayatollah and the secular West.

Khomeini's hatred of America and of Jews was legendary. He invented the term *world arrogance* to designate America and preached holy war (jihad) against America and its allies, which included Western Europe, most Muslim states, and, of course, Israel. Soon after seizing power, Khomeini ordered the first translation into Persian of *The Protocols of the Elders of Zion,* previously unknown in Iran, and changed schoolbooks to reflect his anti-Semitic and anti-American beliefs. If Persians were noteworthy for conspiratorial thinking, until Khomeini, state-enforced anti-Semitism was not part of the mix. As recounted in the Old Testament Book of Esther, in the fifth century B.C., following the Babylonian captivity, Emperor Cyrus the Great saved Jews from extermination. Learning that his vizier Haman had commanded the king's lieutenants throughout the empire "to destroy, to kill, and to cause to perish all Jews, both young and old, little children and women, in one day" (Esther 3:13), Xerxes ordered Haman to be executed and granted the Jews all of his possessions and those of his supporters as spoils of war.[17] Ever since that time, Jews have enjoyed a long and glorious history as Persian nationalists and the respect of Persian leaders. Under Khomeini, that was about to change.

The revolutionary regime's new textbook, *Civil Instructions,* used in high schools across the country, devoted an entire chapter to "America's crimes against Islam and humanity" and concluded that "struggling against this symbol of global arrogance is one of the primary duties of all Muslims." According to Iranian journalist Amir Taheri, it also included numerous citations from Khomeini's "magnum opus, *Kashf al-Asrar (Key to the Secrets)*, which presents history as a story of 'Jewish conspiracies against true believers.' In it Khomeini claimed that Socrates, the ancient Athenian philosopher, was 'one of the first true monotheists' and that he was 'callously murdered in a conspiracy hatched by the Jews.' "[18] Khomeini's hatred for America erupted from the same source as his hatred of Jews. Both represented unacceptable challenges to his belief in an absolutist Islamic government ruled with an iron fist by God's chosen representative on earth. In Khomeini's world there was no room for the rules of men or the people's will. Democracy was an evil plot, hatched by Jews, to frustrate God's will.

I learned much about Khomeini's philosophy from one of his fiercest opponents, Ayatollah Mehdi Rouhani, the leader of the Shiite community in Europe, whom I got to know in the early 1980s in Paris. Rouhani came from a leading clerical family in Qom and was a distant cousin of Khomeini's. His older brother, Grand Ayatollah Mohammad Sadegh Rouhani, had taught many of the revolutionaries who seized control of Iran with Khomeini in 1979. Mehdi Rouhani prided himself on his ecumenism and had a large portrait of himself meeting at the Vatican with Pope Paul VI in 1967. Unlike the radical clerics in Tehran, he also met openly with Jewish leaders and preached tolerance and dialogue.[19]

"The best way to get rid of Khomeini is through the clergy," Rouhani liked to say. "Khomeini claims to be a defender of Islam, but he is not even a good Muslim." Rouhani always referred to the clerical regime in Iran as the "so-called Islamic Republic," because he considered their theology to be a travesty of Islam. He was in Paris in 1978 when Khomeini set up camp in a suburban villa at Neauphle-le-Château at the invitation of a naive French government, which thought it could supplant the United States as Iran's primary business partner after the revolution by openly supporting Khomeini. "I refused to meet Khomeini, although he was staying only twenty miles away from me and I had been contacted by members of his entourage," Rouhani told me. "Khomeini was an extremist, a revolutionary, and I was a man of moderation. There was no possible meeting of the minds."

But even Rouhani acknowledged that Islam was a lifestyle, not just a religion, and that clerics derived their power from *ijtihad,* the study of Islamic law governing all aspects of daily life. The main difference between his view of Islam and that of Khomeini was that he believed clerics should inspire government, but not govern. "It's no wonder the economy is a wreck when you put village clerics who don't even have a fourth-grade education in charge of it," he said.

Rouhani and his followers inside Iran were mercilessly persecuted by Khomeini's radical regime, which saw in them a challenge to their legitimacy from the very heart of the faith. Virtually every Grand Ayatollah in Iran was placed under house arrest by Khomeini and his successors because they agreed with Rouhani that the clerics should return to the mosque and attend to the spiritual and moral needs of the people, but not aspire to governance. But Khomeini's view won out. He used all the power of the state in Iran to preach hatred of Jews and hatred of the West, elevating his visceral rejection of a cosmopolitan modern world into an austere and uncompromising political doctrine. Indeed, Khomeini used this hatred to confer legitimacy upon his so-called Islamic Republic and to justify its excesses. In his view, terror and violence against the "enemies of Islam" was the legitimate defense of the faith.

I hosted Ayatollah Rouhani on several occasions at my home in Maryland before he died in Paris on January 9, 2000. On one occasion, just a few years before his death, I escorted him to an unclassified conference at the Defense Intelligence Agency at Bolling Air Force Base, where I translated for him as he gave a stunning presentation to an audience of intelligence professionals and Iran experts on the underlying philosophy of the ruling clerics in Tehran. "They divide the world into two forces, Dar al-Islam and Dar al-Harb," Rouhani said. "The House of Islam, which they pretend to rule, is the world of their followers. It is open to all those who accept their hegemony. This is a very small portion of the Iranian population—perhaps five percent at most. Everyone else belongs to Dar al-Harb, the House of War. You need to understand that this is how they view the entire world. Either you are followers of their perverse vision of

Islam, or you are damned. Against Dar al-Harb they urge their followers to commit all forms of abomination and violence, claiming it will be blessed in the eyes of Allah. This is not Islam; it is sacrilege."[20]

When the mullahs in Tehran sent young children into the minefields against Iraq, it was to do battle against Dar al-Harb. When they ordered terrorists to blow up the U.S. embassy in Beirut in 1983, or a Jewish Community Center in Buenos Aires in 1994, they justified these attacks as part of a global struggle against the nonbelievers. As Uri Lubrani, another respected student of Khomeini's Iran, liked to say, "How can you argue with people who take their cue from God?"[21]

Ayatollah Khomeini identified his enemies clearly. The United States was the Great Satan, because it had supported the regime of the former shah. Israel was the Little Satan, because it was ruled by the Jews. He vowed that the Islamic Republic of Iran would vanquish both and deployed all the power and influence of the state apparatus to that purpose through terrorism, aggressive intelligence operations, and propaganda. Government officials welcomed French Holocaust deniers Roger Garaudy and Robert Faurisson to Tehran and distributed their works at Iranian-backed Islamic Centers in the United States, along with videotaped sermons that spewed Nazi-style propaganda against America and against the Jews.[22] This ideological assault has continued under Khomeini's successor, Ali Khamenei, a minor cleric with no credentials other than a militant, left-wing anti-Americanism.[23] In a typical Friday prayer sermon, Khamenei explained the driving force behind the current regime:

> We are at war with America as our Prophet was at war against the corrupt empires of his time. Because we believe that Islam is the One and Only true faith, it is incumbent on us to fight until the entire humanity either converts or submits to Islamic authority. This natural march of human history is resisted by America, which is offering a life of corruption and debauchery and waging war against Islamic values in the world.[24]

Khomeini and his successors dealt with Iran's Jewish population much as Muslim leaders in Gaza and elsewhere promised they would do if victorious against Israel: they began by forcing most of the community into exile, then intimidated the Jews who remained into silence or active support for the regime. Of the estimated 120,000 Jews who lived in Iran at the time of the revolution, a scant 11,000 remain today. This community of *dhimmis* is allowed its member of Parliament, who until recently spouted the party line and condemned America whenever the mullahs demanded. Since 1999, however, the regime has taken off the gloves and begun arresting Jews on false charges of espionage, prompting many Iranian Jews to more activism in the belief that they have nothing left to lose.[25]

Ironically, despite all the efforts of the regime, the rabid anti-Semitism and anti-Americanism Khomeini and his successors preached took greater hold in Muslim communities overseas than in Iran itself, where people were fleeing the mosques in droves. As economic conditions in Iran worsened during the 1990s, the ruling clerics were increasingly discredited and viewed with contempt by ordinary Iranians. Those who flocked to the stage-managed Friday prayer ceremonies to hear regime leaders condemn America and denounce the Jews were diehard supporters of the regime anyway. Regime leaders were not making any converts inside Iran with their propaganda, which was treated with derision. In July 1999, university campuses across Iran erupted with antiregime demonstrations, a movement that has continued to grow. For those who track events inside Iran, such as recently exiled student leader Rouzbeh Farihanipour, the regime today hangs on to power by the slightest thread, which could be snapped by a gentle but forceful breeze from the West.[26] Indeed, a public opinion poll in September 2002 of 1,500 Iranians, released by the official Islamic Republic News Agency, showed a regime on the rocks. The official National Institute for Research Studies and Opinion Polls found that 74 percent of those polled favored dialogue with the United States and 45.8 percent believed America's policy of isolating the clerical regime in Tehran is "to some extent correct." Those results were so frightening to the ruling clerics that they ordered the judiciary to prosecute the directors of the government institute that conducted the poll for "publishing lies to excite public opinion."[27]

Outside Iran, it was a different story. For more than twenty years, Tehran became the center of international terrorism, the militant cutting edge of Jew-hatred and anti-Americanism. In their desire to spearhead a worldwide Islamic revival, Tehran's leaders financed terrorist groups from the Persian Gulf to Argentina. In the early days, Khomeini attempted to export the revolution to neighboring Iraq, Kuwait, and Bahrain, in scantly clad coup attempts.[28] After these initial failures, and as the pointless 1980–1988 war with Iraq decimated Iran's prestige and its economic resources, the Islamic Republic invested in guerrilla movements in Lebanon and Palestine, in an effort to position distant Iran on the front lines of the Arab-Israeli conflict and thus confer legitimacy on the regime in the eyes of fellow Muslims. First to benefit from Tehran's largesse was the Hezbollah movement in Lebanon, whose figurehead was a charismatic cleric named Hussein Fadlallah. Issuing anti-American and anti-Jewish fatwas from his base in the southern suburbs of Beirut, Fadlallah became the "spiritual guide" of the terrorists who blew up the U.S. embassy in 1983, murdered U.S. and French Marines in 1984, and took U.S. and French hostages throughout the remainder of that decade. Sheikh Fadlallah was also a rabid anti-Semite, who believed that Jews were "the enemy of the entire human race" bent on global domination.[29]

Fadlallah would never have emerged as an important leader in Lebanon had it not been for Tehran's support. In a country where prestige was counted in foreign bank accounts and weapons shipments, Fadlallah had to compete with proxies of half a dozen nations. Only Iran provided him with the support and influence that allowed him to establish Hezbollah as a militia on the front lines with Israel, a terrorist organization attacking Jewish and American interests worldwide, and ultimately, many years later, as the civil war wound down in the 1990s, a Lebanese political party.

Throughout the 1980s and up until today, the Iranian regime has sponsored annual terrorist conclaves on "Jerusalem Day," bringing together the top leaders of dozens of terrorist groups from around the world. In February 1989, the flavor of the day was Ahmed Jibril, leader of the Palestinian terrorist group suspected of involvement in the downing of Pan Am 103 over Lockerbie in December 1988. Joining him for the festivities were representatives of Abu Nidal, Hezbollah, Hamas, and a handful of Lebanese terror gangs.[30] The goal of these terrorist conclaves was always the same: to promote violence against America and against Jews. After leading the crowd in chanting "Death to America," at a similar event in 1994, Supreme Leader Ali Khamenei vowed that Iran would help Hamas and Palestinian Islamic Jihad (PIJ) "put an end to Israel."[31]

There was no discernible decrease in Iranian aid to terrorist groups after the "moderate" president Mohammad Khatami took office in August 1997. Indeed, Hojjatoleslam Khatami's first foray into foreign policy was a public speech to family members of fallen Hezbollah fighters in September 1997, when he called Israel "the greatest manifestation of international terrorism."[32] One month later, Khatami met personally with Hezbollah secretary-general Sheikh Hassan Nasrallah in Tehran. The goal of Iran's leaders was crystal-clear: to undermine the U.S.-backed Arab-Israeli "peace process" by promoting terror, the ultimate expression of hate.

At a meeting in Tehran in May 1998 with Hamas leader Sheikh Ahmad Yassin, Supreme Leader Ali Khamenei called Israel a "cancerous tumor created in the Middle East by colonial powers" and vowed to continue financial and military assistance to Hamas. "In our support for the Muslim nation of Palestine, we won't be deterred by any political or propaganda pressures," he said on state-run television. It was a clear reference to efforts by the Clinton administration to change the "behavior" of the regime in Tehran by offering trade incentives in exchange for an end to support for terrorist groups.[33] Mohammad Khatami also met with Yassin, cheerfully calling Zionism "an extension of Fascism" and noting that Israel's government had been "created by looting and killing." The English-language daily *Kayhan International,* a publication of the intelligence ministry (known officially as the Ministry of Information and Security, or VEVAK), noted in typically turgid prose that Yassin's weeklong visit had revived hopes of "mobilizing Arab and Islamic powers to overthrow the Zionist-Imperialist alliance." It called for destroying Israel "by adopting the option of armed resistance and by mobilizing the popular forces of the Palestinian people under the banner of Islam and holy jihad."[34]

It was not just rhetoric. During the first nine months of 1997, Israel detected "no fewer than 45 jumbo jets full of weapons" destined for Hezbollah arriving from Iran at the Damascus airport.[35] In its annual budget as presented for parliamentary approval, the Iranian government allocated $100 million to Hamas, Hezbollah, and Palestinian Islamic Jihad. More and more of that money was being spent to sponsor suicide bombers and their families in an effort to end the U.S.-sponsored "peace process." After another meeting in Tehran with top Hamas leaders shortly after the second Palestinian uprising began in the fall of 2000, President

Khatami declared that the only way for real peace in the Middle East was to end the state of Israel. "Real peace can only be achieved through an end to occupation and the return of all Palestinians to their homeland and through respect for the rights of all Palestinians, including Muslims, Christians, and Jews, to determine their own future," he told state radio. That future, he added, would not include the existence of a Jewish state. "They are basically an occupying entity. Naturally, any government that is based on oppression and injustice may stay in power for a while, but ultimately it is doomed to failure."[36]

Supreme Leader Ali Khamenei hastened to add that the latest uprising, which began with schoolchildren bused into Jerusalem by the Palestinian Authority with orders to throw stones at Jews praying at the Wailing Wall, had raised the flag of jihad. "There is only one remedy and there is only one cure" to the Middle East crisis, and that is to "destroy the root and cause of the crisis. What is the root?" he asked. "The answer is, the Zionist regime: a regime which has been imposed on the region. . . . The crisis will be present as long as its root and cause remains intact." Khamenei then urged Palestinians "to continue their jihad," adding that "combatants of Hamas, the [PIJ] and Fatah . . . must not abandon the arena." Later that same week, leaders of the Iranian Revolutionary Guards Corps called for "removing the tumorous cancer Israel off the region's map."[37]

Where does anti-Zionism end and anti-Semitism begin? Islamic Iran's leaders offer a very simple answer: when political opposition to Israeli policies expresses itself in the murder of individual Jews, for no other reason than their faith.

Iranian-backed terrorism has claimed thousands of lives over the past two decades. Leaving aside the hundreds of thousands of Iranians slaughtered during the 1980–1988 war with Iraq, and at least fifty thousand Iranians murdered because of their political opposition to the regime, several hundred Israelis have been murdered by Palestinian suicide bombers sponsored by the Iranian regime since 1994, simply because they were Jews. Americans such as Alisa Flatow, a nineteen-year-old student from New Jersey, have also perished thanks to the murderous policies of Iran's leaders. Alisa was traveling through Gaza on a public bus on April 4, 1995, when a terrorist recruited by the Iranian-sponsored Palestinian Islamic Jihad detonated an explosives-laden van along the roadside at Kfar Darom, killing her and six Israelis. Less than one year later, visiting American students Matthew Eisenfeld and Sarah Duker were murdered by another PIJ attacker as they were boarding the number 18 bus in Jerusalem on February 25, 1996. As in the case of Alisa Flatow, a U.S. court determined that the attack had been directly financed by the government of the Islamic Republic of Iran and ordered the regime to pay punitive damages. Hundreds of others have perished in Iranian-sponsored terrorist attacks in Lebanon, Argentina, and France, some because they were Americans, others because they were Jews.[38]

From the very start of the revolution, Iran's radical clerics boasted of the support they were providing to anti-Western movements around the world. As recently as 1998, Ali Khamenei took out a full-page advertisement in London's *Sunday Times* in which he claimed credit for the success of "Islamic" regimes in Bosnia, Turkey, and Sudan and decried the works of "global arrogance"—that is, the United States.[39]

During the late 1990s, under the sponsorship of Henry Sokolski's Nonproliferation Policy Education Center, I presented what was considered a novel analysis of the Iranian regime to various U.S. government agencies. At the time, many in the intelligence and national security community were fascinated by the possibility that a "moderate" Iranian president could gradually bring about meaningful reforms to a system that had exported terror and was building dangerous weapons of mass murder. They believed that with the right incentives from Washington, they could change the behavior of the regime. I suggested testing the notion that "moderate" and "hard-line" factions existed within the ruling clergy by examining the basic goals of the different groups and what types of changes they were willing to tolerate. The conclusion was simple and far-reaching for U.S. policy. All factions were united on five key goals, starting with maintaining the system of *Velayat-e faghih* (absolute clerical rule) at all costs. For any meaningful change to occur in Iran, and for representative democracy to take root, the dictatorship of the clergy must end. The behavior of Iran's leaders was not something that was haphazard or superficial, but represented core values that all the factions shared. "It's the regime, stupid," I concluded.[40]

Imagine for an instant where the Middle East would be without a radical regime in Tehran spawning terrorist groups whose sole purpose is to murder Americans and Jews. Imagine what would happen to those groups without the financial, intelligence, and logistics support they receive from Tehran. Since 1979, the murderers have benefited from the sponsorship of a major state. Without the Islamic Republic of Iran to show the way, arguably there would have been no suicide bombers, no Hezbollah, no international network of terror committing murder under the cloaks of God-fearing righteousness.

That was the first major change.

†††

The second event that transformed the Middle East and elevated anti-Semitism and anti-American hatred into state-sponsored doctrines went virtually unnoticed in the West.

Nineteen-seventy-nine was filled with upheaval and a violence whose impact would be felt for decades to come. It began with the fall of the shah of Iran and ended with the rumbling of Soviet tanks invading Afghanistan, a country that, if known at all to Americans at the time, was reputed for its hashish. Sandwiched between these earthquakes of history was another event that helped radicalize the Muslim world and contributed to giving anti-Semitism and anti-American hatred a second state sponsor, Saudi Arabia.

On November 20, 1979, a group of radical Islamic fundamentalists posing as religious pilgrims seized control of the Great Mosque in Mecca and proclaimed an end to the al-Saud dynasty and the coming end of the world. For more than two weeks, as Saudi troops struggled to quell their resistance inside the labyrinthine cellars of the mosque with the help of French gendarmes, the Saudi regime shook to its very foundations. But as one Saudi critic of the Wahhabite regime noted recently, in the aftermath of the carnage, the Saudis forged a closer alliance with the radical clerical leaders in their country as an insurance policy to head off future revolts.[41] The most detailed account of the actual fighting comes from Captain Paul Barril, the French gendarme who led the counterterrorist force that ultimately beat back the rebels.[42] By official estimates, 177 rebels were killed during the fighting, in addition to 127 government troops, but most observers believe the real casualties were far more numerous.

It was 5:20 A.M. on November 20, 1979, when Sheikh Mohammad bin Soubbayil ascended the minaret to call the faithful to prayer. Fifty thousand pilgrims were still sleeping within the walls of the Great Mosque, despite the fact that the annual pilgrimage to Mecca had ended three weeks earlier. Before Sheikh Mohammad could finish his song, a wild-eyed man in his early thirties snatched the microphone from his hands and pushed the older man away. "My name is Jouhayman al-Otaibi," he told the crowds in the courtyard below, who had begun to wash their hands and feet in preparation for their morning prayers. "Here with me is Mohammad al-Qahtani. He is the Mahdi who has come to bring justice to the world. Bow down to the Mahdi who will cleanse the kingdom of corruption!"[43]

As he spoke, several hundred men mixed in among the crowd seized key positions, firing on the handful of policemen stationed inside the mosque with automatic rifles they had hidden beneath their pilgrim's robes. Panic seized the crowd. Pilgrims began running in every direction as al-Otaibi denounced the moral depravity and corruption of the Saudi royal family and the Westernization they had brought to the land of God's two holy mosques. Al-Otaibi cited by name the governor of Mecca, Prince Fawaz bin Abdul Aziz, accusing him of debauchery and drunkenness. His message was relayed by hundreds of loudspeakers and was audible halfway across the city.

In the confusion, the imam of the mosque managed to escape, slipping off his clerical garments, and telephoned the authorities. King Khaled was woken up at 7 A.M. to hear the bad news. A weak and ineffectual leader, known for gambling away millions in Monaco, Khaled had delegated most of his power to his brothers.[44] But on this fateful day, the most powerful of his brothers were nowhere to be found. Crown Prince Fahd was attending an Arab summit in Tunis. Prince Abdallah, head of the National Guard, was in Morocco. So Khaled sent Prince Sultan, the defense minister, and Prince Nayef, his interior minister, to coordinate operations against the insurgents. Prince Nayef was convinced that the attack was an Iranian plot and immediately cut off all international telephone and telex lines. The day of the assault was also the beginning of the month of Muharram, the Shiite Muslim month of mourning—not a festival celebrated or revered in the Wahhabite kingdom of the al-Saud, which held that Shiites were a deviant sect established as the result of "a Jewish conspiracy . . . to create discord or fighting *(fitnah)* among Muslims."[45]

As it turned out, the fears of Prince Nayef were unfounded. What was happening was much worse. The rebels were not Iranians or even Shiites; they were members of the Wahhabi sect, the extremist Sunni clerics who had formed a pact with King Abdul Aziz in the 1920s that brought the al-Saud family to power.

Horrified by the violence inside Islam's holiest site, King Khaled summoned the highest religious authorities of the kingdom to his palace and got them to issue a fatwa authorizing a counterattack. Despite this holy armor, the royal troops made little headway. The insurgents had posted snipers in all seven minarets of the mosque complex, picking off any government troops who ventured within range. The innumerable arcades, half-concealed corridors, and underground galleries became so many hiding places for al-Otaibi and his men, now believed to number close to two thousand. They were well armed, having smuggled in weapons and explosives in coffins and stockpiled them in the cellars over a period of several weeks in preparation for the attack. According to one Saudi source, the rebels "believed they would be joined by a host of angels from heaven who would bring about the kingdom of heaven."[46]

After three days, the king and his brothers realized they needed outside help. Having seen how the Carter administration had betrayed the shah of Iran, they called on the French, who dispatched a unit of the elite antiterrorist force known as the GIGN (Groupe d'Intervention de la Gendarmerie Nationale), under the command of Captain Paul Barril. On November 23, 1979, Barril and the three gendarmes who eventually accompanied him onto the grounds of the Great Mosque to lead the counterattack were hastily converted to Islam, to allow the king to pretend that he had not broken the taboo on allowing non-Muslims into Mecca. Nevertheless, it took Barril and the Saudi National Guard nearly two weeks to subdue the rebels. At first, they had tried to drown the rebels by flooding the cellars of the mosque. When that failed, Barril and his men drilled holes through the floor and pumped tear gas into the cellars, forcing al-Otaibi and 170 of his followers to come up for air in the early morning hours of December 5.

Despite all their precautions, the Great Mosque was in a shambles.

According to one eyewitness, who visited the mosque four months after the attackers had been subdued, "minarets had been blown off, artillery fire had punched holes in the exterior walls, and there were huge holes in the floors."[47] In the end, Barril and his gendarmes were helped by the company that had recently expanded the mosque complex on contract to the royal family. They turned over the blueprints of the cellars, allowing Barril and his men to localize the insurgents without a frontal assault. The company, run by a Yemenite family often called the "commoner branch of the Royal Family," was the Saudi bin Laden Group.

A French intelligence report on the bin Laden family claims that the company was eager to help because inadvertently their trucks had been used to bring weapons to the rebels. "Because the bin Laden company had the exclusive contract for repairs in the Holy Places, its trucks entered and left Mecca at all hours without being inspected," the report states. "And the rebels used 'bin Laden' trucks to get weapons into the city. One of the bin Laden sons, Mahrous, was actually arrested on account of his ties with the Islamists, but was later freed."[48]

On January 9, 1980, Jouhayman al-Otaibi and sixty-two others were decapitated in eight cities across the kingdom, to serve as an example. The "Mahdi" had been killed during the counterassault. The insurgent leaders came from two of the most prominent Saudi tribes. Jouhayman was an al-Otaibi, while the "Mahdi" came from the al-Qahtani. Both had supplied numerous foot soldiers to the Ikhwan, the Muslim Brotherhood, which had formed the shock troops for Ibn Saud during his conquest of the Arabian Peninsula from 1902 until he seized Mecca in 1924. In one of history's ironies, Ibn Saud turned against the al-Ikhwan in 1929, totally decimating them as a fighting force, after they had protested his relationship with Great Britain and his failure to persecute Shiite Muslims. Among the tribes who suffered heavy losses at Ibn Saud's hands during the 1929 revolt were precisely the al-Otaibi and the al-Qahtani. This led Prince Nayef and Crown Prince Fahd to fear that the assault of Mecca by their descendants was an attempt to revive the Ikhwan.

Even worse: Once the insurrection had been quelled, Saudi interrogators discovered that Jouhayman was no stranger to the security services, suggesting that he might have well-placed accomplices who quietly approved of his activities. After serving briefly in the National Guard, he studied for two years at the Islamic University of Medina under Sheikh Abdul Aziz bin Abdullah bin Baz, the blind Wahhabite imam who was the official chief priest of the kingdom, or grand mufti. (In 1969, Baz distinguished himself by issuing a fatwa declaring that "the earth is a flat disk around which the sun revolves and that any belief otherwise was heresy." He only rescinded his edict in 1985, when a Saudi prince returned from a spin around the globe on board the U.S. space shuttle and told him that he had "personally witnessed the roundness of the earth.")[49]

After his studies with Sheikh bin Baz, al-Otaibi founded his own religious group and published several pamphlets from neighboring Kuwait, denouncing the corruption of the Saudi royal family. He was arrested during the summer of 1978, just one year before the assault on the Grand Mosque, along with ninety-eight of his followers. Sheikh bin Baz attended his interrogation by the security services and argued in favor of his release, saying that the young fanatic was a "loyal Muslim who has gone astray." It was a near fatal mistake.

† † †

In one sense, the Soviet invasion of Afghanistan on December 26, 1979, couldn't have come at a more opportune moment for the Saudi regime. Still reeling from the attack on the Great Mosque, the Saudis desperately needed to reforge their alliance with the radical Wahhabite clerics, whose support they needed to remain in power. Without the clerics behind them, they feared a revival of the even more radical Ikhwan, who condemned Saudi ties to the West, rejected the modern world, and vowed to close off the kingdom to any foreign and especially any non-Muslim influence.

Keeping the Wahhabis on their side required more than just money. The royal family needed to display adequate passion and commitment to spreading Wahhabi doctrine to Muslim communities around the world. In 1962, to placate the clerics, the Saudis established the Muslim World League to build Wahhabite mosques around the world and propagate the faith. In 1973, they added the activist World Assembly of Muslim Youth (WAMY), which opened offices in sixty countries, distributing scholarships to young Muslims who accepted the Wahhabi doctrine that "Jews are the source of all conflicts of the world, that Shia'a Muslims are part of a Jewish conspiracy, and that Muslims, Jews, and Christians cannot live together."⁵⁰ These organizations spread the works of Ibn Abd al-Wahhab, the sect's eighteenth-century founder, as well as those of the leading contemporary Wahhabi scholar, Sayyid Abul-Ala al-Mawdudi (1903–1979), who condemned all Muslims not embracing the Wahhabi doctrine as apostates and unbelievers. This excommunication from the faith began with Shias and extended to every school of the majority Sunni thought that did not explicitly embrace the austere, fundamentalist Wahhabi doctrine. The Wahhabis reserved special damnation for "Crusaders" and Jews, who were considered the implacable enemies of Islam.⁵¹

Al-Mawdudi also argued for abolishing the protected *dhimmi* status of religious minorities living in Islamic countries, a suggestion the Saudi royal family adopted happily. Saudi officials regularly boast to foreigners that the kingdom is "100 percent Muslim." U.S. expatriates living in Saudi Arabia have learned that this means no outward displays of religion will be tolerated, even in private. U.S. diplomats have complained to Congress that they are forced to hold church services on Sundays like secret conspirators, in specially guarded rooms in the U.S. embassy in Riyadh, or face arrest by the Wahhabi religious police, the *mutawiyin* (formally known as the Committee for the Encouragement of Virtue and Prevention of Vice). When CIA director William Casey, a devout Catholic, became a regular guest of Saudi King Fahd to plot the anti-Soviet war in Afghanistan in the early 1980s, he discovered that even a visiting dignitary of his importance was not allowed to practice his faith openly. Casey insisted on taking communion every Sunday, much to the alarm of King Fahd, who hastily gave his personal approval—and protection—so the CIA chief could hold a private Catholic mass in the home of a U.S. diplomat.⁵²

Al-Mawdudi's doctrine of jihad and his messianic vision of Islam conquering the world inspired a generation of young jihadis who flocked to his native Pakistan following the Soviet invasion of Afghanistan. Like Ibn Abd al-Wahhab before him, al-Mawdudi made clear that his notion of Islamic Holy War was not an internal spiritual struggle, but war. "The Islamic party does not hesitate to utilize the means of war to implement its goal," he wrote in a 1927 text. "Islam seeks the world. It is not satisfied by a piece of land but demands the whole universe." Al-Mawdudi's doctrines can be heard today wherever the disciples of Wahhabism hold sway.

In London, at an anniversary "celebration" of the 9/11 attacks, I watched his followers at the radical Finsbury Park mosque hang out banners proclaiming "Islam will dominate the world," while vowing to transform Britain into an "Islamic Republic."[53]

In a cynical move that would ultimately backfire, the Saudis saw the anti-Soviet jihad in Afghanistan as "a unique opportunity . . . to dispose of restless Wahhabi youths in their own country, who could be sent to martyrdom abroad."[54] One of the first young Wahhibi fanatics who flocked to Afghanistan—"within days of the Soviet invasion," he would claim later—was Osama bin Laden.

As the jihad gathered force, the Saudis seized the occasion to imprint the Afghan resistance with their own Wahhabi stamp. Under the personal direction of Crown Prince Fahd, who became king upon Khaled's death in 1982, the Saudi government spent billions of dollars to fund the jihadis. Prince Salman, the governor of Riyadh and a full brother of the king, was put in charge of raising money at the mosques and from wealthy Saudis and distributing it through ostensibly private agencies, including the Muwafaq (Blessed Relief) Foundation, the International Islamic Relief Organization (IIRO), and the Islamic Salvation Foundation (ISF).[55] His role was so public and so central, the editor of an Arabic-language newspaper told me in London, that the fund-raising effort was called "the Prince Salman Committee" and published its account number to facilitate bank transfers.[56] The young bin Laden was ultimately put in charge of the Islamic Salvation Foundation office in Peshawar. As the local representative of Prince Salman, he became the ex officio Saudi ambassador of jihad.

Prince Turki bin Faisal, head of Saudi intelligence, was tasked with coordinating military supplies and training of the mujahedeen with the CIA and with Pakistan's Inter-Services Intelligence agency (ISI). Although there were eight main factions of the Afghan resistance, all of them fighting in the name of Islam, the Saudis funneled their money to two Wahhabi extremists: a Palestinian cleric named Abdallah Azzam and a fanatical Afghan guerrilla leader, Gulbuddin Hekmatyar, who agreed to enlist Arab volunteers in large numbers. Frank Anderson, a former CIA deputy director of operations in charge of supporting the anti-Soviet jihad, told me that he started complaining to the Pakistanis early on about the amount of U.S. and Saudi aid that was winding up in the hands of the most radical

Islamic factions in Afghanistan. The United States was particularly concerned by the large numbers of Arabs streaming into Peshawar and ultimately into Afghanistan, because it had no contact with them and no control over their activities. "The only time I saw an Arab fighter in Afghanistan was by accident," Anderson told me. "He threatened to kill me because I was an American."[57] American journalist Edward Girardet, who covered the Afghan war for the *Christian Science Monitor,* says that he was personally accosted by an Arab-Afghan fighter in February 1989, who threatened to kill him because he was an American. Later, asking his interpreter about the encounter, Girardet learned the identity of the tall, hysterical Arab who had wanted to kill him: it was Osama bin Laden.[58]

Prince Turki also maintained close ties with the young bin Laden, who brought hundreds of millions of dollars' worth of construction equipment into Pakistan from the family business to build caves and underground bunkers for the mujahedeen, some right in the outskirts of Kabul.[59] According to a member of the Saudi royal family, whom I spoke to regularly over a period of five years, Prince Turki's full brother Mohammad bin Faisal bin Abdul Aziz became a business partner of the bin Laden family. Prince Turki retired abruptly after a lifetime at the head of the Saudi foreign intelligence service on August 31, 2001, reportedly because of his close ties to bin Laden. He was just fifty-six years old.

As many as twenty thousand young Arabs from Morocco to Saudi Arabia flooded into Pakistan in the 1980s to dip their swords in the blood of the infidel Soviets. "The Arabs were fascinated by the Afghan jihad," a former chief of Pakistan's Inter-Services Intelligence service, General Hamid Gul, told me in the living room of his modest villa in a military housing development in Rawalpindi. "In it they found an expression for their bottled-up feelings of being thrashed three times by Israel. They are brave people with a martial tradition. Jihad is still simmering and will express itself elsewhere."[60]

Former jihadis popped up all over the world once the Soviets withdrew from Afghanistan in February 1989. Some fought another war with Russians in Chechnya. Others returned home to Egypt, Saudi Arabia, and even the Philippines and Indonesia and took up arms against the governments there. Afghan veterans in Algeria formed the Armed Islamic Group, which has been responsible for horrific massacres that have claimed over one hundred thousand lives, carving up entire villages of women, old men, and children in their struggle against the Algerian military regime. "At the end of the Afghan war, you had a long queue of unemployed mercenaries who were looking for new masters," a confidant of Egyptian president Mubarak, Nabil Osman, told me in Cairo. "Who created this monster? Those who provided the religious connotation of jihad, those who provided the training, those who provided the armaments, those who had a specific interest."[61]

Not only did the Saudis buy food, clothing, and weapons for the mujahedeen—with their billions they built an entire network of religious schools in Pakistan, where the next generation of Wahhabi fanatics would be trained. Young men sent to these schools learned little about the outside world, focusing instead on Wahhabi interpretations of the Koran. It was here that the Taliban was spawned, brought up to hate non-Wahhabi Muslims, the West, and, of course, the Jews.

The most famous of these schools, Jihad and Dawa University, was ultimately closed down by the Pakistani authorities in the late 1990s "because we felt it was unnecessarily giving a bad name to Pakistan," a senior government official in Islamabad told me in March 1998. Located behind a truck stop along the Trunk Road from Islamabad to Peshawar, the school was the headquarters of Abdul Rasool Sayyaf, an Afghan Wahhabi who was another major recipient of Saudi government aid during the anti-Soviet jihad. Sayyaf vetted the thousands of wanna-be Arab fighters who flocked to Peshawar at the behest of Osama bin Laden and his masters in Riyadh and dispatched those deemed worthy of martyrdom to military training camps inside Afghanistan. It was here that bin Laden reportedly recruited Khaled Sheikh Mohammad, the man who went on to mastermind the September 11 attacks. In one of his earlier attempts to attack America, Mohammad sent a young nephew from Baluchestan who called himself Ramzi Yousef to orchestrate the first World Trade Center attack in 1993. Once Yousef was arrested in Pakistan in February 1995, Western journalists began sniffing around the "university" and ultimately profiled its activities in places like *New York* magazine and the *Atlantic Monthly*.

No one really knows how much the Saudis spent to back the Afghan mujahedeen. Estimates vary from $3 billion to $6 billion. Nor are any accounts available for the amount the Saudis spent to build the scores of radical religious schools in Pakistan. But in March 1998, at a time when the Saudis were backing off their aide in the face of growing pressure from the United States, I passed a Saudi convoy of ten-ton trucks headed for the Afghan border carrying sacks of wheat and other foodstuffs to the Taliban regime. I counted 110 trucks, stretching bumper to bumper for well over a kilometer, packed to the gills with sacks of wheat. As with the aid during the time of jihad, Saudi Arabia's assistance to the Taliban was being coordinated by Prince Salman bin Abdul Aziz, the governor of Riyadh, according to import documents Pakistan officials shared with me in Islamabad. Saudi dissident Ali al-Ahmad believes the Saudis pumped $22 billion into Afghanistan between 1980 and 2001.[62]

The Saudis had several goals in backing the mujahedeen in the highly public manner that became their trademark, according to former U.S. officials, former and current Pakistani intelligence chiefs, and other observers who followed the jihad on the ground.

First and foremost, they sought to defuse internal dissent within the clergy, and within the royal family, by giving radicals an outlet to vent their anti-Western zeal. In so doing, they sought to exercise control over the militant Wahhabi leadership by making them dependent on Saudi-bought guns and aid. Next, they sought to improve the external image of the Saudi regime, which many Muslims criticized as a Mafia of spoiled oil princes who grew fat while other Muslims died of hunger or were killed by infidels. Third, they sought to create a higher profile for the kingdom as the primary state sponsor of Islamic propagation, by financing the construction of a network of Wahhabi academies, or *madrasas,* in Pakistan to train the next generation. Finally, a lesser-known but no less important goal was to discredit the Shiite revolution of Ayatollah Khomeini in Iran and, especially, to prevent Iran from creating a bond with the Shiite population in the kingdom's oil-rich eastern province or with disaffected Saudi Sunnis, by positioning Saudi Arabia as the only true standard-bearer of Islam. It was one reason why King Fahd, on assuming power in 1982, added a new title to his attributions: "Custodian of the Two Holy Mosques." "The Shiite/Sunni competition, especially that between Iran and Saudi Arabia, created a spiral that rapidly became uncontrollable and sucked in most of the other Muslim countries," says Patrick Ali Pahlavi, a critic of the Tehran regime but also an avid Koranic scholar.[63]

Simply put, the Saudi royal family found in the anti-Soviet jihad the perfect vehicle for asserting themselves as the leader of the world Islamic community and, most important, for maintaining their rule over the fabulous oil wealth of the Arabian Peninsula.

†††

After the quadrupling of world oil prices in 1974, the Saudis spent heavily to spread the Wahhabi sect around the world with a zeal that went unnoticed at first. They sought to dominate Islamic institutions through diplomacy at the Organization of the Islamic Conference. But they also used less transparent means, setting up an extensive network of apparently nongovernmental agencies that in reality were bred, funded, and controlled by Riyadh. "They call this effort to spread the Wahhabi sect *jihad al-talab,* the holy war against unbelievers," says Saudi dissident Ali al-Ahmad. "The Saudis believe that all non-Wahhabis are infidels. Their philosophy is very simple: Conquest, subjugate, or die."

Al-Ahmad, a Shiite Muslim from Saudi Arabia's eastern province, was brought up as a child on religious texts in school that denigrated his Shiite faith. "When you're taught from the age of twelve that you are a member of a Jewish conspiracy, it leaves a mark," he says with only a trace of irony. Al-Ahmad's version of Wahhabi rule, while contested by the Saudi regime and their supporters in America, has long been known to international human rights organizations and to the U.S. Department of State, which lists Saudi Arabia as one of the most egregious violators of religious freedoms in the world.[64]

The same relief organizations, government ministries, and "private" Saudis that supported Osama bin Laden and the anti-Soviet jihad in Afghanistan today funnel billions of dollars to Saudi-backed institutions from Malaysia to Los Angeles. Primary among them are the World Assembly of Muslim Youth and the Muslim World League, known more familiarly as the Rabita, the Arabic word for "league." Because of its ties to al-Qaeda and international terrorism, the Bush administration blacklisted

the Lahore, Pakistan, office of the Rabita Trust on October 12, 2001, blocking its assets and preventing U.S. entities, including banks and financial
institutions, from doing business with it.[65] Wael Hamza Jalaidan, secretary-
general of the Trust, was a founding member of al-Qaeda who fought
alongside bin Laden against the Soviets in Afghanistan and was considered by the U.S. Department of Treasury as a top al-Qaeda logistics officer.
At one point, he also headed the Saudi Red Crescent Society and the Muslim World League. Yet the Saudi government continued to defend him.
When the United States announced it was freezing his assets in September
2002, Saudi interior minister Nayef bin Abdul Aziz responded angrily,
"Those who make this accusation should provide convincing evidence."[66]
Clearly, the direct ties between Jalaidan and top Saudi officials, business-
men, and members of the royal family were embarrassing.[67]

Officials of the Rabita travel regularly around the world, checkbooks
in hand, buying off local imams and the leaders of Islamic communities.
As Western governments begin to look closer into the League's activities,
however, the welcome mat is beginning to wear thin. Abdallah Turki,
secretary-general of the World Muslim League, spent a frustrating week in
France in October 2002, rebuffed by French officials and mocked in the
establishment daily *Le Monde,* not known for its lockstep support of the
United States. After citing the French officials who refused to meet him,
Le Monde noted that Turki, a former Saudi minister of religious affairs,
was invited to France by Kamel Kabtane, rector of the Grand Mosque of
Lyon, "whose construction was financed 80 percent by the Saudis." Yamin
Makri, spokesman for the Union of Young Muslims, told the French daily
that Turki's visit shows "all the contradictions of institutionalized Islam in
France, which is represented solely by the mosques in Paris and Lyon paid
for by foreign states. That Islam, we reject." Interior Minister Nicolas
Sarkozy, who finally agreed to meet Turki on October 8, warned him publicly not to fund "organizations whose goals are incompatible with the values of the Republic." At a reception for French Islamic groups in the Paris
Hilton, hosted by the Saudi embassy, "everyone came to present his
respects and . . . his financing needs to His Excellency," *Le Monde* wrote
acidly. "Abdallah Turki didn't exactly come with envelopes, but he left
with requests for financing that will be examined in Saudi Arabia," said
one guest. The Union of Islamic Organizations in France said money from

the League was only a "drop in the bucket" compared to funds donated directly by private Saudis. "Other sources say the Rabita, as it's called in Arabic, pays out $4 billion each year," *Le Monde* added."[68]

Turki went on a similar trip to distribute aid to Saudi vassals in the United States from June 25 to July 15, 2002. He was accompanied by Dr. Ahmad Turkistani, a Saudi government diplomat who is director of the Institute of Islamic and Arabic Sciences in America (IIASA), and Muzamil Siddiqi, who until November 2001 was president of the Islamic Society of North America (ISNA), a leading Wahhabi front organization in the United States. Siddiqi denies he is remunerated by the World Muslim League but he is listed on their Web site as one of the League's official U.S. representatives.[69] Those ties are significant because they demonstrate how closely Siddiqi and other Wahhabite lobbyists have coordinated a Saudi support network within the American Muslim community.

According to one private investigator who tracked Saudi expenditures on Islamic movements around the world for a major financial institution, "The Saudis themselves claim in official reports that they have provided $65 billion to Islamic causes between 1973 and 1993."[70] Indeed, the Saudis like to boast of their liberality. "The determination of the Kingdom to support Islam and Islamic institutions to the best of its ability was evidenced from the formation of the Kingdom by King Abdul Aziz, but it was only when oil revenues began to generate real wealth that the Kingdom could fulfill its ambitions of spreading the word of Islam to every corner of the world," an extraordinary article in the Saudi government English-language weekly, *Ain-al-Yaqeen*, begins.[71] Some of the Saudi aid was development assistance to "Muslim countries less well endowed economically," the article states. But a vast amount was spent in building mosques, distributing Wahhabite literature, and supporting jihad from Richardson, Texas, to Manila through the same institutions that pumped aid into Afghanistan during the 1980s and fund suicide bombings in Israel today.[72] Imagine if the United States government were to spend billions of dollars in virtually every country around the world building Baptist or Methodist churches and then appointed U.S. government officials to run the World Council of Churches? Yet that is precisely what the Saudis have been doing. When the Saudi government speaks of "the voice of Islam," what it really means is the radical anti-Western and anti-Semitic teaching of the Wahhabi sect.

The cost of King's Fahd's efforts in this field has been astronomical, amounting to many billions of Saudi riyals. In terms of Islamic institutions, the result is some 210 Islamic centers wholly or partly financed by Saudi Arabia, more than 1,500 mosques and 202 colleges and almost 2,000 schools for educating Muslim children in non-Islamic countries in Europe, North and South America, Australia and Asia. . . . All over the world the King of Saudi Arabia has supported and contributed in the establishment of mosques and Islamic centers."[73]

In the United States, King Fahd built fifteen Islamic centers and major mosques.[74] In Canada, the Saudi government built mosques in Calgary and Ottawa and contributes $1.5 million each year to the operating costs of the Islamic Center in Toronto. In Europe, the Saudis have been active for decades, building mosques, cultural centers, lecture halls, and *madrasas*. King Fahd personally donated $50 million to cover 70 percent of the building costs of an Islamic Center in Rome "that comprises a mosque, a library, and a lecture hall." The Islamic Center in Geneva receives an annual subsidy from Riyadh of 19 million Saudi riyals ($1 = SR 3.75). In Madrid, the Saudis have pumped in 27 million riyals to build "a very capacious mosque, a [separate] prayer hall for women, a library, a lecture hall, and a medical clinic." Construction for one of the largest overseas mosques, the King Fahd Islamic Center in Malaga, Spain, began in 1998. "The university-like center embraces academic, education, cultural, and propagatory activities," the article states.

The Saudis officially opened their sixtieth state-sponsored mosque in Los Angeles in October 2002, according to Ali al-Ahmad. Altogether, the Saudi government weekly states, "the Kingdom has established more than 1,359 mosques abroad at a cost of SR 820 million. Other mosques partially financed by the Kingdom included mosques in Zagreb, Lisbon, Vienna, New York, Washington, Chicago, Maryland, Ohio, Virginia and 12 mosques in a number of countries in South America." All of these mosques are run by Saudi-trained imams and spread Wahhabi doctrine to the exclusion of traditionalist Sunni teachings.

But even these figures just scratch the surface. As the United States sent Treasury Department officials to the kingdom to help stanch the flow of Saudi money to terrorist organizations, Grand Mufti Sheikh Abdul Aziz al-Sheikh called the U.S. efforts "a smear campaign" aimed at discrediting Saudi charitable societies. "Our charities are supporting the poor and working for the good of humanity," he told a gala fund-raiser held at the Inter-Continental Hotel in Riyadh on November 13, 2002. Organized by IIRO, WAMY, and al-Haramain Charitable Foundation[75]—the very charities in Washington's gun sights for having supported bin Laden—the event was hosted by Riyadh governor Prince Salman bin Abdul Aziz, the same Saudi prince who oversaw fund-raising for the anti-Soviet (and anti-Western) jihad.

Ali bin Abdullah al-Jerais, the director of IIRO's office in Riyadh, said his organization alone had "established 4,400 mosques and sponsored about 209,000 orphans in various parts of the world," *Arab News* reported. In addition, IIRO had "constructed 1,615 wells and published millions of copies of Islamic books and pamphlets." Separately, WAMY had spent "more than SR 429 million during the past five years on various Islamic and charitable projects around the world." The precision of al-Jerais's figures, while impossible to verify, are of interest. In parts of the world where access to clean water makes all the difference between health and the misery of chronic dysentery, these Saudi charities have built 2.7 mosques for every well—and at considerably greater expense.[76] None of these Saudi government-financed institutions has made headlines for promoting interfaith dialogue. Instead, they preach hatred of the West, hatred of Christians, hatred of Jews, and the subservience of women. Not incidentally, it was IIRO mosques and *madrasas* in Pakistan that spawned the Taliban in the early 1990s and feed the breeding ground for al-Qaeda supporters.

††††

The U.S. government's Foreign Broadcast Information Service has begun to translate Friday prayer sermons from Mecca that are broadcast live around the world by the Saudi government over satellite radio and television networks in Europe and the United States. On May 31, 2002, Sheikh Abdul Rahman bin Abdul Aziz al-Sudais, chief imam of the Great Mosque of Mecca, called on the Muslim world to unite against a vast conspiracy of Jews, Christians, and "idol-worshipping Hindus" he claimed was seeking to subvert Islam through Western-style globalization.

The nation has never been in such a dire need to follow the example of the Prophet in this age of tribulations, sedition, open challenges, and mean plotting by the enemies of Islam. I mean especially [the Jews] whom God cursed, got angry with, and turned into monkeys, pigs, and tyrant worshippers. . . . Their course is supported by the advocates of credit and worshippers of the Cross, as well as by those who are infatuated with them and influenced by their rotten ideas and poisonous culture among the advocates of secularism and westernization."[77]

The Jews "have tyrannized, terrorized, and indulged in tyranny and corruption," al-Sudais told his followers on this worldwide broadcast. "O God, deal with them for they are within your power." Two weeks later, al-Sudais returned to the theme, ending his sermon with "a prayer to God to support Islam and Muslims, humble infidelity and infidels, destroy the enemies of religion, and make this and other Muslim countries safe and stable." He called for faithful Muslims to support Muslim mujahedeen fighters wherever they could be found. "O God, support them in Palestine, Kashmir, and Chechnya. O God, deal with the Jews and Zionists for they are within Your power. O God, scatter their assemblies, make them a lesson for others, and let them and their property be a booty for Muslims."[78]

The theme of murdering Jews is repeated constantly. "O God, destroy the tyrant Jews," Sheikh Usama bin Abdallah Khayyat declaimed from Mecca on July 12, 2002. "O God, deal with the Jews and their supporters. O God, destroy them, for they are within your power."[79] Again, on October 11, 2002: "O God, deal with the oppressive Jews, as they are within your power, and spare us their evil," he hectored.[80]

There is nothing unusual about these sermons. Hundreds of examples of this type of hate speech from state-appointed Saudi clerics can be found through FBIS, MEMRI, and other organizations that today track the official Saudi media. They are the usual fare of hate on an average Friday in the state-funded mosques of Saudi Arabia.

At the Saudi-funded Institute of Islamic and Arabic Sciences in America in Fairfax, Virginia, hate literature printed at Saudi government expense is routinely distributed to students. In his treatise *Deen al-Haqq* (*The True Religion*), Abdul Rahman ben Hamad al-Omer elaborates on the theme that "Judaism and Christianity are deviant religions." Good Muslims should never befriend unbelievers, he warns, because it is against the faith. Instead, every effort should be made to convert them. "We say to every Christian and every Jew and all those outside Islam, 'Your children are born into Islam, but you and their mother took them away from Islam with your corrupt rearing.' "[81] This has been interpreted by many Saudis who have married non-Muslim women in Europe and the United States as an open invitation to kidnap their children and bring them forcibly to Saudi Arabia. For several years reporter Tim Maier of *Insight* magazine has been tracking these kidnappings and the virtual refusal of the State Department to intervene with the Saudi government to bring these American children home.[82]

The world beyond Saudi Arabia, especially the non-Muslim world, is regularly portrayed in official Saudi publications and by prayer leaders as threatening, foreign, and dangerous. Another state-sponsored author, Dr. Abdulla al-Tarakee, warns Muslims to shun "suspicious calls to religious coexistence" in an Emily Post–style guide distributed to American Muslims by IIASA. In *A Muslim's Relations with Non-Muslims: Emnity or Friendship,* he writes: "The unbelievers, idolators, and others like them must be hated and despised. . . . We must stay away from them and create barriers between us and them." This is not a radical view but is enshrined in the basic teachings of Islam, he argues. "Qur'an forbade taking Jews and Christians as friends, and that applies to every Jew and Christian, with no consideration as to whether they are at war with Islam or not. . . . Muslims are forbidden from participation in their prayers, funerals, or holidays."[83]

Even the hajj, the annual pilgrimage to Mecca that all Muslims are taught they must perform at least once during their lifetime, is used to spread hatred of Jews. During the 2002 hajj, the Grand Mosque of Mecca "echoed with voices of 1.5 million pilgrims who reiterated after the Imam of the Haram supplications full of curses upon the Jews," according to one admiring account. "O Allah! It is You Who send the clouds, vanquish the enemies, sift in reckoning. O Allah! Vanquish the Jews and ward their harms off," Sheikh Usama Khayyat supplicated his followers. "O Allah! Remove this humiliation and oppression imposed on the Muslim Ummah."[84]

Hedieh Mirahmadi is an American Muslim, born of an Iranian father, who joined the traditionalist Islamic Supreme Council of America after attending Saudi-financed mosques in California. "Anti-Semitism is in their books," she told me. "If you teach kids from the age of five that Jews are your enemy, what do you expect? The Wahhabis say it's not violent, that they never say, 'Go out and kill the Jew.' But this ideology of hate lends itself to violence. That's why we are fighting the Wahhabis here in America. They create uncritical responses in young people to hate other groups. That is the opposite of what religion is supposed to be."[85]

Compare the statements of the Saudi ulema—kill the Jews, kill the infidels—to the statements and fatwas issued by Osama bin Laden. "We knew that the Americans support the Jews in Palestine and that they are our enemies," bin Laden told British reporter Robert Fisk in 1996, explaining why his Afghan Arabs never accepted U.S. assistance during the anti-Soviet war.[86] "The present U.S. government is under the influence of Jews," he said one year later. "The U.S. secretaries of defense and state are both Jews. Cooperation with United States is in fact cooperation with the Jews."[87] In the same interview, bin Laden explained that all Muslims needed to join his jihad because "the Ka'aba, facing which they say their prayers, is under the siege of Jews and Christians." On August 20, 1998, just hours before the United States bombed an al-Qaeda training camp in Afghanistan in retaliation for the bombings of the U.S. embassies in Kenya and Tanzania three weeks earlier, bin Laden deputy Ayman al-Zawahiri telephoned a Pakistani journalist to read a statement in English. "Osama bin Laden calls on all Muslims to continue Jihad against Jews and Americans to liberate their holy places," he said.[88] To justify the bombing of the French tanker *Limburg* on October 6, 2002, off the coast of Yemen, al-Qaeda issued a statement bearing bin Laden's handwritten signature that called the oil tanker target "the umbilical cord of the Christians."[89]

Given this extraordinary effort to spread hatred of Jews and the West by the government of Saudi Arabia, which continues today, it's not surprising that Osama bin Laden and his followers have found it easy to build a clandestine network of dedicated terrorists that the U.S. intelligence community estimates is active in more than sixty countries around the world. All bin Laden had to do was tap into the official network of the government of Saudi Arabia, as he did during the anti-Soviet jihad in

Afghanistan, and recruit young men who had already been prepared mentally and spiritually to join his fight "against the Crusaders and the Jews."

It all comes full circle. From the very earliest ages, when it teaches hate to children, as Doaa ʿAmer and the three-year-old Basmallah illustrate on IQRAA-TV, the Wahhabi system of hate is a well-oiled machine with far-reaching consequences. On September 11, Osama bin Laden demonstrated forcefully that when it comes to hate, what begins with the Jews never ends with the Jews.

ARAFAT'S REIGN OF TERROR 7

All the boys at the graduation ceremony stand at attention on the stage, dressed in combat fatigues. Some carry toy Russian-made Kalashnikovs; others carry models of M-16s and rocket launchers. At one point, they hit the ground, rifles at the ready, and demonstrate how they will kill the enemy. At another, they dip their hands into bowls of red paint and raise them to the audience, in imitation of the Palestinian youth who lynched two Israeli soldiers in Ramallah, then appeared at the window, screaming in ecstasy, to show the crowd his bloody hands. But these are not teenagers or young adults, hardened to street combat, and this is not a military school. These boys are five and six years old, graduating from a private kindergarten run by the Islamic Society in Gaza.[1] They are being trained to kill Jews.

Sheikh Ahmad Bahar, the Egyptian-trained Islamic scholar who heads the charitable association that runs the martyr's school, addresses the boys and their parents, glorifying terrorist attacks against Israel. On the walls are pictures of "martyrs" who have already blown themselves up. The boys should imitate the martyr Mahmoud Marmash, Dr. Bahar says, referring to the young man who blew himself up at the entrance of the Sharon mall in Netanya on May 18, 2001, killing five shoppers and wounding seventy-four others, and inspired Passover bomber Abd al-Basat Odeh. Mothers should educate their children with "Islamic values," he says. For Dr. Bahar and his Hamas brethren, love in Islam means "love of jihad and resistance." Mothers should follow the example of Khansa, the famous Arab poetess who lived in the time of the Prophet Muhammad, Dr. Bahar says. Khansa was a convert to Islam who lost four of her six sons in the battle of Qadissiya between the Muslims and the Persians in A.D. 637 in what today is southern Iraq. In much of today's Arab world, her name has become a synonym for mothers who give their children to suicide attacks.

Girls, who attend separate classes, are also included in the graduation ceremonies and can be seen assisting future martyrs in skits choreographed like passion plays. Dr. Bahar is proud of his preschool, its forty-one classes and 1,650 students. He writes of the political and religious indoctrination the children receive on his Arabic-language Web site, jislamia.org, which displays dozens of pictures of child graduates in full-dress battle uniforms. Most of the money for Dr. Bahar's Islamic Society comes from the government of Saudi Arabia. Muslim charities in America such as the Holy Land Foundation (HLF) also collect tax-deductible funds for these preschools of hate from U.S. citizens, according to U.S. prosecutors and documents captured by the Israelis from Islamic "charities" and Palestinian Authority offices in the spring and summer of 2002. The kindergartens have received delegations from nongovernmental institutions in Sweden and South Africa and grants from the Mennonite Central Committee, the British charity MAP (Medical Aid for Palestinians), and an Italian organization named CRIC.[2]

Hate training in Arafat's Palestinian Authority begins at an early age and is not limited to these Hamas schools. In the official institutions run by Arafat's Ministry of Education, hate and incitement to murder are essential elements of the curriculum.

✝✝✝

Ayatollah Khomeini is believed to have introduced suicide bombing as an international terrorist technique, with fanatical religious beliefs as the driving force behind it. On April 18, 1983, a truck heavily laden with explosives crashed into the crowded cafeteria of the U.S. Embassy in Beirut during the lunch hour, killing more than sixty persons. As one of the first reporters on the scene, I still recall the look of disbelief on the dust- and blood-streaked faces of the U.S. Marines guarding the embassy as they carried the wounded out to the ambulances. Beyond them lay the smoking hulk of the embassy, its entire front blown away, staircases and trapped bodies dangling into emptiness.

For most of us brought up in a Western humanist tradition, something in the mind balks when it comes to suicide attacks. The first theories of what happened in Beirut suggested a remotely detonated car bomb. However, it soon became clear that an individual—a live human being—had driven the truck through the embassy gates to his death. Again, there was denial. The local press, informed by half a dozen intelligence services, speculated that the Lebanese Shiite driver had been duped into thinking he was going to park the truck beside the embassy and leave. They suggested he had been double-crossed by someone sitting in the passenger seat, who dove out of the truck at the last minute and detonated the bomb.

Later, when these stories were discounted and the identity of the suicide driver became known, his action was pinned to the urge to martyrdom "inherent" within Shiite Islam. According to this theory, Shiite believers yearned for martyrdom in emulation of Hussein, an early founder of their sect. They rehearsed their death wish every year in the ritual self-flagellation of Muharram, the Shiite month of mourning, when Hussein's hopeless battle against a far superior army is acted out in a ten-day passion play ending in his death. But as a French intelligence officer once remarked to me during a discussion of Iran's use of suicide troops, this explanation also fell short of the mark. "Ayatollah Khomeini thinks martyrdom is great—for other people. You don't live to be eighty-eight years old with a death wish."

And then, of course, there's the uncomfortable fact that today's suicide bombers are almost exclusively Sunnis, the majority sect of Islam that is said to overwhelmingly reject suicide as against the teachings of the Koran.

It turns out that the network that carried out the April 1983 bombing of the U.S. embassy in Beirut was handed over to the Iranians by none other than Yasser Arafat, after his forcible expulsion from Beirut by the Israelis in late August 1982. According to former CIA Middle East operations officer Robert Baer, Arafat also gave the Iranians his top operative: a young Lebanese Shiite named Imad Mughniyah, who had been trained in terror in Palestinian camps and graduated to murder Americans and Jews in a series of attacks around the globe.[3] Twenty years later, Mughniyah remains high on the U.S. "Most Wanted List" and continues to shuttle between Lebanon and Iran.

With the murderous entry onto the scene of Arafat's Al-Aqsa brigade in 2001, it finally became clear that Arafat considered suicide bombers just another weapon in the cynical arsenal of terror, foot soldiers who served his goal of eradicating Israel and murdering Jews. The use—or condemnation—of suicide bombers has nothing to do with the Koran and nothing to do with the differences between the Sunni and Shiite branches of Islam. Modern Islamic thinkers who are at peace with the West condemn such attacks, whether they are Iranian Shias, or Sunnis from Egypt, Gaza, or Dearborn, Michigan. Radical Islamic fundamentalists who believe that Islam is the one true religion to which the entire world must be made to submit by force applaud them. It is now clear to which camp Yasser Arafat belongs.

†††

Shortly after Arafat entered Gaza on July 1, 1994, he instructed the newly created Education Ministry to examine the textbooks then being used in Palestinian schools. Since the Six-Day War in 1967, Israel had supervised the educational system in the Territories using schoolbooks inherited from Jordan, which had illegally annexed the West Bank after 1948, and from Egypt, which had administered the Gaza Strip. Although Israel officially considered that its borders had remained "in dispute" since 1948 and that therefore it was not an occupying power, nevertheless it established a civil administration in the territories after 1967 that respected United Nations conventions forbidding occupying powers from altering the local education systems, demography, or infrastructure. Under Israel's administration, the degrees earned by Palestinian students continued as before to be fully recognized by Jordan and Egypt.

When the Israeli government examined the Jordanian and Egyptian textbooks being used in Palestinian schools, however, it found an incredible quantity of rabid anti-Semitic material, as well as material that called for the destruction of Israel or that openly incited violence against Jews. Israel deleted that material before reprinting the books. "It didn't take a rocket scientist to find this stuff. It stood out very clearly," says former Labor Party bureaucrat Itamar Marcus, who now runs Palestinian Media Watch. In the early 1970s, Jordan complained to the United Nations that Israel had modified the schoolbooks, in violation of UN agreements, so the Israeli government showed the UN what they had taken out. "When the United Nations committee that investigated this issue saw the deleted material their jaws dropped, and they agreed that Israel had acted legitimately," Marcus told me in Jerusalem.[4]

The first thing the Palestinian Authority's Ministry of Education did when it reprinted the textbooks in 1994 was to restore all that excised anti-Semitic material, on Yasser Arafat's personal orders.

The Oslo Accords contained a commitment by the Israelis and Palestinians to end incitement and hate speech by government officials, the media, and the schools.[5] This end to incitement was considered one of the critical building blocks of any true peace between Jews and Arabs. Without it, future generations would continue to be brought up on a steady diet of violence and hate. In 1994, the Israelis went through their own school textbooks and deleted all references to the Palestine Liberation Organization as a "terrorist organization" and inserted sections explaining the "legitimate rights" of the Palestinian people and their history.[6] When Israeli prime minister Benjamin Netanyahu got wind that Arafat had done just the opposite, he demanded that the Palestinian Authority examine incitement jointly with the United States and Israel at the Wye Conference on Maryland's Eastern shore in 1998.

Itamar Marcus was appointed as the Israeli representative to a trilateral committee set up after Wye to examine incitement in Israel and the Palestinian Authority. He had prepared a report on the Jordanian and Egyptian textbooks that Arafat had ordered the PA to use and gave copies to his colleagues. "Father Hepsburgh of Notre Dame, the U.S. delegate, came back two weeks later and said the material he had just read made him want to vomit," Marcus said. "The Palestinian delegate then spent two hours arguing over whether we could even discuss the textbooks in the trilateral committee. He argued that since any official account of our discussions had to be unanimous, and since they didn't agree to discuss the textbooks, we couldn't even bring up the subject."

In 1999, the U.S. government offered Arafat's Palestinian Authority a cash grant to reprint the Egyptian and Jordanian textbooks without the anti-Semitic material, but Arafat refused. "The Palestinians told us, 'it's our heritage,'" Marcus recalls. Even today, despite grants from the European Union and the United States to write a completely new set of texts, many of the older books with their anti-Semitic material are still being used in the PA schools. "All their arguments today, that these are old books and they are not responsible, are totally false," Marcus says. "They are printing these books today by choice, and they are using them by choice."

Arafat considered the indoctrination of the next generation of students so important for his future plans that he personally assumed the portfolio of education minister when the first set of PA textbooks was reedited and issued to the schools. The hate material Arafat insisted on reintroducing into the schools starting in 1994 was varied but vicious. Marcus reviewed 140 books used in a wide variety of classes, from civics, grammar, language, and literature to history, geography, and Islamic studies. He looked at the books used to teach youngsters to read, as well as high school textbooks. What he found was a systematic portrayal of Jews as "the enemies of the Prophets and the Believers," against whom all good Muslims are obligated to wage a jihad, or holy war.[7]

In third grade, children learn hate through vocabulary. "The Zionist enemy—[attacked]—civilians with its aircraft." (*Our Arabic Language for Third Grade*, part 2, #523, p. 9) In sixth grade, hate becomes a drill. "Who is the thief who has torn our homeland?" (*Our Arabic Language for Sixth Grade*, part 1, #553, p. 15) By seventh grade, students are expected to have internalized anti-Semitism so they can recite it on their own. "Why do the Jews hate Muslim unity and want to cause division among them? Give an example of the evil attempts of the Jews, from events happening today." (*Islamic Education for Seventh Grade*, #745, p. 19) In ninth grade students are told, "One must beware of the Jews, for they are treacherous and disloyal." (*Islamic Education for Ninth Grade*, #589, p. 79)

Traditional Koranic sources are also used. This is critical, since Muslims believe the Koran is the Word of God and thus irrefutable, absolute truth. In fourth grade, children are taught, "I learn from this lesson: I believe that the Jews are the enemies of the Prophets and the believers." (*Islamic Education for Fourth Grade*, part 2, #531, p. 67) In seventh grade, the teachings of Jewish treachery become more detailed. "The Jews adopted a position of hostility and deception towards the new religion. They called Muhammad a liar and denied him, they fought against his religion in all ways and by all means, a war that has not yet ended until today, and they conspired with the hypocrites and the idolaters against him and they are still behaving in the same way. . . ." (*Islamic Education for Seventh Grade*, #564, p. 125) In ninth grade, the lessons include cautionary tales. "Lessons to be learned: One must beware of civil war, which the Jews try to incite, and of their scheming against the Muslims." (*Islamic Education for Ninth Grade*, # 589, p. 94)

Arab society is highly traditional. In the Palestinian Authority, Islam is the religion of state. Arafat personally appoints all religious leaders from the grand mufti of Jerusalem down to the Friday prayer imam of the smallest village. Teaching children that Jews are the enemies of God and his prophet is a powerful message that is direct incitement to murder.

A second important theme in the books is denying the legitimacy of the Jewish presence in Israel by erasing Jews from the history books. "PA books describe Muslim and Christian religious, historical, and archaeological sites but omit any reference to Jewish sites," Marcus writes in a summary of an eighth-grade history book. "Tourists who visit are Christian and Muslim but there is no mention of the Jewish tourists. The Western Wall of the Temple is called 'al-Buraq Wall,' but there is no mention of its Jewish history. A history book describes World War II, Hitler and Nazi racism while ignoring the Jews and the Holocaust." (*World History on Modern Times for Eighth Grade*, #586, pp. 34–45) The state of Israel, Arafat's partner for peace, is consistently portrayed as "occupied Palestine." (*Modern Arab History and Contemporary Problems for Tenth Grade*, part 2, p. 95)

From an early age, children in Arafat's schools are taught that they have a duty to fight Israel. "Know, my son, that Palestine is your country . . . that its pure soil is drenched with the blood of Martyrs. . . . Why must we fight the Jews and drive them out of our land?" (*Our Arabic Language for Fifth Grade,* pp. 64–66) A few pages later, the same textbook elaborates on the same theme: ". . . there will be a Jihad and our country shall be freed. . . . This is our story with the thieving conquerors. You must know, my boy, that Palestine is your grave responsibility. . . ." (Ibid., pp. 69–70)

In the eighth grade, students are made to memorize the poem "Palestine," which calls for jihad against Israel. "My brothers! The oppressors [Israel] have overstepped the boundary. Therefore Jihad and sacrifice are a duty . . . are we to let them steal its Arab nature? . . . Draw your sword . . . let us gather for war with red blood and blazing fire. . . . Death shall call and the sword shall be crazed from much slaughter. . . . Oh Palestine, the youth will redeem your land. . . ." The lesson drills in the message through a series of questions. "Who are the 'oppressors' to whom the poet is referring in the first verse? What is the road to victory over the enemy that the poet mentions? The poet urges the Arabs to undertake Jihad. Indicate the verse in which he does so." (*Reader and Literary Texts for Eighth Grade,* #578, pp. 120–122)

Jihad as the individual religious duty of every Muslim man and woman also is a constant theme. In the seventh-grade Islamic education class, children are taught: "If the enemy has conquered part of its land and those fighting for it are unable to repel the enemy, then Jihad becomes the individual religious duty of every Muslim man and woman, until the attack is successfully repulsed and the land liberated from conquest and to defend Muslim honor. . . ." (*Islamic Education for Seventh Grade,* #564, p. 108)

Yet another theme is the ultimate victory of Islam over the Jews. "Remember: The final and inevitable result will be the victory of the Muslims over the Jews," fifth graders are taught in Arabic-language class. (*Our Arabic Language for Fifth Grade,* p. 67) Christians will also fall prey to a conquering Islam. "This religion will defeat all other religions and it will be disseminated, by Allah's will, through the Muslim Jihad fighters." (*Islamic Education for Seventh Grade,* #564, p. 125) By the eleventh grade, students are taught to meditate on the ultimate superiority of Islam and the decadence of the West. "We do not claim that the collapse of Western civilization, and the transfer of the center of civilization to us [Islam] will happen in the next decade or two or even in fifty years, for the rise and fall of civilizations follow natural processes. . . . Nevertheless [Western civilization] has begun to collapse and to become a pile of debris." (*Our Civilization for Eleventh Grade,* p. 16)

Despite the Oslo Accords, which outlined a road map toward peace between Israel and the Palestinians, all the geographical maps published in the schoolbooks, and, indeed, visible in government offices throughout the Arab world, make no mention of Israel. The maps show Israel and the Palestinian territories as a single state called "Palestine," while Israeli cities such as Tel Aviv are identified by the Arab names of their neighbors (Jaffa). Imagine if Germany after World War II published maps of Europe that showed Poland, France, and Czechoslovakia as part of the German Reich? Yet that is what Arafat has done.

† † †

As a result of the trilateral committee and pressure from the United States, Canada, and the European Union, who were funding his government, Arafat appointed a committee to develop a new Palestinian curriculum and write new textbooks. The first of the new schoolbooks was distributed to Palestinian children in September 2000. While much of the overt anti-Semitic material was taken out, the improvements were only marginal. "They took what was explicit in the old books and made it implicit, but the message is still very clear," says Marcus. "All of Palestine belongs to the Arabs, and every Muslim has a duty to liberate it."

The new textbooks "make no attempt to educate for peace and coexistence with Israel," Marcus found. "Indeed, the opposite is true." Not only is peace with Israel never presented as a goal or even as an option for the Palestinians, but the peace process that established Arafat's Palestinian Authority is not even mentioned. "The Oslo Accords are mentioned once, but are not defined as a peace process, rather as a point in time connected to the PLO's 'liberation army forces' entering 'Palestine,' " Marcus says.

The new books continued to delegitimize Israel by defining it as foreign to the Middle East and as a colonial power that "occupied" Palestine in 1948 in the same manner Britain occupied Palestine in 1917. "Israel is mentioned only in contexts that breed contempt, such as having expelled and massacred Palestinians," Marcus says. The new books "continue to teach nonrecognition of Israel" and omit Israel's name from maps, while citing Jerusalem as the "capital of the State of Palestine," not Israel. Clearly, you cannot make peace with a partner that does not exist, and that is precisely the point. "The concept of peace with Israel is not to be found anywhere in the Palestinian schoolbooks," his study found.[8]

The methodology of the new curriculum is tendentious, and while more subtle than the earlier schoolbooks, it leads just as clearly to hatred and murder. After teaching that Israel has conquered "Palestine" in history and civics books, the new *Islamic Education* textbooks written by Arafat's scholars continue to teach children that "defense of the homeland is a mandatory religious obligation for every Muslim if a centimeter is stolen from his land." By giving a religious overtone to what otherwise is a national conflict over borders, Arafat's scholars are playing with fire.

A separate study of the new second- and seventh-grade textbooks carried out by Israeli Defense Ministry analysts notes three important concepts that appear throughout the curriculum. First is the notion that all of Israel constitutes illegal settlement, not just those settlements established after the 1967 war. Zionism, which is studied repeatedly in Palestinian classrooms, is depicted as "a movement whose motto is the exploitation and confiscation of Palestinian land." Jewish settlements, established in the late nineteenth century on lands purchased for local Arabs, are referred to as "imperialist occupation," whereas Arab settlements are called "villages" or "towns." The new textbooks do not distinguish between settlements in the West Bank and Gaza and those established inside the 1967 borders. Israeli towns, farms, and villages within the 1967 borders are all referred to as *istitan*—an Arabic term usually translated into English as "illegal settlements."[9] This use of the loaded term *istitan* to designate the state of Israel itself "emphasizes the utterly illegitimate and transient character of Jewish settlement, and the moral obligation to eradicate it" that is being drilled into the minds of young Palestinian children, Dr. Reuven Ehrlich, the lead Israeli analyst, points out.

This leads directly to the other two terms that recur at every level and in every subject of the new Palestinian curriculum: "jihad," or Holy War against Israeli occupation, and *"istishhad,"* which signifies "martyrdom for the sanctification of Allah." Martyrs who kill themselves as part of the holy war against Israel are glorified, and their behavior is held up as an example for all students to follow. "Students are taught about jihad warriors throughout Palestinian history, such as [the Syrian-born] Sheikh Izz al-Din al-Qassam who was killed by the British in 1935," whose name has been adopted by Hamas to designate their "military wing" of suicide bombers. "The seventh-grade students who recite the poem named 'the Shahid' are taught to say, 'I [would] rather die than live without my stolen rights and homeland, I take pleasure in the sound, and the flowing [of] blood. . . .'" They are taught that "'dying an honorable death' means dying for the sanctification of Allah (shahada) and the defense of the homeland."[10]

The demonization of Israelis occurs at every level. In a second-grade language lesson, children compare two pictures to answer the question, *What are they doing?* At the top, Arab construction workers carry sand and stones to build a house. *These men are building* is the correct answer. Beneath them, uniformed Israeli soldiers watch as a bulldozer demolishes a house. The response: *These tractors are destroying.* (*Our Beautiful Language,* part 1, p. 88) "These are messages they want their children, tragically, to grow up with," says Marcus.[11]

The same textbook tells the story of a young Arab woman on a "typical" day, as she goes to visit her father in an Israeli prison. She gets up before dawn, packs a lunch, and spends hours in a bus before she arrives at the Israeli prison, guarded by evil-looking soldiers. "After three hours, one of the soldiers looked at them and said: 'No visits permitted today.'" (Ibid., p. 72) A grammar book teaches children how to form the singular and the plural with this example: "One martyr [shahid] is honored by Allah. Two martyrs [shuhada] are honored by Allah."

The result of all this indoctrination is seen in the number of suicide bombers, "martyrs," who are willing to blow themselves up in order to murder Jews. But Marcus believes it takes other, more subtle forms. A public opinion poll released by the PA on August 13, 2002, asked what form of government the respondents preferred in a Palestinian state. Forty-two percent said they preferred a multiparty democracy, while another 42 percent said they favored single-party Islamic rule. "What was fascinating about the poll," Marcus says, "was the breakdown of respondents by age." A majority of those who had been exposed to Arafat's school curriculum, aged eighteen to twenty-four, favored a single-party Islamic state, whereas the older generation, brought up "pre-Oslo, who had seen democracy at work in Israel," favored a multiparty democracy. "Under the Palestinian Authority, the younger generation is not being exposed to democracy," Marcus says. As a result, they are becoming "more Islamic, more anti-Democratic. The processes we were hoping would take place under the Palestinian Authority toward democratization are exactly the opposite of what is happening. The Oslo Accords have made the Palestinians less interested in democracy than they were when they lived under Israel. This is a long-term tragedy. It clearly shows the effect of Palestinian self-rule." In the same poll, 61 percent of the respondents said they supported "boycotting U.S. governmental funding agencies" such as USAID (United States Agency for International Development), which has helped fund the Palestinian school system and build roads, sewers, health clinics, and other basic services for the Palestinian Authority. Sixty-two percent said they favored a boycott of Israeli products, while 63 percent said they favored a total boycott of all American products.[12]

Time and again in interviews with Palestinian politicians and intellectuals over the years, I had heard the argument that the Palestinians experienced the same trauma from losing their land in 1948, when the newly reborn state of Israel beat back a massive Arab attack, as Jews had experienced during the Holocaust. Many Israeli leftists feel sympathy with that view. This prompted left-wing education minister Yossi Sarid to include Palestinian nationalist poems in the Israeli school curriculum after Oslo, in order to promote greater understanding of the depth of the Arab trauma over losing their land.

A debate among members of the Palestinian Authority over whether PA schools should reciprocate by teaching the Holocaust is instructive for what it reveals. At a symposium held in Nicosia, Cyprus, in April 2000, where Palestinians and Israelis gathered to discuss "How to Strengthen Peace Through Education," Palestinian Authority undersecretary of planning and international cooperation Anis al-Qaq broached this sensitive issue. "I believe that Palestine and the entire Arab world need to learn about the Holocaust, and therefore this subject should be included in the school curriculum," he said.[13]

It was a courageous statement that was immediately denounced by the other Palestinian Authority leaders. Dr. Musa al-Zu'but, chairman of the

Education Committee of the Palestinian Legislative Council (PLC), rejected it flat out. "There will be no such attempt to include the history of the Holocaust in the Palestinian curriculum," he said. "The Holocaust has been exaggerated in order to present the Jews as victims of a great crime, to justify [the claim] that Palestine is necessary as a homeland for them, and to give them the right to demand compensation." He concluded: "We have no interest in teaching the Holocaust."

Ziyad Abu Amr, considered a moderate who supports peace with Israel, chairs the Political Committee of the PLC. He noted that al-Qaq had offered to teach the Holocaust because Israeli education minister Yossi Sarid had agreed to include poems by Palestinian nationalist Mahmoud Darwish in the Israeli curriculum, to teach young Israelis about Palestinian national aspirations. Nevertheless, he said, "why must we teach the literature of a people and a state who occupied our land? When the situation changes, we will be able to be more open to their literature and heritage, just as we are now in regard to other countries." Besides, he added, "people who studied the history of the Holocaust in the past have come to very different conclusions," a scarcely veiled allusion to Holocaust deniers who claim that the Jews have exaggerated the number of victims of the Holocaust in order to gain international sympathy.

Hatem Abd al-Qader, a PLC member and Fatah leader, said teaching the Holocaust "is a great danger to the developing Palestinian mentality. It would be dangerous to change the Palestinian curriculum in such a direction. First, the Jews should learn about our disaster, the massacres, the murder, and the exile, because this disaster is still alive. As for the so-called Holocaust, it has already been moved into the museum of history." He added: "This land was promised to us by Allah, while it was promised to the Jews by Balfour. If such a decision [about teaching the Holocaust] is made, it will undoubtedly ruin the Palestinian dream and aspirations. It will entirely obliterate the past, present, and future of the Palestinians." The Palestinian press did not report on the symposium, "with the exception of one newspaper that omitted al-Qaq's speech" calling for teaching the Holocaust, according to MEMRI.[14]

The schoolbooks are important because "they represent the future," says MEMRI director Yigal Carmon. The ideas and ethics taught children at an early age by their teachers will remain with them through their adolescence and possibly beyond, especially if reinforced by parents, the media, and other sources of respect, such as religious leaders. In those areas as well, Arafat and his Palestinian Authority have demonstrated no inclination to breed a culture of peace.

† † †

Shortly after 9 A.M. on October 15, 2002, three unmarked police cars drove into the courtyard of the main Jerusalem police station in the Russian quarter off the Jaffa Road. Escorted by a dozen policemen, most of them in civilian clothes, an elegantly dressed Arab man wearing a white turban emerged from the backseat, straightened his black clerical robes, and followed the policemen inside. Sheikh Ikrima Sabri, the grand mufti of Jerusalem, appointed by Yasser Arafat as the supreme religious leader in the Palestinian Authority, was under arrest for the third time in less than two years. The charge: incitement to murder.

In a June 1 interview with *Al-Ayyam,* considered the official mouthpiece of the Palestinian Authority, the sixty-three-year-old state cleric called suicide bombings "legitimate acts of self-defense" by Palestinians. He repeated the remarks in a separate interview with the *Al-Bayan* daily in the United Arab Emirates, noting that there was "no legal or religious objection" to suicide attacks. To the police, however, he asserted his remarks had been "misinterpreted" and that he was advocating a "verbal, not a physical" struggle against Israel, a police spokesman said three hours later when he was released.[15]

Sheikh Ikrima Sabri is no newcomer to controversy. Well before September 11, he prayed in public for the destruction of America. "Oh, Allah, destroy America as it is controlled by Zionist Jews," he told listeners during his weekly sermon at Al-Aqsa Mosque on July 11, 1997. Two months later, he repeated his appeal, adding: "Cast [the Americans] into their own traps and cover the White House with black!" The Palestinian grand mufti repeated this comment again just two weeks before the September 11 attacks, calling on God to paint the White House black.[16]

When I met the mufti in his stone office abutting the Western Wall, one week after his latest arrest, he insisted that his words had been misinterpreted. "I never said 'destroyed,'" he told me. "I said I was against the *policy* of the United States in the Middle East. Then I prayed to God that He should put a black cloth over the White House. This was a prayer between a human being and God. God answered that prayer on September 11—but I had nothing to do with it!" He thought this was witty and laughed.

Israel's minister of public security, Uzi Landau, who ordered the police to haul in the mufti for questioning, acknowledged that Israel's laws governing free speech were so broad that it was difficult to prosecute the mufti, "even when he calls for the destruction of Israel, the United States, and Britain." But the three hours of questioning left Sabri somewhat chastened and more cautious in his choice of words. "We have a difference of opinion on Palestine, but that does not mean I support using force against the state of Israel," he insisted when talking to me.[17]

Judge for yourself. In an extensive interview in Arabic with the Egyptian weekly *Al-Ahram al-Arabi* in late October 2000, just one month after the resumption of violence by the Palestinians known as the Al-Aqsa *intifada,* Sabri called the fighting "a religious outburst." All Palestinians were engaged in a holy war, he said, and their just goal was to expel the Jews from the region. "The land of Palestine is not only Jerusalem; this land stretches from the [Jordan] River to the [Mediterranean] Sea," he said. "Naturally, the [Palestinian] problem relates to all of this land. We cannot establish a homeland by only liberating Jerusalem."

Asked about suicide bombers, he couldn't find words of praise eloquent enough to express his admiration for their feats. "I feel the martyr is lucky because the angels usher him to his wedding in heaven. I feel the earth moves under the occupiers' feet. . . . The younger the martyr, the greater and the more I respect him."

The mothers of these "martyrs" also deserve praise and admiration, Sabri said. "They willingly sacrifice their offspring for the sake of freedom. It is a great display of the power of belief. The mother is participating in the great reward of the jihad to liberate Al-Aqsa. . . . I talked to a young man . . . [who] said: '. . . I want to marry the black-eyed [beautiful] women of heaven.' The next day he became a martyr. I am sure his mother was filled with joy about his heavenly marriage. Such a son must have such a mother."[18]

The literal interpretation of the phrase *black-eyed women* upsets some

Muslim lobbyists in America, who pretend it has nothing to do with "virgins" or "sexual fantasies." Yet Islamic scholars from Egypt to Saudi Arabia insist that young men who murder Jews will be instantly "married" in heaven to seventy-two dark-eyed virgin brides. Palestinian newspapers regularly publish death notices of suicide bombers that resemble wedding, not funeral, announcements. "Blessings will be accepted immediately after the burial and until 10 P.M. . . . at the home of the martyr's uncle," reads one suicide bomber's death notice. "With great pride, the Palestinian Islamic Jihad marries the member of its military wing . . . the martyr and hero Yasser al-Adhami, to 'the black-eyed,'" reads another.[19] If young Palestinian men and women believe the dead will be rewarded in Paradise for murder, it is in large part because religious leaders such as Sheikh Ikrima Sabri are teaching them such beliefs.

On May 25, 2001, Sabri gave a lengthy homily in praise of "martyrdom" operations in a Friday prayer sermon delivered at Al-Aqsa that was broadcast on the official Voice of Palestine radio. After criticizing a top Saudi cleric who had issued a fatwa against suicide bombings, Sabri addressed the Jews. "We tell them: Inasmuch as you love life, the Muslim loves death and martyrdom. There is a great difference between he who loves the hereafter and he who loves this world. The Muslim loves death and [strives for] martyrdom. He does not fear the oppression of the arrogant or the weapons of the blood-letters. The blessed and sacred soil of Palestine has vomited all the invaders and all the colonialists throughout history and it will soon vomit, with Allah's help, the [present] occupiers."[20] These were the same words I had first heard in Gaza in 1994 from the mouth of a suicide bomber in training.

One week after this incitement to murder, a young Palestinian man waded into a crowd outside the Dolphinarium discotheque along Tel Aviv's popular seaside promenade. It was just after midnight when he pressed the button, blowing himself up and murdering twenty-one people, many of them teenage boys and girls; 120 others were wounded by shrapnel from the bomb, some of them maimed for life.

Sheikh Ikrima Sabri does not have a political dispute with the Israeli government: he hates Jews. Every time he enters the Al-Aqsa Mosque, he says, "I am filled with rage toward the Jews. I have never greeted a Jew when I came near one. I never will. They cannot even dream that I will.

The Jews do not dare to bother me, because they are the most cowardly creatures Allah has ever created. . . ."[21]

Sabri also likes to contest the facts of Jewish history in Palestine. "Give me one proof that the Jews had a temple here—just one proof! Archaeologists, even Jewish ones, have never found any proof of the Hebrew times, either in Al-Aqsa Mosque, around the mosque, or in the whole city of Jerusalem. They haven't found anything! In the Old City, there is not one stone—not one!—that shows the Jews had a presence here in history," he says. When I asked him about the Western Wall, he answered: "We call it al-Burak. It's a part of the wall of the Al-Aqsa Mosque. In 1930, the League of Nations declared that al-Burak was part of the Muslim properties. Ask any Jewish archaeologist if one single stone in the Western Wall belongs to their history. Archaeologists have dug down ten meters beneath the Western Wall, and they have only found stones from the Omayyad period. The stones that we see on the Western Wall all belong to the Islamic period of time."

This, of course, is a stunningly bald-faced lie, but out of curiosity I decided to visit the recent excavations around the western and southern walls of the Temple Mount. In the Davidson Archaeological Park, any tourist can walk upon recently exposed paving stones—slabs of polished marble nearly one-foot thick—that were once part of a kilometer-long street that ran along the base of the Temple Mount. These are the actual stones on which Jesus and his disciples walked. One can also see the arcades where Jewish shopkeepers sold animals for sacrifice in the Temple. The street, the stone stalls, and the ceremonial archway whose remnants still jut out from the Temple wall some twenty meters above the street were built by Herod the Great, the Jewish king put in power by the Romans, as part of his expansion of the Second Temple between 37 and 34 B.C. Huge stones from the Temple walls remain in a jumbled heap in the exact location where they were hurled down by the Romans in A.D. 70, when they destroyed the Second Temple after crushing the Jewish revolt. For centuries they remained buried beneath mounds of dirt and garbage. Some thirteen rows of the massive, original stones from the Second Temple remain in place today and are clearly visible at the base of the Temple Mount. On top of this foundation, Muslim conquerers rebuilt the wall using distinctly smaller stones, then erected a mosque on the spot

where the Temple had stood. The Mosque of Omar was intended to com-
memorate the spot where the Prophet Muhammad claimed he had tied his
horse, al-Burak, before ascending to heaven *in a dream.* Muslim scholars
acknowledge that Muhammad never actually visited Jerusalem, let alone
conquered it. The only historic claim Muslims make on Jerusalem as a
holy place is the dream Muhammad relates to his followers.

An Israeli guide is giving a private tour to three Americans, and we
strike up a conversation. I tell him what the mufti said about "not one
stone" of Jerusalem bearing any relation to Jewish history. He just laughs.
"Sure, I'll say the same thing if you pay me as much."

But in this ancient land, touched by God and where His word became
flesh, words also have the power to kill.

It wasn't supposed to be like this, although looking back, I suppose the
signs were there from the start. Israeli television commentator Ehud Ya'ari,
an early supporter of the Oslo process who later soured on Arafat, recalls
Arafat's entry into Gaza in July 1994. "He comes to Rafah terminal in
Gaza, and a young Israeli soldier turns to another and says, 'Gee, I didn't
know Arafat was so tall.' Arafat arrived in a Mercedes and his keffiyeh
was scraping the ceiling of the car. You have to be an NBA player for that
to happen." Arafat, who is short of stature, obviously didn't fit the bill. "It
turned out that Arafat was sitting on somebody whom he was smuggling
in—Jihad Amarin—and Mamduh Nofal, the former military commander
of the Democratic Front, was hiding in the trunk. They also had a few
Kalashnikov rifles and night-vision equipment in the car."[22]

Between July 1994 and September 2000 when Arafat ordered the beginning of the second *intifada* against Israel, the United States and the international donor community pledged $7.5 billion to aid Arafat and the PA in
the hope they would become partners for peace. "In both absolute and per
capita terms, the donor effort for the Palestinians has been one of the
largest ever undertaken by the international community," a Council on
Foreign Relations task force states.[23] Instead, that money has helped to create yet another Arab dictatorship, where the law is dispensed at the end of
a gun, where ordinary citizens and foreign investors are regularly extorted

by government officials, and where the people are fed a steady diet of anti-Semitic and anti-American hatred. Arafat holds the world record for domestic security organizations (twelve), with more security personnel per capita (60,000 for 2.5 million persons) than Iran, Syria, Sudan, North Korea, or Iraq under Saddam Hussein.

Before the second *intifada* put a damper on criticism, I often heard the lament from Palestinian shopkeepers and cabdrivers, Arab village leaders, human rights activists, members of the Palestinian Legislative Council, and even PA officials in Gaza and the West Bank, that life was better under the Israelis. They shared a widespread belief that corruption and Arafat's autocratic rule had made a mockery of the independence they had worked so hard to achieve. Yet neither the Israeli government of Ehud Barak nor the international donor community put serious pressure on Arafat to clean up his act or to scale back the abuses of the security forces under his control. Indeed, with money from the European Union and the Clinton administration, Arafat expanded those forces, many of whom were later found to have taken an active part in organizing suicide bombings and other terror attacks against Israel. Under the active supervision of Swedish police officer Nils Ericsson, who was promoted by the European Union to ambassadorial rank in 1997, the Palestinian police were trained in a variety of riot control and intelligence techniques that in many cases helped them elude capture by the Israelis. Other European governments, notably Germany, provided similar assistance. Among the main demands of the "road map" released by the Bush administration on April 29, 2003, were the demilitarization of the Palestinian police and political and financial transparency.

"The donors don't want to raise the issue of corruption too loudly because it would generate criticism back home," Tim Rothermel, an American who headed the United Nations Development Program for the West Bank and Gaza, told me. "They are afraid people will demand that donor money be cut off if it is seen to be lining Arafat's pockets."[24] That would mean the end to tax-free salaries, all-expenses-paid housing, and the luxury automobiles many in the "aid" community enjoyed.

For years, the corruption of Arafat and "the boys from Tunis," as the returnees were called, was a scarcely disguised secret. Everyone in Gaza and the West Bank knew who they were and the outrageous privileges they were accorded. In response to public criticism and donor complaints, in 1996 Arafat instructed the chief of his personal office, Tayeb Abdel Rahim, to investigate allegations of corruption. Rahim submitted a 248-page report, detailing the favors granted to government ministers and their entourages.[25]

In one example that galled Palestinians who had lived under Israeli occupation and watched the returnees snap up newly available wealth, the report noted that the PA distributed 4,300 automobiles tax-free to government ministers, employees, and other "returnees." These cars are easily identified by their red license plates. "That favor alone cost the public treasury $130 million in lost tax revenue," a senior PA official told me. "That was bad policy, but it was not corruption."[26] Nevertheless, Arafat never released the report, which I eventually obtained in the Arabic original from an Israeli government official. "These people were so poor when they arrived here from Tunis, we had to give them bread," a Palestinian village leader told me. "Today, they own property everywhere and travel in big cars. *Min ayna laqa haza?*—Where did they get that?" he asked. As I would learn, it was a popular refrain among native Palestinians when referring to the newly arrived Tunis elite. It was a phrase of disdain to designate the hopelessly corrupt.

When I met Hussam Khader, a PLC member from Nablus, at his office in the Balata refugee camp in November 1999, he told me many stories of how Arafat cronies had established monopolies on the import of various commodities and used the security forces to discourage competitors. "If you are lucky enough to be in the police, in six months you'll be able to buy a building—not an apartment, but a whole building," he said ruefully. Just a few weeks after I published his comment in a *Wall Street Journal* article, Khader was placed under house arrest by Arafat. After his release, he became a loyal Arafat supporter.

In 1994, I had shared a simple lunch with Justice Minister Freih Abu Midain and his family at their modest four-room flat in Gaza. Three years later, he had built himself a magnificent villa just around the corner from Arafat's office. Not content with that, he arranged to close the street behind it to traffic, so today it has the feel of a private compound. In 1997, Israeli police stopped one of his deputies, Mousa Abu Sabha, driving a brand-new Mercedes that had been reported stolen in Israel. "The PA promised to prosecute him," a former Israeli intelligence official told me, "but they never did." Not long afterward Brigadier General Zakaria Ba'aloushia, a top Palestinian officer, was caught driving a stolen BMW. Again, nothing happened.[27] PA officials drove through Gaza at high speed, swerving around traffic, just as they had done during Arafat's years in Beirut. Security men drove shiny new Mercedes sedans with no license plates at all, in the purest Beirut tradition.

The head of preventive security in Gaza, Mohammad Dahlan, grew up in a refugee camp in Gaza and became an Arafat confidant during the Tunis years in the 1980s. Soon after coming to Gaza with Arafat in 1994, he began building a multimillion-dollar palace of pink stone just down the beach from Arafat's office on the Gaza beachfront. Dahlan didn't get rich from hard work or business acumen. His newfound fortune came with his job.

Although Dahlan was forced to abandon his palace because of public criticism in 1998, his brother built a three-hundred-room luxury hotel in Gaza, where Dahlan took foreign guests for lunch. Among his guests were EU ambassador Nils Ericsson, CIA director George Tenet, and then U.S. ambassador Martin Indyk.[28] Meanwhile, many Gaza streets remained unpaved, sewers had not gone in, and electricity lines were down, although all these projects had been funded by USAID or by the European Union. In May 2003, Dahlan was being touted as the only man who could reform Arafat's security services.

† † †

A key figure to have emerged in this universe of corruption is Mohammad Rashid, Arafat's economic adviser, also known as Khaled Salem. Born in Iraqi Kurdistan, he began working for Arafat in Beirut in the early 1980s, moving with him to Tunis after the PLO was evicted from Lebanon in November 1983.[29] As Arafat's top economic adviser, Rashid took part in all international economic negotiations. He also has sole control over the Palestinian Commercial Services Company (PCSC), a private company that had never been registered and had no known board of directors, but which presented itself as operating on behalf of Arafat and the PLO.

Through PCSC and Al-Bahr, a private company owned jointly with

Arafat's wife, Suha, Rashid operated monopolies on the import of at least three commodities: cement, flour, and cigarettes. These activities brought in anywhere from $150 million to $350 million per year, not a penny of which went to the public treasury, despite repeated promises by Arafat to provide a public accounting of monopoly trade.[30] PA officials quietly told me that Arafat used this money to support PLO activities overseas and to buy political influence at home, but they refused to be quoted by name. "Private companies have complained about the monopolies," researcher Khalil Shikaki told me in Ramallah. "But nobody goes to court against the PA. Basically, they just complain, then leave."

Occasionally, the abuses made it into Israeli courts. In October 1994, a consortium of Israeli oil companies known as Padesco filed suit after PA security officers physically prevented their tankers from restocking Palestinian gas stations, despite a long-standing supply contract. The PA argued it had signed an exclusive supply arrangement with another Israeli company, Dor Energy, to replace the earlier deal with Padesco. In fact, the new contract established a monopoly over the import of petroleum products that was controlled by Mohammad Rashid for the benefit of Suha Arafat, according to court documents, former intelligence officials, and published sources.[31]

The Palestinians imported the vast majority of their consumer goods and construction materials such as cement from Israel through similar monopoly structures. In many cases, the arrangements amounted to private deals made between Rashid and the man used by Israeli prime minister Ehud Barak as his personal emissary to President Arafat, retired Shin Bet general Yossi Ginossar.[32] Ginossar was "so intimately involved in the business end of the PA that when Ehud Barak brought him in as a pinch hitter at the Camp David summit, press reports at the time described the participants joking that they didn't know whether he was there to represent Israel or Arafat."[33] These cozy back door deals were one of the reasons the Israelis never really complained about Arafat's corrupt system. By all appearances, they got their cut as well.

Arafat himself drained the Gaza Employees Pension Fund in a series of unexplained transfers between 1995 and 1997. Documents I obtained from Palestinian and Israeli sources showed that Rashid dismissed investment adviser Morgan Stanley in early 1996 at Arafat's bidding, then moved the money to a numbered account with Credit Suisse in Zurich. One year later, Rashid dismissed Belesta Asset Management, the Irish firm he had appointed to replace Morgan Stanley, after they had raised objections to PA raids on the fund's capital. Arafat used the money for a variety of purposes. In mid-1997, Arafat claimed he needed $28 million from the fund to pay police salaries. Although the Swedes and other European donors stepped in and paid $34 million to cover these salaries, the $28 million was transferred to Gaza nevertheless. Palestinian minister of justice Freih Abu Midain told the *Financial Times* that the PA wanted to invest the $28 million to develop telecommunications infrastructure.[34] The vice president of the Palestinian Telecommunications Company, PalTel, turned out to be none other than Mohammad Rashid. In all, Arafat drained an estimated $140 million from the fund. To this day, no one knows where the money went.

When I tried to meet Rashid at his corporate headquarters in Gaza, a modest building just across the street from the Ministry of Finance, an aide told me he was in Ramallah for the week. When I went to his office in Ramallah three days later, an aide apologized that he wasn't available because he was in Gaza. The business card she handed me didn't mention his company, PCSC, but gave his title as "Economic Adviser to the President." At least everyone was clear about that.

In April 1999, Palestinian real estate developer Garbed Margossian put his prime property up for sale, the Grand Park Hotel in Ramallah. Known to journalists because it was the only luxury-class hotel then operating on the West Bank, it had become a favorite watering hole. Margossian had paid $3 million for the property in 1997 and invested another $2 million to upgrade it. He was hoping that with the advent of an independent Palestinian state, the property would have great appeal to international investors. His asking price was $7 million.

Several international hotel chains did express interest in the property, but Margossian never got the chance to shop for buyers. Within days of putting out the "For Sale" sign, Margossian sold the hotel to Mohammad Rashid at a break-even price of $5 million. "We were happy to find a buyer for the hotel," Margossian told me nervously when I spoke to him in Ramallah. "Mr. Rashid is a very clever man, very helpful, and very sincere."[35]

The Israeli newspaper *Haaretz* revealed in April 1997 that Rashid and Arafat personally controlled a secret bank account used by Israel to transfer tax payments to the Palestinians. As part of the 1994 Paris Protocols, which established the mechanism for these transfers, Israeli prime minister Yitzhak Rabin had agreed to Arafat's demand that part of the money be deposited in a private account established in his name at the Allenby Street branch of Israel's state-owned Bank Leumi. From 1994 until late 1999, Israel paid more than $600 million into Arafat's secret account, according to Israeli Customs documents and interviews with Israeli, PA, and International Monetary Fund (IMF) officials in Gaza.[36] But according to these same officials, none of that money went into the public treasury of the PA but was used instead as a "slush fund" by Arafat to fund the overseas operations of the PLO, buy political patronage in Gaza and the West Bank, and finance his personal investments, which were handled by Rashid. As we know now, thanks to PLO documents captured by the Israelis after the Passover bombing, the money was also used to finance terrorist attacks that killed Israeli and American Jews.

✝✝✝

One European banker I met who opened a bank in the West Bank said he was approached by a top official with the Palestinian Monetary Authority, who demanded a 20 percent ownership stake in the new bank and threatened to block its operating license if the banker refused. "This is the price of doing business," he said the official told him.

Conflict of interest is nothing new for top PA officials. Consider the case of Munib al-Masri. At the same time he served as a director of the Arab Bank, the largest in the region, he was also vice chairman of Palestine Development and Investment Ltd., PADICO, a private company that was partly owned by PA officials, including Mohammad Rashid. His cousin Maher al-Masri served on PADICO's board while sitting in Arafat's cabinet as commerce minister.

The al-Masri family owns the pro-government newspaper (and publishing house) *Al-Ayyam,* which received a $1.8 million loan from the World Bank in 1998. *Al-Ayyam* columnists regularly called for attacks against America and praised Iraqi dictator Saddam Hussein. When I asked the

World Bank in Washington about the loan, a spokesman called *Al-Ayyam* a "very moderate" paper. *Al-Ayyam* won a contract with the PA Ministry of Education to reprint the old Jordanian and Egyptian schoolbooks once the anti-Semitic material was restored, a project that was funded by the European Union.[37]

For many years, stories such as these were never reported because the political fix was in. Protecting Arafat and his cronies were Foreign Minister Shimon Peres and Prime Minister Ehud Barak of Israel and President Bill Clinton of the United States. They turned a blind eye to corruption, human rights abuses, and the rabid anti-Semitism from the official Palestinian media, the mosques, and the schools and failed to hold Arafat accountable for the growing number of terror attacks against civilians. While each argued the strategic reasons behind his support for Arafat, evidence has emerged on the public record suggesting the possibility of other motives as well.

Hani al-Masri headed his clan's U.S. branch and was a close Arafat confidant. When Arafat came to Washington, he stayed in al-Masri's house in Virginia. To journalists, al-Masri was known as Arafat's personal spokesman. When in Gaza, he sat on a key subcommittee of the PA Ministry of Information responsible for reviewing television broadcasts within the PA, a position akin to that of chief censor. Al-Masri had a double role in promoting hate speech in the PA areas, as part owner of the al-Ayyam publishing house and through his position at the Ministry of Information.

From 1994 to 1996, as PADICO was seeking seed money from the U.S. government to invest in the Palestinian economy, al-Masri and his wife, Cheryl, donated more than $160,000 to the Democratic National Committee (DNC) and to individual Democratic candidates, Federal Election Commission (FEC) records I reviewed show. Al-Masri also paid top dollar to attend the famous White House coffees with President Clinton. In September 1996, Hani al-Masri helped found "Arab Americans for Clinton/Gore '96," a group chaired by James Zogby, a well-known Arab American political activist. In recognition of his fund-raising skills, he was named a trustee of the DNC. FEC records show that al-Masri's largest donations to the DNC were written on corporate checks from Virginia-based Capital Investment Management Corporation, a company set up in 1993 to handle investment in Gaza and the West Bank.

In November 1997, the Overseas Private Investment Corporation (OPIC), a U.S. government entity, returned the favor, granting Capital Investment a $60 million loan guaranty to invest in PADICO and other Arafat-controlled entities in Gaza and the West Bank. Normally such government subsidies are put out for bidding. But not in al-Masri's case. "This was not competitively bid," OPIC spokesman Larry Spinelli told me.[38]

PADICO owned a controlling interest of the Palestinian stock exchange, the country's telephone company (PalTel), the electric company, two tourism companies, and the only company licensed by the state to build projects financed by World Bank, USAID, and European Union loans. In October 1999, for example, the West Bank city of Al-Bira awarded a $10 million bus station rehabilitation project to the Palestine Real Estate Investment Company, a subsidiary of PADICO. The Al-Bira contract was awarded without any competing bids or an outside evaluation of what the project should cost.

While Shimon Peres was serving as foreign minister in June 1999, his Peres Center for Peace announced that it was taking a $60 million stake in PalTel, through a joint venture with renegade U.S. financier Marc Rich, called the Peace Technology Fund. (Marc Rich was represented on the board of governors of the Peres Center by Andrei Azulay, president of the Marc Rich Foundation in Israel, and had not yet been pardoned by Bill Clinton.)[39] The fund's aim, according to the Peres Center Web site, was to make "equity investments in Palestinian companies and joint ventures." The other recipient of the fund's largesse was the Palestinian Mortgage Housing Corporation, tainted by scandal in 1998 "when the EU discovered that $20 million it had donated for the construction of low-cost housing in Gaza had been used instead to build luxury apartments" for Arafat cronies.[40] The kibbutz organization and the Israeli industrial group KORR became business partners with PA institutions and companies set up by Arafat cronies such as PalTel vice president (and Arafat financial adviser) Mohammad Rashid.

Also sitting on the board of governors of the Peres Center were Labor Party insider Yossi Ginossar and the UN "Special Coordinator" for the territories, Norwegian Terje Roed-Larsen. Norway provided a start-up grant of 10 million Norwegian kronor ($1.2 million) to the Peres Center and was one of Arafat's main backers in Europe. Making matters more incestuous was the fact that Roed-Larsen's wife, Mona Juul, was Norway's ambassador to Israel. Neither spouse had an interest in blowing the whistle on Arafat's cozy relations with certain hierarchs of the Israeli Labor Party.[41]

Concerns over cronyism and the misuse of funds dominated an international donors conference in Tokyo in October 1999, with some participants pressing Arafat to crack down on government-backed monopolies and to adopt a fair and open budget process. In public, PA officials promised to clean up their act. "In private discussions, however, Palestinian Authority representatives joked in the corridors of the conference that they will continue to do whatever they like with the money that they receive," a contemporaneous report by a team of Israeli and Arab investigative reporters states.[42] As long as the Labor Party remained in power in Israel, they knew the money would continue to flow.

In August 2002, the lid finally came off Arafat's clandestine financial empire when the former secretary-general of the Palestinian National Fund, Jawad Ghossein al-Russyan, seventy-one, surfaced in London after escaping from a PA prison. Al-Russyan became Arafat's secret banker in 1984 but says he resigned his position in April 1996 because of corruption. "The contributing countries started asking me questions about the money that had disappeared. I couldn't give them any answers," he said. "I resigned and warned some of the contributing countries about what was going on." He was kidnapped by Arafat's men from his home in Abu Dhabi on April 20, 2001, and whisked back to a secret PA prison to keep him quiet. During a medical visit in East Jerusalem, he escaped to Jordan with Israel's help, then went to London, where he began meeting with journalists.[43]

Al-Russyan, a prominent Palestinian businessman who operated one of the largest privately owned companies in the United Arab Emirates, told reporters that Arafat began moving $8 million into his personal accounts each month starting in 1993, from aid that had been sent to the PA by other Arab countries, Europe, the United States, and Japan. This was in addition to the $600 million in Customs duties Arafat and Mohammad Rashid had squirreled away in the Bank Leumi accounts with Israel's agreement. He also confirmed long-standing rumors that among Arafat's secret financial holdings were duty-free shops in the airports of Kenya, Nigeria, Mozambique, and Tanzania, holdings in the airlines of Maldives and Guinea-Bissau, stock in the holding company that owned Mercedes-Benz, refineries, farms, real estate in England, France, Spain, Lebanon, Greece, and Cyprus, radio stations, and shoe factories. Despite Arafat's collaboration with Saddam Hussein's invasion of Kuwait in August 1990, the State Department reported in 1995 that Arafat continued to receive cash from Saudi Arabia and Qatar under the Palestinian Liberation Tax Fund—a 3.5 to 7 percent tax on Palestinian workers in Arab states.[44] Already in 1995, the Government Accounting Office (GAO) in Washington, D.C., estimated that Arafat's financial empire, which he always claimed he controlled on behalf of the "Palestinian people," contained assets valued at between $5 billion and $10 billion.[45] None of it ever appears to have been used to improve the lot of Palestinians living under his rule in the West Bank and Gaza.

Under pressure from the Bush administration and from donors in Europe, Arafat was forced in August 2002 to sign an agreement allowing the audit of parts of his personal empire and of semi-public corporations controlled by financial wizard Mohammad Rashid and other Arafat surrogates. Handling the audit was the nonprofit Democracy Council in California and a team of American auditors from Standard & Poor's. The green eyeshades began by examining allegations of corruption in Rashid's monopolies on the import of cement, flour, and petroleum products.

"The U.S. government and the international donor community decided it was time to convince the Palestinians to come clean on their world holdings in order to set a benchmark for the future," a source knowledgeable about the investigation told me.[46] Prior to the project, nobody knew whether Mohammad Rashid controlled $10 million or $10 billion, or what Arafat was really worth. The Israeli press abounded with rumors that up to $300 million had gone missing from Arafat's secret empire and was transferred to Swiss bank accounts.

One of the key demands of the auditors was that Arafat and Rashid disclose the names of investors and board members of their various companies and provide a certified list of assets that were to be rolled into a newly created Palestine Investment Fund on January 1, 2003. The new fund was to belong to the Palestinian Authority, not Arafat or Rashid. Before the turnover date, there were reports that Arafat shifted assets around to hide them and that some board members jumped ship so their names wouldn't be revealed. Rashid was named managing director of the new fund.

The goal of the project was to bring the money into the light and to provide a baseline for future accounting of PA assets. "If Arafat wanted to use these assets, he had to declare them. If it wasn't declared on January 1, it didn't exist. And if it didn't exist, he couldn't use it," the source told me. "The next time the Palestinian security forces showed up in new uniforms, or payments were traced to Arafat's office, they would have to be able to prove where the money came from. No more slush funds."

The new fund was intended to do away with Arafat's long-standing alleged practice of demanding up to a 20 percent cut of every piece of business done in Gaza and the West Bank, either directly or through conduits. In the past, no one knew for sure how much money was secretly transferred to Arafat through these backdoor deals and from bribes extorted by his security services, but he was believed to get a cut on every cell phone, every telephone line, every sack of cement, and every tank of gas sold in the territories. In a preliminary report released in March 2003, the auditors noted: "There is significant evidence that the Palestinian Authority actively supports [Rashid's] PCSC Company, thereby artificially stifling competition." The report also noted that "agents or employees of various agencies of the PA . . . routinely demand cash payments in order to facilitate the import and transportation of cement into Gaza." Cement was one of Rashid's monopolies.[47] While the language was polite, the conclusion that the PA was rife with corruption was clear.

The list of more than eighty commercial assets Arafat delivered to the auditors included $74 million in cash, $165 million in investments in telecommunications companies in Algeria and Tunisia, holdings in a variety of U.S.-based venture capital funds, and a $28 million stake in the Oasis Casino and Resort in Jericho, which it turned out was half-owned by Martin Schlaff, an Austrian businessman with close ties to senior advisers to Ariel Sharon. When it came to propping up his financial empire, Arafat didn't seem to care whether his partners were from Labor or from Likud. It was precisely this connivance that perpetuated Arafat's reign.

††††

An early crackdown on corruption by the donor community might have helped. But the economic abuses went hand in hand with human rights outrages and the expansion of Arafat's security forces, who regularly extorted the local Palestinian population.

Bassam Eid, a Palestinian activist who for years worked with B'tselem, an NGO that monitored Israeli human rights abuses, felt things started going wrong within months of Arafat's arrival in Gaza in May 1994. "I left B'tselem in 1996," Eid told me in Jerusalem in late 1999, "because I felt there was a need for a human rights organization that tracked the abuses of Arafat's new Authority against Palestinians."

Almost as soon as the PA took over in May 1994, Eid says, Palestinians were put to the whip. "Since then, twenty people have died in police custody. Twenty-four people have been sentenced to death for political crimes, and three of them executed. In the past two years alone two hundred and fifty political prisoners have been arrested without charges, trial, or the right of defense. On seventeen separate occasions, the Palestinian High Court has ordered the authorities to release some of these prisoners, but the PA has simply ignored the court. In two cases—in August 1996 and in February 1997—Arafat responded by firing the judge who signed the release orders."[48] Worst of all, Eid says, was the consistent refusal of Arafat's government to establish a working judicial system under the rule of law. "We have a judicial system we inherited from the Israelis, but the PA refuses to implement it. Nor will they replace it with new laws."

The European Union and the United States urged Arafat to adopt a new legal code and to apply the basic law drafted by the PLC, a rudimentary Palestinian Constitution delineating the relative powers of the executive, legislative, and judicial branches. But Arafat refused any measures that would impose limits on his power. "This place is being run by people who are not schooled in governance," the UN's Rothermel said politely. Haifa University researcher Dan Schueftan put it more bluntly: "Arafat's only experience in running anything was Lebanon, where he made the Mafia look clean. Easy money in the Arab world just makes things worse, whether it's from the oil boom or from dumb Israelis or from international donors. It all goes to create a huge bureaucracy and a secret police organization. Give them $2 billion more, and you will have eight more secret police forces. This is the only place in the world today where the secret police has a state."

Mohammad Hamdan, thirty-six, is a local *muktar,* or Arab village leader, from a farming area near Bethlehem. When I met him secretly in November 1999, his village was still under Israeli control but was scheduled to become part of the Palestinian Authority. Mohammad and the friends of his I met all said they would prefer to remain under Israeli rule. "With the Israelis, we knew that we had to make trouble in order to get trouble. With the PA, we are in constant fear. If they know you have money, they arrest you and keep you in prison until you pay. I have many, many friends who have been jailed and had to pay their way out."

"If we had a real election today, Arafat would not get five percent. But people are afraid. They know that the security forces are everywhere, so they will vote for Arafat. We are locked inside Arafat's house. The future for us is black. We are like blind people: we cannot see what lies ahead."

Ibrahim Hussein al-Shawahin learned firsthand that corruption and abuse of power go hand in hand. He was arrested on October 14, 1996, by the general intelligence service and held in Jericho prison for seventeen months. During that time he was never allowed to see a lawyer, nor was he formally accused of any crime. He lost several teeth during repeated beatings by his jailers, who broke a finger of his left hand and subjected him to the *shabeh,* a form of torture where the hands and legs are handcuffed together behind the prisoner's back while he is beaten.[49] They finally released him after he paid them $61,000 in cash and checks, which they claimed he owed in back taxes.

When he went to the tax office after his release, al-Shawahin discovered that he had owed only $2,100. The head of the tax office called the Jericho prosecutor in front of al-Shawahin and asked him about the discrepancy, but he received no response, "I did not receive the rest of the money from the tax authorities because the money I'd paid wasn't even transferred to the treasury," he told human rights investigator Bassam Eid.[50] There was no trace of the $61,000 al-Shawahin had paid in order to get out of jail.

Al-Shawahin was but one of thirty-six persons interviewed by Palestinian human rights investigators, who all told similar cases of abuse. The PA never responded to these allegations of abuse and shut down the human rights investigators once the second *intifada* began on September 28, 2000. Since then, the security forces and militias have murdered fellow Palestinians at will on charges of "collaboration" with Israel. According to one report, issued in July 2002, 185 Palestinians had been murdered in this manner, fully "one out of every eight Palestinians killed" in the conflict thus far.[51]

In February 2003, a French Socialist Party member of the European Parliament finally came out and said openly what had been known to insiders for years. "There is reasonable and solid suspicion that a considerable part of the 1.4 billion euros the European Union has transferred to the Palestinian Authority since the Oslo Agreement has been abused by senior PA officials and in part reached terrorist organizations," François Zimeray told the World Jewish Congress in New York. "Only recently has the EU become more alert regarding the funds going to the PA. Until three or four months ago, the EU did not show special interest in what the PA was doing with the money."[52]

In such an atmosphere, the resurgence of anti-Semitism in Gaza since Arafat's return in 1994 was no accident. Arafat himself became the most powerful promoter of anti-Semitic lies, to cover his own corruption and the abject failure of his Palestinian Authority to deliver peace and prosperity to his people. Arafat transformed the dream of Palestinian independence into a nightmarish police state, while indoctrinating a new, captive population to kill Jews. Ironically, he was helped in this by successive Israeli governments, a naive U.S. administration, and the European Union.

THE BIG LIE

8

Do Arafat and his Palestinian Authority want peace with Israel? Do Arab leaders want their nations to live in harmony with the West? Do Muslim clerics believe Islam can live side by side with Jews and Christians and persons of other faiths? Do we even think in the same terms, cherish the same values?

I had been asking these questions on both sides of the Arab-Israeli divide for many years. But let me present one more voice, that of a second-generation Russian immigrant who refers to himself as an "old villager" because of the decades he has spent on the land, working side by side with Palestinian Arabs. Dov Weinstock, fifty-seven, known to his friends as "Dubak," believes there can be no peace until we in the West and those in Israel who think like us "change the diskette," the moral operating system we use to understand the Arab Muslim world.

Most journalists would call Dubak a "settler," a term often intended to conjure up images of religious fanatics carrying Uzis who storm into Arab villages and shoot women and children. The first time I met Dubak, in November 1999, we spent two days driving together through the Judean desert and through the farmland around Hebron and Bethlehem, sipping tea and eating grapes with his Arab neighbors, hearing stories from village leaders and bedouin who were terrified of coming under Arafat's rule. We ate simple meals of raw tomatoes, green peppers, olive oil, onions, and bread off the back of his dusty Land Rover, as his "kids" tended to the live-oak trees struggling to reemerge from the ancient terraces of the ravine he has cultivated into a park with their help. Armed with three cell phones and two short-wave radios, Dubak didn't carry a gun.

But even then, times were changing. "From 1967 until 1993—the Oslo Accords—we never had a shooting here," he told me that first time. "Since Oslo, we've had seventeen shootings. Now our children's buses are armored to protect them from bullets. When peace broke out, the army came here and built an eight-foot-high barbed-wire fence around our set-tlement, where we never had one before. We call it the Oslo fence."

Since the second *intifada* broke out in late September 2000, the shoot-ings in this area have been too numerous to count. "In Hebrew, we say this land is sour with blood," Dubak tells me. "And yet, in the war on terror, you have to think like a village of fishermen. Every year the sea takes someone from you. You have to fight it, but there is no solution. It is part of our condition. We have to live with terror. It is a price, and we must be ready to pay it."

During an evening spent to honor Shiloh Gal, the former mayor of Kfar Etzion, the main village of the settlement cluster, Dubak holds forth like an oracle as he carves a brace of turkeys that have been simmering all afternoon in a dugout pit. A hundred tiny candles burn like a celebration where his "kids" have set them into natural ledges in the rock wall behind the outdoor picnic table. "I asked an American reporter once, what would you do if you lived in New Jersey and someone puts rocks in your drive-way, nails in the road to blow your tires, and took potshots at you every night? He said, Why, of course, I'd move away. So how do you explain the fact that we are still here? Jews came back to Gush Etzion four times, each time after it had been destroyed by Arabs. We came back to the places where our fathers were murdered and built again. Where is the logic in that?"

Dubak believes that the problem with Israel is that a defeatist Western logic has arrived here, too. "How do we end this? One of us will be stronger and will win. There is no peace process, no paper. This is not Europe. It is not America. You must be strong to survive." The U.S.-led war on terror, he predicts, "will be a war of all civilians, just as in Israel. How do you deal with terror? When every driver looks to the driver on the left, to the driver on the right. You can see the fear in the eyes of someone about to commit a terrorist act. Security is the responsibility of everyone. Don't expect someone else to do it for you."

Despite the armed attacks, most of the two hundred thousand Jews who have settled in the hills surrounding Jerusalem live without fear and with a sense of community most Americans would envy. On a Shabbat evening I spend in the nearby Orthodox settlement of Efrat, over a hundred teenagers congregate out in the well-lit streets after the evening meal to stroll and socialize—without the fears or anxieties that stalk most Americans of their age. No shopping malls beckon. There are no speeding cars to dodge, no police, no parents, no drug dealers. Bonds that will last a lifetime are forged on these warm autumn evenings of talk and laughter, in the clean air overlooking the Judean desert.

Readers of *The New York Times* or *The Washington Post* probably think that most of the Israeli settlements in the West Bank and Gaza were built on land "stolen" from the Palestinians and that these "illegal" settlements are a major "stumbling block" to a future peace agreement. Think again. "When the Palestinians say 'illegal settlements,' what they mean are Jewish towns and villages that replaced Arab villages," says David Bedein, an Israeli investigative reporter who has lived in Efrat for nearly twenty years with his wife, Sarah, and their six children. "There were never any Arab settlements at Kfar Etzion or at Efrat. The same goes for most of the settlements in Judea and Samaria. They are built on the hilltops. The Arabs didn't like the hilltops because they were difficult to farm. They were full of stones, scorpions, and snakes," Bedein says. Indeed, the entire Gush Etzion bloc is considered a "legal" settlement by Arafat and figures on the PA maps of Palestine as a Jewish area.[1]

So where are the "illegal" settlements? "They are in places like Kibbutz Metzer, inside the Green Line," says Bedein. "Or places like Tel Aviv," built around the Arab fishing village of Jaffa, "or Haifa, or East Jerusalem. The maps of 'illegal' settlements provided by the PA target only the Jewish settlements that 'overran' Arab villages from 1948, with no mention of the Jewish settlements in Judea and Samaria."[2] The PA has identified 531 Arab villages that existed before 1948 where "illegal Jewish settlements" now stand. All became part of Israel in 1948.

On the night of November 10, 2002, a gunman entered Kibbutz Metzer, where thirty-four-year-old Revital Ohayon was reading a bedtime story to her two small children, Matan, aged five, and Noam, aged three, and pumped fourteen bullets into their bodies. Within minutes, the local bureau of the French Press Agency received a call, claiming responsibility in the name of Yasser Arafat's Al-Aqsa brigades. Announcing the events the next morning, the official Voice of Palestine radio confirmed that Fatah had carried out an armed attack against a Jewish "colony." That "colony's" name is Israel.

✝✝✝

The five-minute video clip is dreamy and haunting. Scenes of dead children, joy, and mourning drift eerily across the screen, accompanied by a hypnotic melody sung by an enchanting male voice. It begins with a handsome young schoolboy writing a farewell letter to his parents, then going off on a mission. After his death, the letter is handed to his father, who tears his hair at the news. In the background, scenes of the boy's last day scroll across the television screen as the singer puts the words of his letter to music. "Do not be sad, my dear, and do not cry over my parting. Oh, my dear father . . . how sweet is *shahada* [martyrdom]. How sweet is *shahada* when I embrace you, Oh my land . . ." As that line is sung, a child actor staggers to his death and embraces the ground, his arms stretched out as upon a cross. The boy's death is gentle, innocent, heroic—not the brutal obliteration that awaits suicide bombers.

From the grave, the boy now addresses his mother. "Mother, my most dear, Be joyous over my blood. And do not cry for me."[3] That same line— "Mother, do not cry for me"—has appeared in at least three farewell letters from fourteen- to seventeen-year-old Palestinians who have carried out suicide bombings since the film clip first aired on Palestinian television in May 2001, says Itamar Marcus. Clearly the clip, which aired every day between cartoons, after school, and in the early evening between regularly scheduled programs, without any explanatory note, introduction, or warning, was intended to incite children to commit murder.

"For the six years we'd been following PA TV, we'd seen on average fifteen minutes of violent, anti-Israeli, and anti-Semitic video clips, interspersed between regular programming throughout the day," Marcus said. "Suddenly, in the summer of 2000, it went up to two hours per day, just as Barak was getting ready to give away 98 percent of the territory the PA wanted at Camp David."

And it is not the only such video clip aired regularly by Arafat's official television. Another clip features the eight-year-old Mohammad al-Dura, the most famous Palestinian "martyr," whose death in an apparent crossfire between Israeli soldiers and Palestinian policemen at the start of the second *intifada* was captured live by a French film crew and broadcast around the world on October 2, 2000.[4] The opening screen is a handwritten message "signed" by the young Mohammad: "I am waving to you not to say good-bye, but to say, 'Follow me.'" A child actor portrays the death of the young Mohammad, then shows him in paradise, riding on a Ferris wheel, flying a kite, playing on the beach. A haunting lyric accompanies these pictures, with lines such as these: "How sweet is the fragrance of the *shahids*, How sweet is the scent of the earth, its thirst quenched by the gush of blood flowing from the youthful body." Then the vocalist does a call and repeat with the choir:

> *Vocalist:* "Oh Father, till we meet. Oh Father, till we meet. I shall go with no fear, no tears. How sweet is the fragrance of the *shahids*."
>
> *Choir:* "How sweet is the fragrance of the *shahids*."[5]

One of many myths is that suicide bombers come from poor families where "hopelessness" drives them to despair and suicide. Think again. Since Arafat has been breeding Jew-hatred and the cult of martyrdom through all the mechanisms of his Palestinian Authority, it has spread to all sectors of Palestinian society.

On June 9, 2002, two well-dressed eleven-year-old girls named Wala and Yussra were interviewed on a talk show broadcast by Palestinian Authority TV about their personal yearning to achieve death through *shahada*, which they said was the desire of "every Palestinian child." These were children not of the camps, but of the middle classes. They explained that their goal was not to experience the good life, not to become doctors or teachers or lawyers, but to achieve the proper death through martyrdom for Allah.

> *Host:* You described *shahada* as something beautiful. Do you think it is beautiful?
> *Wala: Shahada* is very, very beautiful. Everyone yearns for *shahada.* What could be better than going to paradise?
> *Host:* What is better, peace and full rights for the Palestinian people, or *shahada?*
> *Wala: Shahada.* I will achieve my rights after becoming a *shahida.*
> *Yussra:* Of course *shahada* is a good thing. We don't want this world, we want the afterlife. We benefit not from this life, but from the afterlife. The children of Palestine have accepted the concept that this is *shahada,* and that death by *shahada* is very good. Every Palestinian child aged, say, twelve, says, 'Oh Lord, I would like to become a *shahid.*' "[6]

Even the name of the official newspaper of Arafat's Palestinian Authority reflects this emphasis on martyrdom. *Al-Hayat al-Jadida* means "the New Life." This mirrors yet another film clip aimed at children that glorifies martyrdom. It ends with a black screen stamped with the official emblem of the Palestinian Authority, a slogan in Arabic, and its translation, in large letters, in English: "Ask for death, the life will be given to you."

There is no precedent for this type of indoctrination. "Not even Hitler did this," Itamar Marcus says as he shows me these scenes. "The Hitler Youth were taught to kill, not to be killed. This is the ultimate in child abuse. Here you have a whole generation of kids who think the most they can accomplish in life is to die for Allah. This is a tragedy with implications that no one in the West has begun to contemplate."

Palestinian psychologist Dr. Shafiq Massalha conducted an experiment in the spring of 2001 with a random sample of 150 boys and girls aged ten and eleven to whom he had distributed notebooks, asking them to record their dreams every morning for ten days and to illustrate them.

The results, though predictable, were still shocking. "A Palestinian girl aged eleven dreamt she went into a market in Israel with bombs all over her body. She stopped in the crowd of shoppers, counted to ten, then blew herself up," according to an account of his findings. He found that 78 percent of the dreams were political, and most of them included physical violence. Half of the children dreamed of becoming suicide bombers.[7]

Arafat has never wavered in making his message clear. In an interview on PA TV that January, he was asked what message he wanted to send to Palestinian children. His reply was quick and to the point: "The child who is grasping the stone, facing the tank; is it not the greatest message to the world when that hero becomes a *shahid*? We are proud of them."[8]

And just in case that was not clear enough, children were told how to achieve martyrdom in the mosques. In the Palestinian Authority, as in the rest of the Arab world, prayer leaders at the mosques are not "men of God," despite the illusions of people such as Jimmy Carter; they are appointed representatives of the political leader.[9] Arafat used his men in the pulpit to transmit his message to the masses. It was not a political message about Israel, not a call to struggle, but a message from God himself, obliging them to take up the holy war against the Jews or face eternal damnation. This is where the anti-Semitism transmitted in a clear line from Haj Mohammad Amin al-Husseini and his mentors to Arafat appears most clearly for what it is: a direct call to murder Jews, for no other reason than their faith.

Addressing "the Palestinian nation" in a televised sermon on July 28, 2000, prayer leader Dr. Ahmed Yusuf Abu Halabiya told them: "Our fate from Allah is to be the edge of the sword in the war against the Jews until the resurrection of the dead. As the Prophet Muhammad said, 'The resurrection of the dead will not arrive until you will fight the Jews and kill them.' "[10]

In these sermons it is clear that killing Jews is not a political need, but a religious requirement on all believers; it is not an order from Arafat, but the will of God himself. This is the message Arafat's men in the pulpit have been drilling into their listeners week after week, year after year. If they want to be good Muslims, they have to kill Jews.

The Jews are the Jews. There never was among them a supporter of peace. They are all liars. . . . They are terrorists. Therefore *it is necessary* to slaughter them and murder them, according to the words of Allah. . . . It is forbidden to have mercy in your hearts for the Jews in any place and in any land. Make war on them any place that you find yourself. Any place that you meet them—kill them. Kill the Jews and those Americans that are like them. . . . The Jews only understand might. Have no mercy on the Jews, murder them everywhere. . . ."[11]

The inclusion of Americans as targets of the wrath of the Muslims was not a clerical error. Dr. Abu Halabiya elaborated on this theme at some length as he harangued his followers in the Zayed bin Sultan al-Nahyan Mosque in Gaza. "This is the truth, O Brothers in belief. From here, Allah the almighty has called upon us not to ally with the Jews or the Christians, not to like them, not to become their partners, not to support them, and not to sign agreements with them. And he who does that is one of them, as Allah said: 'O you who believe, do not take the Jews and the Christians as allies, for they are allies of one another. Who from among you takes them as allies will indeed be one of them. . . .' "

This is an important lesson we in the West would do well to heed. The enmity being preached against America and the West has nothing to do with politics or support for Israel. It stems from the simple fact that we are not Muslims. This is the message that preachers across the Muslim world have been drilling into the minds and hearts of the faithful. "The Jews are the allies of the Christians, and the Christians are the allies of the Jews, [and] they are against you, O Muslims," Sheikh Halabiya preached. "Wherever you are, kill the Jews and those Americans who are like them—and those who stand by them—they are all in one trench, against the Arabs and the Muslims."

Itamar Marcus believes Arafat is using the mosques to spread a systematic anti-Semitism that goes way beyond the current conflict and that will take a generation at least to repair. "The message of this PA religious ideology can be summed up as follows: The enmity of Muslims to Jews and Israel today is not because of the current political conflict, but just the opposite. The current political conflict is a result of the eternal enmity of Muslims to Jews." This is a dangerous escalation of the conflict in the Middle East, transforming what began in essence as a border conflict between Israel and the Palestinians into an eternal battle of Good versus

Evil. "Jews, they teach, are inherently evil and cursed forever by God," Marcus says. "By killing Jews, they are doing God's work. The ultimate battle, upon which the Resurrection depends, is Islam against the Jews."

In such a conflict there can be no peace, no negotiation, no accommodation, no coexistence. From the pulpits of Gaza and the West Bank, this is the message Palestinians are being taught: The conflict between Muslims and Jews is total, it is eternal, and it will end only when the Muslims have murdered the last Jew hiding behind a tree or a stone, wherever he may be. In this struggle to eliminate the Jews from the earth, "anyone who does not attain martyrdom in these days should wake up in the middle of the night and say, 'My God, why have you deprived me of martyrdom for your sake?' "[12]

† † †

Well-meaning journalists and Middle East analysts throw up their hands when they talk about Arafat's rejection of the peace offer handcrafted by President Clinton and Prime Minister Ehud Barak in July 2000 at Camp David, Maryland. With Clinton standing over his shoulder, Barak offered the Palestinians an end to Israeli occupation and full statehood in most of Gaza and the West Bank. It had all the appearances of the "peace of the brave" Arafat has claimed since 1993 that he sought. The new Palestinian state would have a flag, a seaport, an airport. It would be able to establish relations with foreign countries, and it would be responsible for its own security, thanks to a large armed police force. Refugees would be allowed to return, and parts of East Jerusalem would be its capital. Yet Arafat refused. No matter how hard Clinton tried to twist his arm during late night talks, he balked. Why?

In public, Arafat continued to call for peace, but back in Gaza he ordered the PA propaganda machine to prepare for war. Palestinian television broadcast carefully edited video clips from earlier periods of violence, depicting Israeli soldiers as bloodthirsty rapists and murderers, while repeatedly airing a well-known song, "Where Are the Millions," used in the past to call people to the streets. Prayer leaders in the mosques switched from vague threats against Jews to specific calls to violence, abjuring the faithful to fulfill their obligations as Muslims. Dr. Ahmed

Yusuf Abu Halabiya told worshipers on July 28 that their fate "is to be the edge of the sword in the war against the Jews until the resurrection of the dead." Two weeks later, once the full details of Barak's offer were known, he specifically condemned the Camp David talks. "It does not matter how many agreements will be signed or how many contracts will be confirmed. The truth is in the Koran, which is verified in the words of the Prophet Muhammad, that the deciding battle will be in Jerusalem and its surroundings."[13] Hamas leader Sheikh Ahmed Yassin, the head of the Islamic "opposition," told the official PA daily, *Al-Hayat al-Jadida:* "We are talking about *hudna* [a cease-fire] for an interval, but not about ending the struggle." *Hudna* was not a word or a concept well-known or understood in the West, and Sheikh Yassin's statement and others like it were ignored.

The anti-Semitic propaganda following Camp David reached "unprecedented levels," creating "an atmosphere of the eve of outbreak of war," Itamar Marcus wrote on September 11, 2000.[14] "I hesitated before writing that sentence," he says now. "We'd been following PA television for six years, and we'd never seen anything quite like it." Two weeks later, on September 29, 2000, Palestinian schoolchildren bused purposefully to the Temple Mount hurled stones at Jews praying down below at the Western Wall. In response, Israeli soldiers opened fire, killing seven and wounding scores more. The Al-Aqsa *intifada* had begun.

The Western media, repeating official PA propaganda, blamed the outbreak of violence on the visit by Ariel Sharon to the Temple Mount the day before.[15] In fact, Sharon's visit had been cleared well in advance with PA officials, and his delegation included prominent Muslim as well as Jewish leaders. "Sharon's visit, which was coordinated with [PA West Bank security chief] Jibril Rajoub, was directed at me, not the Palestinians," Barak said later, "to show that he cared more about Jerusalem than I did. We know, from hard intelligence, that Arafat intended to unleash a violent confrontation, terrorism. [Sharon's visit and the riots that followed] fell into his hands like an excellent excuse, a pretext. . . ."[16]

Arafat's communications minister, Imad al-Falouji, agreed. Speaking at a symposium in Gaza on December 5, 2000, al-Falouji confirmed that the Palestinian Authority had begun preparations for the outbreak of violence from the moment the Camp David talks concluded on July 28, "in accordance with instructions given by Chairman Arafat himself." Al-Falouji went on to state that Arafat "launched this Intifada as a culminating stage to the immutable Palestinian stance in the negotiations, and was not meant merely as a protest of Israeli opposition leader Ariel Sharon's visit to the Temple Mount."[17] He repeated his comments before a PLO gathering at the Ain el-Helweh refugee camp in Lebanon five months later. "The intifada was set in motion after the collapse of the Camp David talks. It's a mistake to think that the intifada was set off by the visit of Ariel Sharon to Al-Aqsa."[18] Mamduh Nofal, a leader of the Democratic Front for the Liberation of Palestinian, added that Arafat gave the final orders to trigger the *intifada before* Sharon's visit. "A few days before the visit of Sharon to Al-Aqsa, Yasser Arafat told us to be ready to fight."[19]

Despite the violence, Barak and Clinton resumed negotiations with Arafat that autumn and presented an even more generous offer to Arafat's men at meetings in Washington that began on December 23, 2000. Former Clinton administration negotiator Dennis Ross later told the story to Brit Hume on *Fox News Sunday*. The final deal, which Clinton read out to Palestinian negotiators "at dictation speed," included 97 percent of the West Bank, a new Palestinian capital in East Jerusalem, the return of Palestinian refugees to the new state, and a $30 billion fund to compensate refugees. Israel also agreed to a land swap with the new state, to allow the Palestinians to establish a "land bridge" between Gaza and the West Bank. When Arafat met with Clinton and Ross in the Oval Office to discuss to deal on January 2, 2001, he initially said yes. "Then he added reservations that basically meant he rejected every single one of the things he was supposed to give," Ross said. He rejected Israeli sovereignty over the Western Wall and over other Jewish religious sites. He even rejected "the basic ideas on security. . . . So every single one of the ideas that was asked of him, he rejected."[20] Palestinian negotiators had "understood this was the best they were ever going to get," Ross recalls. "They wanted [Arafat] to accept it." Still, Arafat refused. "For him to end the conflict is to end himself," Ross surmised. Why? Because for Arafat, God has commanded Muslims to destroy the Jews, not to make peace with them. Indeed, salvation itself depends upon carrying out this commandment.

In fact, Arafat and the Palestinian leadership have always believed that peace treaties and agreements with Israel were *hudna*. Evidence of

19419419419419419419419194194 4

this has been available in the public domain for years but gets systematically ignored.

Four weeks before Arafat ordered the beginning of the second *intifada,* Israeli Arab Knesset member Abd al-Malek Dahamshe appeared on Palestinian television to comment on the Camp David talks. Responding to a viewer's call that "our problem with Israel is not a border problem, but one of existence," Dahamshe agreed. "We exaggerate when we say 'peace' . . . what we are [really] speaking about is *hudna.* "[21]

PA minister of supplies Abdul-Aziz Shahian gave a more detailed explanation of the process to *Al-Ayyam,* the "moderate" weekly controlled by the al-Masri clan. "The Palestinian people accepted the Oslo agreements as a first step and not as a permanent settlement, based on the premise that the war and struggle in the land is more efficient than a struggle from a distant land," a reference to Tunisia, where the PLO was based before Oslo.[22]

The theory of gaining a foothold in Palestine as the first step toward seizing all of Israel goes back to what the PLO used to call its "phased plan" for the conquest of Palestine. This is precisely the strategy the PLO was supposed to *have abandoned* with Oslo. But Arafat deputy for political guidance and national affairs Otham Abu Arbiah explained in a 1999 interview with the official Palestinian daily *Al-Hayat al-Jadida* that the Palestinian leadership had not only retained the plan, but actually had updated it since coming to Gaza in 1994. He did this by quoting the original plan and comparing it to current events.

> The goal of this stage is the establishment of the independent Palestinian State, with its capital in Jerusalem. When we achieve this, it will be a positive [step] and it will advance us to the next stage via other ways and means. . . . 'Every Palestinian must know clearly and unequivocally that the independent Palestinian State, with Jerusalem as its capital, is not the end of the road.' The [rise of] the Palestinian State is a stage after which there will be another stage and that is the democratic state in all of Palestine [that is, in place of Israel]."[23]

As Arafat and his negotiators prepared to leave for Camp David, telling newsmen in English that they expected to draft a "final peace agreement" with Israel, Palestinian National Council (PNC) Politburo member Abdullah al-Hourani told Palestinians in Arabic that it was all a sham. "Whether they return to negotiations or not, and whether they fulfill the agreements or not," he said, "the political plan is a temporary agreement, and the conflict remains eternal, will not be locked, and the agreements being talked about are regarding the current balance of power. As to the struggle, it will continue. It may pause at times, but in the final analysis, Palestine is ours from the [Mediterranean] Sea to the [Jordan] River."[24]

Arafat's representative in Jerusalem, Faisal al-Husseini, gave the most detailed explanation of how Arafat and the Palestinian leadership viewed the Oslo "process" and the negotiations with Israel in an interview with an Egyptian paper that appeared shortly after his death of a heart attack on May 31, 2001. In an elaborate metaphor, he compared the Oslo Accords to the Trojan horse left behind by a beaten Greek army, which the people of Troy brought inside the city gates, thinking it was the spoils of war. "Had the U.S. and Israel not realized, before Oslo, that all that was left of the Palestinian National movement and the pan-Arab movement was a wooden horse called Arafat or the PLO, they would never have opened their fortified gates and let it inside their walls," he said.

At the time, al-Husseini went on, he had urged all Palestinian leaders to "climb into the horse," regardless of whether they supported or opposed the Oslo Accords. "When we are asking all the Palestinian forces and factions to look at the Oslo agreement and at other agreements as 'temporary' procedures, or phased goals, this means that we are ambushing the Israelis and cheating them." In so doing, he said, Palestinians were behaving "exactly" as the Israelis had done when,

> in 1947, in accordance with [the UN] Partition Plan, they decided to declare statehood on 55 percent of the land of Palestine. . . . Similarly, if we agree to declare our state over what is now only 22 percent of Palestine—meaning the West Bank and Gaza—our ultimate goal is [still] the liberation of all historical Palestine from the [Jordan] River to the [Mediterranean] Sea, even if this means that the conflict will last for another thousand years or for many generations.
>
> In short, we are exactly like they are. We distinguish the strategic, longterm goals from the political phased goals, which we are compelled to

temporarily accept due to international pressure. If you are asking me as a Pan-Arab nationalist what are the Palestinian borders according to the higher strategy, I will immediately reply: 'From the river to the sea.' . . . If you are asking me as a man who belongs to the Islamic faith, my answer is also, 'From the river to the sea,' the entire land is an Islamic Waqf which cannot be bought or sold, and it is impossible to remain silent while someone is stealing it. . . ."[25]

✝ ✝ ✝

Since leaving Kuwait in the mid-1960s to launch the armed struggle against Israel, Arafat has not been known to read a book. For relaxation, say biographers Janet and John Wallach, he watches Tom & Jerry cartoons. But anyone who has examined Arafat's speeches since his return to Gaza in July 1994 cannot help but notice the repeated use of Islamic themes, metaphors, and even direct quotations from the Koran.

One of Arafat's favorite episodes from the life of the Prophet revolves around the Hudaibiya Conciliation Accord. He referred to it after signing the Cairo agreement with Prime Minister Yitzhak Rabin on May 4, 1994, which paved the way for the PLO to enter Gaza and the West Bank. Traveling to Johannesburg, South Africa, where he addressed a local mosque just six days later, Arafat gave this explanation of his actions: "This agreement, I am not considering it more than the agreement which had been signed between our prophet Muhammed and the Quraish, and you remember the Caliph Omar had refused this agreement and [considered] it a despicable truce." The struggle with Israel was a jihad, he said, that good Muslims were obligated to carry out to the end. Arafat's remarks, taped by someone from the South African Jewish Community, were broadcast shortly afterward on Israeli radio. Yet apparently no one listened.[26]

Arafat referred again to the Hudaibiya agreement in a speech carried by PA TV on August 21, 1995. "Did the Prophet, Allah's Messenger, the Last of the Prophets, really accept a humiliation [as Omar bin al-Khattab blamed him]? No, and no again. He did not accept a humiliation. But every situation has its own circumstances."[27]

So what was this agreement, and why is it so important to understanding Arafat's view toward the peace process?

In A.D. 628, the Prophet Muhammad signed a ten-year pact with the powerful Quraish tribe, after having been chased from Mecca to Medina. The Quraish were not a Jewish tribe, but pagans. Because Muhammad and his followers were then weak, he needed to make peace with at least some of his enemies to gain time to consolidate his forces. Muslims refer to the "painful" concessions the Hudaibiya agreement contained and note that Muhammad removed the words *messenger of Allah* from beneath his signature, thus making it an "inferior peace agreement." Just two years after signing the peace, Muhammad attacked Mecca and slaughtered all the members of the Quraish, in direct violation of the treaty. Since then, "Hudaibiya" has been taken to mean a temporary peace or tactical agreement, intended to be swept aside whenever expedient.

Whenever Arafat evokes the Hudaibiya pact, he is speaking in codes fully understood by faithful Muslims, not just his own constituents. He is really saying this: We will get strong and then we will destroy Israel, just as Muhammad destroyed the Quraish, but today we must eat the bitter herbs of humiliation. Arafat explained how he viewed the "despicable truce" he had signed with Israel in a meeting with Arab diplomats in Stockholm's Grand Hotel on January 30, 1996.

> You understand that we plan to eliminate the State of Israel and establish a purely Palestinian State. We will make life unbearable for Jews by psychological warfare and population explosion. Jews won't want to live among us Arabs. . . . I have no use for Jews; they are and remain Jews! We now need all the help we can get from you in our battle for a united Palestine under total Arab-Muslim domination."[28]

He spoke those words less than three months after the assassination of Prime Minister Rabin and just days before a murderous round of suicide bombings conducted by his Hamas allies, aimed at influencing the Israeli electorate.[29] As Israeli public opinion swung against Oslo, a leading PLO "moderate," Nabil Shaath—a minister in Arafat's government and his main negotiator with Israel—explained the strategy at a symposium aired on PA TV. "We decided to liberate our homeland step by step. Should Israel continue—no problem. And so, we honor the peace treaties and nonviolence. But if and when Israel says, 'That's it, we won't talk about

Jerusalem, we won't return refugees, we won't dismantle settlements, and we won't retreat from borders,' then we will return to violence. But this time it will be with 30,000 armed Palestinian soldiers who will operate in areas in which we have unprecedented elements of freedom."[30]

One year later, a leading Russian newspaper, *Novoye Vremya,* popped the question to Arafat again, asking him if the Palestinians would resume the armed struggle against Israel. "Anything is possible," he replied. Hamas was not a terrorist group, but "one of many patriotic movements," he said. Even its military wing? the reporter asked. "Even its military wing. One should not forget that the movement took an active part in the *intifada.*"[31]

Arafat gave his most explicit description of how he saw the Hudaibiya truce in an interview with Egypt's Orbit television on April 18, 1998.

> When the prophet Mohammad made the Hudaibiya agreement, he agreed to remove his title "messenger of Allah" from the agreement. Then, Omar bin Khattib and the others referred to this agreement as the "inferior peace agreement." Of course, I do not compare myself to the prophet, but I do say that we must learn from his steps and those of Salah al-Din. The peace agreement which we signed is an 'inferior peace.' . . . We respect agreements the way that Prophet Mohammad and Salah al-Din respected the agreements that they signed. . . . All the options are open to the Palestinian people.[32]

In the overheated world of the Middle East, words are important. These statements by Arafat and by other Palestinian leaders clearly demonstrate that none of the historical leadership of the PLO had any intention of accepting the "land for peace" formula of Oslo. For Israel, the "peace of the brave" meant a historic compromise with the Palestinians, recognizing their rights to the land and giving them a state, in exchange for full peace and normalized relations with the Arab world. For Arafat, it was merely a stepping-stone on the road to war and the total destruction of the Jews.

Even Mahmoud Abbas (Abu Mazen), the new, "moderate" Palestinian prime minister who was handpicked by the United States as a counterweight to Arafat, endorses Arafat's view that the Oslo Agreements are merely a stepping-stone that will lead to the replacement of Israel by a Palestinian state. In an interview published on March 4, 2003, in the London-based daily *Al-Sharq al-Awsat,* he condemned suicide bombings but clearly stated that Jews who lived in settlements were appropriate military targets whose murder was justified as part of "the right of resistance."[33] Just three days after that interview appeared, Palestinian gunmen burst into the home of American-born Rabbi Eli Horowitz in Kiryat Arba, just outside the West Bank city of Hebron, murdering him and his wife, Dina, as they sat down to Shabbat dinner on March 7, 2003. Dina's mother, Bernice Wolf, also a U.S. citizen, filed a formal complaint with the Israeli police against Abbas for incitement to murder and on May 1, 2003, hand-delivered a letter to the U.S. Consulate in East Jerusalem, asking the U.S. government to "cut off all ties to Abu Mazen, since Abu Mazen continues to advocate the murder of Jews."[34]

Abbas also espouses the openly anti-Semitic views of the grand mufti of Jerusalem, Sheikh Ikrima Sabri, in denying the existence of a Jewish Temple in Jerusalem. "[The Israelis] demand that we forget what happened 50 years ago to the refugees—and I speak as a living, breathing refugee—while at the same time they claim that 2,000 years ago they had a temple," he told the Israeli-Arab weekly *Kul al-Arab.* "I challenge the claim that this is so. But even if it is so, we do not accept it."[35] On March 30, 2003—less than two weeks after he was named as prime minister—Abbas met with Hamas and Islamic Jihad leaders in Gaza. Hamas spokesman Abdul Aziz Rantisi, who attended the meeting, told *The New York Times* that "the meeting was positive" and that Abbas "made no demands." On the contrary, he even offered Hamas the Education Ministry in his new cabinet, allowing them to reach even more Palestinian children with their doctrine of hate.[36] When an Israeli helicopter fired rockets into Rantissi's car on June 10, 2003, as his son was driving him to meetings in Gaza, Prime Minister Abbas was furious, telling Palestinian Satellite TV that the Israeli strike was a "terrorist attack in the full meaning of the word because it targeted innocent people." Israel's failed assassination against Rantissi came two days after a suicide attack against Israeli soldiers at the Erez crossing in Gaza that killed four Israelis and was jointly claimed by Hamas, Islamic Jihad, and Abass's own Fatah group. Israel claimed that Rantissi had ordered the attack.

✝✝✝

The record of duplicity of Arafat's Palestinian Authority began to emerge in March 2002, after Minister of Public Security Uzi Landau ordered the definitive closure of Orient House, the quasi-official but illegal seat of the PA in Arab East Jerusalem. Israel seized computer disks, hard drives, and file boxes containing nearly half a million documents. From the very first, says Michael Widlanski, who was working for Landau at the time, it was apparent that they had stumbled onto a mother lode of information that revealed the day-to-day management of terror by Arafat and his proxy, cousin, and sometimes rival, Faisal al-Husseini.

Among the captured documents were reports addressed to al-Husseini from a joint "Field Committee" of Palestinian organizations detailing terrorist operations carried out in Jerusalem, along with a budget request to cover operational costs for the coming month. "After al-Husseini initialed this document, he wrote a separate letter to Arafat relaying the request and recommending that he approve the expenditure," Widlanski said.

Other documents, also relayed by al-Husseini to Arafat, showed requests for money to organize the murder of Israelis living in the Bethlehem area. The man asking for the money, Atef Abayat, was well-known to the Israelis as the leader of the Tanzeem in Bethlehem, a militia that was part of Arafat's Fatah oganization. "Atef Abayat and his two brothers were directly involved in the murder of at least five Israelis," said Widlanski. "The Abayat clan was the backbone of the Bethlehem Tanzeem organization. Yet when the Israeli government formally asked Arafat to hand Abayat over, Arafat claimed he didn't know who he was. We found his pay slips, countersigned by Arafat, in Orient House."

Tanzeem commander Marwan Barghouti figures prominently in the captured documents. In a June 5, 1997, letter, Barghouti requested that Arafat grant a formal PA military commission and salary to a Tanzeem agent who worked for Faisal al-Husseini at Orient House. In a separate letter, al-Husseini supported the recommendation, asking that the man receive a high rank and salary. Barghouti's letter was countersigned in Arafat's handwriting, with the following referral: "Yasser Arafat: Majaida, Haj Mutliq, Haj Ismail, do what is needed in regard to this."

These and hundreds of documents like them show that the Tanzeem militia "is an integral part of the PA military," Widlanski said. "Its men operate essentially as a non-uniformed army, contrary to international law." The documents also show that "Yasser Arafat has formal and practical control of the Tanzeem, contrary to analyses that have contended that Tanzeem is independent of Arafat's control. While Fatah Tanzeem militiamen carry the bombs and shoot the guns, Yasser Arafat has been paying the tab."[37]

The Israelis arrested Barghouti in Ramallah on April 15, 2002, making him the highest-ranking Palestinian leader to be taken into custody during Operation Defensive Shield. Two weeks later, the Associated Press reported from Jerusalem, Barghouti confirmed to Israeli interrogators what the Orient House documents had already shown, namely that "Palestinian leader Yasser Arafat personally approved weapons funding for attacks against Israelis."[38]

Once the Israelis went into West Bank towns and refugee camps following the Passover massacre in Netanya, they stumbled on operational files showing in minute detail how Arafat put Al-Aqsa brigade members involved in the murder of Israeli civilians on the payroll of the PA security forces, so they could devote all their time to murder. Many of the documents authorizing payment to these Fatah activists also bear annotations in Arafat's handwriting. List after list of individuals identified by the Israelis as having committed specific acts of terrorism was forwarded to Arafat by Tanzeem leader Marwan Barghouti with the note "I request your decision, in an exceptional manner, to employ and reregister in the security apparatus the following brothers [who are] active honorable members of the movement."[39]

The salaries of the PA security forces are financed by direct monthly grants from the European Union (10 million euros) and the Arab states ($55 million). By putting members of Tanzeem and the Al-Aqsa brigade on the payroll of the security forces, the PA is using money that was supposed to help fight terrorism to actually carry out terrorist acts against Jews. Thus the Oslo process, instead of promoting peace, has enabled the Palestinian Authority to wage war more effectively.

As the suicide bombings became more frequent, Arab nations kicked in enormous amounts of money to encourage them. This was not "development assistance" or aid to build schools and hospitals, but money intended and used to sponsor the murder of Jews. The Saudis contributed payments of $5,000 to the families of suicide bombers. Arafat's PA gave $2,000, and the governments of the United Arab Emirates and Qatar kicked in $500 each. But the lion's share of the blood money came from the government of Saddam Hussein, which awarded a "bonus" of $25,000 to the families of suicide bombers who carried out "quality operations," a euphemism for a suicide attack that killed Jews. In the hierarchy of mayhem, families of less successful murderers were rewarded with checks from Baghdad for $15,000, $10,000, or $5,000, depending on the number of victims and whether the perpetrator died inadvertently or by intentional suicide during the attack. The higher payments were clearly intended to encourage suicide attacks, the captured documents show.[40] With Saddam's fall in April 2003, one major state sponsor of terror vanished from the world scene.

For Minister of Public Security Uzi Landau, the documents captured at Orient House and during Operation Defensive Shield provided confirmation of what Israel had known all along. "Well before this, in our debates within the government, it was quite clear that Arafat was the man behind it," he told me. Landau recalled a briefing from 1995, when military intelligence chief Major General Moshe Ya'alon (who went on to become Israeli chief of staff) came before the Knesset Defense and Foreign Affairs Committee. "He told us there is no difference between the strategic objectives of Arafat and [those of] the extreme Hamas and Islamic Jihad. They only differ in the means they adopt. In fact, [Ya'alon said] Arafat is using the Hamas extremists as a strategic weapon of the Palestinian Authority, to stage attacks as if he is not involved. So we've known this for years, but it's been ignored by politicians who did not want to be bothered by facts, because it would ruin their concept." The captured documents, Landau said, provided "inside information and detailed correspondence that show exactly how their strategy for destroying Israel was translated into day-to-day activities. But for me, there was no surprise whatsoever."[41]

††††

The official anti-Semitic myths, stereotypes, and lies of Arafat's Palestinian Authority are not just propaganda: they are deadly. Their immediate purpose is to dehumanize Jews, by painting them as inherently evil and the enemies of Allah, to justify the murder of Jews as the will of God. In so doing, they consistently paint America as a willing accomplice of the Jews and thus as a legitimate target of the soldiers of Allah.

When hatred is taught to the young and spread to unwitting populations through every public media, including the mosques, it breeds an evil that goes way beyond today's political goals. That is precisely why the Oslo Accords specifically committed Israel and the Palestinian Authority to ban hate speech from the airwaves and to eradicate it from the larger society. Instead, Arafat has made hate speech the preferred language of his government. For this reason alone, his Palestinian Authority deserves to be disbanded. He and the PA have proved beyond a shadow of a doubt that they are unsuited for peace.

Uzi Landau believes a Palestinian state would be a "destabilizing element" for the entire region. "Palestinians can of course have self-rule and self-government and generous autonomy, but not a state with those elements of sovereignty such as an independent army or the right to have agreements with other countries. Suppose they signed a security agreement with Iran that says if one of the parties is attacked, the other will come to its rescue. We could see an Iranian flotilla off the coast of Gaza and thousands of troops coming on shore. What shall we do then? Contact a future Palestinian Authority and say, Hey, you're not allowed to do that under the agreement? What will a future Arafat do? Say, Oh, I'm really sorry, I will remove them?

"If you have a port in Gaza which they can run freely, they would be able to bring in almost anything. Without a port, they brought in Katyushas and SAMs on the *Karine A*. With a port they could smuggle in extended-range missiles that would be capable of covering all of Israel. We would not be able to take off and land from Ben Gurion Airport. Our air force bases would be within their range. What country can accept that? What kind of stable Middle East does anybody think they're going to gain if they allow an independent Palestinian state?"

Yet that is precisely what the European Union and the U.S. government continue to advise. "I hope that our friends in the West will not be seduced by ideas that might be good for central Europe or North America, but would be disastrous here, where our neighbors are very different. If we were to have Swiss people or Canadians as our neighbors, I can assure you we would have had peace a long time ago."[42]

† † †

Peace is made not between friends, but between enemies. Rare are the examples in the history of the world when peace has come through treaty alone, imposed by outside powers, or agreed upon by mutual accord. War without a victor and a vanquished is still war, as the twelve years of hostilities that followed the first Gulf War in 1991 show. The type of lasting peace America has known with Germany and Japan since the end of World War II, and arguably with Russia since the end of the Cold War, comes when one side wins so decisively that it can dictate the terms of the peace and treat the vanquished with generosity. Yet every time Israel has defeated Arab armies on the battlefield, Europe and America have rushed in to guarantee that the Arabs will rise to fight again. It is time to reconsider such policies.

Many academics and pundits continue to promote a "two state" solution, where an Arab and a Jewish state would live side by side in peace. Others dream of a unified, democratic, secular state of Palestine in which Jews, Muslims, and Christians would live with equal rights. This was a vision promoted by Soviet foreign minister Andrey Gromyko during the Cold War and picked up by well-oiled Palestinian spinmeisters in Beirut, who understood exactly what the Euro-Left wanted to hear.

But do these visions coincide with what the Arab side really wants? The original PLO Charter—which has never been abrogated, despite Arafat's pledge to do so in September 1993—calls for the destruction of Israel. Arafat's handpicked clerics and his official media continue to speak of Israel itself as occupied Arab land, not a peace partner. Hamas leaders, in perfect tune with this thinking, admonish Jews to "return" to Europe or to set up a Jewish homeland in America, while Palestinian schoolchildren are being taught to hate Jews and to prepare for another generation of war. Muslim clerics and political leaders continue to believe, and the West encourages them in this belief, that they can reverse the defeat of 1948 and turn back the clock to a world before Israel came into existence.

Every time Israeli troops enter an Arab town or refugee camp, the Arab side accuses Israel of seeking a new "Holocaust." They claim that Israel seeks to build an empire stretching from the Nile in Egypt to the Euphrates in Iraq. In dozens of interviews, Arafat has claimed that a map of this Israeli empire hangs over the entry to the Knesset in Jerusalem.[43] Sorry. No such map exists, nor has any Israeli leader ever seriously proposed conquering or annexing Arab lands beyond Israel's 1967 borders.

Not even the Jewish extremist group Kahane Chai can equal the Arab vision of a Middle East that is *Judenrein,* free of Jews. They dream of a Jewish homeland that is free of Arabs, not the conquest of the Arab world and the slaughter of its inhabitants. While alive, Rabbi Meir Kahane called for the forced but peaceful "transfer" of populations from within Israel's pre-1967 borders to achieve ethnic homogeneity. Even in this most radical Jewish vision, there is no room for massacres or Serbian-style ethnic cleansing. Population transfer, while abhorrent to most observers, is not murder. It has been carried out repeatedly by Arab regimes, who have expelled their Jewish populations since 1948 without a word of protest from the United Nations or the world community. So accepted were these forced transfers by the professional Arabists at the U.S. Department of State that until now no U.S.-backed peace proposal has ever broached the subject of material compensation for these Jewish refugees and their descendants.

As suicide bombings intensified, a poll by the Jaffee Center for Strategic Studies at Tel Aviv University in June 2002 found a dramatic upsurge of support for transfer, with 46 percent of those polled supporting it.[44] But population transfer is not the policy of the state of Israel and has long been rejected by all Israel's mainstream parties, including Likud.[45] Most analysts believed the poll results showed fear and confusion more than anything else. "To some extent, this is Israel's wet dream," says professor Efraim Inbar, director of the Begin-Sadat Center for Strategic Studies at Bar-Ilan University. "Many people may say they like the idea of transfer. But deep down, they know it is nothing more than wishful thinking. It is just a fantasy that they might wake up one day and find all the Palestinians gone."[46]

If anything, Israelis tend to lack a vision of "victory." Their equivalent of the PNC Charter—the Basel Declaration of 1897—sought the creation of a Jewish state "secured by public law," not by war. Optimists such as Shimon Peres once believed that by offering economic and technological benefits to its neighbors, Israel could entice them to abandon war. With the beginning of the second *intifada* in September 2000, those hopes faded. More likely, visions of an Israeli victory would resemble what we have seen over the past fifty years: Jewish sovereignty over borders defined by Israel as defensible, with full citizenship offered to Arabs who chose to live peacefully within them. Such a "victory" would amount to a cold, armed peace between Israel and her Arab neighbors, which in the eyes of most Israelis will include a Palestinian state in parts of the West Bank and Gaza. It is a vision that projects constant vigilance, hopefully an end to violence, but not exultation.

Between those two visions of victory—the Arab and the Israeli— where is the risk of a new "Holocaust"? Under whose rule would the vanquished have the most rights—starting with the most basic, the right to life?

Today's Arab leaders are teaching their children that peace can come only when no more Jews remain in the region and when U.S. and Western influence has been stamped out. They are teaching this in the schools, in the mosques, and over the airwaves. Should they prove victorious, given today's advanced weaponry, the sixty million dead of World War II could appear as a footnote to the horrors to come.

THE "NEW" ANTI-SEMITISM IN EUROPE 9

Since 1964, the Anti-Defamation League (ADL) has conducted annual polls in the United States to measure anti-Semitic beliefs and prejudices. In the wake of anti-Semitic violence not seen since World War II, the ADL began conducting similar polls in Europe. The results showed disturbing trends. Asked about the causes of the recent violence against Jews, 62 percent answered that they believed it was the result of anti-Israel sentiment and not traditional anti-Jewish feelings. Yet 30 percent of those polled agreed with six of eleven anti-Semitic statements. "These findings are especially disturbing because they show that the old, classical form of anti-Semitism has been joined by a new form fueled by anti-Israel sentiment, creating a potent and dangerous mix," said Abraham F. Foxman, ADL national director. "The resiliency of anti-Semitism, coupled with the emergence of strong anti-Israel sentiment in European countries with enormous Muslim/Arab populations, demands our serious and immediate attention."

Among the findings of a June 2002 poll were these:

- 30 percent harbor traditional anti-Semitic stereotypes.
- 45 percent believe Jews are more loyal to Israel than their own country.
- 30 percent believe that Jews have too much power in the business world.
- 19 percent say Jews don't care about anyone but their own kind.
- 16 percent say Jews are more willing than others to use shady practices to get what they want.
- 39 percent of Europeans believe Jews still talk too much about the Holocaust.

"These beliefs, such as the charge that Jews are more loyal to Israel than to their home country, help to fuel and legitimize anti-Semitic violence," Foxman said. "It is disingenuous to blame the anti-Jewish violence in Europe simply on a popular reaction to Israel's policies, when it is apparent that the violence is directly targeting Jews. That is anti-Semitism. Yet many European leaders continue to shrug off the violence as an episode in the Mideast conflict, and not as a reflection of a serious problem closer to home."[1] This initial survey of 2,500—500 each in Belgium, Denmark, France, Germany, and the United Kingdom—was conducted by telephone in the native language of each of the countries from May 16 to June 4, 2002, by First International Resources for ADL.

A follow-on poll of 2,500 individuals conducted in September surveyed opinion in five additional countries: Austria, Italy, the Netherlands, Spain, and Switzerland. In these countries, 21 percent of respondents harbored anti-Semitic views, while 56 percent believed that Jews were more loyal to Israel than to their own country. Spain, with 12,000 Jews out of a population of 39.6 million, had the highest percentage of anti-Semitic views of the countries polled, with 34 percent holding "strong anti-Semitic views."

While a majority believed their governments were doing enough to ensure the safety and security of Jewish citizens, 30 percent of Italian and Spanish respondents felt otherwise, the highest percentage of any of the countries surveyed. "It is encouraging that such a large majority feel concerned about violence against Jews. That is the good news," said Foxman. "The bad news is that not enough people of goodwill have been willing to stand up to reject anti-Semitism. It is especially disturbing that only sixty years after the Holocaust, Europe's leaders and citizenry are being diffident when confronted with anti-Semitism."[2]

✝✝✝

Today, for the first time since the Holocaust, Jews in Europe are afraid. The cries of "Never again" that once had been Europe's pride are being drowned out by angry crowds chanting, "Death to the Jews!" All across Europe, it again has become acceptable—in some cases even fashionable—to express the ancestral hatred of Jews that was common during the Third Reich. Anti-Semitism has come back to the lands where it was first created like a virus that has mutated, adapting to survive.

Newspapers in Italy, Greece, and Norway run explicit anti-Semitic cartoons, depicting Ariel Sharon as the killer of Christ and Israeli soldiers as Nazi murderers. In Belgium, the mayor of Antwerp advises Jews to stay home and lock their doors on the Sabbath, because the authorities can no longer protect them from angry mobs.[3] In France, anti-Semitism has become so widespread that it illicits shrugs. "We have the right to be anti-Jew, don't we?" a high school sophomore complains when reprimanded by a teacher for remarks he had made in class.[4]

Violent attacks against Jews and Jewish institutions have occurred since September 2000 in France, Britain, Belgium, Italy, Greece, Finland, and Germany, for the first time in more than a generation. At the same time, the taboos prohibiting hate speech have disappeared, making it legitimate for the first time since the Nazi era to openly discuss alleged Jewish conspiracies to dominate the world. Germany knows more about the evils of anti-Semitism than any other nation on earth. Yet Rudolph Scharping, until July 2002 the defense minister in the government of Prime Minister Gerhard Schroeder, dragged out that ancient canard in a policy talk to American scholars in Hamburg on August 27, 2003, claiming that "the Jews" were driving President George W. Bush to launch "a massive American attack on Baghdad" in exchange for Jewish votes in the upcoming election.[5] On the extreme Right, Holocaust denial has become brazen and commonplace. Among Europe's limousine liberals, it has become fashionable to talk of Israel as a "criminal" state, responsible for all Middle East violence, that should be punished by the international community, if not simply eradicated. In countries where the media and political elites should know better, they have engaged in hate speech directed outwardly toward Israel but ultimately toward Jews. "Look at their language," a senior Israeli diplomat told me in Washington. "They accuse the Israeli army of behaving as Nazis. They demonize Sharon and call him a dictator, although he was popularly elected and now has 60 percent approval ratings. They show him dressed as Hitler, and call him 'Adolf Sharon.' Clearly it is easier to carry the burden of the Holocaust by saying that your former victims are now victimizers in their own right."[6] Conservative French deputy Pierre Lellouche agrees. "I think we are seeing anti-Semitism on a daily basis, amplified by a deformed image of Israel in the press . . . [that has] imposed a form of collective guilt on the Jewish community in France." Day after day, Lellouche notes, the major French dailies Le Monde and Libération spew anti-Israeli hate. "The rejection of the legitimacy of the state of Israel has become the mask most frequently used to hide a virulent anti-Semitism," he says.[7]

The anti-Israel climate in Europe goes way beyond a simple disagreement over Israeli government policies. Speaking to a prominent British columnist at a dinner party in December 2001, the French ambassador to Britain, Daniel Bernard, calmly referred to Israel as "that shitty little country" responsible for all the tensions between the Muslim world and the West. "Why," he asked, "should the world be in danger of World War Three because of those people?" When his comments appeared in print, he suggested tepidly that he had been misquoted. He was never reprimanded by the French Foreign Ministry, but the reporter who revealed his comments—Barbara Amiel, the wife of media magnate Conrad Black—was hounded by fellow columnists in Britain, France, and Germany for her "gaffe."[8] Ambassador Bernard's comments were enthusiastically reprised by one London columnist, who opined, "Anti-Semitism is disliking all Jews, anywhere, and anti-Zionism is just disliking the existence of Israel and opposing those who support it. This may be an academic rather than a practical distinction, and one which has no connection with holding the honest view that in my experience Israel is shitty and little."[9] A member of the House of Lords, quoted by Petronella Wyatt in London's *Spectator* magazine, was relieved to find that a new environment had replaced the old taboos since September 11. "Well, the Jews have been asking for it and now, thank God, we can say what we think at last." Anti-Semitism "has become respectable once more . . . at London dinner tables," she concluded.[10]

There is a general tendency in the European media and in government to dismiss the outcry generated by the new wave of anti-Semitic attacks, claiming that critics of Europe's failure to crack down on hate crimes confuse anti-Zionism with anti-Semitism. But the two are often confounded in the media and by Europe's leaders. "Criticizing specific Israeli policies is, of course, legitimate; self-criticism is an Israeli national pastime," writes Israeli journalist Yossi Klein Halevi. "But . . . when the very existence of a Jewish state becomes immoral and the only form of nationalism considered racist is Zionism—then the line is crossed from legitimate criticism to demonization. And the ground is prepared for murder."[11]

Official Europe views Israel as unnecessary, at best. When the Israeli army goes into Palestinian towns to hunt down terrorists who have orchestrated suicide attacks against civilians, headlines across Europe scream of "genocide" but fail to condemn Palestinian terrorism. Cherie Blair, wife of the British prime minister, gushes to journalists about how she "understands" the motives of Palestinian suicide bombers. In Holland, Greta Duisenberg, the wife of the European Central Bank chairman, Wim Duisenberg, hangs a Palestinian flag from her balcony in Amsterdam and blames "rich American Jews" for the woes of Palestinians. Within days, twenty thousand Palestinian flags were seen hanging from balconies in several Dutch cities in solidarity.[12] At the United Nations conference on racism in Durban, Belgian foreign minister Louis Michel, speaking on behalf of the European Union, argues in favor of deleting specific proposals to combat anti-Semitism and Holocaust denial. In March 2002, upon the EU's recommendation, the UN General Assembly deletes "anti-Semitism" as a specific concern of the United Nations.[13] The net effect of this attitude among Europe's cultural and political elite, says Swedish author and commentator Per Ahlmark, has been to promote anti-Semitism to the realm of legitimate discourse. "Anti-Semitism is a non-Jewish disease that kills Jews," he says. "But it's our disease, so we have a responsibility to fight it."[14]

Nowhere has the violence been more intense and the complacency of the government more visible than in France, home to the largest Jewish community in Europe after the Holocaust.

In a moving speech commemorating the sixtieth anniversary of the infamous roundup of French Jews in 1942, French premier Jean-Pierre Raffarin spoke hard truths to his fellow Frenchmen. For two generations, the French have cloaked themselves in the memory of a Resistance movement against the Nazi occupation that was neither widespread nor terribly glorious. Now, said Raffarin, it was time for the French to own up to the truth and make amends.

"The French state, in organizing these systematic roundups, plunged into collaboration and betrayed the founding principles of our nation," Raffarin said.[15] He spoke at a July 21, 2002, ceremony at the Square of the Martyrs, a Paris memorial built where a bicycle stadium–turned–transit camp once stood.

Citing names that live on in infamy as centers for the deportation, Raffarin went on: "Yes, the Vel' d'Hiv, Drancy, Compiègne, and all the transit camps, these antechambers of death, were organized, managed, and protected by Frenchmen. Yes, the first act of the Shoah played itself out here, with the complicity of the French state. . . . Seventy-six thousand Jews were deported from France. So few ever came back."

On the night of July 16–17, 1942, 13,152 Jews were rounded up and taken to the Paris bicycle stadium, the Velodrome d'Hiver, or Vel' d'Hiv, and subsequently deported to Nazi death camps. Yet even today defensive French officials insist that the French government protected French Jews during the occupation. "There were only [sic] seventy-six thousand Jews deported from France, because the French government, even under Vichy, made an effort to save the essential part of the French population," a senior official told me.[16] Only 2,500 of the 76,000 Jews deported from France survived.

Raffarin saluted the memory of the Free French, who heeded the call of General Charles de Gaulle from his exile in Britain to rise up against the German occupant and the French collaborationist government in Vichy. But he also spoke out forcefully and unequivocally against the rage of anti-Semitic attacks that had ravaged French synagogues and Jewish cemeteries and struck fear in the hearts of French Jews for the first time in sixty years. "Attacking the Jewish community is to attack France, to attack the values of our republic, where there is no room for anti-Semitism, racism, or xenophobia," he said. He pledged that his government, which came to power in the wake of the presidential and parliamentary elections in spring 2002, would "take all necessary measures" against the perpetrators of "these acts that insult our country."

The previous French government had been sharply criticized by intellectuals and Jewish organizations for failing to take action against the most extensive and sustained wave of anti-Semitic attacks in Europe since the Holocaust. During the last three months of 2000 alone, physical violence against Jews included forty-four fire bombings, forty-three attacks on synagogues, and thirty-nine assaults on Jews as they were leaving places of worship. Over an eighteen-month period, the Representative Council of French Jewry (CRIF) cataloged more than one thousand anti-Semitic acts. It was an unprecedented outbreak of Jew-hatred in a country that prided itself on having purged the anti-Semitic virus for good. "History has shown that, against the Jews, anything is possible," wrote the authors of a "white book" on the racist violence. "Antisemitism is not an opinion like any other: it is an opinion that kills."[17] Yet in over eighteen months, the French police made just a few dozen arrests. The French Interior Ministry concluded that the violence was the work of "petty criminals," not anti-Semites.

Until late April 2002, the government was headed by Socialist premier Lionel Jospin, who was humiliated during the first round of presidential elections when he was edged out by neo-fascist candidate Jean-Marie Le Pen. The specter of a respectable showing by Le Pen so terrified the French establishment that every political party, newspaper, and community organization rallied behind President Jacques Chirac in the runoff against Le Pen. Huge rallies organized against Le Pen brought together representatives of Muslim and Jewish organizations, Communists, and free-market conservatives, and Chirac was reelected with more than 80 percent of the vote. With his political opponents in disarray, Chirac also won an overwhelming majority in the snap parliamentary elections that followed.

Chirac's new interior minister, Nicolas Sarkozy, donned a bulletproof vest immediately after he was appointed and visited violence-prone housing projects in the predominantly Muslim suburbs of Paris. These were areas that the French police previously had feared to enter. He warned French Muslim leaders that fresh violence would be met firmly and that police intelligence units (known as the Renseignements Généraux) would keep close tabs on local mosques, to ensure they stopped preaching hatred and violence against Jews. He and his subordinates met repeatedly with French and American Jewish leaders and pledged to prosecute the perpetrators of anti-Semitic attacks.

"Yes, we have a problem with anti-Semitic attacks against the Jewish community," Sarkozy told Shimon Samuels and Rabbi Abraham Cooper of the Simon Wiesenthal Center. "When a synagogue is firebombed on Yom Kippur, it is absurd to claim that it does not constitute a hate crime because the attackers failed to spray-paint the words *Death to the Jews* on the temple walls."[18]

Despite these very positive steps, President Chirac undercut his own government just two weeks later during a July 29 meeting in Paris with Israeli prime minister Shimon Peres. He called criticism of France's belated reaction to anti-Semitic attacks "an insult" and accused Israel of organizing a worldwide anti-French campaign through the intermediary of American Jewish organizations. Jack Rosen, president of the American Jewish Congress, fired back. "Chirac's very accusation—that Jerusalem directed orders to American Jews—is reminiscent of ancient anti-Semitic stereotypes of worldwide Jewish conspiracies," he said. "I'm surprised that Chirac was so callous in protesting France's lack of anti-Semitism that he invoked that classic anti-Semitic canard."[19]

†††

The wave of anti-Jewish attacks in France began in late September 2000, almost simultaneous to the renewed violence in the Middle East, and quickly turned ugly. In the Paris suburb of Aubervilliers, a car drove full speed into a crowd of Jews leaving the synagogue after a prayer service on

October 1. Molotov cocktails were thrown against Jewish schools and synagogues. Rabbis and Jews wearing distinctive clothing were assaulted with clubs in the streets. Vandals spray-painted "Death to the Jews" across synagogue walls in Marseilles. On October 7, worshipers were pelted with stones as they left prayer services in Lyon and other cities. On October 10, at the end of Yom Kippur, two synagogues were attacked in Paris, while two others in suburban towns were firebombed and totally destroyed.[20]

The mounting tension exploded in Trappes, a distant suburb of Paris controlled by the Communist Party. As the Left gabbed about creating a "multicultural" society in France, ethic groups that refused to tolerate one another came to blows in Trappes, turning the housing projects that fed the surrounding factories into centers of ethnic tension.

Trappes is where the French melting pot fell off the stove before its new citizens were willing to cast off their old identities and prejudices. Eighty different ethnic groups live in town, according to French census figures, but the largest among them are North African Muslims, who account for one-third of the population. Bitter memories of the French colonial war in Algeria have left deep scars in the older generation that have turned to hate in their young, born in France but never accepted and never really wanting to belong. In their midst live a handful of Jews—just ten families in all.

Michel Mimouni, sixty-five, shared many of their memories of French Algeria. But in his modest living room after the Shabbat meal, he also recalls the night his parents bundled him and his younger brother into a dark car sixty years ago, to cross the border separating Nazi-occupied France from the liberated zone in southern France. His father, a French Jew born in Algeria, was on leave from the army. The night before they fled Paris, someone had slipped a note under the door of their apartment, warning them to leave immediately because the Nazis were planning to round up Jews. "The smuggler told us to hush, and I still remember the deathly quiet in the car as we approached the crossing point at Monceau-les-Mines. We could hear the watchdogs of the German border patrol and knew they had captured many people who had crossed illegally, just as we were doing."[21]

By chance, we meet on the sixtieth anniversary of his departure, a date that has burned into his memory, for they escaped just three days before the French police herded Jews into the Vel d'Hiv. "Not everybody was as lucky as we were," Mimouni says. "My mother's parents were deported from Drancy, and she never got over it. After we fled to Marseilles and to Algeria, she began to have heart problems. She died a few years later, at the age of thirty-two. Another friend lost twenty-seven members of his family. The French like to say that they protected the French Jews, that only foreign Jews got deported. But that wasn't always true. And the roundups never could have happened without the collaboration of the French authorities and the French police who carried them out."

Mimouni returned to France in 1961 with the first wave of Jews expelled from Algeria, a refugee for the second time at the age of twenty-four. He has been going to the discreet little synagogue in Trappes ever since. Located in a small house owned by the local housing authority, the synagogue bore no distinctive signs; indeed, the only inscription visible from the street identified the superintendent's office, which occupied the other half of the house, where the predominantly Muslim residents of the housing project came once a month to pay their rent.

Tensions were already running high as they approached the Yom Kippur holidays, with screaming headlines and television reports that systematically portrayed Israeli soldiers as war criminals and bloodthirsty child murderers. Just a few days earlier, one of the most infamous scenes of the Palestinian uprising occurred: the shooting death, captured live by a Palestinian camera crew working for French television, of a young Palestinian boy named Mohammad al-Dura. "The French media was whipping up a frenzy against Jews," Mimouni recalls. "They told all kinds of horror stories, so that people wanted to go out and kill the first Jew they saw."

On Sunday morning, October 8, the small Jewish section of the local cemetery was vandalized. "Everything was ripped apart," Mimouni says. "Because of the tension and media barrage against Israel, we were afraid. We'd been asking the police for protection for ten days." After Yom Kippur services on Monday, Muslims from the housing project stood around in groups, hurling insults at the Jews as they left the synagogue.

On Tuesday, Mimouni went to the local police commissioner, asking him what he planned to do to protect the small Jewish community. Reassured by his pledge to give them police protection during services,

Mimouni made the hour's drive up to Paris to take part in a pro-Israel demonstration in front of the Israeli embassy early that evening.

"We got back late and I went immediately to bed. At eleven P.M. I was awakened by a phone call from the police. 'Monsieur, your synagogue is burning,' they said. I couldn't believe it. Outside, it was raining cats and dogs. I jumped into my car, and must have run every red light between my home and the synagogue three kilometers away. When I got there the synagogue was burning like a heap of straw and I burst into tears. Not even during the Nazi occupation were synagogues attacked in France. The last time a synagogue was burned was in the Middle Ages!"

The next morning, the local paper carried a front-page picture of a fire at a six-story building in nearby Elancourt.[22] No one was hurt in the blaze; the site had no special significance; yet the media dispatched photographers to capture the event. But no newsmen came to Trappes to witness the first burning of a synagogue in France since the Middle Ages; and neither Mimouni nor the police thought to bring a camera to capture the crime as it occurred. The only pictures of the burned synagogue were taken the next day after the fire was out, showing the skeletal roof and the charred windows.

Local officials in Trappes had no doubt as to the criminal origin of the fire or the desecration of Jewish graves that had preceded it. The police found the remains of two petrol bombs inside the ruined building, one of which hadn't gone off. An eyewitness identified six Muslim youths who had left the synagogue just as the fire began, and within days they were behind bars. Deputy Mayor Karim Chacal denounced the attacks in a statement to local newsmen. "When you don't respect the dead, you don't respect the living. When you destroy a place of worship, you threaten all believers." The Communist mayor immediately offered the Jewish community free of charge a new locale for their synagogue, which Mimouni accepted. From as far away as Malibu, California, retired actor Jerry Daniels heard about the attacks and sent two sizable checks to help rebuild the synagogue.

A few months later, the state prosecutor dropped charges against the six Muslim youths, citing a lack of evidence. Michel Mimouni was accosted by a young Arab man on the street. "You Jews," he shouted, "we'll get you." He went up to the bearded Mimouni, cocking his fingers like a gun. "We'll get you—bang!—with a bullet in the back."

And so it went for eighteen months. The small synagogue in Trappes was merely one of the first. That week alone, fifteen more synagogues burned across France. Jewish schools were attacked, school buses packed with small children were firebombed, and Jews were beaten with baseball bats in the streets. In the southern suburb of Les Ulis, I saw where the attackers had been so brazen that they hurled Molotov cocktails into the synagogue despite the fact it was located just fifty meters from the police station. The resulting fire destroyed the entire upper floor of the building. The attacks continued all through 2001, with little or no intervention from the police. Nationwide, forty-seven suspects were arrested in 2000 and another thirty-five in 2001, few of whom were ever prosecuted. A sizable portion of those arrested were classified as "ultra-Zionists," accused of attacking Arabs.[23]

In Garges-les-Gonesses, in the northern suburbs of Paris, the Orthodox Ben Yaakov synagogue was attacked repeatedly. When it was built in the 1960s, few Arabs lived in the neighborhood. When I visited in July 2002, hostile Muslim youths were living on all sides.

The first violent attack occurred on October 13, 2000, when someone threw a fire bomb at the synagogue, says community president Alain Ben-Simon. Two months later, on December 22, two Arabs rammed their car into a school bus full of Jewish children. One of them jumped inside, threatening to kill the driver and the children with guns. As they fled the scene, they fired into the windshield, shattering it completely and wounding one of the schoolgirls with flying glass. The bus driver reported the attack to the police, but they wouldn't allow him to file a complaint, claiming that it had only involved a "broken windshield."

The complacency of the authorities only encouraged the attackers. More fire bombs were thrown at the synagogue in January 2001, and in March 2002 unknown assailants set fire to the congregation's two school buses, destroying them entirely "They came back and finished the job," says Ben-Simon.

Until April 2002, when the French government finally delivered on its promise to park antiriot squad vehicles and troops on the street during Shabbat ceremonies, congregants and schoolchildren were regularly pelted with bottles and other objects thrown by Arabs from apartments over-looking the synagogue. "Things have gotten better recently," says Ben-Simon, pointing to the four-foot-high green metal panels freshly installed on top of an existing four-foot-high wall. "We put up the new wall, and installed surveillance cameras." But the police have been withdrawn—"for lack of resources," a local police officer tells me when I stop by the police station.

Jews in Garges-les-Gonesses retain bitter memories of French president Jacques Chirac, who never visited them—or, for that matter, any synagogue that was attacked—during the initial eighteen-month wave of anti-Semitic violence. "But he did come here to open his election campaign" in the spring of 2002, recalls Shalom Temim, a Tunisian Jew who came to France in the 1960s at the age of twenty. "Chirac brought the television cameras, right here, just one hundred meters from the synagogue, to get his picture taken with a young Arab wearing a keffiyeh. He never invited the president of our community, or the rabbi, or anyone. The only time he officially met with leaders of the Jewish community was in Le Havre a few weeks later in a synagogue that is used three times per year."

As we chat out on the quiet sidewalk by the synagogue after Shabbat services, a car pulls up alongside us and stops. The driver leans on his horn for nearly thirty seconds. No one turns his head. The driver inches forward and honks repeatedly; still the Jews say nothing. The driver eventually passes by us, stops, honks again, and calls in Arabic toward a nearby building. Five minutes later, another car comes by and repeats the same maneuver. It is just an ordinary Shabbat in the mixed neighborhoods of the Paris suburbs for the embattled Jews of France.

††††

Writing in *Le Monde* in January 2002, University of Paris French literature professor Eric Marty suggested that the Jews of Paris had once again become *dhimmis,* the protected second-class citizens of traditional Islam. "They are subjects whose presence is tolerated but who, whenever the need arises, can be mistreated without hesitation, perpetual hostages of the political necessities of the moment," he wrote. The French political and media elites bore a direct responsibility for the violence against Jews, he argued, because of "the perception that, even if not authorized, there has been a certain indulgence or understanding." The authorities had failed to arrest the perpetrators, while the media "scarcely ever mentions these incidents, or by all sorts of euphemisms minimizes them." Even worse, Marty wrote, "Not a single voice, from any center of authority, has been raised to say 'no,' to say that on French soil, it is out of the question that someone will lay hands on a Jew because he is a Jew. . . ." Marty's conclusion was devastating: "Every Jewish building in Paris requires protection, every Jewish festival is an occasion for concern and anguish, anyone walking in Paris or its suburbs wearing a *kippah* is imprudent and any child leaving school may be beaten because he is Jewish, only because he is a Jew."[24]

†††

"We are living through a new and deeply dangerous period of anti-Semitism, of increasingly violent commando operations carried out against Jews and Jewish interests," said the president of the Jewish community in Lyon, Alain Jakubowicz, after the firebombing of a synagogue in Lyon. "If anyone wanted a demonstration of the reality and the gravity of what the Jews of France live through, they have it now."

When the French government still did nothing, the Simon Wiesenthal Center in Los Angeles issued a "travel advisory" warning American Jews against traveling to France. The American Jewish Congress urged U.S. filmmakers and distributors to boycott the Cannes Film Festival. The American Jewish Committee ran a chilling ad that featured a photograph of the charred ruins of the Marseilles synagogue, superimposed on a memorial bearing a chiseled list of the attacks for the single month of April 2002. Above it appeared just two words: "Short Memory." President Chirac, in the middle of what appeared to be a difficult reelection campaign, furiously protested that France was not anti-Semitic.

"President Chirac was upset," said American Jewish Congress president Jack Rosen, describing the pleas his organization and other U.S. Jewish groups had made to the French government. "He and others in the French government realized that the public scrutiny exposed them and that they needed to react."[25]

For nearly eighteen months, the French government had simply looked the other way, pretending nothing was happening. If there was violence, it wasn't serious; if it was serious, it wasn't anti-Semitism, just Arab youths upset over Israel's treatment of Palestinians. Yet several surveys showed that few young North Africans in France cared about the Arab-Israeli fighting or knew much about it.[26] All they knew was that they were attacking Jews and the French government didn't seem to care. "There are those who commit these acts," a senior Israeli diplomat suggested, "and those who permit them."[27] The atmosphere of tolerance only encouraged them to more violence.

The tolerance at the top was exacerbated by the constant coverage in the French and European media that portrayed Israel as the source of all evil. "When young North African Muslims see TV reporting that glorifies suicide bombers, it incites them to action, to become avengers," said Moïse Cohen, president of the Paris Jewish Council.[28]

Ambassador Rene Roudaut, a French diplomat who volunteered to troubleshoot the tensions between the government and religious communities, defends France from being the sole locus of anti-Semitic attacks. "The same thing is happening on campuses across America," he reminded me. If there was an impression that the French government was minimizing the attacks, it "was not intentional, but due to a difference of appreciation" between the government and Jewish organizations over what constituted an anti-Semitic attack. But he acknowledged that the previous government had waited too long to crack down. "The government was simply unaware of the problem, and unconscious of the causes. And it ignored the Jewish community." Changes came after foreign Jewish organizations buttressed complaints from French community leaders in meeting after meeting with French officials, including Roudaut. In the spring of 2002, the French government got the message and agreed to deploy 1,200 antiriot police to protect Jewish institutions.

"The police have new instructions from the Ministry of the Interior to go after these crimes," he said. "The courts have instructions from the Ministry of Justice to prosecute them. New orders have been transmitted to the police to follow up and investigate." A detailed compilation of these cases, made available by French officials, showed 105 arrests in 41 separate prosecutions between March 30 and July 2, 2002. In most cases, those found guilty of anti-Semitic violence received suspended prison sentences, were granted probation, or were simply let go. Nevetheless, once word got out that the French authorities intended to haul the perpetrators into court, the violence fell off dramatically.

But why had it occurred in the first place? One reason, Roudaut acknowledged, was "media coverage of the Middle East conflict that glorifies violence and arouses anti-Israeli feelings." But even more was a new form of anti-Semitism now fashionable on the Left, one that masquerades as a political argument. "What's new is anti-Semitism that attacks not the Jew, but the state of Israel, and in attacking Israel, then attacks the Jew."

Mimouni's wife, Adjedj, saw the effects of this latest form of anti-Semitism up close. She worked at an office of the French Census Bureau (INSE) near Trappes. After the synagogue burning, she says she was harassed by co-workers, including her immediate supervisor, who made derogatory comments about Israelis and Jews. "For six straight weeks this went on. My supervisor told me at one point, 'What we ought to do is simply wipe Israel from the map.' " When she heard that comment, Mrs. Mimouni says, she burst into tears and called her husband to come pick her up. The date was November 28, 2000—just six weeks after the synagogue burned. "I told my supervisor she wouldn't see me again until I retired. I felt physically threatened."

Roger Cukierman, president of the Representative Council of French Jewry, believes a dangerous cocktail of ancient and more modern forces was at work. "We have the traditional anti-Semitism of the extreme Right, and now a mix of antiglobalization, anti-American, and anti-Zionist elements on the extreme Left that have become openly anti-Semitic," he said.[29] "Added to these is a third element, the pro-Palestinians who are members of the Muslim community."

Retired French general Michel Darmon heads the France-Israel Association. Part of the blame belongs with Socialist officials such as former foreign minister Hubert Vedrine, he believes. "The French Foreign Ministry is not just anti-Israel, but anti-Semitic. The Quai d'Orsay has become the center of official anti-Semitism within the French bureaucracy, taking on the role formerly played by the Army General Staff during the Dreyfus affair one hundred years ago." Left-wing Christians have jumped on the anti-Israel bandwagon, encouraged by Vatican officials who find the very idea of a Jewish state "simply unacceptable, because they cannot stomach Jewish sovereignty over Jerusalem and the Holy Sepulchre, the tomb of Christ," Darmon said. The French government bears a crushing responsibility for continuing the Middle East conflict, he believes, "because they actively encourage the Arabs to the worst forms of anti-Semitism" through public diplomacy and international broadcasting. "The French message is that hate speech is legitimate." French policies in the Middle East are designed to create "maximum instability," he believes. Why? "The core goal of French diplomacy is to change the status of Jerusalem, to make it an international city."[30]

The new anti-Semitism on the Left was crudely expressed by a prominent member of the Socialist Party central committee, Pascal Boniface, in a "letter to an Israeli friend" that appeared in the French daily *Le Monde*. French Jews had only themselves to blame for anti-Semitic attacks, he argued, because of their "blind" support of an Israeli government "considered by more and more people as unjust, if not odious." Today, he argued, "the principal victims are the Palestinians, not the Israelis. . . . You can't put the occupier and the occupied on the same footing."[31] Just two months before his article appeared, 21 Jewish teenagers were slaughtered when a suicide bomber murdered them at the Dolphinarium disco in Tel Aviv; 120 others were wounded. Five days after the article appeared, 15 people were killed, including 7 children, and about 130 injured at the Sbarro pizzeria in downtown Jerusalem.

I briefly met Boniface in the summer of 1984 in Baghdad, where he had taken a Swiss girlfriend on an all-expenses-paid fact-finding mission at the invitation of the government of Saddam Hussein. I'm sure he must have a "friend in Israel" to whom he could write, but the target of his warning was the Jews of France, not Israel. "In France, by permitting the Israeli government to act with impunity, the Jewish community could also lose out in the longer term," he wrote. "The Arab and/or Muslim community is certainly less well organized [politically] but seeks to counterbalance [the Jews], and will quickly make its larger numbers felt, if that is not already happening." In an internal memo to Socialist party leaders, Boniface expanded on these comments, which were widely denounced as anti-Semitic, by urging party leaders to abandon the seven-hundred-thousand-strong Jewish community and appeal directly for votes to

France's five million Arab immigrants by adopting strong anti-Israel posi-tions. The downside to his proposal, which was leaked to the press, came on April 9, 2002, when Jews voted massively against the Socialists in the first round of the presidential elections and the Arabs stayed home.

Thierry Keller is the treasurer of SOS Racism, a left-wing group seek-ing dialogue between Jewish youths and second-generation Arab immi-grants, or *beurs*. Keller agrees that French anti-Semitism did not die with Hitler and Marshal Pétain, who headed the Nazi puppet government in Vichy. "The fact that young *beurs* are carrying out these attacks is very convenient for the anti-Semitic Catholic elites. The *beurs* are inadvertently doing their dirty work for them," he says. Keller was brought up Catholic himself and recalls the religious teachings of his childhood about Jews as the killers of Christ. He believes anti-Semitism is reemerging in France "because the old taboos against attacking Jews in public have been lifted. This legitimizes those who make intellectual arguments against Jews, and makes it an open season for Holocaust denial and anti-Semitic attacks. So you have a crossover between the old line anti-Semitic intellectuals in France and the Arab street in the suburbs, an objective alliance between the Islamists and the extreme Right."[32]

While Keller and his organization place greater emphasis on the mis-deeds of their political enemies on the Right, they nevertheless recognize the migration of the virus to the Left. "José Bové is a notorious anti-Semite. He has publicly accused the Mossad of burning the synagogues. So this is not just Muslim anti-Semitism." (Bové is a well-known leftist and opponent of "globalization," who served a prison term for attacking a McDonald's restaurant in France.) "We have been fighting for an inte-grated France, but not for U.S.-style quotas and affirmative action," says Keller. "We tried to unite people during the wave of anti-Semitic attacks by telling Arabs that these attacks were simply insane, and telling Jews that you are first French. You can't be pro-Israeli while seeking the death of Palestinians, or pro-Palestinian while burning synagogues. But this message is very hard to get across in France."

National Front leader Jean-Marie Le Pen has been condemned several times in French courts for anti-Semitic statements and Holocaust denial, but his favorite target in recent years has been the Muslim immigrants liv-ing in France, who account for roughly 10 percent of the country's population. Le Pen's upset victory in the first round of the French presidential elections on April 9, 2002, led to massive demonstrations against racism, and an abrupt end to most violent anti-Semitic attacks. "Le Pen made both Jews and Arabs afraid, so they fought a common enemy," Keller says. "But the attacks could start again as soon as there is a new flare-up in the Middle East." And indeed they did, in early 2003.

A senior deputy to Le Pen, Dominique Chaboche, called the waves of anti-Semitic attacks "very limited acts. We're talking about a few fires, a few slogans, a few insults," he told me at the party's fortresslike headquarters in St. Cloud on the outskirts of Paris. "It's intolerable that French Jews are Jews first and French second."

Asked several times about reports that his party questioned the existence of the Nazi gas chambers, Chaboche insisted that it was "perfectly legitimate" to question the facts of the Holocaust. "You can't forbid people from thinking. I don't understand why the Holocaust is the only period in history where it's not allowed to do historical research. So to challenge the existence of the gas chambers, to research their existence, is perfectly legitimate." In March 2001, a prominent party official, Georges Theil, was condemned by a court in Grenoble for Holocaust denial after he told a public meeting that the Nazi gas chambers "could not have existed, for physical and chemical reasons."[33] He was by no means the first, and he was never punished by his party, which won 17 percent in the first round of the presidential elections.

Like many leaders of his party, Chaboche takes the old anti-Semitic canards for gospel truth. "It's obvious that Israel is running the United States. The Jewish lobby is so powerful, you could never imagine a U.S. government imposing its policy on Israel." The same Jewish lobby, he believes, also runs France. "That's obvious, too. The Jews control most of the financial institutions, the banks. They hold key positions in the media. When we criticize Jewish control of the media, we are called anti-Semites. It's not true. Just because I don't like Chagall doesn't make me an anti-Semite."

Chaboche quickly makes the leap between anti-Semitic statements and weird conspiracy theories involving the United States. He is convinced the United States planned to attack Afghanistan as of July 2001, in order to control the oil resources of Central Asia. When I ask him the basis of his belief, he tells me he has a source in French military intelligence who claimed to have reported on U.S. war plans well before September 11. "The September 11 attacks were just a pretext. The United States made this war in order to construct a pipeline across Afghanistan, as part of its plan to dominate world oil supplies."

He truly believes the United States has a strategic goal to dominate Afghanistan in order to control the oil resources of Central Asia and that without this pipeline (which has yet to be built), U.S. automobiles and factories would grind to a halt—apparently ignoring the fact that an international consortium is investing $3 billion to build a massive pipeline to bring the same oil and gas from Central Asia to Western markets through Azerbaijan, Russia, and Turkey—in exactly the opposite direction. In conversation with ordinary Frenchmen over the following six months, I hear a similar argument repeated by people from the Left to the Right. It is absolutely mind-boggling.

✝ ✝ ✝

Thierry Meyssan, a French conspiracy theorist, is the author of a blockbuster best-seller with a thesis that leaves one equally breathless. He believes that the Pentagon was blown up by U.S. intelligence agencies on September 11 as part of a still secret coup d'état and that no commercial airliner was flown into the building. The basis of his fantasy? The "fact" that no debris from the airliner was found at the crash site and that the hole in the Pentagon was "too small" to have been caused by a Boeing 757. Eyewitnesses who saw the plane crash into the Pentagon were all plants, he alleged. Network television correspondents, such as ABC's John McQuethy, who broke off live reports from inside the Pentagon because of a "loud noise" coming from the far side of the building, all had been coached and were willing co-conspirators, he claimed. Cell phone calls from American Airlines Flight 77 just minutes before it crashed into the Pentagon from noted author Barbara Olson to her husband, Ted Olson—the Solicitor General of the United States—were just "hearsay," he argued. To justify the notion that U.S. intelligence agencies carried out the 9/11 attacks as part of a diabolical right-wing plot, he cited a declassified public diplomacy position paper from March 13, 1962, titled "Justification for U.S. Military Intervention in Cuba."[34] He also reproduced as fact the allegations of former U.S. representative Cynthia McKinney, widely derided by her colleagues in the Congressional Black Caucus, that President Bush had conspired with Osama bin Laden for personal gain against the national interests of the United States.

Even more unbelievable than Meyssan's travesty of reality is the fact that in the first two months after his book appeared in March 2002, some 142,000 copies had been sold, according to booksellers at the FNAC, the largest chain store in France. For so many people in a modern European country to go out and purchase a book of conspiracy theory is a sign that something is deeply amiss with French democracy.[35]

Meyssan's thesis was given instant credibility when it was featured on a mainstream French television magazine, similar to NBC's *Dateline* or CBS's *48 Hours*.[36] Reaction from the French press came immediately and was universally hostile—but that didn't perturb Meyssan or his audience, since the press was assumed to be part of the conspiracy anyway. In the left-wing daily *Le Monde,* no fewer than eight articles, including a lead editorial, appeared within a week, condemning Meyssan's contemporary version of Goebbels's Big Lie. The defense correspondent of the center-left daily *Libération,* Jean Guisnel, coauthored a rebuttal with intelligence specialist Guillaume Dasquié that exposed Meyssan's ties to far right Holocaust deniers and compared his methods to theirs. One of Meyssan's sources, Emmanuel Ratier, had recently published an updated French version of *The Protocols of the Elders of Zion,* they revealed.[37] Another source of the "information" fueling Meyssan's conspiracy theory turned out to be the well-known American fringe presidential candidate Lyndon LaRouche, who suggested that the 9/11 attacks were a "provocation" carried out by a pro-Israeli faction of the U.S. government "to enrage the United States into going in full force in support of the launching of the Israeli Defense Forces against neighboring Arab nations."[38] Meyssan picked up the hint and ran with it. "The bombings were thus not the work of a fanatic who believed he was carrying out a divine punishment, but of a group within the U.S. government apparatus who succeeded in dictating [their] policy to President Bush," he wrote.[39]

For conspiracy theorists such as Lyndon LaRouche and Thierry Meyssan, Holocaust denial forms a single equation with the notion of a "secret government" controlled by international Jewish elements. If you believe in one side of the equation, the other term appears just as well-founded. Philosopher and commentator Alain Finkelkraut called Meyssan's inventions "real-time revisionism. . . . We now have to confront new versions of *The Protocols of the Elders of Zion* that denounce official history as a farce and expose a secret sphere of influence while telling us that visible reality is just a smokescreen intended to fool people."[40]

On Meyssan's many Web sites, he claims to speak truth to power. In fact, he speaks lies on behalf of powerful backers. He found support in the United Arab Emirates, where the Zayed Centre for Coordination and Follow-Up invited him on April 8, 2002, to present his thesis to a sympathetic audience "under the auspices of the Arab League." The center was established in December 1997 under the sponsorship of UAE ruler Sheikh Zayed bin Sultan al-Nahyan to promote "the concept of Arab solidarity" through seminars and publications. In his presentation, Meyssan calmly stated that the U.S. government was inciting the public to murder Arabs and had no evidence to support its allegation that the planes had been hijacked or that the perpetrators all were Arab nationals. "The official version [of the September 11 attacks] amounts to an enormous lie," he stated. It was evident from the "facts" that the United States had "no basis in international law" for launching its war on terrorism. It was a comforting message for his hosts.[41]

Without interviewing a single eyewitness, or apparently even traveling to the United States to investigate, Meyssan unblushingly turned facts on their head. "It is obviously impossible that a Boeing 757 could, for some 500 kilometers, escape detection by civil and military radar, by fighter-bomber planes sent in pursuit of it and by observation satellites that had just been activated. It is also obviously impossible that a Boeing 757 could enter the Pentagon's air space without being destroyed by one or more of the five missile batteries protecting the building. . . . One must acknowledge the evidence: it is impossible that the attack against the Pentagon on September 11, killing 125 persons, was carried out by a jet airliner." Instead, he claimed that the U.S. military had fired one of its own air-launched cruise missiles against the Pentagon. The Zayed Centre reproduced his allegations without commentary and published a full-length Arabic-language translation of Meyssan's book on July 3, 2002. In the five years since its inception, the center has attempted to give an intellectual imprimatur to Holocaust denial and anti-American propaganda that regularly accuses the United States of being a "racist" state that "persecutes" Arab citizens, while promoting terrorism as "legitimate resistance." And this, from the United Arab Emirates, a country touted as one of America's "best friends" in the Arab world.[42]

Meyssan claims to gather his information from former intelligence officers and "patriots" who have joined him in a mysterious "Voltaire Network" (www.reseauvoltaire.net), a subscription-only Web site. But most of his information appears to have been lifted directly from Lyndon LaRouche.[43] Meyssan portrays himself as a leftist crusader for truth, where anti-Americanism is common. But his 9/11 books also appealed to the anti-Semitic and anti-American fringes on the far Right, living proof that when it comes to hate, the political extremes invariably join. Increasingly, the view is spreading across the French political spectrum that the world is run by occult powers, against whom the honest citizen is powerless. Such beliefs are fact-resistant and impervious to logic, with hate, suspicion, and powerlessness replacing reason. The rebirth of conspiracy theories in Europe, such as those prevalent in the Muslim world today, should set off alarm bells. The only element missing in Meyssan's portrayal from the lethal brew that brought Hitler to power is the designation of a single enemy pulling the strings behind the scenes. Unlike Lyndon LaRouche, whose ideas he parrots, Meyssan cleverly omitted to mention the enemy's name: the Jews.

† † †

Austria will always have a special place in the life and near extermination of European Jewry. It was here in Vienna that the notion of a Jewish homeland was born in 1896, when journalist Theodor Herzl published his historic booklet, *The Jewish State*. And it was here, in March 1938, that Hitler first expanded the Third Reich beyond Germany's borders when he marched triumphantly into Vienna to broad public acclaim. The first act of the "Anschluss" was to strip Austria's two hundred thousand Jews of their citizenship, jobs, and property. Over sixty-five thousand Austrian Jews perished in German death camps and ghettos. The rest fled or were expelled. Sixty-five years later, just seven thousand people belong to the Austrian Jewish Community. To this day, most have never received compensation or even recognition of the horrors they suffered under the Third Reich. "It's not easy to be a Jew in Austria," says Victor Wagner, who heads the local chapter of B'nai B'rith.[44]

The failure of postwar Austrian governments to acknowledge Austria's complicity in the Holocaust prompted the president of the Austrian Jewish Community, Dr. Ariel Muzicant, to press the government in 1998 to establish a Historical Commission to reexamine Austria's past. "It is important that Austria finally tries to live up to its past, not just what happened from 1938 to 1945, which is pretty well-known, but to what didn't happen after 1945, and the enormous amount of Jewish property that was never returned or compensated," Dr. Muzicant told me in Vienna.

In the summer of 2002, that commission released a damning report. Despite no fewer than seven laws passed since 1945 that called for restitution of property stolen from Austria's Jews—the flower of Vienna's economic, social, and cultural life—it determined that very little property was ever returned. The main reason, commission spokesperson Eva Blimlinger said, was simple and far-reaching. "Austria did not want to admit any wrongdoing during the war." Postwar governments portrayed Austria as a "victim" of Nazi evil, not as the willing partner that it was, and actively discouraged exiled Jews from returning. With tacit government approval, those who had stolen Jewish property were allowed to keep it. Some of Austria's biggest fortunes were built on property stolen from the country's dead or exiled Jews.

That position was reaffirmed spectacularly in November 2000 by conservative prime minister Wolfgang Schuessel, shortly after he invited Jorg Haider, leader of the far-right Freedom Party (FPO), into his government. "The sovereign state of Austria was literally the first victim of the Nazi regime," he said. "They [the Austrians] were the very first victims."[45] Despite this position, it was under Schuessel's leadership, and with the active cooperation of the Freedom Party, that the Historical Commission began its work and the first compensation payments to the families of Holocaust victims were made. Such are the contradictions of postwar Austria.

The World Jewish Committee (WJC) also discouraged Austrian Holocaust survivors to return after the war, although for different reasons. The WJC believed the open anti-Semitism in Austria showed that the country and especially its early postwar leaders had never fully broken with Nazism. "It was 200 percent easier for Jews to go back to Germany than to Austria after the war," recalls Victor Wagner. "My own family in Germany even got back the furniture that had been stolen from their flats, plus money, back rent, and pensions. Without any doubt, Austrian Jews had it the worst."

✝✝✝

Austria's Historical Commission hired scholars from around the world in an effort to set the record straight and in 2002 issued several reports listing "aryanized" property stolen from Austria's Jews. The commission also pledged to place a monetary value on at least some of the theft. "Our own historians estimate the amount of property seized from Austria's Jews at roughly $14 billion, of which 60 percent was never returned and never compensated," Dr. Muzicant says. "This estimate includes businesses, homes, money, stock, insurance policies, leases, household goods, art, silver and gold, jewelry, books. We're talking about twenty-five different categories, down to little things, such as pianos, stolen from people's homes."[46] Muzicant said he expected the Historical Commission to place a monetary value on only 2 to 6 percent of the property seized, primarily that now belonging to the Austrian state. But as public interest grew, so did the curiosity of journalists and researchers. Lothar Hoebling, who helps trace property ownership at the Holocaust Victims Information Center, says the actual research isn't all that difficult. "All the documents were centralized in Vienna as of 1938 because 180,000 of Austria's 200,000 Jews lived in Vienna. So you have real estate registries, the central registry for businesses, city and national archives, tax records. People were killed, but the documents survived. That's how the Nazis organized the state."[47]

A preliminary listing of prominent properties stolen from Austria's Jews came out in 2001, the work of historians Tina Walzer and Stephan Templ. Its title alone—*Unser Wien (Our Vienna)*—evoked the secret that everyone in Vienna had known for decades but never spoke about openly.[48]

So widespread was the theft organized by the Austrian Nazis that a significant portion of Vienna's postwar economy—even today—was built upon stolen property. Yet the current owners appear oblivious to the origin of their good fortune. "They say nothing about this," Dr. Muzicant says. That was "our Vienna."

Unser Wien explains in black and white how entire businesses were simply stolen from Jews, transferred to "Aryan" owners, and never returned after the war. Among them are some eighty Viennese pharmacies, seventy-four theaters, numerous bookstores, and some of Vienna's most prestigious hotels and eateries. At Albertinaplatz 2, tourists often stop for a pastry at the Café Mozart. In the 1930s, it was owned by two Jewish women—Jeanette Kessler and Ethel Hornik. After the Anschluss, it was "aryanized" and given to two Nazi Party sympathizers, Fritz Quester and Fritz Gindelhuber.[49] Vienna's legendary Hotel Imperial, where Hitler stayed on the night of March 14, 1938, to savor the fruits of the Anschluss, belonged to Jewish businessmen Samuel Schallinger and Paul Abel. One week after Hitler's one-night stay, their trading company was blacklisted and their properties "aryanized" in the names of Ernst Hoffmann, Hermann Klimpfinger, Günghter Rustler, and Friedrich von Schoeller.[50] Even the Ferris wheel on Vienna's Prater, the enormous park along the Danube, had belonged to Jews, as did hundreds of factories, department stores, hotels, jewelry stores, and national monuments, none of which have been returned to their owners or their heirs.

✝ ✝ ✝

Austria's political parties from across the spectrum have courted the votes of former Nazis since the postwar years. According to official estimates, five hundred thousand Austrians had belonged to the Nazi Party, 20 percent of the population—more even than in Germany itself. (Unofficial estimates put the number of Austrian Nazis at twice that.) Early Socialist governments included former Nazis as cabinet ministers and protected them from prosecution. In 1986, former Wehrmacht officer Kurt Waldheim was elected Austria's president on a platform that implicitly excused Austrians from accusations of war crimes.

Austria's peculiar contradictions are not about to disappear. "When you look at newsreels of people waving from balconies as Hitler made his triumphal entry into Vienna in 1938, don't tell me the Austrians had nothing to do with National Socialism," a Western diplomat in Vienna told me. "In the late 1980s, the Austrian government put up a plaque on the main prison in Vienna, commemorating the beheading of one thousand people between 1938 and 1945 because of their race or religion. Beheaded, mind you, not shot or hung."

In stump speeches in the early 1990s, Freedom Party leader Jorg Haider praised Hitler's "sound employment policies" and once called Waffen SS veterans "men of character," remarks for which he apologized repeatedly. When conservative prime minister Wolfgang Schuessel invited Haider's party to join his governing coalition in February 2000, after they edged out his own People's Party with 27 percent in parliamentary elections the previous October, it caused an uproar throughout Europe. Left-wing politicians vowed to toss Austria out of the European Union unless Schuessel disowned them. To head off a collision, Haider resigned as party leader.[51]

But was Haider any less democratic or any more anti-Semitic than, say, French Socialist premier Lionel Jospin, who never lifted a finger for eighteen months as Jewish synagogues were torched and Jewish schools attacked across France, and who urged the unelected European Commission to reverse the elections in Austria? The question is taboo in Europe, where Haider is hounded as an incarnation of Adolf Hitler because of his populist demagoguery, his pledge to end immigration, and the open support he receives from neo-Nazi skinheads. Haider's success has been attributed to the "failure of the Austrians to face up to their role as Hitler's 'willing executioners' after the Second World War."[52] Yet with Haider's party in government, not a single anti-Semitic attack was reported in Austria during the wave of violence that swept across Europe starting in September 2000.

On July 4, 2002, when a top FPO parliamentarian, Ewald Stadler, compared the U.S. troops occupying Austria after World War II to the Nazi occupation during the war, he was roundly condemned. Ironically, the first to rebuke him was the deputy general secretary of his own party,

Peter Sichrovsky, who told Austrian reporters that the Freedom Party's days of Nazi apologetics were over. Sichrovsky is virtually unknown outside of Austria, and his remarks were never picked up by the European press, although Stadler's outrageous comparison made headlines.

"We have a new generation of leaders, who have more liberal ideas," Sichrovsky told me. "They are not the typical postwar generation that grew up with parents heavily involved with the Nazis. The Freedom Party has changed."[53]

Sichrovsky's claim drew scorn from Austrian Jewish Community leader Dr. Muzicant. "Sichrovsky is Jewish. If that is what he believes, how can he be in a party with such people? There are dozens like Stadler in the Freedom Party, saying these things loudly." Sichrovsky has been ridiculed by the ADL and has been the subject of negative profiles in the Israeli media, where his political adversaries called him a "traitor."[54]

I asked Sichrovsky whether the fact he is Jewish had made his life difficult in the FPO. "The problems I have had would have been the same in all parties," he said. Little has actually changed in Europe over the past fifty years except for the public discourse, he believes. "For years, people kept quiet. They were forced to control themselves. It was taboo to talk about Jews, to blame the Jews. What's changed is that now we've got European governments attacking Israel constantly, so people feel more free to say what they really think. It's like blowing away a cloud, allowing what was hidden behind it to show through. It shows that anti-Semitism is a problem that has never been solved."

He cited the case of German Liberal Party leader Jurgen Möllemann, who in early 2002 called on the head of the German Jewish community to denounce Israel, in terms similar to those used by French Socialist Pascal Boniface in *Le Monde*. "The political establishment in some countries no longer makes the distinction between criticizing Israel and criticizing Jews. This is what's new. They are holding Jews responsible for Israel's actions. . . . Anti-Semitism is on all sides, but especially on the Left."

Sichrovsky pointed out that for years Austria's Socialist governments had refused to discuss compensation for Holocaust victims. It was only the right-wing coalition under Schuessel that carried it out. "It's become a cliché to say that anti-Semitism comes from the Right. In fact, the worst crimes against Jews after World War Two were carried out in Eastern Europe, which was supposed to be Socialist."

Victor Wagner, the head of B'nai B'rith in Vienna, believes the Right and the Left are "absolutely the same" when it comes to anti-Semitism. "It's an old tradition here. Look at [Socialist premier] Bruno Kreisky. He was Jewish himself. But under Kreisky, Austrian Jews lost their rights. Kreisky wanted to show he had no connection to his Jewish past. In his first government, in 1970, he had four ministers who were former SS officers."

Wagner is one of the tiny community of Austrian Holocaust survivors still living in Austria. After the war, it took his father until 1953 to reclaim the family business. "I have no problems to live in Austria. I'm not religious. I wear no beard, so people don't know that I'm Jewish. But if I ran a firm, that would be different. Then I would have problems," he tells me. "There is a quiet anti-Semitism here in Austria. It's there all the time. It's the way people speak at home, in cafés, to one another, but not in public. They criticize Israel because they want to criticize Jews. Otherwise they have absolutely no interest in Israel or the Middle East."

In early 2002, Wagner was accused of being an agent of the Israeli government by the Socialist Fritz Edlinger. The theme of "dual loyalty" is a frequent charge of anti-Semites who claim there is a world Jewish conspiracy. "He wrote me about 'my' prime minister, Ariel Sharon," Wagner said. "So now I have to give up my Austrian nationality just because I am a Jew?"

Edlinger runs the Society for Austro-Arab Relations, an interest group that's leading a campaign to delegitimize the state of Israel. On his board is Freedom Party secretary-general Karl Schweizer. Although Edlinger is a dedicated leftist, one of his biggest supporters in opposing the U.S.-led war in Iraq is Jorg Haider, who branded President Bush and British Prime Minister Tony Blair "war criminals" for launching the war without United Nations approval.[55] The apparent admiration they share for Saddam Hussein and their contempt for America and her freedoms are yet other areas where the extreme Right and the hard Left in Austria join.

"We feel Europe should hit Israel where they are most sensitive," Edlinger says. His group is urging the Austrian government and the

European Union to enforce legislation banning the import of Israeli goods made in settlements, to cut off scientific cooperation, and to demand repayment of all European-funded projects that have been destroyed by the Israeli army in the recent fighting. He was even considering raising funds to rebuild a destroyed Palestinian building in the hopes PA gunmen again would use it as a base, inviting Israeli retaliation, so his group can sue Israel in international courts. "Yesterday I gave instructions to our lawyers to explore this possibility. I want to hire American lawyers—even better, Jewish ones!" he said, laughing. To this limousine liberal, the best joke he could play on the center of world imperialism is to use our freedoms and our respect for the law against us. When Vienna is drenched in rain on July 4, he jokes that he "ordered it specially" to celebrate Independence Day.

But when I asked him about the anti-Semitism of Palestinian leaders and clerics, he became defensive. "You have to be careful about using this label," he said. "In Europe, anti-Semitism has a hundred years of tradition and a specific historic meaning. The Palestinians have been under occupation for fifty-four years. When they turn against Israel or the Israeli army, it's not the same as what we mean by anti-Semitism. They are anti-Israeli, or anti-Zionist, but not anti-Semitic."

What about the Palestinian textbooks? I asked, citing some of the conclusions from a report from the Center for Monitoring the Impact of Peace, the U.S. nonprofit group that regularly studies textbooks in Israel and the Palestinian Authority. "Again, you must be careful," Edlinger said. "That study was done by a very right-wing Israeli organization. The EU [European Union] has evaluated the textbooks, and didn't find them anti-Semitic. It's not anti-Semitic to never mention Israel. Nor is it anti-Semitic not to mention Israel's borders."[56] From delegitimizing Israel, which Edlinger openly avows is his goal, it may be a leap to Israel's destruction, but that is not a risk most Jews are willing to take.

Simon Wiesenthal, who turned ninety-five in 2003, has fought many battles over the years to preserve the memory of Austria's Jewish community, and in support of Israel. As a private researcher, he tracked the Austrian Nazi Adolf Eichmann to Argentina, where Israeli Mossad agents ultimately arrested him in 1961 and brought him to Jerusalem to stand trial. Wiesenthal returned to Vienna almost immediately after he was liberated from Auschwitz by the Allies in 1945 and has never left. His Jewish Documentation Center has become a repository for information on Nazi war criminals. He best explained the attachment many European Jews feel for Israel. "If the state of Israel had existed at the time of the Holocaust, there wouldn't have been six million dead," he told me.[57] Regardless of what one thinks of the policies of any particular Israeli government, without Israel today, the doors to a new Holocaust would stand open.

✝✝✝

As the Middle East violence intensified in the spring of 2002, with Palestinian suicide bombers murdering hundreds of Israelis and the Israel Defense Forces retaliating with force against the communities that harbored them, one woman in tiny Norway stood up against the violence. Her name was Hanna Kvanmo. A leading left-wing parliamentarian until 1989, she had been a member of the Nobel committee that awarded the Nobel Peace Prize in 1994 jointly to Shimon Peres and Yasser Arafat. In April 2002, the seventy-six-year-old Kvanmo told Norwegian reporters she regretted her decision in 1994 and now felt that the prize should be withdrawn—from Shimon Peres, not Yasser Arafat. Three months later, when I phoned Kvanmo in southern Norway, she said she "regretted" her statement—not because she had changed her mind, but because "so many people have been calling me about it. It's gotten so much attention."[58]

In Norway, Jew-hatred is as old as the state, according to Christian author and journalist Vebjørn K. Selbekk. It was enshrined in Norway's Constitution of 1814 at a time when there were no Jews in Norway and no synagogue. "How could they be so afraid of Jews when they hadn't met a Jew in their lives?" Selbekk asks. "And yet, fear of Jews led to the adoption of an anti-Semitic clause in the Constitution, Article two, that forbids freedom of religion to two groups: Jesuits and Jews. It shows you can have anti-Semitism without Jews."[59]

It wasn't the only time Norway was in the forefront of official anti-Semitism, Selbekk says. In 1931, Norway passed a law that forbade Jewish ritual slaughter, two years before Hitler did the same in Germany. "If you read the debate in Parliament, it was clearly anti-Semitic. They said, If the Jews don't like it, they can leave Norway." Germany changed its laws banning ritual slaughter in 1945, but Norway never has. Even today, Norway's tiny Jewish community of some 1,720 souls must import kosher meat, whereas Muslim immigrants are allowed to slaughter meat according to Muslim law. Even Norway's Lapp community, frequently a target of race hatred, is allowed to slaughter meat using a procedure identical to Jewish ritual butchery, but not the Jews.

The head of the Centerpartiet in the 1930s, Jens Hundseid, believed in the supremacy of the Nordic race and wanted to ban entry to Norway of Jews and other foreigners. Hundseid became prime minister in 1932. "So one year before Germany got Hitler as chancellor, we had an anti-Semite and a race supremacist as prime minister of Norway," Selbekk explains.

✝ ✝ ✝

The most infamous chapter of modern Norwegian history was the Nazi puppet regime of Vidkun Quisling, a former military officer whose name has become a synonym for traitor. After briefly serving as defense minister in Hundseid's government, Quisling formed his own Nazi Party in 1933, known as the Nasjonal Samling (National Union Party). At a meeting with Hitler in December 1939, Quisling touted allegedly secret British plans to seize Norwegian air bases of Stavanger and Kristiansand and urged an immediate German invasion. When Hitler's troops arrived in April 1940, the British couldn't be found. But Quisling burst into the studios of Norwegian radio and proclaimed himself prime minister.

Within a week, the Germans realized they couldn't force the Norwegian king to approve Quisling's appointment and set him aside. But once the king and the Parliament went into exile, they installed Quisling in a sumptuous forty-two-room palace in Bygdøy, an exclusive peninsula in Oslo Harbor with a staggering view over the fjord, as head of the puppet occupation government. On June 23, 1941—the day after the German army launched the massive invasion of the Soviet Union known as Barbarossa— the "Norwegian führer" announced in a speech that Norway's "Jewish problem" would soon be resolved. Indeed, the first arrests of Jews had already begun.[60]

"Quisling and the Holocaust were not just German imports," Selbekk says, "but had deep roots in Norway." Starting in January 1942, Jews were given special identity cards, stamped with a large "J" to designate their religion. "It was Norwegians who did all the bureaucratic work of registering the Jews, who made the lists that led to the October 26, 1942, roundup of Jews that was carried out by the Norwegian police," Selbekk said.

Quisling was executed as a traitor after a trial in Norway at the end of the war. Three reparations committees, working immediately afterward, used Quisling's own estimates for seized Jewish property and in many cases determined that the estates of murdered Jews actually *owed* the government money. As with Austria, it took fifty years for Norway to examine its wartime past. In 1997, the Skarpnes Commission, named after its chairman, Oluf Skarpnes, stated the facts in devastating terms. "The economic liquidation of the Norwegian Jews during World War II was total," the minority report adopted by the commission report states. Following Quisling's Norwegian Act of October 26, 1942, which confiscated Jewish assets, "Norwegian Jews were deprived of all rights of ownership and any kind of business base." Of the 2,173 Jews who lived in Norway at that time, "a total of 767 Jews were deported from Norway. Thirty survived. The remainder of the Jews who had lived in Norway fled the country."[61]

This little-known wartime history is important because Norway has played a central role in the Oslo "peace process" between Israel and what until then had been considered a terrorist movement, the PLO. While the center-right government of Prime Minister Kjell Magne Bondevik has tried to be evenhanded, the same Norwegian politicians on the Left who urged the Israelis to recognize the PLO now accuse Israel of genocide and openly compare Israeli leaders to the Nazis. "Norwegians like to see themselves as the conscience of the world, so they cannot accept the black spots in their own history," says Selbekk. "Norway is not an anti-Semitic society, but we have a strong anti-Semitic heritage and dangerous anti-Semitic elements in the mainstream press and in politics. We must not deny the fact that we also had a part in what happened during the Nazi period."

The Nazi references emerge frequently and easily in today's Norway, and they are directed mainly at Israel, but also at the United States. At a huge demonstration in central Oslo to protest Israel's independence on April 20, 2002, former Labor Party prime minister Jens Stoltenberg addressed pro-Palestinian groups waving Nazi flags. Without blinking, he endorsed their cause. "There is one occupant, and one occupier," he told them.[62] (It was his party, under the leadership of Gro Harlem Brundtland and Foreign Minister Johan Jorgen Holst, that oversaw the Oslo Declaration of Principles in September 1993.) The former leader of the center-left Center Party, Gunnar Stålsett, now the state-appointed Lutheran bishop of Oslo, addressed a crowd of anti-Israeli demonstrators waving Nazi flags on April 6, 2002. "He asked that they pull down the swastikas before he spoke," an Israeli diplomat in Oslo told me. When the crowd kept on waving them, he spoke anyway. The same newspaper that prominently featured his speech also carried a photograph of an unidentified Arab who threw a Molotov cocktail at the Israeli embassy. "He was arrested, but never prosecuted," the Israeli diplomat said.[63]

Anti-Israel demonstrations and Israeli "misdeeds" in the West Bank and Gaza get extensive coverage in a Norwegian press whose brazen anti-Semitism goes way beyond any tolerable expression of a political disagreement with Israel. For years, Norwegian reporters and cartoonists have compared Israel to Hitler's Third Reich and have used classical anti-Semitic themes that arguably should be outlawed under Norway's 1975 hate crimes legislation.

Norway's only "conservative" daily, *Aftenposten*, shows Arafat and President Clinton gazing with shock at a Christmas tree. The reason for their shock? The Jews had replaced the Christian star at the top of the tree with the Star of David (December 16, 1998). In a similar theme, three Israeli tanks are on their way to Bethlehem (instead of the three Wise Men) and score a direct hit that pulverizes the star of Bethlehem that announces the birth of Christ (April 5, 2002). Five days later, storm trooper Ariel Sharon is down on his knees, strangling Yasser Arafat, a common theme. By this point, however, the U.S. president has changed and is no longer the "sympathetic" Clinton. The "villain" Bush is dressed as a Wild West sheriff, wearing a Star of David in place of his badge. Sharon calls to him to help finish the job.

The second major paper, *Dagbladet*, also draws inspiration from the ancient blood libels. A December 24, 2001 headline mocks the birth of Christ: A CHILD IS SHOT IN BETHLEHEM. Two weeks later Sharon is portrayed as a Nazi concentration camp warden, shouting at his inmate, Arafat (January 16, 2002). On April 4, 2002, Sharon appears in an SS storm trooper uniform, carrying under an arm a captive George W. Bush, reduced to a bawling infant, and tramples Arafat with his knee-high boots. Around his neck, he wears the Nazi Iron Cross, with the cross replaced by the Jewish star. A May 16, 2002, cartoon shows Sharon addressing his barber, the Norwegian prime minister. "Quisling!" he calls, as if beckoning a dog. It's the familiar theme of Jews as Nazis and their supporters as collaborators. Smaller Norwegian papers run similar political cartoons.[64]

The ugliness of these caricatures is mirrored in the news coverage, which stands out as the worst in Europe for its one-sided portrayal of the Middle East conflict. "Almost anyone who reads our newspapers and watches Norwegian television begins to see Israel as an evil state," says Martin Bodd, a spokesman for the tiny Jewish community. "This impacts on us as Jews."

When Bodd appealed to one editor to provide more balanced coverage, he received a snide reply via e-mail. "Hello Martin!" wrote Tomm Kristiansen, foreign editor of state-run Norwegian National Broadcasting Company (NRK) television. "I realize you have joined the 'Israel-friendly' campaign. You are interviewed in a bunch of newspapers, saying that [the NRK's Middle East correspondent Lars-Erik] Sunnanaa has not interviewed a single Jew for half a year. . . . Martin, honestly, you should approach the press and apologize or correct the picture you have given. If not, I will do it." In a postscript, he added: "On a personal level, I hope that your God, who is more strict than mine (i.e., Jesus), gives those who killed a priest in Bethlehem and shot down the statue of the Virgin Mary on the roof of the Church of the Nativity the necessary punishment."[65] As a news editor, Kristiansen should have known that both allegations were slanderous falsehoods.

Rolf Kirschner, the fifty-five-year-old president of the Norwegian Jewish Community, felt the anti-Semitism firsthand. Not long after the second *intifada* began, his name appeared on a "death list" of eight leading Jews that was sent to newspapers and widely circulated in Norway's large Muslim community. Kirschner thought nothing about it until early April 2002, when an unidentified caller telephoned his home, asking for him by name. Just minutes after he had responded to that call, a rock smashed into his bedroom window. That's when Kirschner asked for police protection.[66]

Attacks on Jews occur frequently but rarely get reported to the police. "Norway's Jews try to keep a low profile," the outgoing chief rabbi Jason Rappoport told me. "The average Norwegian has never met a Jew."[67] But Norway's growing Muslim immigrant community has. A young Norwegian boy, whose father was Israeli, was approached on the street by three teenagers of Iranian background shortly after Easter 2002. "We are going to kill you, Jew," they shouted at him. At a local Oslo soccer club for twelve-year-old boys, the trainer from an Arab country harassed two Jewish boys, accusing them of being murderers. Instead of fighting back, the parents pulled them from the club. At one Oslo school, Arab immigrant children were caught throwing stones at two young Jews. At another, the wife of an American diplomat was warned that her daughter should not come to school wearing her Star of David, because it was too "provocative." Another Jewish teen told me a harrowing tale of being repeatedly harassed by young Arabs in the streets and at school, who sought to rip the star of David from around her neck. Erez Uriely, an Israeli who has lived in Norway for over a decade with his wife, Rachal Suissa, a university lecturer, says the rabbi at Oslo's lone synagogue has warned him not to wear his *kippah* out on the street. "It can be dangerous. When I leave it on sometimes after synagogue, other Jews come after me, saying that I forgot to take off my *kippah*. They are afraid I will attract attention to them. It can be dangerous to show outward signs of Jewishness in Norway."

✝✝✝

Many commentators who have expressed shock at the dramatic return of anti-Semitic violence in Europe since September 2000 have been quick to pin the blame on fringe groups on the far Right, where anti-Semitism and conspiracy theories abound. In Norway, a group of skinheads known as the "Boot Boys" emerged from the gutter in the late 1990s and attempted to celebrate the anniversary of the death of Rudolf Hess by parading in front of the Israeli embassy in Oslo. Others, such as Alfredo Olson, preach Jew-hatred over the Internet. In 1999, *The Protocols of the Elders of Zion* reappeared in a Norwegian translation for the first time since the Quisling era, the work of an obscure group that called itself the Norwegian National Socialist Front.

While such groups are potentially dangerous, they are marginal and have been under police surveillance for years. Their every move is monitored carefully and treated with scorn by the press. They have no mass following and no ideology; indeed, they are more objects of ridicule than admiration. Far more dangerous is what has been happening on the Left, where warmed-over radicals from the 1968 generation have taken over the mainstream Labor Party and now occupy top policy positions in government ministries, in the national education system, and in the media. "The extreme Right are too few to be a real problem, and they are not organized," says Jan Gregersen, an activist with the Norsk-Israeli Center. "The danger is on the Left, which has both the numbers and the organization."[68]

Nils Butenschoen and Kjell Bygstad have spent their lives combating America and the state of Israel in the Socialist Left Party and associated Marxist-Leninist groups. In separate interviews they explained the radical agenda animating the Norwegian press and, most important, their former colleague, Terje Roed-Larsen, architect of the Oslo "peace process."[69] While Larsen's past association with hard-left groups is no secret—he was a member of the Workers Communist Party (Marxist-Leninist) in the 1970s—it is not well-known outside of Norway and never seems to have disqualified him as an "honest broker" between an Israeli state whose very existence he once rejected and a Palestine Liberation Organization whose goal of eradicating Israel he had publicly endorsed.

Butenschoen directs the Institute for Human Rights at Oslo University and today is considered a mainstream analyst of Middle East politics. He appears regularly on Norwegian television as a "neutral" commentator whenever there is a flare-up in the violence between Israelis and Palestinians. Yet Butenschoen is far from neutral. As he explained to me, he was a leading member along with Kjell Bygstad of a pro-PLO activist group in Norway that in the early 1970s advocated the destruction of the state of Israel.

The group's founder was a young Norwegian radical named Finn Sjue, who traveled to Jordan in hopes of becoming a Fatah guerrilla. Arafat's men were so pleased with their new recruit that they gave him the nom de guerre "Abu Yasser" before taking him with them on a failed guerrilla attack against a kibbutz in the Jordan Valley. When he returned to Norway, Sjue established the Palestine Committee on September 29, 1970, with the goal of destroying the state of Israel. Its official program called for "full support of the struggle of the Palestinian people . . . active opposition to U.S. imperialism and the Zionist state of Israel," and "opposition to all superpower solutions that guarantee the Zionist state's existence."[70]

"We initially advocated a single, secular state in all of Palestine with equality between all races and religion," Bygstad told me, careful to use the politically correct terms of today's Euro-Left to describe their agenda. When Arafat directed the PLO to adopt a two-state solution in 1974, Bygstad and his group abruptly shifted gears. "We couldn't be more Palestinian than the PLO, so we changed our position to coincide with theirs," he said.[71] Nevertheless, the group's mimeographed broadsheet, *Palestine News,* continued to advocate the destruction of the state of Israel. A young Communist activist named Terje Roed-Larsen "was attached to *Palestine News* in 1977 when they had the following solution for the Middle East problem: 'Say no to a two-state solution! Support the fight for liberating all of Palestine!' "[72]

At the same time these hard-left movements were organizing for Palestine, the more mainstream Labor Party was also evolving. Norway's Socialists had been strongly pro-Israel since 1948, but made an about-face after Israel's victory in the 1967 war. In 1971, the Labor Party Youth League (AUF) passed a resolution at its annual convention calling for the abolition of the Jewish state. "Norwegian socialists had been dreaming of a socialist utopia in Israel, not a Jewish state," says Selbekk. When the conservative Likud Party came to power in Israel in 1977, the gloves came off.

Arafat was then engaged in a vicious war in Lebanon that began when PLO gunmen massacred an entire busload of Christian civilians on their way to a funeral. Having established a "state within a state," the PLO regularly launched Katyusha rockets into Israeli towns and villages from southern Lebanon, randomly killing civilians. Butenschoen says he first met Arafat in 1978, traveling as chairman of Norway's Palestinian Front to Arafat's bunker in the Fakahani district of Beirut. The Israelis had just launched a limited invasion of southern Lebanon to push the PLO back beyond artillery range from Israel's borders, and Arafat needed help.

Butenschoen remains cagey over just what transpired at that meeting with Arafat. But when the United Nations agreed to insert an international "monitoring" force into a buffer zone just north of the Israeli border, Norway quickly volunteered troops. "The Palestinians called me occasionally to help establish contact with the Norwegian military and foreign office," Butenschoen says. The United Nations Interim Force in Lebanon (UNIFIL) has remained in place ever since 1978 and still includes a Norwegian battalion (Norbat). During one of several trips I made to the area, UNIFIL spokesman Timor Goksel acknowledged that UN troops had never intercepted Palestinian or Hezbollah guerrillas before or after raids on Israel but regularly reported Israeli retaliation attacks to the UN.[73]

Soon after Butenschoen's trip, Labor Party heavyweights began traveling to Lebanon to pay homage to Arafat. Among them were Thorvald Stoltenberg, the future foreign minister, and Gro Harlem Brundtland. Although she was older than the 1968 generation radicals, Brundtland took them under her wing. Under her leadership, many of the former Socialist Left Party activists joined the Labor Party. She promoted them to the party leadership, while adopting their anti-Israel agenda. In April 1983, when Brundtland headed the Association of Scandinavian Labor Parties, she invited Arafat to visit Stockholm. It was a major diplomatic coup that broadened his support in Europe. After an eight-month initial stint as prime minister in 1981, Brundtland twice returned to power, from May 1986 to October 1989 and, again, from September 1990 to October 1996, when Oslo was negotiated and implemented.

One of the former Socialist Left Party activists promoted by Brundtland was Einar Foerde, who eventually became head of the Norwegian National Broadcasting Company. Until his retirement in 2001, "Foerde continued the tradition of picking key persons who shared his political views and placing them throughout the NRK," says Jan Gregersen. Another hard-leftist Brundtland brought into the Labor Party fold was Terje Roed-Larsen, the anti-Israel Communist from the Palestinian Front.[74]

Roed-Larsen (whose first name is pronounced "Terry") became the deputy director of Fafo, the Labor Party Institute of Applied Social Science, and followed his wife, Mona Juul, when she was named to the Norwegian embassy in Cairo. In 1991, he saw an opportunity to put his old Palestinian contacts to work. "It was in Cairo that Larsen got involved in the back-channel talks with the PLO that eventually led to Oslo," says Butenschoen.

Arafat biographer Said Abu Rish says the first substantive meeting with the Israelis that led to the secret Oslo back channel took place at a small Indian restaurant in Tel Aviv in May 1992, shortly before the Israeli Labor Party was returned to power. Larsen's luncheon partner was Yossi Beilin, a confidant of Shimon Peres. "Almost in passing . . . the Norwegian suggested the use of his country as a conduit for direct Palestinian-Israeli contacts." When Labor won the elections three days later, Peres became foreign minister, with Beilin as his deputy. Terje Roed-Larsen, the former Communist and anti-Israel activist, had new friends in powerful places.[75]

✝✝✝

The Oslo Accords catapulted Larsen into the public eye, and with the fame came substantial rewards. In 1994, his institute was given a onetime special $100,000 "peace award" from the Carter-Menil Human Rights Foundation for its "work in brokering the September 1993 declaration of principles." Presenting the award were Jimmy Carter, philanthropist Dominique de Menil, and Israeli foreign minister Shimon Peres.[76]

In 1996, the Labor Party government of Norwegian prime minister Thorbjoern Jagland named Larsen minister of national planning, a newly created post that carried tremendous prestige. But less than three months later, his past caught up to him as reporters and government investigators discovered a trail of financial scandal that ultimately forced him to resign from government on November 28, 1996.

While he was receiving secret Norwegian government grants, for which he provided no accounting, it was revealed that Roed-Larsen had also acquired stock options in a fish-processing plant known as Fideco.[77] Although the company was on the verge of bankruptcy, Larsen neverthe-less managed to sell his options in 1991 for a tidy 600,000-krone profit, then worth around $100,000. According to Svein Milford, the managing director of a company known as Bird Technology, his company had been "pressured" to buy out Larsen's worthless Fideco shareholdings, which he believed Larsen had received as a gift.[78] The episode became known as "Larsen's fish story" in the Norwegian press.

And that was just the beginning. The Norwegian Parliament was soon informed that for years the Foreign Ministry had financed Roed-Larsen's personal lifestyle in the Middle East by diverting millions of kroner in "development assistance" to pay for his travel and personal staff, at a time when he was theoretically serving as a United Nations special envoy.[79]

In 1997, on the verge of financial ruin and in political disgrace, Roed-Larsen returned to Israel, where his wife, Mona Juul, had become Norway's ambassador. Roed-Larsen's friendship with Peres soon blossomed into a business relationship. In 1999, he and his wife were given an award by the Peres Center for Peace. Despite his repeated claims as a sometimes United Nations envoy that Israel was guilty of "war crimes," no one in Israel found anything untoward in the honor.

When Israeli reporter David Bedein revealed in April 2002 that the prize had also carried a cash award of $100,000, heads began to turn. Roed-Larsen protested that he had fully disclosed the money to the Norwegian government. But a Norwegian Foreign Ministry spokesman publicly challenged his veracity. "No one in the Foreign Ministry has known about these sums of money. . . . When he says that the Norwegian diplomats present at the awards ceremony in 1999 were informed about the money, that is completely incorrect." The ministry said it planned to investigate "how closely [Roed-Larsen's wife] Mona Juul was involved in the decision-making process which led to Norway contributing over 10 million Norwegian kroner to the Peres Peace Center, which awarded the prize."[80]

Given that Roed-Larsen also sat on the board of governors of the Peres Center when the award was made, and that his wife represented a principal foreign funder, the payment had all the appearances of self-dealing. The Norwegian Foreign Ministry issued a formal written reprimand to Mona Juhl on May 23, 2002, and the next day she agreed to return her half of the $100,000 prize.[81] But Roed-Larsen escaped sanction by the Norwegian government for violating civil service regulations by hiding behind his on-again, off-again United Nations affiliation.[82] Bedein says he discovered record of the payments to Roed-Larsen in official papers filed by the Peres Center with the Interior Ministry's Registrar of Non-Profit Organizations. "The Peres PR people put it in the open record to show how proud they were of such an accomplishment," he said.[83]

Roed-Larsen has never wavered in his support for Arafat, nor has he refrained from getting involved in Israel's domestic politics on behalf of his friends on the Left. Once Ariel Sharon was elected prime minister in Israel in early 2001, Roed-Larsen became a vocal critic. When Sharon's government cut off transfers of tax revenues to Arafat, Roed-Larsen helped convince the European Union to make general support payments to the Palestinian Authority, money that Arafat used to pay for terrorist attacks, as the Israelis discovered from captured PA documents. Roed-Larsen also got the EU to fund Arafat's anti-Semitic textbooks. So determined was he to promote his political agenda, he told reporters once the scandal broke, that he had used the money from the Peres prize "to continue working in the region during times when he was not employed to do so."[84]

But he is best known to reporters as Europe's man on the scene, always the first to call journalists whenever he heard the sound of Israeli tank treads. After the battle of Jenin in April 2002, it was Roed-Larsen who took sympathetic reporters and VIP visitors from Europe to tour Palestinian houses destroyed by Israeli forces. "Israel has lost all moral authority," he thundered as he exposed this latest "massacre." Roed-Larsen was filmed touring the bulldozed streets and houses of a United Nations Relief and Works Agency (UNRWA) refugee camp in Jenin, turning up his nose in fine European disgust at the brutality of the Israeli army. British reporters touring with him conveniently came upon an "eyewitness"—one—who described a horrific scene. Identified as "Kamal Anis, a labourer" *(The Times),* "Kamal Anis, 28" *(Daily Telegraph),* and "A quiet, sad-looking young man called Kamal Anis" *(The Independent),* he claimed he had personally witnessed Israeli soldiers "pile 30 bodies beneath a half-wrecked house," then bulldoze the building, "bringing the ruins down on the corpses." In order to finish the job, he claimed the evil Jews "flattened the area with a tank" to make sure that international human rights investigators would never ever find the evidence. After that "historic" testimony, Kamal Anis disappeared along with the corpses and was never heard of again.

To put a number on the dead, reporters went to PA official Saab Erekat, who picked the number three thousand out of his hat. A few days later, he said five hundred had been killed. When the dust cleared, the PA said fifty-six Palestinians had died, most of them PA policemen killed in fierce fighting within the refugee camp. Palestinian fighters interviewed by American reporters called Jenin a "great victory over the Jews" because they had managed to kill twenty-three Israeli soldiers. They were especially proud when a ten-year-old child managed to kill an entire patrol of Israeli reservists on April 9—thirteen soldiers in all—by detonating himself in their midst. Not wanting to fire on an innocent child, the soldiers had allowed him to approach.[85]

The Israeli cabinet was so outraged by Roed-Larsen's manipulation of the truth that they actually discussed declaring him persona non grata—surely a world first for the husband of a sitting foreign ambassador, Attorney General Elyakim Rubinstein told reporters. Coming to Roed-Larsen's defense was his old friend and benefactor Shimon Peres. "A procedure like this," the foreign minister said, "would do injustice to a man who has made a special contribution toward peace in our region for years." His solicitude gave rise to suggestions from "high-ranking members of his own Labor Party" that the $100,000 payment in 1999 to Roed-Larsen and his wife was "a kickback for their intervention on his behalf with the Nobel Committee in 1994." Peres "vigorously denied" the story almost the instant it was aired by Israeli journalist Yoav Yitzhak on Channel 1 television.[86] But it was soon reported that Peres had helped to funnel even more money to Roed-Larsen that year, when he sat on a panel of seven judges who named Roed-Larsen a winner of the $100,000 International Activist Award from the Gleitsman Foundation.[87]

The Israeli sharks began circling around Peres. Up in Oslo, however, it was the other recipient of the 1994 Nobel Peace Prize who rankled the most.

† † †

Now in his late seventies, with a crest of thick wavy white hair and lively blue eyes, former Christian Democratic Party chairman Kåre Kristiansen has been Israel's most outspoken supporter in Norway for the past forty years. An Evangelical Christian, he believes in the historical and biblical claims of the Jews to the land of Israel, and during the dark hours of the 1973 war, he established the Friends of Israel group in the Storting, Norway's Parliament. At the time, 108 of the Storting's 165 members joined, a clear majority. Over his long career, Kristiansen has frequently sparred over Middle East policy with "the other" Kåre of Norwegian politics, Conservative Party leader Kåre Willoch.

"When Willoch became prime minister in 1983, my party entered the government coalition," Kristiansen told me over a late lunch outside Oslo in July 2002. "Because I headed the Foreign Affairs Committee in Parliament, I was in line to become foreign minister, but Willoch said I was too pro-Israel." He became minister of oil and energy instead.[88]

When he left Parliament in 1989, he was appointed to the five-member Nobel Peace Prize Committee—ironically, not by his own party, but on the recommendation of Progress Party leader Carl I. Hagen. Left-wing observers of European politics have almost invariably tried to marginalize Hagen and his party as anti-Semitic, right-wing extremists. But it was Hagen who took the initiative to revive the Friends of Israel group in Parliament in the spring of 2002, to counter efforts by the Left to delegitimize the Jewish state.[89] Norwegian journalist Vejbjørn Selbekk asked Hagen recently why he had supported Kristiansen's appointment to the Nobel Committee. "He said he chose Kåre specifically to keep Arafat from getting the peace prize," Selbekk told me. "Hagen never mentioned this specifically," Kristiansen demurred. "But I knew his positions. At that time, none of us thought it could occur. Give the Nobel Peace Prize to Arafat? What a silly thing! Instead of the man who'd done the most for peace, he was in my opinion the man who had done the most to destroy peace."

At the beginning of 1994, the five members of the Nobel Peace Prize Committee met to share their respective lists. "Arafat was never on my list," says Kristiansen, "and Peres was never at the top of my list. I made it clear I would never accept Arafat as a candidate. By statute, the vote must be unanimous. Until the last round, I opposed giving Arafat the prize."

But Kristiansen and committee chairman Francis Sejersted were the only non-Socialists of the five-member prize committee. "I went to the chairman and said, Either you join me in opposing Arafat, or I have to resign." In the end, they worked out a deal. Sejersted announced the prize recipients at the same time Kristiansen held a press conference to announce his resignation. He could say truthfully that he never voted for Arafat, and the chairman could say the vote was unanimous. "Terje Roed-

Larsen and the Labor Party thought that giving the peace prize to Arafat and Peres would strengthen the Oslo process and enhance Norway's prestige," Kristiansen said. "They actually believed Arafat would become more liberal if he got the Nobel Peace Prize, just as today, they believe he will become a more peaceful man if only he gets a new state. This is just a naive way of thinking."

Pushing for Arafat on the committee were two anti-Israel radicals, Sissel Runbeck and Hanna Kvanmo. Runbeck was the former wife of Bjorn Tore Godal, who became minister of foreign affairs that year after the death of Oslo architect Johan Jorgen Holst. Both Godal and his former wife had been leaders of the Labor Party Youth League, the AUF, when it adopted a resolution that called for the destruction of the Israeli state.[90] As for Hanna Kvanmo, the Socialist left parliamentarian, her own past, now largely forgotten, had been a national scandal when she was first elected to Parliament in 1973.

"Dear Aryan Kindred," begins an article devoted to Hanna Kvanmo on a Web site of Nazi nostalgia. "Today I will tell you a very terrible story about some 1,000 young girls who [put] their lives [at] stake to help wounded soldiers and were imprisoned for their humanity after WW2." The wounded soldiers were all Germans, fighting in Hitler's army. One of the volunteer Nazi nurses from Norway was the sixteen-year-old Hanna Kvanmo.[91]

Hanna Kvanmo was convicted for collaborating with the Nazis in 1948 and sent to jail. Although she now refers to her past as youthful indiscretions, she revealed in an autobiographical account published in 1990 that she had actually volunteered on three separate occasions to serve as a Nazi nurse, at ages sixteen, eighteen, and nineteen. She also acknowledged that she had joined the Nazi Party in Germany and had worked as a translator for the Gestapo when they conducted interrogations of Norwegian Resistance fighters.[92]

"Hanna Kvanmo and I were already antagonists in Parliament well before joining swords in the Nobel Prize Committee," Kristiansen says. Her political journey from Nazi Party member and wartime collaborator to the anti-Semitic hard Left "clearly shows that the extreme Left and the extreme Right meet at the bottom," Kristiansen said.

Even in retirement, Kåre Kristiansen continues to fight for decency in

Norwegian politics. "Kåre Willoch is bad, but the state bishop of Oslo is worse," he says. The appointment of former Center Party leader Gunnar Stålsett to become bishop of Oslo on May 24, 1998, "almost broke up the government," Kristiansen says. Stålsett had for many years been chairman of Geneva's Lutheran World Federation, a group that has taken strong positions against the Jewish state. "Our prime minister, Bondevik, claimed he had to recuse himself from the cabinet vote on the appointment, because the only other candidate was his own uncle. I argued that this was not a conflict of interest, but he didn't agree. I believe he secretly wanted Stålsett to get the job. The final vote was ten to nine."

Besides appearing with Nazi flags at anti-Israel demonstrations, Bishop Stålsett regularly derides the legitimacy of a Jewish state on national television. "I recall challenging him once on Israel. After the cameras went dark, he blew up. 'Du er frekte!'—rude—he shouted. How dare I oppose him, a bishop! Not being a member of his church, I disagreed. 'You have no authority over me. You are not the guardian of my soul.' He began trembling with rage. 'In the name of Jesus Christ, I appeal to you to alter your opinion.'" Kristiansen says he wrote the bishop afterward, saying he had never before heard such an outrageous mixing of religion with politics. "Anti-Semitism in Norway goes very far back. It is where fascism and communism meet," he believes. "Anti-Semitism is the mother of all race hatreds, the darkest corner of the human soul."

Before he departs, Kristiansen tells me a story he says he frequently uses in speeches around Norway, one he has adopted from a nineteenth-century Norwegian politician who was involved in helping to get legal restrictions lifted against Norway's tiny Jewish population.

"There was once a Jewish trader who came to a Norwegian village at Christmastime bringing gifts. One year he didn't arrive, and everyone wondered where he was. On his way to the village, there was a driving snowstorm, and he heard something in the woods. He stopped and heard the cry again. He went toward it and found a little girl, nearly frozen to death. So he dropped his bundles and wrapped her in his coat and headed off to find someplace warm.

"That evening, Christmas Eve, he arrived at a cottage and knocked at the door. A woman answered. When she recognized the itinerate trader, she slammed the door. 'What, a Jew! Why is a filthy Jew coming here on such a holy night?' The next morning she came out of her cottage and found him slumped in the snow. 'What's this filthy Jew doing here still?' Then she saw something in his coat and, opening it, broke down in tears. 'Why, that's our little Annie, who disappeared in the woods.'

"The moral of this story," says Kristiansen. "Take care of the Jew, and you take care of your own future. Take care of the weak, of those who need your help, and you help yourself."

✝ ✝ ✝

What's happened in France, Austria, and Norway is happening elsewhere in Europe, and indeed in the United States as well. The same political faction that has been pushing Israel into a "peace process" with the PLO is also leading an international campaign to demonize and delegitimize the Jewish state. Even if you grant every charge of the Left's indictment of Israel—it represses the Palestinians, it is violating international law, it has failed to achieve the democracy to which it aspires—that still cannot explain the virulence of the attacks on Israel or the massive press coverage Israel's alleged "misdeeds" receive, argues French writer Gilles William Goldnadel. No similar outrage greeted Syria's massacre of twenty thousand Islamists in Hama in 1982, the gassing of several thousand Kurds by Saddam Hussein in Halabja in 1988, or the massacre by Islamic fundamentalists in Iran of tens of thousands of their opponents after the 1979 revolution against the shah. "Just as the Jewish people were the object of a particular hate until the creation of the State of Israel," Goldnadel writes, "so today the Jewish state is the object of a hatred that is just as particular. . . . It is a single hate, common to the people and to the state."[93]

The "new" anti-Semitism in Europe began with Israel's victory in 1967, Goldnadel argues, an event that ended the myth of the weak Jew cherished by the Left. Forgotten were "Israel's narrow, indefensible borders . . . and the overwhelming demographic superiority of the Arabs," he writes. The European Left continues to love the "ideal Jew"—the meek, assimilated Jew of the Diaspora, who agrees to live in *dhimmi*-tude under Arab rule—while the Right loves the "real" Jew, the proud, militant Israeli state.

Per Ahlmark argues that the "new" anti-Semites also have a long track record of anti-Americanism and during the Cold War were fierce apologists for Communist tyranny. "For the 1968 generation, anti-Zionism has become a substitute for their pro-Marxist ideologies," he says. In a remarkable book called *Tyranny and the Left,* Ahlmark examined the statements and writings of Sweden's top left-wing intellectuals, politicians, and journalists and found almost unanimously that they "were praising totalitarian governments or condoning their most flagrant crimes." Not only did they defend Mao, they also defended Pol Pot. Not only did they oppose American and Israeli "imperialism," they proposed Cuban and Arab "nationalism" in their place.

Former prime minister Olof Palme was the most famous of these leaders and one of the first to voice publicly what has become the standard exercise of Holocaust denial by the Euro-Left. In a July 1, 1982, speech, in the midst of the war in Lebanon, Palme compared Israel to Nazi Germany.

> Those of my generation who, when we were very young indeed, saw pictures of Jewish children in the concentration camps and ghettos and realized the unspeakable crime which had been committed against them, from which we experienced a pain that accompanies us through life—we naturally feel beside ourselves with the same pain when we see pictures of the Palestinian children, *persecuted in exactly the same way* [Ahlmark's italics]. But this time it is Israel which is behind the outrages.[94]

In the past, remarked Ahlmark, "the most dangerous anti-Semites were those who wanted to make the world *Judenrein,* free of Jews. Today the most dangerous anti-Semites might be those who want to make the world *Judenstaatrein,* free of a Jewish state."[95] For without a Jewish state, what becomes of the Jews?

THE ISLAMIC REPUBLIC OF AMERICA

10

Perhaps most astonishing of all, at least on the surface, is the spread of open anti-Semitism in America. Over the past decade, anti-Semitic hate speech has become a common occurrence on America's campuses, where the cardinals of political correctness have decreed an end to all forms of hate speech but two: hatred of America and hatred of Jews. It is even more common in certain segments of America's divided Muslim community, where no nuance separates anti-Semitism from hatred of Israel and only the most fragile "truce" prevents leading spokesmen from calling for violence against America. As in Europe, the facilitators have come not from the extreme Right, but from the hard Left. Indeed, in the History and Political Science Departments of most U.S. campuses, it is hard enough finding a professor who admits to sympathizing with the Republican Party, let alone with neo-Nazi skinheads. But sympathizing with Palestinian suicide bombers and their "cause" is common.

Laurie Zoloth has been director of Jewish studies at San Francisco State University (SFSU) for seven years and has lived in the community for two decades. But she had never seen anything like the actions by a riotous crowd on May 7, 2002, that cornered some fifty students and faculty after a pro-Israel demonstration on her campus. As the counterdemonstrators poured into the plaza, they screamed at the Jews: "Get out or we will kill you," "Hitler did not finish the job," and "Go back to Russia, Jew!" Students waved posters showing cans of "Palestinian Children Meat." On the label was a baby with its stomach sliced open, with the inscription: "Made in Israel according to Jewish rites under American license." The label said this horror had been "manufactured by Prime Minister Ariel Sharon." A shocked SFSU president Robert A. Corrigan later told reporters the slogans were "too hate filled to repeat." But police and administrators heard them and were not shocked enough to remove the counterdemonstrators even as they backed the Jews into a corner of the plaza, physically menacing them. "The police told me that they had been told not to arrest anyone, and that if they did, 'it would start a riot.' I told them that it already was a riot," Zoloth says.[1]

The pro-Israel demonstrators were eventually escorted through the hostile crowd to the Jewish Studies Center by armed San Francisco police. In the weeks that followed, the slurs and the threats continued unabated, despite pledges by SFSU administrators to find those responsible for the near violence and sanction them.

> I cannot fully express what it feels like to have to walk across campus daily, past maps of the Middle East that do not include Israel . . . past poster after poster calling out "Zionism=racism," and "Jews=Nazis." This is not civic discourse, this is not free speech; this is the Weimar Republic with brown shirts it cannot control. This is the casual introduction of the medieval blood libel and virulent hatred smeared around our campus in a manner so ordinary that it hardly excites concern—except if you are a Jew, and you understand that hateful words have always led to hateful deeds."[2]

Zoloth's anger was mixed with sadness, as the failure of any of her fellow faculty members to stand by her sank in. "I knew that if a crowd of Palestinian or African American students had been there, surrounded by a crowd of white racists screaming racist threats, shielded by police, the faculty and staff would have no trouble deciding which side to stand on," she said. "In fact, the scene recalled for me many moments in the civil rights movement, or the United Farm Workers movement, when, as a student, I stood with black and Latino colleagues, surrounded by hateful mobs. . . . How ironic that it all took place under the picture of Cesar Chavez, who led the very demonstrations that I took part in as a student."

What happened to Laurie Zoloth and the Jews of the Hillel community at San Francisco State was not an isolated incident. In just the month of April 2002, more than twenty similar incidents occurred on campuses across America in which Jews were either physically assaulted or where campus groups publicly distributed Holocaust denial materials or prominently compared Israelis to Nazis.

At UC Santa Barbara, and at George Washington University in downtown Washington, D.C., dormitories were defaced with anti-Semitic graffiti including phrases such as "God Hates Jews," "Burn the Torah," and "Israel=SS."[3]

At the University of Illinois, unknown assailants smashed the front window of the home of an Israeli couple, where the couple had displayed an Israeli flag earlier in the day. Their car, parked out front, was also vandalized.

At UC Berkeley and UC San Diego, Muslim student groups distributed flyers with fabricated or out-of-context quotations from the Talmud, aimed at breeding hatred of Jews. One flyer claimed, "A Jew is permitted to rape, cheat, and perjure himself but he must take care that he is not found out, so that Israel may not suffer." Another alleged that according to Jewish Scripture, "A Gentile girl who is three years old can be violated." Yet another claimed this "Jewish" doctrine: "The Jews are human beings, but the nations of the world are not human beings but beasts."[4]

The Jew-hatred erupted at the Ivy Leagues and at state universities, from the East Coast to the West. It was encouraged and at times even guided by faculty members who have fed their students a steady diet of anti-Israel and anti-American propaganda. "For three decades," writes Middle East scholar Daniel Pipes, "left-wing extremists have dominated American academics, spouting odd but seemingly harmless theories about 'deconstruction,' post-modernism,' 'race, gender and class,' while venting against the United States, its government and its allies. Only these ideas are not so harmless. . . . Not surprisingly, some interpret all this as implicit permission to harass Jewish and pro-Israel students."[5] Pipes provides a disturbing repertory of anti-Semitic statements by prominent faculty members at Columbia University, SUNY Binghamton, Kent State University in Ohio, and the University of Oregon. In offering a class on "The Politics and Poetics of Palestinian Resistance" at UC Berkeley, the English Department's Snehal Shingavi warned conservatives "to seek other sections" if they didn't agree with his opinions. Instead of encouraging intellectual rigor and open-mindedness, America's universities are providing a safe haven for intolerance and bigotry.

In Canada, radical pro-Palestinian students at Concordia University broke windows and battled with riot police in downtown Montreal, to prevent former Israeli prime minister Benjamin Netanyahu from giving a university lecture. "What are they afraid of? Hearing the truth?" Netanyahu asked. The students boasted that they had "achieved their rights" and would " continue to work like that."[6]

At the University of Chicago, harassment of Jewish students has become a daily event, writes Joseph Farah of *WorldNetDaily*. Here are a few samples of the types of incidents that have been occurring since the spring of 2002:

- A car drove up to a Jewish student on campus and a passenger screamed: "Death to Jews. Hitler should have finished you all off when he had the chance."
- On a public listserv in the Humanities Department, a pro-Palestinian graduate student joked openly about Auschwitz.
- A Jewish senior was told by a university-appointed preceptor that he couldn't be "bothered" reading her BA paper because it focused on topics relating to Judaism and Zionism.
- Flyers posted in a dorm to publicize a pro-Israel rally were defaced with obscenities and vile, anti-Semitic suggestions.[7]

After a series of anti-Muslim incidents that erupted in the wake of 9/11, university president Don Randel issued a "zero tolerance" policy forbidding discrimination against Muslims. But when Jewish students appealed to him for help, he refused to condemn the rampant anti-Jewish bigotry. "If this were an isolated instance, we could chalk it up to one university sadly out of touch or too timid to respond to the new political correctness on campus," Farah writes. "But the University of Chicago is no different in this regard to dozens of other campuses I hear from on a daily basis."

Farah's conclusion is chilling. "This is how it begins," he writes, referring back to the Germany of the 1920s. "The bullies are winning the day."

Washington Institute fellow Martin Kramer has studied the growth of Middle East studies programs at U.S. universities over the past thirty-five years. Although some 125 universities and colleges offer degrees in the area, there are few Jewish studies programs, and Hebrew is virtually untaught as a language. Many of the programs are funded by Arab governments, including Libya, and their professors fill the academic journals and appear regularly on the nightly news, presenting views that correspond with those of their sponsors. Kramer calls them "factories of error."[8]

Some high-profile "Orientalists" almost flaunt their anti-Semitic views. Such is the case of Professor Edward Said, who holds an endowed chair in English literature at Columbia University and who boasts of his membership in the Palestinian National Council. On February 14, 2003, he published an article with *Al-Ahram al-Arabi* weekly in Egypt titled "A Monument to Hypocrisy," which accused "the Perles and Wolfowitzes of this country" of leading America into war with Iraq, a war "planned by a docile, professionalized staff in places like Washington and Tel Aviv." (The specific references were to Richard Perle, a prominent "hawk" who was chairman of the Defense Policy Board, a nonpaying job outside of government, and to Deputy Defense Secretary Paul Wolfowitz, but obviously the larger reference was to "Jews.")

Professor Said went well beyond the slander of less talented anti-Semites such as Congressman James Moran (D-Va.) who, in a March 3, 2003, speech to the St. Anne's Episcopal Church in Reston, Virginia, blamed the American Jewish community of pushing the nation to war.[9] Professor Said alleged that White House spokesman Ari Fleischer was an Israeli agent who secretly controlled the policy of the government of the United States. President Bush and his advisers, Said wrote, were "slaves of power perfectly embodied in the repetitive monotone of their collective spokesman Ari Fleischer, who I believe is also an Israeli citizen." Fleischer says that is not true, and Professor Said would not respond to a reporter's inquiries as to why he had made the allegation. Similar allegations have been made by a publication called *The End Times,* which claims it is dedicated to righting the Jewish effort to establish a satanic "Anti-Christ Beast System Rule of the Earth," and by the White Aryan Resistance (WAR), which has published a list of prominent Zionist agents that included Fleischer and Secretary of State Colin Powell.[10]

† † †

Graduation ceremonies at America's prestigious institutions of higher learning have always attracted famous speakers. During the Clinton presidency, both the president and the First Lady were prized speakers, and colleges and universities often competed to see who would succeed in attracting them. President Bush returned to less flamboyant traditions, announcing well ahead of time that he would deliver the commencement address at the U.S. Military Academy at West Point, as it prepared to graduate the first crop of officers in a generation who were knowingly preparing for war. But as the Harvard class of 2002 prepared their final salute to Harvard Yard, nine months after the attacks on the World Trade Center and the Pentagon, the buzz was all about a twenty-two-year-old senior named Zayed M. Yasin.

"Imagine it's June 1942—just a few months after Adolf Hitler declared war on the United States," Middle East scholar Daniel Pipes wrote. "At Harvard University, a faculty committee has chosen a German-American to give one of three student orations at the festive commencement ceremony. He titles it 'American Kampf,' purposefully echoing the title of Hitler's book, *Mein Kampf (My Struggle)* in order to show the positive side of 'Kampf.' When this prompts protests, a Harvard dean defends it as a 'thoughtful oration' that defines the concept of Kampf as a personal struggle 'to promote justice and understanding in ourselves and in our society.' "

To make matters worse, Pipes says, imagine that the student "turns out to be past president of the Harvard German Society, a group with a pro-Nazi taint—but the administration still isn't bothered. Nor is it perturbed that he praised a Nazi front group for its 'incredible work' as well as its 'professionalism, compassion and dedication to helping people in dire need,' then raised money for it."

Pro-Saudi Muslim spokesmen and liberal academics screamed that Pipes had gone over the line in his portrait of Zayed Yasin as an enemy collaborator.[11] But had he? Here are the facts:

- Zayed Yasin's speech, originally titled "American Jihad," drew its central theme from a term frequently used by Yasser Arafat to promote suicide bombers and by Osama bin Laden to justify the murder of Americans, Christians, and Jews around the world. Yasin explained that his goal was to convince his audience that "jihad is not something that should make someone feel uncomfortable," but a personal, spiritual struggle for self-betterment. Pipes retorted that jihad has historically meant one thing: "military action with the object of the expansion of Islam." That was indeed the type of thing "that should make someone feel uncomfortable," he said.
- As president of the Harvard Islamic Society, in November 2000 Yasin co-hosted a fund-raiser for the Holy Land Foundation,[12] an Islamic "charity" closed down by President Bush because it was sending funds to Hamas. When the controversy erupted over his speech, Yasin defended the foundation and his actions on its behalf. "I felt that it was very wrong for this very important kind of humanitarian assistance to be shut down. That's still the way I feel," he said.

Pipes claims that hiding jihad's legacy of murder and destruction of non-Muslim societies is "standard operating procedure at Harvard." A Harvard professor of Islamic history portrays jihad as "a struggle without arms," while the Harvard Islamic Society's faculty adviser defines true jihad as nothing more than a wish "to do good in society." Behind the smokescreen, Pipes argues, is a pattern of behavior "pretending Islam had nothing to do with 9/11."

Jihad was a popular subject at Harvard, where Islamic student groups have enjoyed an organized presence for years. As the commencement controversy brewed, a group of Harvard faculty circulated a petition calling on the university's massive $19 billion endowment fund to divest from Israel and from American companies that sell arms to Israel.

Harvard professor of Yiddish literature Ruth Wisse, an authority on the history of anti-Semitism, believes the divestment campaign was clearly anti-Semitic, because it was aimed at delegitimizing the Jewish state. Comparing the petition to the near mauling of Jewish demonstrators at San Francisco State University, she wrote that it was "corrupt and cowardly in ways that a mob assault is not. . . . How very clever to call upon Israel to obey this or that resolution of the UN when Arab states remain in perpetual defiance of the entire UN Charter!"[13]

Even more important, Wisse argued, were the parallels between the anti-Semitic intent of these academics and the anti-Americanism of the Left. The main signatories were "noted for their long-standing agitation against the so-called crimes of American capitalism, against American 'colonization' of third world countries, against putative American abuse of human rights." Since the 9/11 attacks, however, they were "finding it tough to promote al-Qaeda as effectively as they once did Ho Chi Minh," although some continued to express admiration for "the brave fighter Osama bin Laden." With America's wounds still fresh, they found "it is much safer to condemn imperfect democracy by prosecuting Israel rather than America." She called the supporters of the disinvestment campaign "the Campus Coalition for Tyranny."

Anti-Semitism on campus is fueled by the twin engines of a growing Muslim population that is becoming increasingly radicalized and the more traditional "hate America first" crowd. After listening to the overheated rhetoric for many months, Harvard's new president, former Clinton administration secretary of the Treasury Lawrence Summers, spoke out at a September 17, 2002, prayer breakfast. He chose his words with care. "I speak with you today not as President of the University but as a concerned member of our community about something that I never thought I would become seriously worried about—the issue of anti-Semitism. I am Jewish, identified but hardly devout." To be *identified* as a Jew by others was something he had given little thought to until then. But as he watched the "synagogue burnings, physical assaults on Jews, or the painting of swastikas on Jewish memorials in every country in Europe," suddenly history began to suggest disturbing parallels. And most shocking of all to this former Clinton administration liberal was the realization of where it was coming from—not "poorly educated right-wing populists . . . [but] progressive intellectual communities. Serious and thoughtful people are advocating and taking actions that are anti-Semitic in their effect if not their intent."[14]

The examples Summers cited were all too common. In Europe, he said, "hundreds of European academics" had pledged to end all support for Israeli researchers, but not those from any other nation. Israeli scholars now get forced off the boards of international journals, he noted, for no other reason than that they are Jews. At protests against the IMF and global capitalism, protesters now commonly "also lash out at Israel." What Israel has to do with the IMF was a mystery to this former Treasury secretary. Yet "at anti-IMF rallies last spring, chants were heard equating Hitler and Sharon."

Then Summers turned to Harvard, where fund-raising events for organizations "later found to support terrorism have been held by student organizations on this and other campuses with . . . very little criticism." He personally pledged not to cave in to the ongoing disinvestment drive, which "called for the University to single out Israel among all nations as the lone country where it is inappropriate for any part of the university's endowment to be invested."

Summers made his plea for tolerance, mutual respect, and academic freedom after careful reflection. "I have always throughout my life been put off by those who heard the sound of breaking glass, in every insult or slight, and conjured up images of Hitler's Kristallnacht at any disagreement with Israel. Such views have always seemed to me alarmist if not slightly hysterical. But I have to say that while they still seem to me unwarranted, they seem rather less alarmist in the world of today than they did a year ago."

†††

No one better typified the hate-America-first faction of campus radicals than MIT professor Noam Chomsky, who has churned out books and pamphlets and speeches worldwide "with one message alone: America is the Great Satan; it is the fount of evil in the world."[15] Not a single anti-American cause has passed beyond Chomsky's gun sights. During the Vietnam War, he was pro-Vietcong. During the Cold War, he was pro-Soviet. During the 1990–1991 Gulf war, he was pro–Saddam Hussein. And throughout Israel's fifty-year struggle for survival, Avram Noam Chomsky, born in Philadelphia in 1928, the son of noted Hebrew scholar William Zev Chomsky, has been pro-Arab, advocating the destruction of the Jewish state. Former leftist David Horowitz calls Chomsky "without question the most devious, the most dishonest, and—in this hour of his nation's grave crisis—the most treacherous intellect in America." But he is best understood not as an intellectual, Horowitz writes, but "as the leader of a secular religious cult, as the ayatollah of anti-American hate."[16]

In a statement released the day after 9/11, Chomsky compared the devastation at the World Trade Center and the Pentagon to the 1998 U.S. cruise missile strike on a suspected chemical weapons production plant in Sudan. That midnight retaliatory raid, conducted after Osama bin Laden had killed two dozen Americans and more than two hundred Africans in twin bombings of U.S. embassies in Kenya and Tanzania, had been carried out "with no credible pretext, destroying half [Sudan's] pharmaceutical supplies and killing unknown numbers of people," Chomsky asserted.[17] It was vintage Chomsky, making "the victim, America, appear as an even more heinous perpetrator than the criminal himself. However bad this may seem, you have done worse," was Chomsky's message to Americans.

On numerous occasions, Chomsky has also thrown in his lot with prominent Holocaust deniers, asserting their right to question the existence of the Nazi gas chambers as "legitimate" historical research. Researcher and writer Werner Cohn first revealed Chomsky's relationship to French Holocaust denier Robert Faurisson and his group's publishing house in 1988.[18] Known as the Vieille Taupe (the Old Mole), this was the same group of anti-Semites and conspiracy theorists who later championed the outrageous claims of French pseudojournalist Thierry Meyssan. As Cohn documented in his study, Chomsky wasn't content just to provide intellectual support to Faurisson and his coterie of Holocaust deniers, or to have his works published in French under their imprint. "He has promoted the anti-Semitic idea that the Jewish religion is basically antisocial," Cohn wrote. Yet Chomsky has still managed to convince most American leftists that he is one of them. His anti-Semitic statements and activities have gone largely ignored in the United States.

One reason is Chomsky's own deviousness. In many cases, his anti-Semitism comes buried behind careful formulas, caveats, and assorted intellectual muck. But it was right out in the open in this reply to *New York Times* columnist A. M. Rosenthal after Rosenthal had argued against the creation of a Palestinian state in the West Bank and Gaza by reminding readers that Jordan, created from the former British mandate of Palestine, was already a Palestinian state. "We might ask how the *Times* would react to an Arab claim," Chomsky wrote, "that the Jews do not merit a 'second homeland' because they already have New York, with a huge Jewish population, Jewish-run media, a Jewish mayor, and domination of cultural and economic life."[19]

Rosenthal never used the term *second homeland,* but it was standard Chomsky practice to set up straw men, falsely ascribing beliefs to others, and then whack at them with his rhetorical sword. In this case, he used terms that were "staples of traditional anti-Semitism," Cohn wrote. "Chomsky's target here is very simply Jews."[20] Yet no one in the left-wing academic circles Chomsky frequented seemed to care.

Chomsky was also protected by the fact that until the early 1990s, his most malicious statements were reserved for tiny ultraleftist publications, mainly in France, where they remained "hidden from the general American reader."[21] But as time went on, "Chomsky's ties with the Holocaust-denying Institute for Historical Review [IHR] have been strengthened," Cohn found. The Los Angeles–based IHR and its publishing house, Noontide Press, offer for sale a wide variety of anti-Semitic and Nazi propaganda, including the works of Adolf Hitler and Joseph Goebbels and English-language editions of *The Protocols of the Elders of Zion.* In 1995, Noontide began offering no fewer than five Chomsky titles, noting that Chomsky "enlightens as no other writer on Israel, Zionism, and American complicity." Cohn concluded that "[Chomsky's] associates are in the business of justifying the Nazis and that Chomsky helps them to carry on this business, not at all as a defender of freedom of speech but as a warm and reliable friend."

Cohn and Australian writer William D. Rubinstein sent Chomsky detailed proof of Faurisson's anti-Semitism, including the Frenchman's infamous statement that all witnesses to the Holocaust at Auschwitz are liars "because they are Jews." Chomsky's reply was stunning and to my knowledge has never been mentioned by any of his academic colleagues in the United States:

> I see no anti-Semitic implications in denial of the existence of gas chambers, or even denial of the holocaust. Nor would there be anti-Semitic implications, per se, in the claim that the holocaust (whether one believes it took place or not) is being exploited, viciously so, by apologists for Israeli repression and violence. I see no hint of anti-Semitic implications in Faurisson's work. . . ."[22]

In 1987, Pantheon Books brought out a five-hundred-page collection of Chomsky's political writings, calling him "America's leading dissident intellectual."[23] Chomsky's influence on two generations of American academics has been profound and far-reaching. With such a godfather, it is no wonder that U.S. campuses regularly spike their anti-Americanism with a potentially deadly dose of anti-Semitism.

†††

During 1983 and 1984, members of an obscure right-wing terrorist group known as the Order waged a two-year campaign of robbery and counterfeiting in the hopes of sparking "a racial revolution in America." Their goal was to "trigger a rebellion of the white population against the forces of ZOG, the Zionist Occupation Government of the United States."[24] Their blueprint for this bizarre effort was a 1978 novel, *The Turner Diaries,* written by William Pierce, the leader of the National Alliance, a neo-Nazi group based in West Virginia.

The book's hero, Earl Turner, was the leader of an underground guerrilla movement waging a terrorist campaign against a Jewish-controlled American government. This venomous but highly imaginative screed showed the unholy marriage between anti-Semitism and anti-Americanism at the other end of the political spectrum. As we saw in Europe, when it comes to hating the Jews and hating the freedoms for which America stands, extreme Left and extreme Right meet at the bottom.

Widely considered a terrorist's "how to" manual, *The Turner Diaries* describes in great detail a bomb attack on a federal building, carried out as the first step of a nationwide revolt. When Gulf war veteran Timothy McVeigh was arrested shortly after bombing the Murrah Federal Building in Oklahoma City on April 19, 1995, he was carrying a copy of *The Turner Diaries* and was said to have been profoundly influenced by it.

Asked to comment on the blast just hours later, terrorism expert Steven Emerson noted the physical similarities between the way the Murrah Building was attacked and the April 18, 1983, attack on the U.S. embassy in Beirut. The near coincidence of the dates, the type of attack, and the fact that Hamas operatives "were known to be living in the Oklahoma City area" all suggested a possible Middle East connection. "Federal law enforcement officials" were investigating that possibility, he told television viewers, although he made clear that it was too early to say anything for sure.[25]

Once McVeigh's arrest was revealed a few days later, American Muslim leaders jumped on Emerson for having "slandered" them by accusing Islamic terrorists for the attack. Ever since, they have used the Oklahoma City bombing and *The Turner Diaries* as convenient whipping boys. It's not us, they protest: it's right-wing extremists. Even Jesse Jackson joined the chorus. "In Oklahoma City, they said they were looking for a Middle Eastern terrorist, and they found out it was the Middle West."[26] On 9/11, Osama bin Laden proved them all wrong.

While there are dozens of anti-Semitic fringe groups across America, from the American Nazi Party to Pierce's own National Alliance, they navigate far from the mainstream of the American political spectrum and have little if any noticeable influence on American campuses or on the media. Nor do they have institutional, financial, and operational ties with foreign governments or thousands of soldiers engaged in murder and terror who masquerade as "resistance" fighters.

The leaders of organized anti-Semitism in America can be found elsewhere. And it is no coincidence that their hatred of Jews comes wrapped in a profound contempt for the very American society that shelters them.

†††

The fact the meeting took place at all was unusual. Somehow, the event had slipped beneath the radar screen of the "mainstream" organizations, who claimed to represent the U.S. Muslim population. These groups worked very hard to monitor U.S. government activities and had a "war room"–style operation to counter remarks about radical Islam wherever they appeared. They regularly smeared journalists and terrorism experts such as Steve Emerson and Daniel Pipes as "anti-Muslim bigots" and "racists." But Sheikh Mohammad Hisham Kabbani was a fellow Muslim, leader of the Islamic Supreme Council of America. Since 1992, just one year after he arrived in America from his native Lebanon, Sheikh Kabbani had crossed swords with these groups. Until now, however, the blows had fallen within the closeted confines of mosques and Arabic-language media.

The State Department invited Sheikh Kabbani to the January 9, 1999, open forum on Islamic extremism precisely because they had learned he did not fear exposing the Saudi-backed Wahhabi lobby and their apologetics for terrorist groups that were killing Americans and Jews around the world. In his energetic presentation, wearing scholarly robes, the white-turbaned Kabbani warned U.S. officials that an organized effort was under way to hijack the Muslim community in America. It had been launched by Islamic extremists whose goals were totally incompatible with American values and whose methods in many instances violated American law. These Saudi-backed Muslim organizations "are declaring war against anyone who will not go with them" and had taken over "more than 80 percent of the mosques that have been established in the United States," he said. The struggle for the soul of Muslim America that Kabbani had been waging in the dark for the past seven years burst out into the open in a public fireworks display.[27]

Sheikh Kabbani traced the origin of extremist Islam to Muhammad ibn Abd al-Wahhab, the eighteenth-century Saudi cleric whose name today comes frequently to the lips of Osama bin Laden and the Saudi ruling family. Wahhabism was "hijacking the mike" by pouring huge sums of money into the United States to establish mosques, nonprofit foundations, and lobbying groups. Groups that had been active for decades on U.S. campuses informing students about Islam had become the mouthpieces for extremists, thanks to Saudi money and directives. Many of these organizations also were collecting money from major Muslim donors "to send to extremists outside the United States," he said. "They send it under humanitarian aid, but it doesn't go to humanitarian aid." Instead, most of the money was being used to buy weapons and to sponsor terror. "We want to tell you that the Muslim community as a whole is innocent from whatever extremism and extremist ideology is being spread" by such groups. "You are not hearing the authentic voice of Muslims, of moderate Muslims, but you are hearing the extremist voice of Muslims."

The response from the organizations Kabbani had not yet denounced by name came soon enough. On February 26, 1999, eight groups jointly issued a statement demanding that he retract "false and defamatory allegations" that "could have a profoundly negative impact on ordinary American Muslims." The list of signatories formed the visible front end of the vast Wahhabi network in America, whose aim was to infiltrate and control American Islam.[28] They twisted and deformed Kabbani's words until his meaning was unrecognizable, but the Lebanese Sufi imam was not surprised. Ever since Kabbani first began insisting that traditional Islam have a seat at the table of American Muslim institutions, he has been subjected to a pattern of vilification, discrimination, and outright lies.

At times, the efforts by the Wahhabi lobby to discredit Kabbani, who is a descendant of the Prophet, were so petty they appeared ludicrous. In 1994, the Saudi-backed Islamic Society of North America rejected Kabbani's request that they invite traditionalist Islamic scholars to address the annual ISNA convention. So instead Kabbani rented a booth at the conference meeting hall to distribute Koranic literature and respond to questions from visitors. Virtually the moment the booth opened, Kabbani's people were surrounded by ISNA security officers brandishing walkie-talkies, who demanded that they leave. ISNA convention manager Hamid Ghazali eventually confessed pathetically: "Is it not enough that so many people are following you and that you are attracting everybody? Do you also need to have a booth?" ISNA's president said he could not allow Kabbani to distribute traditional Sufi Muslim literature at the conference "due to the source of ISNA's funding."[29]

There was a serious reason behind such tactics. Moderate Muslim leaders such as Kabbani presented a threat to the doctrine of hate being spread by the Wahhabi lobby. At rallies and meetings over more than a decade across the United States, Saudi-financed groups have been drumming up support for terrorist organizations such as Hamas and Islamic Jihad. They have been raising money from American Muslims and recruiting terrorists, according to their own declarations and a growing series of federal government indictments. In 1989, at a convention in Kansas City, Missouri, they worked behind closed doors. Qatar-based Palestinian cleric Yusuf al-Qaradawi addressed an enthusiastic crowd in Arabic: "Our hour of judgment will not come until you fight the Jews [and] kill them. Muslims, wherever they are, should actively participate in the battle." A veiled Palestinian commander stood up, waving the Hamas flag in one hand and the Koran in the other. "Greetings . . . from the occupied land," he began. Then he gave a report "describing in methodical detail Hamas terrorist attacks" that drew enthusiastic cheers from the crowd every time he provided details of how they had killed Jews.[30]

With a huge influx of cash from Saudi Arabia, leaders of the Wahhabi lobby have gone mainstream in the United States and have lost their fear. At an anti-Israel rally in front of the White House on October 28, 2000, American Muslim Council president Abdul Rahman al-Amoudi derided those in the press and in government who had failed to get the radical message cloaked beneath the slick lobbying campaigns in English. "I have been labeled by the media in New York to be a supporter of Hamas. Anybody support Hamas here?" When the crowd burst out with responsive cheers, he shouted: "Hear that, Bill Clinton? We are *all* supporters of Hamas. *Allahu Akbar!*"[31] At the same rally—less than one year before September 11—the president of the Islamic Society of North America, Muzamil Siddiqi, added an open threat. "America has to learn . . . if you remain on the side of injustice, the wrath of God will come. Please, all Americans. Do you remember that? . . . If you continue doing injustice, and tolerate injustice, the wrath of God will come." By "injustice," he meant U.S. support for Israel. His reference to terrorist attacks against the United States was crystal clear to his audience. The poison of anti-Semitism and violence was leaking into the U.S. Muslim community through these Saudi-backed extremists. Sheikh Kabbani was one of the rare leaders who tried to stop it.

In 1998, an ISNA executive suggested that a foreign government was putting pressure on U.S. Muslim groups to prevent them from working with Kabbani's traditionalist Islamic Supreme Council of America. There was no doubt to which government he was referring: it was the kingdom of Saudi Arabia.[32] When Kabbani organized an "International Islamic Unity Conference" in Washington, D.C., in August 1998, the pro-Saudi organizations launched an offensive to discourage other Muslim leaders from attending. They spread slanders accusing Kabbani of being a Mossad agent through the Internet and e-mail lists, including "to a huge number of Muslim individuals responsible for mosques and Islamic organizations."[33] Speakers arriving from overseas told Kabbani they even had been discouraged from attending by an Immigration and Naturalization Service official at Dulles International Airport. "The agent explained that he was a Muslim convert and advised them not to attend, saying it was a *shirk* [idolators] conference and if they want to protect their faith, they should not attend." Just the word *shirk* is enough to instill fear in most Muslims, since idolatry is considered an unforgivable sin. The self-avowed Muslim INS agent gave them the names and telephone numbers of two Islamic "scholars" they could call for more information, both apparently affiliated with the ISNA.[34] Would-be speakers from the United States told Kabbani they received phone calls "from the embassy of one Muslim country," threatening that "if they attended the Islamic Unity conference, their stipends from that nation's Islamic organization would be cut."[35]

Efforts by the government of Saudi Arabia to control the Muslim community in America were already in full swing by the early 1980s, former U.S. diplomat and Muslim convert Dr. Robert Crane explains. Crane says he was approached in 1983 by the Saudi embassy in Washington to run a "cultural center" in the Watergate building. "I soon discovered that this was to be an intelligence operation designed to monitor and influence all the Muslims in America. . . . The objective presumably was to prevent the growing Muslim community in America from opposing the policies and interests of the regime in Saudi Arabia and the private investments of its elites in America." Crane witnessed a similar effort by the Saudi government "to fund, infiltrate, and control all of the national Muslim organizations" a decade later, when he founded and headed the Muslim American Bar Association. "Perhaps it is better that the full story not be told of the Wahhabi threat to America," he concluded.[36]

But that full story is now beginning to emerge thanks to the work of a number of experienced investigators, whose work has given courage to moderate Muslim leaders to denounce the Saudi attempt to hijack American Islam, and to government officials who for years have feared retribution from paid agents of the government of Saudi Arabia if they tracked terrorist support networks in the United States.

Steven Emerson was the first to investigate terrorist groups on American soil that were operating under the cover of humanitarian and charitable organizations. His 1994 television documentary, *Jihad in America*, included clandestine footage of pro-terrorist conclaves in Kansas City, Oklahoma City, Chicago, and other American cities. In his latest book, Emerson draws a map of how these terrorist groups have spread across America and "achieved a new level of coordination, owing to their exploitation of the civil liberties of the United States. None of these small national groups was ever able to coordinate its worldwide efforts with the others until they came to the United States."[37]

Thanks to the openness of U.S. society, Hamas, Palestinian Islamic Jihad, Hezbollah, the Islamic Salvation Front of Algeria, the Muslim Brothers in Egypt, the Jama at Muslimeen of Pakistan, and holy warriors from Chechnya to the Philippines have been able to work and coordinate their activities, raise money together, spread propaganda, and establish clandestine support cells that would ultimately serve the purposes of their most flamboyant avatar, Osama bin Laden. Both Hamas and Islamic Jihad were actually created in the United States with financial support from Saudi Arabia and for years used the United States as a support base. Internal Hamas documents "strongly suggest" that the 1988 Hamas Charter, with its direct citation of *The Protocols of the Elders of Zion*, was written in the United States by activists who were funded by the Wahhabi lobby.[38] The terrorists were among us, and they were joined by two things: hatred of Jews and utter contempt for the liberties enshrined in the American Constitution that allowed them—literally—to get away with murder.

At the University of South Florida (USF), a Palestinian professor of engineering named Osama (Sami) al-Arian had for years been operating as a U.S. base for Palestinian Islamic Jihad, a group that sees Israel and America "as two faces of the same coin."[39] PIJ has claimed responsibility for the murder of hundreds of Jews and Americans. In 1986, al-Arian incorporated the Islamic Concern Project, also known as the Islamic Committee for Palestine (ICP), and a sister organization named the World Islamic Studies Enterprise (WISE). The groups shared office space, a post office box, and interlocking directors.[40]

One board member was a well-respected Palestinian academic named Khalil Shikaki, whose brother Fathi was the secretary-general of Palestinian Islamic Jihad. In January 1993, the ICP magazine ran a full-length interview with Fathi Shikaki, in which the acknowledged terrorist explained his goals of promoting Islam and murdering Jews. On October 26, 1995, in what appeared to be the work of a Mossad hit squad, Fathi Shikaki was assassinated in Malta. Shortly afterward, one of Sami al-Arian's closest colleagues "disappeared" from Florida, then reappeared in Damascus, where he was proclaimed the new secretary-general of Palestinian Islamic Jihad. Ramadan Abdallah Shallah had been an adjunct professor of Middle Eastern Studies at USF, the director of administration of WISE, and a board member of al-Arian's ICP.[41] Now he simply took off the mask he wore in America and appeared openly as the terrorist he had always been. At public events across America, al-Arian's ICP was raising money for Islamic Jihad and signed up American Muslims as "sponsors" of Palestinian "martyrs." For revealing these connections, Emerson was accused of "Muslim bashing" and for launching a "McCarthyesque witch-hunt."

On May 16, 2002, former Justice Department lawyer John Loftus filed a lawsuit against Sami al-Arian in the circuit court for Hillsborough County, Florida, alleging that the Saudis were using the al-Arian network to launder money "for the support of terrorist groups in the Middle East."[42] He cited an FBI videotape of al-Arian watching approvingly while an associate at a fund-raising event "begged for $500 to kill a Jew."[43] A previously classified FBI affidavit described in detail how "ICP has served as a vehicle by which PIJ has raised funds to support terrorist activities in the Occupied Territories."[44]

"The single largest source" of ICP funding came from "what appeared to be a public tax-exempt charity at 555 Grove Street, Herndon, Virginia, which transferred hundreds of thousands of dollars to [ICP] in Florida," Loftus asserted. The address was "used by four interrelated foundations, institutes, and charities with more than $1 billion of assets donated by or through agents of the government of Saudi Arabia. Each year the 555 Grove Street charities donated more than $1 million to selected organizations such as [ICP] inside the United States."[45] The Herndon, Virginia, address was shared by the SAAR Foundation, the World Muslim League, WAMY, and the IIRO. Until September 11, the head of the WAMY office was Abdullah bin Laden, a half-brother of the Saudi terrorist.[46]

The FBI tooks the wraps off its investigation of al-Arian on February 20, 2003, arresting him and three other alleged terrorist colleagues on fifty counts of racketeering and conspiracy and indicting four others overseas, including al-Arian's former colleague at the University of South Florida, Palestinian Islamic Jihad secretary-general Ramadan Abdallah Shallah. The 120-page indictment alleged that al-Arian and his co-conspirators had been "operating a racketeering enterprise from 1984 until the present that engaged in a number of violent activities," including "conspiracy within the United States to kill and maim persons abroad." Al-Arian was "the alleged leader of the PIJ in the United States," as well as a member of the group's "Shura Council," its worldwide governing body. As chief fund-raiser for the terrorist group, he was alleged to have used his position at the University of South Florida to gain visas for terrorists to enter the United States and to have transferred cash into overseas accounts that were used for the planning or support of terrorist operations that killed Americans. A PIJ manifesto discovered during the FBI investigation "indicated that the only goal of the PIJ was to destroy Israel and end all Western influence (of the "Great Satan—America") in the region regardless to the cost of the inhabitants." The documents released by Attorney General John Ashcroft specifically tied al-Arian and his group to the "murders of over 100 people in Israel and the Occupied Territories, including two U.S. citizens, Alisa Flatow, age 20, and Shoshama Ben-Yishai, age 16."[47] Commenting on the indictment, a *Washington Post* lead editorial concluded, "If these allegations prove true, Mr. Al-Arian—far from a victim of a new anti-Muslim McCarthyism—will rank among the more important terrorists ever arrested and prosecuted in this country."[48]

Just in case there was any doubt that al-Arian might have experienced a change of heart after 9/11, the indictment stated that the PIJ killings have continued. On November 4, 2001, two American citizens, Shoshana

Ben-Yishai, sixteen, and Shlomo Kaye, fifteen, were among the victims of a PIJ shooting attack on a bus in the French Hill area of Jerusalem, the indictment alleges. Again on June 5, 2002, Professor al-Arian's co-conspirators "murdered 17 people and wounded approximately 45 in a suicide car bombing of a bus in the vicinity of Megiddo Junction near Afula, Israel," the government states.[49]

Still, no official mention was made of al-Arian's friends in Saudi Arabia, whom Loftus claims were fronting the cash.

Former National Security Council official Oliver North warned of the Saudi role in financing terror against America in his autobiography, *Under Fire: An American Story*, where he claimed that every time he had wanted to go after terrorist organizations he was told to back off because it would embarrass the Saudi government.[50] Former FBI deputy director John O'Neill reportedly told friends that he resigned from government service in 2001 because "he was disgusted with the way the Saudis were being protected."[51] Arguably the U.S. counterterrorism official with the greatest knowledge of the Saudi networks, O'Neill was a major asset to the FBI, and his resignation was a great loss. He started his new job as head of security for the World Trade Center just days before the September 11 attacks and died as he attempted to pull victims from the wreckage.

Despite mounting evidence, the Saudi government continued to believe it could disguise its involvement in anti-U.S. terror. Right after the September 11 attacks, the Saudis hired the PR firm Burson-Marsteller and spent $2.5 million to buy national newspaper ads to counter the negative image of Saudi Arabia as the home of fifteen of the nineteen hijackers. They spent another $3.8 million hiring a Republican spin shop, Qorvis Communications, through one of Washington's best-connected lobbying law firms, Patton Boggs. Fred Dutton, a former White House adviser to President Kennedy, is the dean of registered Saudi agents in Washington and has fought PR battles before. "This is probably a $10 million campaign," he told me in May 2002. "But that's peanuts in our politics. For every dollar the Saudis are spending, the American Jewish community is spending ten dollars to influence politicians and public opinion."[52]

†††

By the time the U.S. government began to close in on the Saudi-backed terror support network in the United States, it was already too late.

On September 5, 2001, federal agents from the Joint Terrorism Task Force in Dallas, Texas, raided the headquarters of InfoCom Corporation, an Internet service provider in Richardson, Texas. It was a massive undertaking, the culmination of an investigation going back several years. Eighty agents from several federal agencies cordoned off the street and invested the offices located at 630-525 International Parkway. One team rushed into the air-conditioned room where the huge servers hummed and blinked and pulled them off-line. They yanked power plugs out of the walls, to prevent tampering with the mass backups. Another team began going through filing cabinets. Yet others started checking the personnel and billing records. The next day, based on documents they had seized, the assistant secretary of commerce for export enforcement issued a temporary denial order—the equivalent of a commercial blacklisting— against one of InfoCom's founders, Ihsan Elashi, for having "shipped and attempted to ship goods to Libya and Syria without authorization from the United States."[53]

But the export violations, which included the sale of computers and communications gear to nations on the State Department's list of terrorist-sponsoring nations, were just the tip of the iceberg. For three days, federal agents copied the contents of computer hard drives and carted out box after box of documents, letting frantic company officials put their servers back on-line one by one, only after the contents had been thoroughly copied. The feds were hoping to find critical evidence that would allow them to begin rolling up terrorist support networks in the United States.

A "coalition" of American Muslim groups, led by Nihad Awad, executive director of the Council on American Islamic Relations, and the American Muslim Counncil—the leading edge of the Wahhabi lobby— screamed bloody murder. At a televised press conference the next day, they claimed the action was part of an "an anti-Muslim witch-hunt promoted by the pro-Israel lobby in America." An FBI spokesperson, Lori Bailey, responded calmly. "This is a criminal investigation, not a political investigation."

The reason for the panic soon became clear. InfoCom shared office space, personnel, and board members with the Holy Land Foundation for

Relief and Development, a 501(c)(3) to whom contributions were tax-exempt. Holy Land and InfoCom were established with seed money from Hamas leader Moussa Abu Marzouk and were run by family members of his wife, Nadia Elashi Marzouk. Marzouk was arrested in the United States in 1995, carrying documents clearly identifying him as a Hamas operational leader and detailing a $10 million commercial and nonprofit empire in the United States, which he controlled allegedly to finance Hamas operations. In 1997, after the Israelis declined to extradite him, he was expelled to Jordan. Two years later, the Jordanians expelled him to Syria, where today he openly claims responsibility for Hamas terrorist attacks in Israel. He was no small fish, but "one of the highest-ranking officials in Hamas ever since its inception."[54]

While living in the Chicago area in the 1980s, Marzouk established a wide-ranging support structure for the Islamic resistance movement against Israel (Harakat al-Muqawama al-Islamiya), an offshoot of the Muslim Brotherhood, which as of 1988 became known by its Arabic acronym, Hamas. Together with his wife's cousin Ghassan Elashi, Marzouk incorporated the Islamic Association for Palestine (IAP), an umbrella group that established offices in Illinois, Indiana, Arizona, and California and published a magazine called *Ila Filistin,* which "routinely called for the death of 'infidels and Jews.' "[55] Ghassan's brother Basman Elashi became IAP's president. The organization distributed the Hamas Charter in the United States, produced training materials for terrorists, and even sponsored "a Hamas-affiliated music troupe" whose theme song boasts, "We buy paradise with the blood of the Jews. . . ."[56] And all of this had been taking place in the United States, where Hamas supporters insisted they were engaged in protected political speech, not murder. Marzouk's United Association for Studies and Research (UASR), also established in Illinois, was called by a Hamas detainee in Israel "the political command of Hamas in the United States."[57] The executive director of UASR, Ahmed bin Yousef, was a childhood friend of Marzouk's from Gaza and denied playing any leadership role in Hamas, although he was mentioned by a detainee in Israel as a "Hamas leader in the United States." Bin Yousef went over to UASR after working as a journalist for the IAP publications.

With $250,000 provided by Marzouk's wife, the Elashi brothers also established InfoCom Corporation in Richardson, Texas. By the time it was shut down, InfoCom hosted more than five hundred Web sites, including Islamic groups and charities around the world. Al-Jazeera television in Qatar hosted its Web site and e-mail server with InfoCom. Because it was regularly used by bin Laden's group to transmit bin Laden's speeches and "Islamic" decrees, Al-Jazeera was often referred to by U.S. government investigators as "Jihad-TV." The four remaining Elashi brothers who worked at InfoCom were arrested on December 18, 2002, in connection with the federal investigation into terrorism fund-raising in the United States.[58]

In the United States, CAIR, ISNA, the Muslim Students Association, the Islamic Association for Palestine, and the Holy Land Foundation all worked with InfoCom and listed Bayan Elashi as the administrative contact for their Web sites. Indeed, as the leaders of these groups repeated to the press for many days, the federal task force that closed InfoCom and its "mynet.net" servers brought down radical Muslim networks worldwide. "We believe the genesis of this raid lies not in Washington, but in Tel Aviv," a statement released by the pro-Saudi groups said. U.S. law enforcement had become "tools in the hands of a foreign government."[59]

The circling of the wagons was pretty impressive. And it may have had good cause. As a joint congressional task force found during its investigation of the intelligence failures that contributed to 9/11, bin Laden's al-Qaeda network was using Arabic-language Web sites and encrypted e-mail to transmit coded messages to operatives around the world, so that unwitting Web site owners became portals for al Qaeda terror.

InfoCom/HLF officer Ghassan Elashi was also one of four founders of the Council on American Islamic Relations in Texas, which was established in 1994 as "an outgrowth of the Islamic Association of Palestine."[60] Both Nihad Awad and Omar Ahmad, who originally worked for Marzouk's IAP, went over to CAIR once it was formed in 1994.[61] When federal judge Kevin Duffy ordered Marzouk's extradition in 1996, CAIR naturally marshaled support. The group established a "Marzouk Legal Fund" and held a press conference to complain that the extradition order was "anti-Islamic" and "anti-American."[62]

Eleven days after September 11, the FBI arrested another InfoCom employee, Ghassan Dahduli, when he refused to answer questions. The feds were intrigued because Dahduli's name and phone number were found in the datebook of Wadi el-Hage, the private secretary of Osama bin Laden who was sentenced to life in prison for his role in the 1998 bombings by al-Qaeda of two U.S. embassies in East Africa. El-Hage's notes included a reference to a "joint venture" between himself and HLF. Dahduli had also been a former head of Marzouk's Islamic Association for Palestine. Together with Omar Ahmad, who became CAIR board chairman, he had run the American Middle East League for Palestine (AMELP), a charity that appeared to exist only on paper. When the feds placed him under arrest, CAIR board member Mohammad Suleman "expresssed concern and support for Dahduli, and argued against his deportation."[63] Dahduli was deported to Jordan on November 26, 2001. The Jordanian authorities released him one week later when he denied involvement with Hamas or al-Qaeda.

The hard drives, banking documents, and internal correspondence seized at InfoCom headquarters were churned at light speed after September 11 and led to multiple raids by an interagency counterterrorism task force called Green Quest, set up to track the funding of terrorist organizations.

In December 2001, Green Quest shut down the Holy Land Foundation and froze its assets. Attorney General John Ashcroft explained the link. "The Holy Land Foundation for Relief and Development, based in Richardson, Texas, shares employees of an Internet company known as InfoCom. . . . InfoCom, like the Holy Land Foundation, received much of its early money from Moussa Abu Marzouk, a top Hamas official who, the U.S. courts have determined, was directly involved in terrorism."[64]

President Bush came down even harder when he announced the crackdown on terror funding at a Rose Garden ceremony on December 2, 2001, although he was careful not to mention the Saudi connection. After calling Hamas "one of the deadliest terrorist organizations in the world today," the president continued:

Hamas has obtained much of the money that it pays for murder abroad right here in the United States, money originally raised by the Holy Land Foundation. The Holy Land Foundation is registered with the IRS as a tax-exempt charity based in Richardson. It raised $13 million from people in America last year. The Holy Land Foundation claims that the money it solicits goes to care for needy Palestinians in the West Bank and Gaza.

Money raised by the Holy Land Foundation is used by Hamas to support schools and indoctrinate children to grow up into suicide bombers. Money raised by the Holy Land Foundation is also used by Hamas to recruit suicide bombers and to support their families.

HLF denied that it "provides any financial support to terrorist groups or individuals," and members of the Wahhabi lobby began meeting with Treasury and Justice Department officials to get them to back off.[65] But the FBI had done its homework. In an affidavit submitted to the Treasury Department in support of freezing HLF assets, Dale Watson, deputy director for counterterrorism, described a pattern of criminal activity going back many years. At one 1993 meeting in Philadelphia secretly recorded by the FBI, Hamas and HLF leaders met and "decided that most or almost all of the funds collected in the future should be directed to enhance the Islamic Resistance Movement." In an effort to evade surveillance, "they referred to HAMAS as "SAMAH," which is HAMAS spelled backward." At a 1994 meeting in Oxford, Mississippi, also secretly taped by the FBI, Hamas leader Moussa Abu Marzouk "designated the HLFRD as the primary fund-raising entity in the United States," Watson wrote. At a 1995 HLF fund-raiser in Los Angeles, Hamas military leader Sheikh Muhammed Siyam told a cheering crowd: "Finish off the Israelis. Kill them all! Exterminate them! No peace ever! Do not bother to talk politics." Immediately after that speech, an HLF official exhorted the crowd to give to "the cause." The FBI revealed that Siyam had made five trips from the Middle East to the United States that were charged to HLF's corporate credit card.[66] This was not "guilt by association," as Wahhabi lobby spokesmen liked to pretend. It was direct involvement in terror.

At the same time, the Treasury Department froze the assets of Beit el-Mal Holdings, an investment company, and its subsidiary, the Al-Aqsa Islamic Bank, which the White House called "a financial arm of HAMAS." Beit el-Mal had offices in East Jerusalem, the West Bank, and the Gaza Strip and "transfers money to and raises funds for associations that the Palestinian Authority itself has identified as belonging to HAMAS," the White House said.[67]

In Chicago that same month, Green Quest investigators raided the offices of Global Relief Foundation (GRF). "It's clearly related to directing funding to terrorist activity and their associates, and specifically to al-Qaeda," Treasury Department spokesman Tony Fratto said. The move against GRF was carried out simultaneously with raids on the foundation's offices in Kosovo, which NATO explained were based on "credible information that individuals working for this organization may have been directly involved in supporting worldwide international terrorist activities" and were "allegedly involved in planning attacks against targets in the U.S. and Europe." GRF denied any links to terrorism. "We are in the business of helping innocent civilians and take every precaution to ensure our aid does not go to support or subsidize any nefarious activity," they said.[68]

The feds also hit Benevolence International Foundation, where they discovered videos and literature glorifying martyrdom in operations against Americans and Jews. "According to the charity's newsletter, seven of its officers were killed in battle last year in Chechnya and Bosnia," Washington Institute for Near East Policy scholar Matthew A. Levitt told a congressional panel.[69] The foundation's executive director, Enaam M. Arnaout, was subsequently indicted in April 2002 on seven counts of racketeering, money laundering, mail fraud, and conspiracy to provide material support to a terrorist enterprise and struck a plea bargain with the U.S. Attorney's Office in Chicago, Illinois, ten months later. "Arnaout had a personal relationship with both bin Laden and many of his key associates dating back more than a decade" and had "reportedly facilitated money and weapons transfers for bin Laden through the foundation," the indictment alleged.[70] Federal prosecutors identified Arnaout as a top official in bin Laden's Maktab al-Khidmat (Services Bureau) who "often drove bin Laden or otherwise accompanied him in Afghanistan." In a proffer made to the court, they stated that he had worked with the Saudi-run Muslim World League prior to setting up Benevolence International Foundation in the United States in 1992 and had purchased arms for bin Laden through his charity.[71]

In the Philippines, Benevolence International had been run as a for-profit corporation by bin Laden's own brother-in-law Mohammad Jamal Khalifa, at the same time he was the official representative of the International Islamic Relief Organization, a Saudi government–sponsored charity. According to a Philippines National Police intelligence report, Khalifa managed more than a dozen charitable and for-profit enterprises on bin Laden's behalf, including Benevolence International Foundation and the Islamic Institute of the Philippines.[72] In a supporting affidavit filed with magistrate judge Ian Levin, the FBI tied the Benevolence International Foundation office in Chicago to Khalifa and to Ramzi Yousef, the terrorist convicted of masterminding the first attack on the World Trade Center in 1993.[73] It was a small world.

† † †

On March 20, 2002, Green Quest struck a body blow to the Saudi financial network the feds alleged was providing "material support to foreign terrorist organizations." Most of the fifteen charities, investment companies, and self-styled "religious" institutions raided that day by more than 150 agents from ten federal agencies and local police departments were located in the suburbs of Washington, D.C., and they were connected in many cases by interlocking boards and executives. In their search for money being laundered in support of terrorism, the feds also carted away documents from Piedmont Poultry, a chicken farm in Gainesville, Georgia, that was part owned by one of the Saudi principals.[74]

At 360 South Washington Street in Falls Church, Virginia, they hit the offices of the International Islamic Relief Organization, the same Saudi charity that had funded Osama bin Laden during his anti-Soviet jihad in the 1980s. Established just before the Afghan war in 1978, IIRO now operates in more than ninety countries out of forty-five overseas offices and has long presented itself as the unofficial conduit for Saudi government aid. The IIRO shared office space with its parent organization, the Muslim World League, whose files were also confiscated.

Simultaneously, the feds raided the School of Islamic and Social Sciences on Miller Drive in Leesburg, Virginia, the only accredited school for training Muslim chaplains for the U.S. Armed Forces. Funded by Saudi Arabia, it was a Wahhabi institution, educating imams in the radical beliefs of the Wahhabi sect. Its president, Dr. Taha Jaber al-Alwani, doubled as head of the International Institute of Islamic Thought (IIIT), whose offices at 500 Grove in Herndon were also raided.

IIIT was under investigation for large donations to the Islamic Committee for Palestine and the World Islamic Studies Enterprise in Florida, the Palestinian Islamic Jihad front network run by Sami al-Arian. That same morning, the apartment of IIIT employee Tarik Hamdi was raided by a separate law enforcement team. Prosecutors in New York had named Hamdi in the summer of 2001 as having personally flown to Pakistan in 1998 to bring special batteries to bin Laden for his satellite telephone, "the phone bin Laden and others will use to carry out their war against the United States."[75] Their words were unfortunately prophetic, yet another reminder that the anti-Semitism and fear of Western-style freedoms that form the backbone of radical Wahhabi fundamentalism is also deadly for ordinary Americans.

But the keys to the kingdom were across the street at 555 Grove Street, which the World Muslim League gave as its mailing address. This was the U.S. headquarters of the SAAR Foundation, a billion-dollar Saudi conglomerate. The SAAR Foundation "was of particular concern because of the close links between the Saudi royal family and its founder, the Saudi banker Sheikh Suleiman Abdul Aziz al-Rajhi (initials SAAR)," scholar Matthew Levitt told members of Congress.

Shortly before the raid, SAAR filed an amended tax return changing its stated income for the year 2000 from $15 million, as previously declared, to a whopping $1.8 billion, then abruptly announced it had ceased doing business in the United States. No accounting was given for the money. Just days after the raid, *Newsweek* reported that federal investigators believed the money had been transferred "to obscure entities on the Isle of Man, a notorious money-laundering haven."[76] Over a period of many years, SAAR reportedly is suspected of having financed Hamas and Palestinian Islamic Jihad operations in the United States and in Israel, directly and through cutouts.[77] Their lawyer, Nancy Luque, denies the allegations and points out that the federal government has not accused them of any crime. She also claims the $1.8 billion on SAAR's tax return never existed, but was generated by a computer error and was later corrected on an amended reutrn.

SAAR and many of the entities raided that day were run by Jamal Barzinji, an Iraqi who was considered a key player in the U.S.-based Wahhabi networks. One of Barzinji's business partners and office mates was Samir Salah, who "formerly ran a branch of al-Taqwa in the Caribbbean, heads a financial firm linked to SAAR, and directed Dar al-Hijra, a mosque in Falls Church, Virginia, notable for hard-line Wahhabi preaching."[78] Al-Taqwa was a shell company based in Lugano, Switzerland, that was blacklisted by the U.S. Treasury Department on November 7, 2001, after U.S. intelligence had "tracked telephone contacts between Al-Taqwa and members of bin Laden's inner circle."[79] On its board was notorious Nazi sympathizer Albert Friedrich Armand Huber, a seventy-four-year-old former Swiss journalist who converted to Islam in the 1960s and now calls himself Ahmad. A longtime friend of François Genoud, the Swiss banker who held the copyrights to writings by Hitler, Goebbels, and other top Nazi officials, Huber boasts of his efforts to bring together radical Muslims and neo-Nazis. He has partnered with Holocaust deniers in Europe such as Ahmed Rami of Radio Islam in Sweden and is a dedicated admirer of Sheikh Mohammad Amin al-Husseini, the grand mufti of Jerusalem who enthusiastically embraced Hitler in the hope of eradicating world Jewry. Al-Taqwa changed its name to Nada Management Organization after September 11, apparently in an effort to confuse federal investigators.

Al-Taqwa's parent corporation, the Al-Taqwa Bank, was headquartered in the Nassau, Bahamas, offices of Arthur Hannah, a former deputy prime minister. Hannah performed a similar service for Dar al-Maal al-Islami, a financial conglomerate controlled by Prince Mohammad bin Faisal al-Saud, the son of former King Faisal who is elsewhere identified as an investor in Osama bin Laden's bank in the Sudan.[80] Deputy Assistant Secretary of the Treasury Juan C. Zarate testified before Congress that in 1997 "the $60 million collected annually for Hamas was moved to accounts with Bank Al-Taqwa." In October 2000, he said, "Bank Al-Taqwa appeared to be providing a clandestine line of credit to a close associate of bin Laden and as of late September 2001, bin Laden and his al-Qaeda organization received financial assistance from the chairman of that bank." The offshore firm's alleged ties to al-Qaeda convinced the U.S. government to freeze Al-Taqwa assets in the United States, Europe, and the Bahamas, he added.[81]

Sharing offices with SAAR was a sister organization called Safa Trust, with virtually the same board, which appeared to be used as a conduit for payments to other organizations. The feds also seized the files from MarJac Investments, a private company owned by Jamal Barzinji, who headed both SAAR and Safa Trust, and from other organizations in the Wahhabi network, such as the Success Foundation, whose board members included Abdul Rahman al-Amoudi, until late 2001 the president of the American Muslim Council.[82] By 4 P.M., journalists, employees, and bystanders watched as scores of federal agents carted out boxes of documents to a U-Haul truck parked outside.

††††

Some of the network's money had gone to buy political influence in the purest American tradition. Al-Amoudi and the Safa Trust each wrote $20,000 checks to the Islamic Institute in Washington, D.C., established in 1998 by GOP activist Grover Norquist and two of al-Amoudi's former employees from AMC, Khaled Saffuri and Abdel Wahhab al-Kebsi. The institute's stated goal was to mobilize American Muslim support for the Republican Party and to promote free markets. But it had also received foreign funding, including $55,000 from Kuwait, more than $200,000 from Qatar, and at least $15,000 directly from Saudi Arabia.[83] Saffuri tried to deny the Saudi funding until *Insight* magazine reproduced copies of the checks from the Saudi Hollandi Bank and the Riyad Bank.[84] He told me later that "all but $5,000" of the money had come from an American Muslim who was "traveling abroad."[85]

As the feds cracked down on the financial networks supporting Islamic extremism, Norquist added his voice to the chorus of condemnation. He helped arrange meetings for top Wahhabi lobbyists with the president, the secretary of the Treasury, the Immigration and Naturalization Service, FBI director Robert Mueller, and top Justice Department officials—all in hopes of getting the administration to back off. To his enemies, Norquist became "the chief enabler of Islamic extremists seeking access to the White House," in the words of author Stephen Schwartz, a former leftist and a convert to Islam.[86] Norquist claimed that his goal was to bring Muslim Americans into the mainstream of the Republican Party, yet he openly ridiculed mainstream Muslim leaders such as Sheikh Kabbani who reject the extremist Wahhabi clique. His interest in the Middle East appears to have begun at family discussions with a brother-in-law who is of Palestinian origin. Norquist boasts that his organizations have received money for the Wahhabi regime in Qatar to set up conferences that "promote democracy and free markets."[87]

At a meeting at the editorial offices of *Insight* magazine on May 13, 2002, which took place at his demand, Norquist complained that *Insight*'s reporting of his ties to the Wahhabi lobby was "unfair" and accused the magazine and its reporters—including myself—of "bizarre anti-Muslim attacks." Saffuri, who accompanied him, tried to distance himself from AMC and al-Amoudi, the pro-Hamas lobbyist. Yet, as I pointed out, while Saffuri worked for al-Amoudi in 1995, the group had invited Yusuf al-Qaradawi to address an AMC conference. Al-Qaradawi is notorious for spouting anti-Semitic lies and preaches violence against America, yet he has been a regular guest at AMC conferences. In a sermon broadcast on Qatar state television on November 1, 2002, he included America among the "enemies of Islam" and called on the faithful to "wipe them out, destroy their power, and prevent them from committing aggression against your servants." He ended on this note: "O God, destroy the aggressor, treacherous Jews. O God, destroy the aggressor Americans. O God, destroy the fanatic pagans. O God, destroy the tyrannical Crusaders."[88]

When I raised the AMC invitations to al-Qaradawi, Norquist flew into a rage. Any attempt to link him to al-Qaradawi or the AMC was "guilt by association." Saffuri had left the AMC "years ago," he added. But by Saffuri's own account, he went to work for Norquist's Islamic Institute almost immediately after he left the AMC.

Norquist's efforts to whitewash the Wahhabi lobby were implicitly rejected by FBI director Robert Mueller, who in a speech at the American Muslim Council national convention on June 28, 2002, upbraided the group and its supporters for failing to draw the line between terrorism and legitimate political discourse. "Unfortunately, persons associated with this organization in the past have made statements that indicate support for terrorism and for terrorist organizations," Mueller said. "I think we can—Muslims and non-Muslims alike—justifiably be outraged by such statements."

Over the past decade, the Wahhabi lobby has bought political influence wherever it would be most useful. During the Clinton presidency, al-Amoudi and other Wahhabi lobbyists raised hundreds of thousands of dollars for the 1996 Clinton-Gore reelection campaign, regularly sought photo opportunities with First Lady Hillary Rodham Clinton, and contributed to her 2000 U.S. Senate campaign.[89] During the 2000 election cycle, Norquist convinced the Bush campaign that the AMC, CAIR, and their allies would help sway the Muslim American vote in favor of Republicans, and Saffuri was named a national adviser to the campaign on Arab and Muslim affairs.[90] Bush and his wife posed for a photograph with University of South Florida professor Sami al-Arian, now under indictment on terrorism-related charges, during a campaign appearance at the Florida Strawberry Festival on March 12, 2000. Al-Arian's wife later told *The Washington Post* that she had campaigned for Bush in Florida mosques.[91]

Although Norquist claims that the votes of Muslim Americans tipped the election in Bush's favor, the record of that support is mixed.[92] Even Norquist protégé Khaled Saffuri contributed to liberal Democrats such as David Bonior and Sam Gejdedson almost as frequently as he did to Republicans, according to Federal Election Commission records. The same was true for al-Amoudi and Islamic Institute director Abdul Wahhab al-Kebsi, who rallied Muslims to back radical leftist Cynthia McKinney (D-Ga.), certainly no friend of the Bush White House. (McKinney ultimately lost her 2002 reelection bid after making viciously anti-Semitic remarks.)[93] In Bush's native Texas, CAIR boasted of having "developed a relationship" with former Democratic mayor of Dallas Ron Kirk in his bid to replace the retiring Republican U.S. senator Phil Gramm in 2002, with top CAIR officials contributing to his campaign. After the March 2002 raids, the Muslim Public Affairs Council (MPAC), one of the groups that had endorsed Bush just weeks before the election, turned around and slammed the president for having "squandered the support of the American Muslim community," said executive director Salam al-Marayati. "The feeling is the endorsement went to the wrong candidate. People feel betrayed by the Bush administration."[94] During an interview with a California public radio station on September 11, al-Marayati raised the possibility that "Israel might have carried out the destruction of the World Trade Center and the assault on the Pentagon."[95] MPAC, CAIR, and other groups Norquist pushed with the White House attempted to mobilize Muslim Americans to oppose the president's policy toward Iraq and in early 2003 joined the so-called antiwar movement led by a hard-left coalition known as International ANSWER, whose leaders had distinguished themselves by barring prominent liberal rabbi Michael Lerner from addressing a rally because he was a Jew. If the aim was to bring the radical Wahhabis into the Republican Party—an aim of dubious merit—even there Norquist would appear to have failed.

Most serious, in the view of national security experts such as former Pentagon official Frank Gaffney, were efforts by Norquist, his Islamic Institute, and other Wahhabi lobbying groups to prevent the use of "secret evidence" by the Justice Department in terrorism cases. On April 5, 2001, the National Coalition to Protect Political Freedom, a far-left group headed by al-Arian, gave Norquist an award for his work in opposing the use of secret evidence.[96] At his meeting with *Insight* magazine reporters and editors, Norquist said that he was "proud" of the award, even though the coalition included among its members the National Lawyers Guild (NLG), a communist front organization established during the Cold War, and an astonishing array of groups reportedly fronting for known terrorist organizations.[97] Among them was the Tampa Bay Coalition for Justice and Peace, a group formed by al-Arian to spring his brother-in-law Mazen al-Najjar from an INS jail. Al-Najjar had been detained using secret evidence in 1997 because of his association with Palestinian Islamic Jihad leader Ramadan Abdallah Shallah. Norquist joined their efforts, and a founding board member of his Islamic Institute, Suhail Khan, was scheduled to address a Washington, D.C., rally for al-Arian's Tampa Bay Coalition in 1999, according to e-mail messages publicizing the event. (Khan, who was on the campaign staff of Representative Tom Campbell [R-Calif.] at the time, says he was out of town when the rally occurred and had not been aware that his name was used on the invitation.) Al-Najjar was released during the waning days of the Clinton administration but rearrested on November 24, 2001, and deported nine months later.[98]

Repealing the use of secret evidence was a priority Norquist shared with the Wahhabi groups. After 9/11, he teamed up with conservative Republican congressman Bob Barr of Georgia and the National Lawyers Guild to oppose the inclusion of secret evidence in the USA Patriot Act. The FBI wanted secret evidence as a tool so they could deport suspected members of terrorist support networks who had overstayed their visas. With secret evidence, the FBI could go to immigration courts without compromising the individuals who had become state's witnesses. Without it, few American Muslims were willing to come forward as witnesses, for fear of retribution from the powerful Wahhabi lobby. Indeed, immediately following 9/11 the major Wahhabi organizations such as CAIR and AMC urged their followers not to cooperate with the FBI. For Hedieh Mirahmadi of the Islamic Supreme Council of America, this was a virtual heresy. "It is our patriotic duty as Americans and our duty as Muslims to speak up against any attempt by extremists to mobilize the Muslim community against our country."[99]

On July 17, 2002, al-Amoudi and his friends filed a lawsuit in federal court against George W. Bush and Secretary of State Colin Powell for complicity in "genocide, war crimes, and crimes against humanity, racketeering, acts of murder and torture, bodily harm, arson, kidnapping," and other crimes allegedly carried out by Israeli prime minister Ariel Sharon. Speaking in Arabic without a translator, al-Amoudi said the suit "sends a message to the American Muslim community" that they need not be afraid of the U.S. government anymore and that they can now "challenge the system" through the courts. "We've been doing it politically and now we're going to do it legally," he said.[100] Here was a leading member of the groups Norquist was trying to bring into the Republican Party, filing a lawsuit against a Republican president. It was a daunting insult.

Stephen Schwartz was fired from Voice of America for his opposition to giving equal airtime to radical Islamists such as CAIR, AMC, and their allies. He believes the Wahhabi lobby has had a devastating impact on the American Muslim community.

A "Muslim establishment" did not exist in America until the mid-1980s when Hamas, the Wahhabi organization fighting Israel, decided to open a political front on U.S. territory, a "Wahhabi lobby." A constellation of carefully designated entities, funded from the same source, suddenly appeared, radiating ideological aggression in all directions. Like the front organizations fostered in the past by Communism, they each had specific tasks and were designed to appeal to various constituencies. But they had a single program: to create a secure base for planning terrorist operations in Israel, to amass funds and recruits, and finally to control all discussion of Islam and Muslim societies in American media and government. No such aim had ever before been put forward by a Muslim group in America, and no single Christian or Jewish institution had ever staked an exclusivist claim of this kind.[101]

Norquist's advocacy of the Wahhabi groups was causing friction within the conservative movement, and national security conservatives, including Frank Gaffney and American Conservative Union president David Keene, began to take their distance. In a stinging op-ed published on February 20, 2003, Keene blasted "the Wahhabis and their apologists," a clear dig at Norquist. "These groups are, in the main, acting as de facto defenders of the sponsors of extremist terrorism," he wrote.[102]

The loop between the Wahhabis and the terrorists was closed in November 2002 when federal investigators leaked classified intelligence information to the press detailing how checks written by Princess Haifa al-Faisal, the wife of Saudi ambassador Bandar bin Sultan bin Abdul Aziz, were then signed over to an associate of two of the September 11 hijackers. Once the story broke, Saudi foreign policy adviser Adel al-Jubeir told the weekend talk shows that the princess had innocently sent a $15,000 check and then made $2,000 monthly payments from November 1999 through May 2002 to a Jordanian woman who needed medical treatment. He said that the Saudi government had just discovered that the woman's husband had signed over some of the checks to Omar al-Bayoumi, a suspected al-Qaeda contact who threw a welcoming party for two of the September 11 hijackers and rented them an apartment next to his own in San Diego.[103]

✝✝✝

What type of America did the Saudi-backed Muslim organizations want to see? Was it the "diverse, open society" they evoked in their official newsletters, written in English and destined for journalists and government officials? In internal meetings and conferences, many of these same leaders communicated a very different message.

"Let us damn America. Let us damn Israel, let us damn their allies until death," Sami al-Arian told the AMC national convention in 1998, where he had been invited as a guest speaker. The Immigration and Naturalization Service showed a videotape of al-Arian's remarks at a bond hearing in 2000. "Why do we stop?" he went on. The Jews were "monkeys and pigs . . . Muhammad is leader. The Koran is our Constitution. Jihad is our path. Victory to Islam. Death to Israel. Revolution! Revolution! Until victory! Rolling, rolling to Jerusalem!"[104]

CAIR chairman Omar Ahmad addressed a crowd of California Muslims in July 1998 with a similar message. "Islam isn't in America to be equal to any other faith, but to become dominant. The Koran . . . should be the highest authority in America, and Islam the only accepted religion on earth."[105] In November 1999, he told a CAIR audience in Chicago that suicide bombers deserved admiration and respect. "Fighting for freedom, fighting for Islam—that is not suicide. They kill themselves for Islam."[106]

CAIR and AMC held a joint rally at Brooklyn College in 1998 that featured Egyptian extremist Wagdi Ghuniem. After a vicious anti-Semitic speech, he led the crowd of five hundred in singing "No to the Jews, descendants of the apes."[107]

Wahhabi lobbying groups have been in the forefront of defending Osama bin Laden from accusations of terrorism. In October 1998, CAIR demanded the removal of a Los Angeles billboard describing Osama bin Laden as "the sworn enemy" of America. In their words, identifying bin Laden as a terrorist was "offensive to Muslims." That same year, CAIR simply denied evidence presented by U.S. prosecutors (and by bin Laden himself in media interviews) of al-Qaeda's responsibility for the twin East African embassy bombings. CAIR national communications director Ibrahim Hooper said that September 11 resulted from "misunderstandings of both sides."[108] He told an interviewer, "I wouldn't want to create the impression that I wouldn't like the government of the United States to be Islamic sometime in the future."[109]

A joint statement by the entire coalition of Wahhabi front groups, led by CAIR and AMC, took out a quarter-page advertisement on the editorial page of *The Washington Post* on the Friday after the attacks. They condemned "senseless acts of terrorism against innocent civilians." Did that mean that terrorist attacks against military targets, such as the Pentagon, were okay? Rather than denounce those who used Islam as an excuse for murder, they urged the media to be "sensitive" whenever they mentioned the expressions of faith of the terrorists.

Yet CAIR officers don't display the same "sensitivity" when it comes to Jews. Daniel Pipes, who is not Jewish but has observed Middle East politics for two decades, notes that CAIR officers use anti-Semitic labels the way others spread jam. "The head of CAIR's Los Angeles office, Hussam Ayloush, routinely uses the term *zionazi* when referring to Israelis," Pipes says. Similarly, he notes, CAIR defends murderers such as Jamil al-Amin (the former H. Rap Brown) and raised money for a "defense fund" after his conviction for the murder of an Atlanta policeman. At the ISNA national convention in Washington, D.C., in late August 2002, an ISNA affiliate called the National Support Committee for Imam Jamil claimed contributions to Brown's defense were tax-deductible. "Your Imam," the group's flyer read, showing H. Rap Brown wearing the humble white headdress of a hajji pilgrim to Mecca. "Caged like an Animal."[110]

CAIR has a long record of defending militant Islamic terrorists. It labeled the conviction of the perpetrators of the 1993 World Trade Center bombing "a travesty of justice." Despite their confessions, CAIR executive director Nihad Awad wrote in the *Muslim World Monitor* that "there is ample evidence indicating that both the Mossad and Egyptian intelligence played a role in the explosion." Similarly, CAIR called the conviction of Omar Abdel Rahman, the blind sheikh who planned to blow up New York City landmarks, a "hate crime." CAIR president Eric Erfan Vickers has repeatedly refused to condemn al-Qaeda and believes that Steve Emerson and his independently financed Investigative Project is "more dangerous to America than terrorism."[111] Suicide bombings are terrible, he tells Fox News, but the real problem is the Israelis. "We support the Palestinian resistance." That is the English translation of Hamas.

On the home page of its Web site after September 11, CAIR featured a section telling visitors "what you can do for the victims of the WTC and Pentagon attacks." CAIR advised: "Donate through the Global Relief Foundation" and "Donate through the Holy Land Foundation," and it provided links to the Web sites of both groups.[112] These were the same "charities" that the FBI Joint Terrorism Task Force closed down in December. The FBI alleged that funds raised by GRF were going directly to al-Qaeda, the same group that was responsible for the 9/11 attacks!

At the same time, the Wahhabi lobby routinely defames moderate Muslims who reject its extremist agenda. In June 2001, CAIR blasted scholar Khalid Duran for writing a *Guide to Islam* for non-Muslims, published by the American Jewish Committee in an effort to promote interfaith dialogue. Duran explains what happened next: "CAIR's attack snowballed into a campaign of personal vilification, which eventuated in a Jordanian political leader calling me an apostate *(murtadd)*. Neither CAIR nor Sheikh Abd al-Mun'im Abu Zant of Jordan's Islamic Action Front had ever read or even seen my book, but the CAIR attack prompted the latter to issue an appeal to Muslims, asking them to unite to kill me."[113]

In the Wahhabi Islamic Republic of America, death edicts and religious fatwas are considered legitimate means of dealing with political adversaries, while terrorism is considered "resistance." It's all part of what they call the "Islamic World Order," the name of a new Internet chat room sponsored by the Islamic Circle of North America, WAMY, and other Muslim groups.

President Bush is right. There are no two sides to terror. Either you are with us, or you are against us. He has said this to Pakistani president Pervez Musharraf. He has said this to Egyptian president Hosni Mubarak. It's time he said it to Crown Prince Abdallah of Saudi Arabia and to the Wahhabi lobby in America.

ISLAM ON THE MARCH

ON THE TRAIL OF OSAMA BIN LADEN

11

In late January 1998, *Reader's Digest* editors Bill Schultz and Ed McFadden invited me to lunch at the Palm, a watering hole frequented by many Washington, D.C., editors, K-street lobbyists, and their political guests. They wanted to talk terrorism. There had been a whole series of spectacular attacks against America since Bill Clinton had taken office, starting with the February 1993 bombing of the World Trade Center. Yet the administration just seemed to keep rolling with the blows, without any counterstrike. Was there a story there?

I mentioned information I had gleaned from top Israeli intelligence officials during a recent trip to Tel Aviv and from a foray to U.S. district court in New York, where I had spent three days combing through thousands of documents from the first World Trade Center bombing trial. At every twist and turn, the name of Saudi millionaire Osama bin Laden—virtually unknown to Western intelligence agencies just a few years earlier—kept popping up. In August 1996 the State Department had issued an unusual four-page "white paper" on him, calling him "one of the most significant financial sponsors of Islamic extremist activities in the world today." The CIA had set up a special "bin Laden station" based in Frankfurt, Germany, and claimed he had backed terrorist operations from Algeria to Saudi Arabia, Yemen, Pakistan, and beyond. The National Security Agency had been listening to every call from his Inmarsat satellite telephone since 1995.

Bin Laden was unusual for many reasons. The twenty-second son of a Saudi billionaire of Yemeni origin, he boasted of close personal ties to top Saudi princes. Yet he had traded a life of indolence in the casinos of Europe for a cave in Afghanistan.

After kicking around a number of different approaches, the *Digest* commissioned me to do a profile of bin Laden so ordinary readers could understand the danger he represented. The crazed Jew-hatred he had learned at Wahhabi mosques as a child had grown into a more generalized hatred of America and the West. In bin Laden's person, hate met capability.

We dubbed him the "Godfather of terror."

† † †

After initial spadework in Washington, where I received the names and phone numbers of several key sources from a now retired *Digest* reporter, Nathan Adams, I prepared for what I knew could be a rough winter trip into Afghanistan in search of the "renegade" Saudi.

I was getting ready to leave when a friend working on a congressional committee called with a piece of stunning news. Bin Laden had just issued a fatwa along with a number of other groups—some known, others not—calling on Muslims to kill Americans and Jews, military personnel and civilians, wherever they were around the world.

> The ruling [fatwa] to kill the Americans and their allies—civilians and military—is an individual duty for every Muslim who can do it in any country in which it is possible to do it. . . . We—with God's help—call on every Muslim . . . to kill the Americans and plunder their money wherever and whenever they find it.[1]

Although the order to "plunder" Western economies was mystifying (it became clear after 9/11), the fatwa gave a sense of urgency to my reporting. My orders from *Digest* editors were to find bin Laden and interview him, if possible. But if that was not doable, I should gather as much hard information as I could on his network, his capabilities, and his intentions so we could get our story out before something big happened.

My first stop was London to meet with an old friend whose sister was married to a senior member of the bin Laden clan. He gave me the "official" family view of their black sheep. "If Osama's share of the family business were liquidated today, he would barely be worth $150 million. He has been cut off and is despised for the damage he has done to the family name." That was true enough, but other sources had estimated his net worth at $300 million, and the CIA had released a list of companies he controlled in Sudan, including a bank, where bin Laden joined forces with Saleh Abdallah Kamel, one of Saudi Arabia's most wealthy investors. Saleh Kamel's royal partner was Prince Mohammad bin Faisal bin Abdul Aziz. How could someone who was completely cut off from his family and despised by the regime remain business partners with prominent Saudis, including top members of the royal family?

This was the Middle East, my friend reminded me. There was an old Arab proverb: Keep your friends close, and your enemies closer, so when the time came to slit their throats, you'd always know where to find them. Osama bin Laden may have declared war against the Saudi royal family, but that didn't mean they had cut off all ties. Indeed, in 1994, while bin Laden was building his guerrilla army—and his fortune—in Sudan, the Saudi government sent the terrorist's mother to Khartoum in an effort to woo the stray sheep back to the fold.[2] Even today, he was still friends with top Saudi royals, who helped him on the sly.

My friend suggested I probe the contacts between bin Laden and the Muwafaq Foundation. It was a familiar name, one that represented serious money and influence. Sitting on the board was Abdul Rahman bin Khaled bin Mahfouz, the scion of another extremely powerful Saudi businessman. The elder bin Mahfouz controlled the Commercial Bank in Jedda and had owned one-third of the failed Bank of Credit and Commerce International (BCCI). "If you were the CIA and you wanted to funnel large amounts of money covertly to the Afghan guerrillas, of course you would use the BCCI," my friend said. "Who else can operate from Luxembourg to Lahore in total confidence? It was the only international bank really operating in

Pakistan in the 1980s." That was the time of the anti-Soviet jihad where bin Laden cut his teeth. But would Muwafaq retain those ties now when bin Laden was considered a renegade?

The next day I took the underground to an anonymous neighborhood in north London to meet Saudi dissident Saad al-Faqih. A surgeon by training, he headed the Movement for Islamic Reform in Arabia (MIRA) and ran a clandestine satellite television service into the Saudi kingdom that broadcast harsh criticism of Saudi leaders. With his long, slender fingers, carefully groomed nails, and immaculate white robe, it was hard to imagine al-Faqih hunkering in bin Laden's cave in Afghanistan. He was a master of communications, both the message and the techniques. And he liked to talk.

He had traveled to Afghanistan only once, he told me. "It was in 1989, at the end of the war. I had gone to help the Fauzan Hospital in Peshawar. One night, they came and took me across the border to the front, where we were pounded with bombs and rockets. It was impressive, scary. But it was fun." It was the type of war tourism bin Laden was famous for offering wealthy Saudi backers.

In 1993, al-Faqih became involved with bin Laden and another dissident named Mohammad al-Massari in an Islamic protest group known as the Committee for the Defense of Legitimate Rights (CDLR). They had presented a petition of demands to the royal family that called for the stricter application of Islamic Sharia law and a crackdown on corruption. By way of comparison, al-Faqih mentioned Saddam Hussein. "Saddam may be a tyrant, but he doesn't feel like he is the owner of Iraq and treat it like a family enterprise, as do the al-Saud." Their petition was met with a nationwide crackdown and massive arrests. Bin Laden fled to Sudan, and the rest of the leadership flew to London, where they reemerged in April 1994. Al-Faqih hardened the political message. Bin Laden prepared the troops.

I had been told that bin Laden was pumping close to $200,000 per month into al-Faqih's London operation, and it was making the Saudis mad with rage. One source even mentioned that the emir of Qatar, a Wahhabi rival of the Saudi royal family, made weekly cash payments to al-Faqih, using an embassy car to make clandestine drops at a north London strip mall. Al-Faqih just smiled.

At this point, information on bin Laden was very sketchy. When suicide bombers hit a Saudi National Guard post in Riyadh in 1995, and the
Khobar Towers in Dhahran in 1996, bin Laden never claimed responsibility
directly, although he "saluted" the bombers. Al-Faqih played the same
game, shadowboxing with the lives of innocents. Like bin Laden at this
stage, he was careful to distance himself from the groups who actually carried out the murders, while positioning himself as a major player in the
Saudi opposition. He was walking a fine line, and both of us knew it.

††††

Osama bin Laden had been brought up by Saudi Wahhabi clerics to hate
Jews. But there were no Jews in Saudi Arabia or Afghanistan, so he
quickly turned his hatred toward the West, which he believed was controlled by a vast Jewish conspiracy. As he told Abdel Bari Atwan, the journalist whose London newspaper had just published bin Laden's latest
fatwa, his hatred of America became acute in 1991, during the first war
against Saddam. Bin Laden had returned to Saudi Arabia and, after a
failed offer to Saudi defense minister Prince Sultan bin Abdul Aziz to
force Saddam out of Kuwait with the swords of his Islamic Jihad fighters,
bin Laden became despondent. "He was bitter and frustrated" by Prince
Sultan's rejection. "He hated to see all these American women in bikinis
on Saudi beaches," Atwan told me. "He considered the Saudi royals as
atheists."[3]

Although I didn't know it at the time, Atwan's paper was widely
believed to be financed by the government of Iraq.[4] Criticizing the Saudis
for allowing U.S. troops to use American-built bases in Saudi Arabia for
the 1991 attack on Iraq obviously served the interests of Saddam Hussein,
as did pumping up the reputation of Osama bin Laden as a defender of the
Arab homeland. As I would learn later when I investigated the April 1995
Oklahoma City bombing, bin Laden networks crossed paths frequently
with Iraqi intelligence operatives and appeared to launch joint terrorist
operations.[5]

A few days later, I spoke to Mohammad al-Massari, who set up the
Advice and Reform Committee with bin Laden and Saad al-Faqih in

1993. Under pressure from the Saudis and from the British government, al Massari was extremely cautious. But at the same time, he wanted to let me know that he was important. His group, he told me, had "continuous telephone contacts between London, Yemen, Sudan, and Afghanistan." Under the noses of the Saudi intelligence, they held "secret meetings of the leadership in Mecca during the hajj omra," a minor pilgrimage to the holy sites of Islam. The latest bin Laden fatwa was more significant than earlier decrees, because it had been signed by the leaders of other prominent jihadi groups, most notably Ayman Zawahiri, head of Egypt's Islamic Jihad, and Taha Ahmad Rifai, head of Egypt's Jammaa Islamiya. "If this type of coordination continues, they will develop into a tremendous striking force." Prophetic words indeed.

† † †

Omar Bakri Mohammad, a forty-year-old red-haired Syrian who claimed to be an expert on Islamic laws, met me in the tiny closet that doubled as his office just behind a chicken joint at the Wood Green subway station. We spend almost four hours together. After singing the praises of bin Laden, who "has devoted his life to supporting the mujahedeen worldwide," Sheikh Omar, as he called himself, tried to convert me to the wisdom of radical Islam. He had answers for everything: how many wives I could have, how I should educate my children, how far I should shave my beard and mustache, how I should punish a disobedient wife. He gave me several books of his *fiqr*—Islamic rulings. The fear of Western freedoms was obvious. To ensure the utter subservience of women, for example, "Sharia [law] forbids a Muslim woman from marrying a non-Muslim man."[6]

But most disturbing were his claims to be actively recruiting terrorists for bin Laden's training camps. "We send people every three months to bin Laden camps in Afghanistan, and to camps in Lebanon, Albania, and Nigeria," he told me. "There are mujahedeen camps around the world. The only cost [for recruits] is travel, since everything else is taken care of locally. There is an international army—Muhammad's army—to combat occupying governments. There are twenty-six million Muslims in Europe.

In the U.K. alone we have 385 fundamentalist organizations, 1,200 mosques, 800 Muslim organizations. We form a fifth column, and we will create chaos. . . . Muslims in Britain want to change society, to make the Islamic flag fly over Downing Street."

†††

Khaled Fuawaz was born in Kuwait in 1966 but had become an ardent follower of bin Laden and a senior member of his organization. He welcomed me to his modest attached house in northern London, just blocks from where I had met Saad al-Faqih a few days earlier. He regaled me with anecdotes of bin Laden's exploits as the "emir" [prince] of the Arab jihadi fighters in Afghanistan. "Osama bin Laden was unique because he didn't just support the jihad financially, but personally, which other business-men did not. He built new supply roads through the mountains. He brought huge bulldozers and trucks to Pakistan, free of charge, and built new roads for the mujahedeen. People laughed at him when they first saw these huge monster machines arriving in Pakistan. Who could they ever get to drive them with Soviet helicopters flying around? So bin Laden drove the bulldozers himself. He was attacked by Soviet helicopters with missiles, he was hurt, but he escaped. So then he trained other muja-hedeen to drive the bulldozers. He built roads, hospitals, and underground shelters in the mountains." Among them was the sprawling Tora Bora complex, close to the Pakistani border, where bin Laden made his last stand against a U.S.-led Afghani force in December 2001.

Like the other bin Laden wanna-bes, Fuawaz also skated across thin ice. On the one hand, he tried to convince me that he had nothing to do with bin Laden's terrorist operations and was "working hard to stop this type of action." But he insisted repeatedly that he believed in jihad and felt radical Islamic fighters would ultimately expel America and the Jews from the Middle East by force. "Jihad is a solution," he said.

Could he help me reach bin Laden? I asked.

Perhaps, perhaps. He told me a long, complicated story of how a pro-posed interview with CBS television correspondent Bob Simon had fallen through, because they couldn't agree on time, place, or the questions. I felt

I was undergoing a test. Fuawaz wanted to sound out my views before helping me out. Nevertheless, he gave me a name—this time not of someone in London, but of bin Laden's fixer in Peshawar, Pakistan. He was the man with the satellite phone.

Khaled Fuawaz was one of the first to be picked up by the British authorities, who arrested him on September 23, 1998, in connection with the African embassy bombings, along with six Egyptians. He was publicly identified as "a member of the al-Qaeda leadership," and his assets were frozen by the U.S. Treasury Department in April 2002.

† † †

I stopped off in Cairo on my way to Pakistan because Egypt had already paid a high price in the war against terror. The Luxor attack in 1997 shut down virtually the entire tourist industry in Egypt, starving this already poor country of $1 billion in much needed foreign currency each year. The Egyptian economy was still reeling under the blows, and President Mubarak was determined to catch the terrorists and punish them. He had an added incentive. The "jihadi" who had planned the attack, Mustafa Ahmed Hamza, was on Egypt's "List of 14" terrorist suspects whose extradition they were seeking for the machine-gun attack on Mubarak's motorcade in Ethiopia in June 1995. "The Egyptians believe Mustafa Hamza has returned to Afghanistan," a U.S. diplomat told me high above the din of Cairo's Tahrir Square in the fortresslike embassy compound. "Egypt has become a bin Laden target because it is secular, and because it was the first to sign peace with Israel."

Mohammad Abdul Moneim is the deputy editor of the daily *Al-Ahram*. From 1989 to 1994, Moneim was Mubarak's spokesman. It was only natural for him to "shift over" to *Al-Ahram* when the Egyptian president opted to give his public affairs shop a face lift.

"Osama bin Laden focused early on Egypt, because he knew that if Egypt fell into the hands of the Islamists, the whole Arab world would fall," he told me. Bin Laden used a variety of groups, providing money, training, directives. "There is a mastermind to these groups. We see coordination among them. When they want operations to come to a full stop, they do. It is a classic intelligence operation: they set up multiple groups under different names, to give the impression that they are different, when in fact they are all working together. We should call these people terrorists, not Islamists," he insisted.

The Luxor attack had been carried out by a group who called themselves the Al'a Idoun, the Returnees. All had trained in bin Laden camps in Afghanistan. They had been sent back to their home countries to wage a war of terror and subversion with the goal of toppling "pro-Western" governments controlled by the international "Jewish conspiracy." It was no accident that the date they chose to strike Egypt was exactly two years after bin Laden's first major strike against the Saudi regime, the November 17, 1995, bombing of a National Guards headquarters in Riyadh.

"Mubarak is the symbol of a country heading toward peace and Western values, that is standing up to this terrorist empire," Moneim said. "That is why he was a target." Progress, openness, Western values of tolerance: all traits of the cosmopolitan Jewish "conspiracy" that drove bin Laden and his followers to rage.

Nabil Osman was chairman of the state information service and a close confidant of the Egyptian president. For over four hours, we talked about bin Laden, but also about Mubarak's anger with Europe for failing to extradite wanted terrorists to stand trial. "There is plenty of hypocrisy all around," Osman said. "How can we condemn terrorism on the one hand, and still allow terrorists safe haven and political asylum?" Yet throughout Europe, that was precisely what was happening. "An Egyptian newspaper recently said there were thirty-five international terrorist groups active in London, collecting money, organizing, moving about freely. The international community has to wake up to the fact that this is a common danger, and that nobody is safe."

Not everyone I spoke to in Egypt was willing to give Mubarak and his regime a free pass. Saad Eddin Ibrahim was a political scientist at the American University of Cairo. An Egyptian Coptic Christian by birth, he was a dual U.S. citizen who had worked for many years with moderate Muslims in Egypt to promote a more tolerant, democratic society based on constitutional law. His think tank, the Ibn Khaldun Center, was known internationally for promoting interfaith dialogue and challenging the

Islamists. He believed Mubarak was partly to blame because his government had not included Egyptian moderates in the political game.

"The government would like to think terrorism is always a foreign conspiracy, but it's homegrown," he told me. "The people who do this come from the lower middle class, but they are high achievers. When they are in college and realize that despite their achievements they are not going to find a rightful place under the sun, they begin to question why. That's when someone comes and whispers in their ears: The system is corrupt. And what's the answer? Islam. Islam is the solution."

The radical Islamists preached that all the problems of the Muslim world resulted from a conspiracy, a secret war being waged against faith and against Allah. It was America, it was Europe, and the puppet regimes they supported. But behind all of them stood the Jews. "That gets the process of recruitment under way," he went on. "Then they are insulated from the mainstream, brainwashed, and indoctrinated until they become deployable. They become walking human time bombs. And one day, they explode."

†††

The climate of intrigue and mayhem that reigned in Pakistan during the Afghan war years had changed very little when I arrived in early March 1998. Instead of the KGB and Afghanistan's Communist KHAD intelligence operatives setting off bombs in the frontier town of Peshawar, it was the Research and Analysis Wing (RAW) of Indian intelligence and Iran's Ministry of Information and Security, VEVAK, both of which were seeking to destabilize Pakistan. As I arrived, two separate bomb blasts ripped through passenger trains just outside of Lahore, killing more than twenty people. Within twenty-four hours, the Pakistani government announced it had arrested Indian-trained agents whom they said confessed to planting the bombs. Having helped win the Cold War, Pakistan was orphaned when its American protector went home, but the neighborhood was as dangerous as ever.

The bin Laden fatwa had not generated much interest in the U.S. media, and I was virtually the only Western reporter in Islamabad or

Peshawar, a Wild West town choked with Afghan refugees and radical Islamic groups that was bin Laden's gateway to the outside world. The Pakistani press was alive with rumors that the United States had launched an all-out manhunt, with more than one thousand FBI agents and U.S. Special Forces troops on the ground inside Afghanistan hunting for bin Laden. The climate of conspiracy made my mission more tenuous than it might have been otherwise. Bin Laden and his Taliban hosts were on the alert. They believed that any American reporter not known to them was most probably a spy. And they hated us—all of us: Americans, British, French, German, and Australians alike. After knocking on every door imaginable, from the head of Pakistan's CIA, the Inter-Services Intelligence, to a variety of fixers equipped with satellite phones, it became apparent that it was simply the wrong time to meet the terror master.

†††

Back in Islamabad, I met with General Hamid Gul to learn more about bin Laden and his men. A former director of ISI, who led the jihadis to the final victory against the Soviets in 1989, General Gul had made several clandestine trips into Afghanistan as an unofficial emissary to the Saudi renegade. "You need to make peace with these people, not hound them," he said of bin Laden. "Pat the mujahed on the back, and you eliminate the terrorist. Let him fight his jihad."

What was the jihad all about now that the war against the Soviet Union was over? It was very clear: America and the Jews, General Gul said. "America has lost all morality. It is a country that has no standards. It supports dictators in Egypt and Saudi Arabia who are oppressing their people. It's all because of the Jews who are running the country. We know this. Everywhere they go they cause so much trouble. The Jews will destroy America if you don't take care of them."

In just a few simple sentences, General Gul had explained how a deep-rooted belief in a world Jewish conspiracy morphed into hatred of America. America had become the leading edge of the world Jewish conspiracy, he believed. Such were the terms of what soon became an open declaration of war as Osama bin Laden asserted his leadership over the jihadi movement in a spectacular way.

† † †

According to CIA director George Tenet, bin Laden's al-Qaeda network is present in "more than sixty countries." An estimated twenty thousand men received military and intelligence training in his camps before returning to their home countries, where today they form the backbone of a deadly worldwide jihad. Often called "Afghan Arabs," bin Laden's jihadis also come from non-Arab countries from Canada to Indonesia. What unites these disparate groups of Muslim men is their hatred of Jews and a hatred of Western culture and Western values. In their own countries, they targeted leaders such as Egypt's Hosni Mubarak, or Abdul Aziz Bouteflika of Algeria, whom they believed were "puppets" of the Western/Jewish conspiracy. Since 9/11, they have attacked U.S. expatriates in Saudi Arabia, a synagogue in Tunisia, a French freighter off the coast of Yemen, a nightclub in Bali, Christian parishers in Pakistan, a U.S. diplomat in Jordan, a seaside resort in Kenya full of Israeli vacationers, tourist sites, and a synagogue in Casablanca, Morocco, and a gated community for expatriates in Western Riyadh, Saudi Arabia. This is in addition to the almost daily murder of Jews in Israel and the territories by suicide bombers claiming to act in the name of Islam.

Thirty-one-year-old Lamine Maroni is an Algerian who lived in Sheffield, England, under an assumed name until he was "activated" by al-Qaeda in August 2000. Standing trial in Germany for his involvement in the plot to blow up the Christmas market in Strasbourg, France, in December 2000, he expressed the group's philosophy with brutal clarity. "You are all Jews!" he screamed when the judge asked him if he wanted a lawyer. "I don't need the court. Allah is my defender."[7]

In a U.S. court, French-born Zacarias Moussaoui faced charges as the alleged twentieth bomber in the 9/11 conspiracy. He also dismissed his court-provided defense lawyers, claiming they were "Jewish zealots," "pigs," and "bloodsuckers."[8] Calling himself a "slave of Allah," Moussaoui wrote to the court, "I am a dedicated enemy of the United States and of course all its good citizens."[9] In public hearings, he railed against "pagans, Jews, Christians, and hypocrites" and said he prayed for "the destruction of the United States" and of "the Jewish people and state." In the eyes of bin Laden's jihadis, we are all Jews.

Moussaoui reportedly learned to hate Jews while studying Islam in Britain with a cleric named Abdallah al-Faysal, a Jamaican-born convert to Islam. Al-Faysal was eventually arrested by British authorities five months after 9/11 and charged with soliciting murder and racial incitement for calling on his disciples to kill Americans and Jews.[10] Richard Reid, the al-Qaeda "shoe bomber," was another of al-Faysal's disciples.

Bin Laden codified his ideology of hate in a manual for al-Qaeda trainees that was found by the Manchester (England) Metropolitan Police during a raid on an al-Qaeda safe house. Translated from Arabic, it became state's evidence in the New York District Court trial of the African embassy bombers. In the dedication, new al-Qaeda recruits are asked to make a "declaration of jihad against the country's rulers."

> The confrontation that we are calling for with the apostate regimes does not know Socratic debates, Platonic ideals, nor Aristotelian diplomacy. It knows the dialogue of bullets, the ideals of assassination, bombing, and destruction, and the diplomacy of the cannon and machine-gun. Islamic governments have never and will never be established through peaceful solutions and cooperative councils. They are established as they [always] have been by pen and gun, by word and bullet, by tongue and teeth.

The manual itself contains a series of lessons, covering the tradecraft of terror. Trainees are taught how to make bombs, improvise weapons, forge false identity documents, and counterfeit currency. They are taught to blend into Western societies, shaving their beards and avoiding any outward signs of "Islamic behavior." They learn how to rent safe houses and how to secure them during "arrest campaigns," and they are taught techniques for identifying and tracking enemy targets. They master clandestine methods of communication and learn to compartmentalize their activities to minimize risk should a member of the cell be captured, as happened with Moussaoui before September 11. "The main mission for which the Military Organization is responsible is the overthrow of the godless regimes and their replacement with an Islamic regime," the manual states.

The list of secondary missions taught the trainees provides a clear road map for al-Qaeda terror attacks since 9/11:

1. Gathering information about the enemy, the land, the installations, and the neighbors.
2. Kidnapping enemy personnel, documents, secrets, and arms.
3. Assassinating enemy personnel as well as foreign tourists.
4. Freeing the brothers who are captured by the enemy.
5. Spreading rumors and writing statements that instigate people against the enemy.
6. Blasting and destroying the places of amusement, immorality, and sin; not a vital target.
7. Blasting and destroying the embassies and attacking vital economic centers.
8. Blasting and destroying bridges leading into and out of the cities.

In his speeches and writings, bin Laden has frequently referred to the "Crusader occupation" of the Iberian Peninsula, his term for the victory of the Spanish crown in 1492 over the last remaining Moorish kingdom in Granada. In a brief but sweeping introductory essay, the al-Qaeda training manual identifies a much more recent event as the starting point of evil and "apostasy" in the Dar al-Islam: the establishment of a secular republic in Turkey on March 3, 1924. That was when the government of Mustafa Kemal (Atatürk) abolished the Islamic caliphate, expelled Turkey's Ottoman dynasty, and, perhaps most significant, passed a law unifying the public education system so that boys and girls could learn together in secular institutions. Atatürk explained why he felt the school reforms were so essential to establishing a modern, secular society. "Knowledge and science are the best guide to everything in the world, to material and to spiritual things, to life, to success," he told teachers later that year. "To seek for a guide outside knowledge and science is to show oneself ignorant, blind, and misguided."[11]

This recourse to secular knowledge, science, and the modern world is what the jihadis hated and feared the most, as the al-Qaeda manual makes clear:

After the fall of our orthodox caliphates on March 3, 1924, and after expelling the colonialists, our Islamic nation was afflicted with apostate rulers who took over in the Moslem nation. These rulers turned out to be more infidel and criminal than the colonialists themselves [and] started spreading godless and atheistic views among the youth. . . . Colonialism and its followers, the apostate rulers, then started to openly erect crusader centers, societies, and organizations like Masonic Lodges, Lions and Rotary clubs, and foreign schools. They aimed at producing a wasted generation that pursued everything that is western and produced rulers, ministers, leaders, physicians, engineers, businessmen, politicians, journalists, and information specialists. [Koranic verse:] "And Allah's enemies plotted and planned, and Allah too planned, and the best of planners is Allah."

To the anti-Semite, Masonic lodges and Lions and Rotary Clubs are yet more devilish inventions of the Jews.

† † †

For Yehudit Barsky, a scholar of Muslim anti-Semitism with the American Jewish Committee in New York, Jew-hatred has become so deeply rooted in Muslim societies over the past eighty years that it now forms part of the culture. "Anti-Semitism is something people grow up with—it's like Mom and apple pie, or like certain popular television programs in the 1950s and 1960s in the United States. It's part of everyone's personal baggage. Everyone can relate to it."

And it is not just cultural, but deeply religious. Because of the pervasive social and educational role played by the mosque in most Muslim countries, the duty to hate Jews is often presented as the verdict of Allah himself, as delivered in the Holy Koran. "It makes no difference whether people understand the context of the Koranic verses condemning Jews; they can be misused. It's not logical—I wish it were," she says.[12]

The great irony is that anti-Semitism is strongest in countries where there are no Jews, such as Saudi Arabia. "So there is this nameless, faceless thing called a Jew onto whom you can project all your ills, and that person doesn't suffer directly from that hate in your society," Barsky told me.

Ruth Wisse has spent the past thirty years tracking how the images of Jews in the Arab world and Europe have changed over time. She sees a deep political lesson in Muslim anti-Semitism that parallels the rise of fascism in Europe. "Modern anti-Semitism was essentially opposition to liberal democracy," she told me. "The Jews, who had represented everything evil to Christian thinking, became the vehicle for antidemocratic impulses. Jews represented competition, pluralism, progress, emancipation. In a way they became the emblem for everything that seemed to be tearing away at what felt secure and protected and familiar and our own. Jews became the representative of what was going to destroy cohesive society. They became the no-fail target, because there was never any cost for opposing them."

The motivations that impelled political leaders in Europe to demagogue Jews for their political benefit are even stronger in the Arab and Muslim world today, she believes. Arab nations are waking up after centuries of isolation and realizing that the world has changed around them and that they must adapt. Radio, television, and the Internet assault them; new technologies and new ideologies beguile them. "These societies are faced with tremendous problems to which they must adjust, and they don't have creative political tools for adaptation. So even more than in Europe in the 1870s, finding the Jew responsible for everything that is going wrong is the handiest political instrument of all. This started well before 1948. But the creation of the state of Israel made it possible for the Arabs to organize their politics around opposition to the Jews. In the Arab world, anti-Semitism plays exactly the same role as it did in Europe. And you see it growing year by year."

Wisse believes there is a direct correlation between democracy and the *absence* of anti-Semitism. "If you want to test the level of democracy in a society," she said, "ask yourself, does it have to become anti-Semitic for the politicians to survive?" She notes that no politician in America has ever been elected to office on a platform of anti-Semitism. "It's not that people didn't try. Look at Jesse Jackson and Louis Farrakhan; they didn't succeed." Conversely, the return of anti-Semitism in Europe signifies a decline in democracy. "It clearly shows that the European Union is really an antidemocratic force. If it were working to invigorate democracy, you wouldn't be seeing the rise of anti-Semitism." Many European politicians agree with her view and cite the concentration of executive powers in the European Commission as a dangerous vesting of an unelected bureaucracy.

Jews certainly have good cause to fear these developments, but so does everyone who has a stake in democratic freedoms, because the ultimate target is not the Jews, but freedom itself. "Hitler's real target was, after all, not the Jews," she argues. "The Jews were just the beginning of his political struggle, but they were not the endgame. In the same way, the forces that are using anti-Semitism in Europe are after something else. If the fight for democracy is not waged here, for protection of the Jews, it will have to be waged at a much more dangerous pitch just a couple of years down the line. That is the real danger."

In the Middle East, it is obvious that Israel has nothing to do with the problems of the Arab world, including the problems of the Palestinians, she argues. Israel has no control over how Saudi leaders squander their oil wealth on casinos and palaces, leaving their populations largely uneducated and unemployed. Israel has not forced Yasser Arafat to divert hundreds of millions of dollars in international aid to his privy purse, instead of using it to develop the Palestinian economy. Israel does not dictate to the governing board of al-Azhar University in Cairo, where I was told that the only entrance requirement is not grades or academic achievement, but rote memorization of the Koran. "It's a testimony to how undemocratic the Arab world really is to see how anti-Semitism has burgeoned to this astonishing degree and become increasingly virulent in recent years," Wisse says.

Amir Taheri is an Iranian exile, living in Europe, who has written many books on the "Islamic" revolution of Ayatollah Khomeini. In addition to a distinguished career as a journalist and essayist, he currently edits the premier French-language foreign policy journal *Politique Internationl*. In the 1980s, he called the phenomenon described in this book "holy terror," since it involved the misuse of Islam, primarily by Ayatollah Khomeini of Iran, to justify murder for political ends. He agrees with Wisse that Israel has little to do with the violence aimed at it by the jihadis and the Palestinian Islamists. They say it's about the Jews, but ultimately it's about fear: fear of progress, fear of Western influence, fear of change, fear of women, fear of freedom.

The hate projected against the West is not linked to any specific political issue such as the Arab-Israeli conflict or sanctions against Iraq, although both are at times used in attempts at justifying the unjustifiable. Even if Israel were wiped off the map, as the patrons of the hate industry desire but seldom openly call for, and sanctions against Saddam Hussein were lifted, as they publicly demand but do not desire, they will not close shop and go home. They will persist because they believe it is their mission to conquer the whole world for their brand of Islam, and they consider the West—and, mostly recently, the United States, labeled as "the Infidel" or the "Great Satan"—as the chief obstacle on their path to total victory.[13]

U.S. District Court Judge William Young came to the same conclusion. As he sought to understand the "unfathomable hate" that led shoe-bomber Richard Reid into his courtroom, Judge Young said he thought he had found an answer. "It seems to me you hate the one thing that is most precious. You hate our freedom. Our individual freedom. Our individual freedom to live as we choose, to come and go as we choose, to believe or not believe as we individually choose."

As he sent Reid off to life plus 120 years in jail, Judge Young admonished him one last time. "See that flag, Mr. Reid? That's the flag of the United Staes of America. That flag will fly there long after this is all forgotten. That flag stands for freedom. You know it always will."[14]

†††

One year after the September 11 attacks, I returned to London to revisit some of the Islamic militants I had met four years earlier. They were commemorating the 9/11 attacks at the Finsbury Park mosque in north London in a very different way from the minute of silence I had observed at Heathrow Airport that morning. Posters announcing their event showed a Boeing 757 airliner about to slam into the south tower of the World Trade Center, under the headline "A Towering Day in History."

The Finsbury Park mosque is well-known as a hotbed of radical Islamic leaders in Britain. It's here, in a three-story modern building that could pass for a small office except for the concrete minaret sprouting from the roof, that shoe bomber Richard Reid and Zacarias Moussaoui came to listen to anti-Semitic preacher Abdallah al-Faysal. British authorities believe the mosque served as a recruitment center for al-Qaeda.

Yet an element of farce and bluster surrounds these jihadi wanna-bes. Camp followers crowding the steps of the mosque cover their faces from police and news photographers with Palestinian headdresses (the wrong color—green), trying to look like fierce revolutionaries. One young man wears sunglasses well into the evening, letting just enough of the head-dress fall away to reveal a week's growth of beard and a thick black mustache. Out on the pavement, a twenty-three-year-old Iraqi named Mourad insists that "Jews are instructed by the Talmud to kill Gentiles and to steal their property." When I ask him how he knows this, he shrugs. "That's what it says in the Holy Koran." As the evening wears on, they make us cool our heels outside in a pen surrounded by police; Omar Bakri's follow-ers hang banners from the windows for the photographers. "Islam Will Dominate the World," "Islam the Future of Britain," they read. Many hours later, we are herded brusquely into a basement conference room by a mosque minder. "Welcome to ground zero!" he jokes. No one laughs.

"To us Muslims, the eleventh of September was a turning point," says Abu Hamza al-Masri, a cleric who was banned from preaching by the British authorities on charges of incitement to violence. Ironically, al-Masri's birth name was Mustafa Kemal. His Egyptian parents named him after Atatürk, the twentieth-century leader most hated by the Islamic extremists because he ushered in a new era of secular rule in the Muslim world.

I ask him whether he believes there will be more attacks, especially if the United States invades Iraq. "You're asking will the nail go into the wall. I say: Ask the hammer."

"Who's the hammer?" I ask.

"America. The West. So don't ask the nail how far he's going to scrape the wall without including the hammer."

Saudi dissident Mohammad al-Massari praises Osama bin Laden and the September 11 attacks. "Yes, it is legitimate," he says. "It is not the wis-est thing, but legitimate, yes. He took retaliation."

The ever present minders intervene, trying to cut him off, but al-Massari won't be silenced. "He's a fighter, and he fought according to his belief. And anyone fighting a legitimate battle is a hero."

Abu Hamza comes back with a warning. Until now, America has "only" been attacked every four or five years, "because you are not on our agenda." But if the United States attacks Iraq, America will "see suicide bombs everywhere, as you see in Israel. So keep away and preserve your people."

I have always wondered why people such as Abu Hamza or Moham- mad al-Massari are still allowed to walk the streets of London. German intelligence has long pointed fingers to "Londonstan" as bin Laden's Euro- pean headquarters, and in my own contacts with British Foreign Office and intelligence officials, no one really denies it. We make a great error in the West when we tolerate groups such as these whose agenda is to over- throw our societies and our governments. Free speech is one thing, sub- version quite another. The irony is that we tolerate groups who have no tolerance for us and no respect for our way of life or our freedoms.[15]

Hoover Institution scholar James Q. Wilson, writing in *The Wall Street Journal,* points out, as have many Muslims, that Islam is still waiting for its reformation. The struggle between Islam and the West stems from the fact that "the West has mastered the problem of reconciling religion and freedom, while several Middle Eastern nations have not," he believes. And in reconciling the two, Western culture displaced Islam as the domi- nant force in Europe and the Middle East.[16]

✝ ✝ ✝

In late October 2002, I returned to Cairo, where I interviewed the grand mufti of Egypt. Sheikh Dr. Ahmad al-Tayyeb was named by President Mubarak to the post earlier that year after his predecessor issued a ruling authorizing suicide bombings against innocent civilians. Throughout a ninety-minute interview, he explained why he agreed with that ruling. He also displayed a remarkable flexibility when it came to defining terrorism. To him, American Christian leader Jerry Falwell was a "terrorist" because he had said things that offended Muslims. Palestinians, on the other hand, were justified in massacring Israelis in cold blood "because they are defending their land and have no other weapons at their disposal." Any Palestinian who refused to become a martyr, he said, was "a traitor."[17]

I decided to ask for a second opinion. Dr. Mohammad Abu Laila is a professor of comparative religion and heads the English Department at al-Azhar, the largest and most respected Islamic university in the Muslim world. He earned his Ph.D. at Britain's Exeter University and did his thesis on Christianity. He introduced me to a group of Islamic scholars. "We don't hate Jews because they are Jews," he said. "We hate what they do against Palestinians. If a Muslim did this, we would hate them, too."

This was just an opening salvo, to make sure that I understood he was not an anti-Semite. He also condemned the 9/11 attacks but accused America of having launched a "war on Islam." President Bush had "never presented evidence" of bin Laden's involvement, he argued. I asked what type of evidence he wanted. "I need him [bin Laden] to appear in court and say, 'I did it.'" Perhaps the United States should have waited to declare war on Japan until it could compel Admiral Isoroku Yamamoto to put in an appearance in the Ninth Circuit, I ventured.

Christian scholars often debate the requirements for a "just war." A similar concept exists in Islam, Dr. Abu Laila said. "If your country or property is under attack, then it is just to defend it through any means," he argued. "This is not terrorism. Holy jihad is defensive. You misunderstand this in the West." Palestinian suicide bombers are "martyrs" in this just war. "The martyr is donating himself for his cause, to defend his family and his land. The Jews stole our land. What else do you want us to do, just go away?"

I am curious that he appears to be placing equal weight on material things—land, house, property—as on human life. In my religion, I say, we believe life is sacred, a gift of God.

"Life is sacred in Islam," Dr. Abu Laila replies. "But we are facing the Israeli state, which is militarily based. Israeli citizens are like warriors. They have their weapons with them at all times. So who are civilians, Palestinians or Israelis?"

Americans and Westerners concerned by the violence in the Middle East need to understand that the two parties to this conflict do not use the same logic, nor do they believe in the same moral code. Those of us who have been brought up in the Judeo-Christian tradition have been taught that respect for life is one of God's most basic commandments. But according to these Islamic scholars—and they are not alone—"justice" is more important than life, and justice is a term that can be conveniently bent out of shape to fit the political agenda of the day.

That evening, I recounted these interviews to an old friend over dinner in Cairo. A member of the Saudi royal family, who travels frequently to the West, he considers himself moderate, Westernized, tolerant. "Which would you prefer to lose," I asked him, "your land or your wife?"

Without hesitation he said, "My wife, because I can always get another one. But my land I can never replace."

I think his comment shattered the last illusion I might have had about the possibility of building bridges between Islam and the West. As Dubak liked to say, to understand the difference in logic "you need to change the diskette." Those acting in the name of Islam use a different moral operating system than we do—a simple statement with far-reaching consequences.

† † †

Is there a conspiracy between America and the Jews? Indeed there is. It's called shared values, a common heritage, a dedication to improving the human condition through compassion, and tolerance of differences: a conspiracy of freedom. From the very start of the American dream, Jews rallied to the flag of freedom. Some four thousand Jews lived in the Colonies at the time of the Revolution, clustered in New York and Philadelphia. Many instinctively understood that their emancipation from official anti-Semitism in Europe, which relegated them to ghetto life and the whim of capricious rulers, depended upon the success of the American dream and invested heavily in making it work. Jews from the Revolutionary period have left a permanent mark—not just on American history, but on our daily lives.

The most famous is Alexander Hamilton, father of the Federal Reserve Bank, who as America's first secretary of the Treasury introduced the use of paper money. Hamilton was born on the Caribbean island of Nevis in the Leeward Islands. According to some accounts, his mother was a Sephardic Jew named Rachel Levy (Levine). According to others, she took the name Levy from her first husband, a Danish Jew named John Michael Lavien, before cohabiting with Hamilton's father, a penniless Scotsman. Because the couple was living in sin, the local Anglican church "denied Alexander membership or education in the church school," so he was sent to a Jewish private school, where he became fluent in both Hebrew and French.[18]

Hamilton's Jewish background has been a cause célèbre among anti-Semites for generations. In the 1920s, Henry Ford railed against him in *The International Jew*. In the 1930s and 1940s, poet Ezra Pound denounced Jewish control of America's financial institutions in Fascist radio broadcasts from Italy and cited Hamilton's Jewish background as proof of an international Jewish conspiracy. Adding to his "sins," Hamilton wrote the original constitution for the Bank of New York, which he co-founded in 1784 with Jewish financier Isaac Moses. For anti-Semites and antigovernment fanatics even today, Hamilton regularly gets singled out as one of the all-time villains because of his close ties to the Jewish community.

Less well-known is Chaim Solomon, a prominent businessman from Philadelphia who saved the Continental Army during the dismal winter of 1777–1778 at Valley Forge, when George Washington and his men were running out of food, ammunition, and hope. A Polish Jew who spoke many languages, including German, Solomon had served as Washington's spy among the German-speaking Hessian mercenaries employed by the British and was captured by the British and briefly imprisoned. He escaped, rebuilt his fortunes, and dedicated his talents to financing the war. The Continental Congress appointed Solomon "Broker to the Office of Finance of the United States," and the French appointed him "Treasurer of the French Army in the United States." Solomon raised "desperately needed cash to bolster the currency by negotiating bills of exchange with France and the Netherlands" and brought in millions of dollars from the American and European Jewish communities to support the troops.[19] Chaim Solomon almost single-handedly financed Washington's army at the turning point of the Revolution, when even the Continental Congress turned a deaf ear to Washington's entreaties for funds.

George Washington was so appreciative of Chaim Solomon's contribution to America's independence that he had the engravers of the Great Seal of America express homage to the Jewish people by placing the Star of David over the head of the American eagle. It has survived to this day on the one dollar bill, stylized as bursts of light, said to signify "the cloud burst of the Shekinah Glory of God that was over the Tabernacle" in ancient Israel.[20] When turned upside down, the crest girdling the eagle's waist portrays the menorah. Whenever Americans engage in commerce or simply buy soda or stamps, the presence of these Jews from the time of the Revolution remains close.

The message from George Washington and the days of the Revolution is simple but far-reaching: If Jews can thrive in America, then any group—no matter how downtrodden or vilified in their country of origin—can take part in the American dream. Conversely, if Jews are attacked, then the doors to oppression and bigotry stand open. Anti-Semitism always starts with the Jews, but it never stops with the Jews. History shows that once the taboo against attacking Jews has been lifted, assaults on other minorities soon follow. The ultimate victim is the freedom of all citizens and the protections of the rule of law, the underpinnings of civilized society.

Appendix A

FRIDAY SERMON ON
PALESTINIAN AUTHORITY TV

MEMRI Special Dispatch Series No. 370
April 17, 2002

The following are excerpts from a Friday sermon delivered by Palestinian Authority imam Sheikh Ibrahim Madhi[1] at the Sheikh Ijlin Mosque in Gaza City, broadcast live on April 12, 2002, by Palestinian Authority television:

> . . . Oh, beloved of Allah. [In the Friday sermon] two weeks ago, I bore in your name a blessing of love to the crowns upon our heads, [that is] to the Arab and Muslim rulers. Among other things, I said: "Oh crowns upon our heads: If Sharon spat in your faces, what would you do?" Today I apologize for these words, because Sharon has not only spat on the heads of the nation, but also trampled us underfoot.
>
> We are convinced of the [future] victory of Allah; we believe that one of these days, we will enter Jerusalem as conquerors, enter Jaffa as conquerors, enter Haifa as conquerors, enter Ramle and Lod as conquerors, the [villages of] Hirbiya and Dir Jerjis and all of Palestine as conquerors, as Allah has decreed. . . . "They will enter Al-Aqsa Mosque as they have entered it the first time. . . ."
>
> Anyone who does not attain martyrdom in these days should wake in the middle of the night and say: "My God, why have you deprived me of martyrdom for your sake? For the martyr lives next to Allah." . . .
>
> Our enemies suffer now more than we do. Why? Because we are convinced that our dead go to paradise, while the dead of the Jews go to hell, to a cruel fate. So we stand firm and steadfast, in obedience to Allah. . . .
>
> "The Jews await the false Jewish messiah, while we await, with Allah's help . . . the Mahdi and Jesus, peace be upon him. Jesus' pure hands will murder the false Jewish messiah. Where? In the city of Lod, in Palestine. Palestine will be, as it was in the past, a graveyard for the invaders— just as it was a graveyard for the Tatars and to the Crusader invaders, [and for the invaders] of the old and new colonialism. . . .

A reliable Hadith [tradition] says: "The Jews will fight you, but you will be set to rule over them." What could be more beautiful than this tradition? "The Jews will fight you"—that is, the Jews have begun to fight us. "You will be set to rule over them"—Who will set the Muslim to rule over the Jew? Allah. . . . Until the Jew hides behind the rock and the tree.

But the rock and tree will say: "O Muslim, O servant of Allah, a Jew hides behind me, come and kill him." Except for the Gharqad tree, which is the tree of the Jews.

We believe in this Hadith. We are convinced also that this Hadith heralds the spread of Islam and its rule over all the land. . . .

Oh beloved, look to the east of the earth, find Japan and the ocean; look to the west of the earth, find [some] country and the ocean. Be assured that these will be owned by the Muslim nation, as the Hadith says . . . "from the ocean to the ocean." . . .

Oh Allah, accept our martyrs in the highest heavens. . . .

Oh Allah, show the Jews a black day. . . .

Oh Allah, annihilate the Jews and their supporters. . . .

Oh Allah, raise the flag of jihad across the land. . . .

Oh Allah, forgive our sins. . . .[2]

Appendix B

THE HAMAS CHARTER *(Excerpts)*
AUGUST 18, 1988

From Rafael Yisraeli, in Y. Alexander and H. Foxman, eds.,
The 1988–1989 Annual on Terrorism (Netherlands: Kluwer Academic Publishers).

The Charter of the Hamas
The Charter of Allah:
The Platform of the Islamic Resistance Movement (HAMAS)

In the Name of Allah, the Merciful, the Compassionate

Introduction

[. . .] This is the Charter of the Islamic Resistance (Hamas) which will reveal its face, unveil its identity, state its position, clarify its purpose, discuss its hopes, call for support to its cause and reinforcement, and for joining its ranks. For our struggle against the Jews is extremely wide-ranging and grave, so much so that it will need all the loyal efforts we can wield, to be followed by further steps and reinforced by successive battalions from the multifarious Arab and Islamic world, until the enemies are defeated and Allah's victory prevails. Thus we shall perceive them approaching in the horizon, and this will be known before long:

[† † †]

Article One

The Islamic Resistance Movement draws its guidelines from Islam; derives from it its thinking, interpretations and views about existence, life and humanity; refers back to it for its conduct; and is inspired by it in whatever step it takes.

Article Five

As the Movement adopts Islam as its way of life, its time dimension extends back as far as the birth of the Islamic Message and of the Righteous Ancestor. Its ultimate goal is Islam, the Prophet its model, the Qur'an its Constitution. Its special dimension extends wherever on earth there are Muslims, who adopt

Islam as their way of life; thus, it penetrates to the deepest reaches of the land and to the highest spheres of Heavens.

Article Seven

[† † †]

Hamas is one of the links in the Chain of Jihad in the confrontation with the Zionist invasion. It links up with the setting out of the Martyr Izz a-din al-Qassam and his brothers in the Muslim Brotherhood who fought the Holy War in 1936; it further relates to another link of the Palestinian Jihad and the Jihad and efforts of the Muslim Brothers during the 1948 War, and to the Jihad operations of the Muslim Brothers in 1968 and thereafter.

But even if the links have become distant from each other, and even if the obstacles erected by those who revolve in the Zionist orbit, aiming at obstructing the road before the Jihad fighters, have rendered the pursuance of Jihad impossible; nevertheless, the Hamas has been looking forward to implement Allah's promise whatever time it might take. The prophet, prayer and peace be upon him, said:

The time will not come until Muslims will fight the Jews (and kill them); until the Jews hide behind rocks and trees, which will cry: O Muslim! there is a Jew hiding behind me, come on and kill him! This will not apply to the Gharqad, which is a Jewish tree (cited by Bukhari and Muslim).

Article Eight: The Slogan of the Hamas

Allah is its goal, the Prophet its model, the Qur'an its Constitution, Jihad its path and death for the case of Allah its most sublime belief.

Article Nine

As to the objectives: discarding the evil, crushing it and defeating it, so that truth may prevail, homelands revert [to their owners], calls for prayer be heard from their mosques, announcing the reinstitution of the Muslim state. Thus, people and things will revert to their true place.

Article Thirteen

[Peace] initiatives, the so-called peaceful solutions, and the international conferences to resolve the Palestinian problem, are all contrary to the beliefs of the Islamic Resistance Movement. . . .There is no solution to the Palestinian problem except by Jihad.

Article Fifteen

That invasion had begun overtaking this area following the defeat of the Crusader armies by Salah a-Din el Ayyubi. The Crusaders had understood that they had no way to vanquish the Muslims unless they prepared the grounds for that with an ideological invasion which would confuse the thinking of Muslims, revile their heritage, discredit their ideals, to be followed by a military invasion. That was to be in preparation for the Imperialist invasion, as in fact [General] Allenby acknowledged it upon his entry to Jerusalem: "Now, the Crusades are over."

Article Seventeen

The Muslim women have a no lesser role than that of men in the war of liberation; they manufacture men and play a great role in guiding and educating the [new] generation. The enemies have understood that role, therefore they realize that if they can guide and educate [the Muslim women] in a way that would distance them from Islam, they would have won that war. Therefore, you can see them making consistent efforts by way of publicity and movies, curricula of education and culture, using as their intermediaries their craftsmen who are part of the various Zionist Organizations which take on all sorts of names and shapes such as: the Freemasons, Rotary Clubs, gangs of spies and the like. All of them are nests of saboteurs and sabotage.

Those Zionist organizations control vast material resources, which enable them to fulfill their mission amidst societies, with a view of implementing Zionist goals and sowing the concepts that can be of use to the enemy. . . . When Islam will retake possession of [the means to] guide the life [of the Muslims], it will wipe out those organizations which are the enemy of humanity and Islam.

Article Eighteen

The women in the house and the family of Jihad fighters, whether they are mothers or sisters, carry out the most important duty of caring for the home and raising the children upon the moral concepts and values which derive from Islam; and of educating their sons to observe the religious injunctions in preparation for the duty of Jihad awaiting them. . . .

[† † †]

Article Twenty

. . . The Nazism of the Jews does not skip women and children, it scares everyone. They make war against people's livelihood, plunder their moneys and threaten their honor. In their horrible actions they mistreat people like the most horrendous war criminals.

Article Twenty-two

Our enemies have planned from time immemorial in order to reach the position they've obtained now. They strive to collect enormous material riches to be used in the realization of their dream. With money, they've gained control of the international media beginning with news agencies, newspapers and publishing houses, broadcasting stations. [They also used this] wealth to stir revolutions in different parts of the world in order to fulfill their interests and reap their fruits. They were behind the French and the Communist Revolutions and were behind most of the revolutions we hear about elsewhere. With their money, they created secret organizations that spread around the world in order to destroy societies and carry out Zionist interests. Such organizations are: the Freemasons, Rotary Clubs, Lions Clubs, B'nai B'rith and the like. All of them are destructive espionage organizations. With their money, they've taken control of the Imperialist states and pushed them to occupy [colonize] many countries in order to exploit the wealth of those countries and spread corruption there.

The same goes for local wars and world wars. They were behind World War I, so as to wipe out the Islamic Caliphate [Turkey]. They collected material gains and took control of many sources of wealth. Then they obtained the Balfour Declaration and established the League of Nations in order to rule the world by means of this organization.

They also were behind World War II, where they made enormous profits from speculation in war materials and prepared for the establishment of their state. They inspired the establishment of the United Nations and the Security Council to replace the League of Nations, in order to rule the world through them. There was no war that broke out anywhere that doesn't have their fingerprints on it. . . .

The forces of Imperialism in both the Capitalist West and the Communist East support the enemy with all their might, in material and human terms, taking turns between themselves. When Islam appears, all the forces of Unbelief unite to confront it, because the Community of Unbelief is one.

Article Twenty-five

[Hamas] reciprocated its respect to them, appreciates their condition and the factors surrounding them and influencing them, and supports them firmly as long as they do not owe their loyalty to the Communist East or to the Crusader West. . . .

Article Twenty-seven

The PLO is among the closest to the Hamas, for it constitutes a father, a brother, a relative, a friend. . . . Under the influence of the circumstances which surrounded the founding of the PLO, and the ideological invasion which has swept the Arab world since the rout of the Crusades, and which has been reinforced by Orientalism and the Christian Mission, the PLO has adopted the idea of a Secular State. Secular thought is diametrically opposed to religious thought. . . .

When the PLO adopts Islam as the guideline for life, then we shall become its soldiers, the fuel of its fire which will burn the enemies. And until that happens, and we pray to Allah that it will happen soon, the position of the Hamas towards the PLO is one of a son towards his father, a brother towards his brother, and a relative towards his relative who suffers the other's pain when a thorn hits him, who supports the other in the confrontation with the enemies and who wishes him divine guidance and integrity of conduct.

Article Twenty-eight

The Zionist invasion is a mischievous one. It does not hesitate to take any road, or to pursue all despicable and repulsive means to fulfill its desires. It relies to a great extent, for its penetration and espionage activities on the secret organizations which it has established, such as the Freemasons, Rotary Clubs, Lions, and other spying associations. All those secret organizations, some which are overt, act for the interests of Zionism and under its directions, strive to demolish societies, to destroy values, to wreck answerableness, to totter virtues and to wipe out Islam. It stands behind the diffusion of drugs and toxics of all kinds in order to facilitate its control and expansion.

[† † †]

Israel, by virtue of its being Jewish and of having a Jewish population, defies Islam and the Muslims.

Article Thirty-one

[† † †]

Under the shadow of Islam it is possible for the members of the three religions: Islam, Christianity and Judaism to coexist in safety and security. Safety and security can only prevail under the shadow of Islam, and recent and ancient history is the best witness to that effect. The members of other religions must desist from struggling against Islam over sovereignty in this region. For if they were to gain the upper hand, fighting, torture and uprooting would follow; they would be fed up with each other, to say nothing of members of other religions. The past and the present are full of evidence to that effect.

[† † †]

Article Thirty-two

World Zionism and Imperialist forces have been attempting, with smart moves and considered planning, to push the Arab countries, one after another, out of the circle of conflict with Zionism, in order, ultimately, to isolate the Palestinian People.

Egypt has already been cast out of the conflict, to a very great extent through the treacherous Camp David Accords, and she has been trying to drag other countries into similar agreements in order to push them out of the circle of conflict.

[. . .] Today it is Palestine and tomorrow it may be another country or other countries. For Zionist scheming has no end, and after Palestine they will covet expansion from the Nile to the Euphrates. Only when they have completed digesting the area on which they will have laid their hand, they will look forward to more expansion. Their scheme has been laid out in the Protocols of the Elders of Zion, and their present [conduct] is the best proof of what is said there.

Appendix C

ARAFAT'S "PHASED PLAN" (1974)

THE PLO'S "PHASED PLAN"

N*ote:* Speaking just after concluding the 1993 Oslo accord, PLO chairman Yasser Arafat announced that the historic agreement "will be a basis for an independent Palestinian state in accordance with the Palestine National Council resolution issued in 1974. . . . " (Radio Monte Carlo, September 1, 1993)

Political Program
Adopted at the 12th Session of the Palestinian National Council
Cairo, June 9, 1974

Text of the Phased Plan Resolution:

The Palestinian National Council:

On the basis of the Palestinian National Charter and the Political Program drawn up at the eleventh session, held from January 6–12, 1973; and from its belief that it is impossible for a permanent and just peace to be established in the area unless our Palestinian people recover all their national rights and, first and foremost, their rights to return and to self-determination on the whole of the soil of their homeland; and in the light of a study of the new political circumstances that have come into existence in the period between the Council's last and present sessions, resolves the following:

1. To reaffirm the Palestine Liberation Organization's previous attitude to Resolution 242, which obliterates the national right of our people and deals with the cause of our people as a problem of refugees. The Council therefore refuses to have anything to do with this resolution at any level, Arab or international, including the Geneva Conference.

2. The Liberation Organization will employ all means, and first and foremost armed struggle, to liberate Palestinian territory and to establish the independent combatant national authority for the people over every part of Palestinian territory that is liberated. This will require further changes being effected in the balance of power in favor of our people and their struggle.

3. The Liberation Organization will struggle against any proposal for a Palestinian entity the price of which is recognition, peace, secure frontiers, renunciation of national rights and the deprival of our people of their right to return and their right to self-determination on the soil of their homeland.

4. Any step taken towards liberation is a step towards the realization of the Liberation Organization's strategy of establishing the democratic Palestinian state specified in the resolutions of previous Palestinian National Councils.

5. Struggle along with the Jordanian national forces to establish a Jordanian-Palestinian national front whose aim will be to set up in Jordan a democratic national authority in close contact with the Palestinian entity that is established through the struggle.

6. The Liberation Organization will struggle to establish unity in struggle between the two peoples and between all the forces of the Arab liberation movement that are in agreement on this programme.

7. In the light of this programme, the Liberation Organization will struggle to strengthen national unity and to raise it to the level where it will be able to perform its national duties and tasks.

8. Once it is established, the Palestinian national authority will strive to achieve a union of the confrontation countries, with the aim of completing the liberation of all Palestinian territory, and as a step along the road to comprehensive Arab unity.

9. The Liberation Organization will strive to strengthen its solidarity with the socialist countries, and with forces of liberation and progress throughout the world, with the aim of frustration all the schemes of Zionism, reaction and imperialism.

10. In light of this programme, the leadership of the revolution will determine the tactics which will serve and make possible the realization of these objectives. The Executive Committee of the Palestine Liberation Organization will make every effort to implement this programme, and should a situation arise affecting the destiny and the future of the Palestinian people, the National Assembly will be convened in extraordinary session.

NOTES

INTRODUCTION

1. Kenneth R. Timmerman, *In Their Own Words: Interviews with Leaders of Hamas, Islamic Jihad, and the Muslim Brotherhood* (Los Angeles: Simon Wiesenthal Center, 1994); forty-two pages, plus ten-page appendix containing the text of the 1988 Charter of the Harakat al-Muqawama al-Islamiya (HAMAS).

2. "For thousands of years, Judaism has consisted of three components: God, Torah, and Israel—that is, the Jewish (conception of) God, Jewish law, and Jewish nationhood. Jews' allegiance to any of these components has been a major source of antisemitism because it has rendered the Jew an outsider, and most important, it has been regarded by non-Jews (often correctly) as challenging the validity of the non-Jews' god(s), law(s), and/or national allegiance." Dennis Prager and Joseph Telushkin, *Why the Jews: The Reason for Antisemitism* (New York: Touchstone, 1985; originally published in 1983 by Simon & Schuster), p. 22.

3. Sometimes translated as "Westoxication," the term was invented by an Iranian Communist named Jalal al-e Ahmad, a well-known short-story writer. According to Patrick Clawson of the Washington Institute for Near East Studies, "After the 1963 riots and his 1964 pilgrimage to Mecca, Ahmad called for rejection of all Western ideologies including Marxism. He vigorously defended the ulema as the bastion for protecting Iran's identity. He was a highly respected intellectual and was central in forming the intellectual/ulemma alliance of the 1970s—and one of the figures the shah had in mind when he spoke about the Red/Black alliance (Communist/ulema) against progress." (Private communication with the author)

4. Prager and Telushkin, *Why the Jews*, pp. 152–153.

1: "THE JEWS DID IT!"

1. Abdel Moneim Said, "Look the Tiger in the Eye," *Al-Ahram Weekly* (Cairo), October 24–30, 2002, p. 15.

2. Mohammed Daraghmeh, "Palestinians Celebrate," Associated Press, September 11, 2001 (*Edmonton Journal*, September 12, 2001).

3. Ibid.

4. Ibid.

5. Matthew McAllester, "Terrorist Attacks: The Reaction," *Newsday,* September 12, 2001.

6. Under the rules of Norquist's meetings, all remarks are considered off the record unless subsequently cleared with their author. I reinterviewed Keene a year later to confirm this interchange, which I had witnessed.

7. "Woman Understands Palestinian Reaction," *The Standard* (St. Catharines), September 12, 2001.

8. Tracy Wilkinson and Mary Curtius, "America Attacked: World Reaction," *Los Angeles Times,* September 12, 2001.

9. Ibid.

10. "Iraq's Saddam: 'America Reaps Thorns Sown by Its Rulers,' " *Deutsche Presse-Agentur,* September 12, 2001. The leaders of most Muslim nations expressed condolences to the American people, but the disconnect between these official statements of mourning and the outpouring of anti-American sentiment on the street was widespread. The one exception was Iran. See Note 16.

11. Daraghmeh, "Palestinians Celebrate."

12. Interviews with Iranian source, Los Angeles, September 11–12, 2001.

13. Interview with U.S. official, September 12, 2001. The time-stamped Al-Manar report was subsequently translated by the Foreign Broadcast Information Service (FBIS).

14. Foreign Broadcast Information Service, September 12, 2001.

15. *Teshreen* columnist Hassan M. Yussef: "There is a possibility that this was an [act of] ancient retribution. . . . The U.S. declared war on Japan—and used the atomic bomb for the first time against Hiroshima and Nagasaki. [The bomb] killed more than 221,983 Japanese, and was the cause of the Japanese defeat and the end of the war in 1945." (*Teshreen,* September 13, 2001—Middle East Media Research Institute, "A New Antisemitic Myth in the Arab Press: The September 11 Attacks Were Perpetrated by the Jews," January 8, 2002 [hereafter MEMRI Special Report No. 6] available at www.memri.org).

16. Adding to the fears of top officials in Iran was a candlelight vigil on the evening of September 11 in Tehran, when several thousand Iranians spontaneously poured into the streets to demonstrate solidarity with the victims in the United States in a clear rebuke to the ruling Islamic government. In their paranoia, the hard-line clerics who rule Iran see a foreign hand in every homegrown opposition movement, as the shah did before them, and identify any expression of solidarity with America as an incipient counterrevolutionary movement. In this particular case, they may have been right.

17. James Bennet, "After the Attacks: The Arabs," *The New York Times,* September 12, 2001.

18. Ibid.

19. Ken Thomas, "Feds Investigating Possible Terrorist-Attack Links in Florida," Associated Press, September 12, 2001.

20. Dr. Anwar Ul Haque, "America on Attack," Islamic News and Information Network, Wednesday, September 12, 2001. The inin.net Web site was administered by a Honolulu, Hawaii, firm, MuntadaNet, Inc., which appears to have filed fictitious administrative contacts when it changed the registration information for the Web site on September 9, 2001. The site was initially registered on October 13, 1999, according to the official Internic registry.

21. The U.S. ambassador to Israel Haque refers to is Martin Indyk, a Clinton protégé whose open hostility to Israeli prime minister Benjamin Netanyahu during the 1996 election campaign undermined his effectiveness as a diplomat and ultimately forced his recall to Washington, since Netanyahu wouldn't speak to him after his election.

22. See www.cpsp.edu.pk/superwiser/ISLAMABAD.htm.

23. Other motives cited by Haque included the following:
- diverting world attention "from the almost continuous and constant daily killings of innocent Palestinians" by Israel.
- "to embarrass Muslims in the United States and other Western countries."
- to divert attention from the nineteenth anniversary of the massacres of Palestinians in Beirut's Sabra and Shatilla refugee camps (a killing spree carried out by Lebanese Christian militiamen under the eyes of Israeli troops).

24. Ibid.

25. See Harold Evans, "The Anti-Semitic Lies that Threaten All of Us," *The Times* (London), June 28, 2002, which quotes a spring 2002 Gallup opinion poll taken in nine Muslim countries representing roughly half the world's Muslim population. Only in Turkey did a small plurality (46 percent) believe U.S. evidence that Arabs had carried out the attacks. "In all the other eight Islamic countries, the populations rejected the idea that Arabs or al-Qaeda were responsible . . . ," Evans writes. "In Pakistan only 4 percent accept that the killers were Arabs."

26. Professor Dr. Anwar Ul Haque, e-mail to the author dated June 28, 2002.

27. In his address to a joint session of Congress on September 20, 2001, President Bush said, "We will not forget the days of mourning in Australia and Africa and Latin America, nor will we forget the citizens of 80 other nations who died with our own, dozens of Pakistanis, more than 130 Israelis, more than 250 citizens of India, men and women from El Salvador, Iran, Mexico, and Japan, and hundreds of British citizens." ("Presidential Speech: President George W. Bush Addresses Congress and the Nation Regarding America's Fight Against Terrorism," September 20, 2001, National Public Radio transcripts)

28. Dr. Harold Brackman, "9/11: Digital Lies," Simon Wiesenthal Center, Los Angeles, 2001, includes similar statements from white supremacists and the radical Left; MEMRI Special Report No. 6.

29. Galal Duweidar, writing in *Al-Akhbar* (Egypt), September 12, 2001, MEMRI Special Report No. 6.

30. Quoted in Brackman, "9/11: Digital Lies" (original source: Palestinian Information Center, in PIC home page, September 13, 2001, www.palestine-info.com/daily_news/prev_editions/2001/Sep01/13sep01.htm).

31. *Al-Dustour* (Jordan), September 13, 2001, MEMRI Special Report No. 6.

32. Ibid.

33. *Al-Rai* (Jordan), September 13, 2001, MEMRI Special Report No. 6.

34. *Tehran Times* (Iran), September 15, 2001.

35. *Al-Ayyam* (Palestinian Authority), September 16, 2001.

36. *Saut al-Haqq Wa al-Hurriya* (Israel), October 19, 2001, MEMRI Special Report No. 6.

37. *Al-Ayyam* (Palestinian Authority), October 2, 2001.

38. Al-Manar TV (Lebanon), September 17, 2001, www.paknews.com, MEMRI Special Report No. 6.

39. Interview with relative of a senior Iranian official, September 11, 2001; Al-Manar TV, September 11, 2001, 1420 GMT, Foreign Broadcast Information Service.

40. One vehicle for spreading the initial Al-Manar TV story was a Web site called InformationTimes.com, which bills itself as "an independent news and information service" based in the National Press Building in Washington, D.C. Former *U.S. News & World Report* editorial director Harold Evans asked the editor of the Web site, Syed Adeeb, "if he had any qualms about relying on Al-Manar because it was a mouthpiece for the terrorist group Hezbollah. Adeeb replied: 'Well, it is a very popular station.' Adeeb clearly believed his story; when I mentioned that there were Jews who died in the towers, he conceded that one or two might have died, but he found it sinister that nobody could tell him just how many." Evans, "The Anti-Semitic Lies that Threaten All of Us."

41. *Al-Manar* (Palestinian Authority), September 24, 2001, MEMRI Special Report No. 6. In another article, entitled "Two Events and a Single Piece of Evidence," the weekly reported, "It is known that the Mossad station in the U.S. maintained a luxurious office in New York under the name of a computer company. The office's clerks left it, with the furnishings, 10 days before the attacks. The Israeli Rafael Security Industries also had offices in the same tower, and its employees left the tower before the incident." (*Al-Manar,* October 22, 2001, MEMRI Special Report No. 6)

42. *Kayhan* (Iran), October 2, 2001, MEMRI Special Report No. 6.

43. *Saut al-Haqq Wa al-Hurriya* (Israel), October 5, 2001, MEMRI Special Report No. 6.

44. *Al-Ahram* (Egypt), October 7, 2001, MEMRI Special Report No. 6.

45. In a column by Syrian commentator Mu'taz al-Khatib in *Al-Hayat* (Saudi), October 9, 2001, MEMRI Special Report No. 6.

332 Notes

46. Islamic Republic News Agency (IRNA), October 24, 2001, MEMRI Special Report No. 6.

47. Al-Manar TV (Lebanon), September 17, 2001, www.paknews.com, MEMRI Special Report No. 6.

48. *Al-Hayat* (London), September 30, 2001, MEMRI Special Report No. 6.

49. See www.lailatalqadr.com/stories/p5041001.shtml, MEMRI Special Report No. 6.

50. Yuval Dror, "Odigo Says Workers Were Warned of Attack," *Haaretz,* daily English edition, September 26, 2001.

51. Brian McWilliams, "Odigo Clarifies Attack Messages," *Newsbytes,* September 28, 2001, www.newsbytes.com/news/01/170653.html.

52. Orkhan Muhammad Ali, writing in *Saut al-Haqq Wa al-Hurriya* (Israel), December 14, 2001. The hard-line Iranian daily *Kayhan* first aired this thesis on October 2, 2001: "The Zionists are the ones who caused the September 11 explosions; perhaps they carried out these operations by means of remote control of the plane." (MEMRI Special Report No. 6)

53. Interview in Cairo, October 31, 2002.

54. Saudi interior minister Prince Nayef bin Abdul Aziz, interview with Islam On-Line (Qatar based), www.islam-online.net/English/News/2001-10-16/article11.shtml, quoted in Brackman, "9/11 Digital Lies."

55. See newstribune.com/stories/020602/wor_0206020962.asp.

56. Interview in Cairo, October 30, 2002.

57. See asia.cnn.com/2002/US/08/01/cia.hijacker.

58. Bob Woodward, "In Hijacker's Bags, a Call to Planning, Prayer and Death," *The Washington Post,* September 28, 2001, p. A1.

59. Dan Eggen and Amy Goldstein, "FBI Names 19 Men As Hijackers," *The Washington Post,* September 15, 2001, p. A1. A second FBI list, released on September 27, contained slightly different spellings for some of the hijackers as well as additional names and aliases.

60. See www.fairus.org/html/04178101.htm.

61. Hanna Rosin, *The Washington Post,* December 14, 2001, p. A32. For segments of the tape, see abcnews.go.com/sections/world/DailyNews/OBLtapereleaseo11213.html.

62. Alaa Shahine, "Saudi Minister: Jews Behind 9/11 Attacks," Associated Press, December 5, 2002. The interview was translated into English by *Ain al-Yaqeen,* an Internet weekly devoted to Saudi affairs. The AP reporter noted that the translation referred to "Zionists" instead of "Jews" ("Yahoodi"), the term Prince Nayef used in the original Arabic.

63. The "Missing Persons List" is accessible from the 9/11 NYC Service Center at the New York City government Web site, home.nyc.gov.

64. Arch Puddington, "The Wages of Durban," *Commentary,* November 1, 2001.

65. Author interviews, July 11–12, 2002, Paris.

66. See www.aijac.org.au/updates/Mar-01/190301.html.

67. Interview with Per Ahlmark, Stockholm, July 8, 2002.

68. Shimon Samuels, "The Road to Durban," *Jerusalem Post,* August 17, 2001.

69. Among her more public concessions was to don an "Islamically correct" head scarf during the Tehran preparatory conference in February 2001 at the demand of the Iranian government. See Robert Evans, "UN Rights Chief Defends Wearing Headscarf in Iran," Reuters, February 23, 2001.

70. Interviews with Shimon Samuels, July 11–12, 2002. Mary Robinson spoke to NGOs on the evening of August 29, 2001.

71. Chris Tomlinson, "Jewish Event Disrupted in S. Africa," Associated Press, August 30, 2001.

72. Herb Keinon and Janine Zacharia, "Robinson in Durban," *Jerusalem Post,* August 30, 2001.

73. Robert S. Wistrich, *Muslim Anti-Semitism: A Clear and Present Danger* (New York: American Jewish Committee, 2002), p. 15.

74. Herb Keinon, "Festival of Hate," *Jerusalem Post,* September 7, 2001.

75. Interviews with Shimon Samuels, July 11–12, 2002.

76. Keinon, "Festival of Hate."

77. Prager and Telushkin, *Why the Jews,* p. 147.

78. Puddington, "The Wages of Durban."

79. Herb Keinon, "U.S. and Israel Quit Durban," *Jerusalem Post,* September 4, 2001.

80. Puddington, "The Wages of Durban." In a bizaare twist of pure Orwellian double-speak, Arab NGOs condemned "Zionist practices against Semitism," arguing that Arabs were victims of anti-Semitism. This peculiar notion, long familiar in the netherworld of radical anti-Israel organizations, suddenly burst into the UN mainstream at Durban, where it went virtually unchallenged. In fact, as the renowned scholar of Islam and Middle Eastern history Bernard Lewis has pointed out, "the term 'Semite' has no meaning as applied to groups as heterogeneous as the Arabs or the Jews." Furthermore, Lewis writes, "anti-Semitism has never anywhere been concerned with anyone but Jews." (Bernard Lewis, *Semites and Anti-Semites* (New York: W. W. Norton, 1986), p. 117 (all page citations are to 1999 Norton paperback edition).

81. See www.wiesenthalcenter.com, press release dated September 1, 2001.

82. Keinon, "Festival of Hate."

83. Ibid.

84. Keinon, "U.S. and Israel Quit Durban."

85. The wording of this quotation comes from Sibylle Sarah Niemoeller von Sell, Martin Niemoeller's wife (see us-israel.org/jsource/biography/niemoeller.html). Other wording expressing the identical sentiment appears in the *Congressional Record,* October 14, 1968, p. 31636.

86. Albert Speer, *Spandau: The Secret Diaries* (New York: Macmillan, 1976), p. 80; quoted in Robert S.Wistrich, *Muslim Anti-Semitism,* p. 15.

2: HORROR AT PASSOVER

1. Interview with Rami Gouvernik, spokesman for Netanya mayor Miriam Fierberg, Netanya, October 21, 2002. My dramatized portrait of Odeh and his movements was derived from interviews with Netanya police chief Avi Biran, Park Hotel staff, various survivors, and Israeli intelligence sources. Other details of Odeh's preparations and the network that supported him were drawn from the indictment released by Israeli Defense Forces judge advocate general brigadier Einat Rom against Nasir Sami al-Raq Yatima (Zitaoui) on October 22, 2002.

2. Glenn Frankel, "A Short Journey from Friend to Foe: Cities Linked by Attack Shared Hopes for Peace, *The Washington Post,* April 14, 2002, p. A1.

3. The text of Odeh's suicide message was quoted in full in the indictment of Nasir Yatimeh.

4. For what Major General Aharon Zeevi, Israeli military Intelligence chief, described as "a technical mishap," the cyanide was never released. Yoav Appel, "Military Intelligence Says Palestinians Tried to Use Cyanide Gas in Bomb Attack," Associated Press, June 5, 2002.

5. "Thanks to Hitler, of blessed memory, who on behalf of the Palestinians, revenged in advance, against the most vile criminals on the face of the earth. Although we do have a complaint against him, for his revenge on them was not enough." (Ahmad Ragab, "Half a Word," *Al-Akhbar* [Cairo], April 18, 2001; translated by MEMRI Special Dispatch Nos. 208 and 212)

6. Jason Keyser, "Amnesty International Chief Visits Israeli Victims," Associated Press, April 29, 2002.

7. Laura King, AP special correspondent, "Passover Attack Memories Still Fresh," AP Online, April 27, 2002.

8. Eric Silver and Anne Penketh, "This Was a Battlefield, Says Bomb Witness," *Independent,* March 28, 2002, p. 17.

9. Ibid.

10. Interview with Chaim Jacouv Deutsch and members of the Kiryat Sanz Zaka unit, Netanya, October 21, 2002.

11. Andrew Levin, "Imbalances of Victimhood," *Jerusalem Post,* June 7, 2002.

12. Edward Cody, "When Resistance Reaches Its Limits," *The Washington Post,* May 9, 2002, p. A1, quoting Hamas leader Ismail Abu Shenab in Gaza.

13. Dr. Khalil Ibrahim Al-Sa'ada, *Al-Jazirah* (Saudi Arabia), April 1, 2002; translated by MEMRI Special Dispatch No. 367.

14. Celean Jacobson, "Chef Who Survived Israel's Worst Suicide Bombing Dies in Attack Six Weeks Later," Associated Press, May 20, 2002.

15. Ibid.

16. Interview with Uzi Landau, Tel Aviv, October 23, 2002.

17. Briefing by Israel Defense Forces (IDF) spokesman, April 1, 2002.

18. Herb Keinon, et al., "Getting Down to Business," *Jerusalem Post,* April 25, 2003.

19. Interview with Major General David Tsur, October 24, 2002.

20. Interview with Lieutenant Colonel Sheikeh Horowitz, October 24, 2002.

3: "THEY HAVE A PLAN!"

1. In September 1992, Hamas and Palestinian Islamic Jihad (PIJ) joined together with eight other Palestinian organizations to create the so-called Damascus Coalition, also known as the Rejectionist Front or the Group of Ten. The ten groups—Hamas, Palestinian Islamic Jihad, the Popular Front for the Liberation of Palestine (General Command, the Palestinian National Liberation Movement), Fatah (Abu Musa faction), Al-Saiqa, the Popular Front for the Liberation of Palestine, the Democratic Front for the Liberation of Palestine, the Revolutionary Palestinian Communist Party, the Palestine Popular Struggle Front, and the Palestine Liberation Front—met regularly in Damascus to coordinate political and military opposition to the peace process. Leaders of the military wings of Hamas and PIJ such as Moussa Abu Marzouk and Fathi Shikaki operated out of Damascus with the full knowledge of the Syrian government.

2. Bernard Lewis, *Semites and Anti-Semites,* p. 81.

3. Ibid., p. 108.

4. The Israelis captured documents from a variety of charitable societies used by Hamas during their military thrust into the West Bank after the Passover massacre that showed how Hamas used charities as a cover to raise funds to directly support terrorist attacks against Israeli civilians. See Kenneth R. Timmerman, "Documents Detail Saudi Terror Links," *Insight,* June 10, 2002, available on-line at www.timmerman2000.com/news/insight_saudis_020517.htm.

5. Interview with Dr. Ahmad Bahar, Gaza, November 5, 1994.

6. Interview with Dr. Saud Shawa, Gaza, November 5, 1994.

7. Interview with Hamzi Mansour, Amman, Jordan, October 31, 1994, conducted in Arabic and translated by Mansour's aides.

8. Confidential source, royal palace, Amman, Jordan, November 1, 1994. My informant was referring to U.S. aid to the Afghan mujahedeen during the 1980s and to Israel's tacit support for Hamas in 1987–1988, at the start of the first *intifada,* when the Israelis believed Arafat could be undermined by a homegrown Palestinian Islamic movement.

9. Interview with Yehia Saqra, Amman, Jordan, October 31, 1994.

10. Interview with Dr. Abdallah Akaillah, Amman, Jordan, November 1, 1994.

11. Interviews with Abu Musa representatives, Damascus, Syria, October 28, 1994.

12. One who didn't—at least, not at this point—was Nayef Hawatmeh. His Democratic Front for the Liberation of Palestinian was a full member, with Hamas and Palestinian Islamic Jihad, of the Group of Ten Palestinian groups that rejected the Oslo Accords. But unlike his coalition partners, Hawatmeh told me that he had abandoned "the illusion of rolling back" Israel and was calling instead for democratic elections on the West Bank and in Gaza so a new Palestinian leadership could emerge to replace Yasser Arafat. (Interview with Nayef Hawatmeh, Damascus, October 29, 1994.)

13. Rabbi Marvin Hier, "The Anti-Semitism of the Terrorist Organizations," Introduction to Timmerman, *In Their Own Words,* p. i.

14. Interview with Abul Aziz Rantissi, Gaza, October 4, 1997.

15. Just minutes after Abbas finished his ostensibly conciliatory June 4, 2003, speech in Aqaba, Rantissi told Reuters, "We will never be ready to lay down arms until the liberation of the last centimeter of the land of Palestine." One week later, he repeated the comments he had made to me. "I swear we will not leave one Jew in Palestine. We will fight them with all our might." Ibrahim Barzak, "Israel tries to kill Hamas head," *Washington Times* (AP), June 11, 2003.

16. Obviously the Torah, which reached its final form more than 1,500 years before the time of Muhammad, makes no mention of Muslims.

17. Charter of Harakat al-Muqawama al-Islamiya (Hamas). Excerpts from the forty-page text were translated into English along with the Arabic original and published by the Simon Wiesenthal Center in September 1988 and reproduced in Timmerman, *In Their Own Words.*

18. Hamas Charter, Article 22. The first paragraph is pulled almost word by word from the Ninth Protocol of the *The Protocols of the Elders of Zion.*

19. Interview with Charles Helou, Beirut, January 22, 1995.

4: THE ELEMENTS OF HATE

1. Abd al-Rahman Sami Ismat, *Al-Sahyuniyya wa'l-Masunniya* (Alexandria, 1950), pp. 45, 50; quoted in Lewis, *Semites and Anti-Semites,* p. 15.

2. Lewis, *Semites and Anti-Semites,* pp. 208–210.

3. *Protokolat mak'aa zionioon wa t'alim al talmood* [Protocols of the elders of zion and the precepts of the talmud] (Cairo, 1968), Preface by Shaouki Abd al-Nasser. The original cover shows a book representing the Talmud on top of which sits a skull and a dagger bearing the Star of David. Cover reproduced in Meir Waintrater, "La montée de l'antisémitisme dans le monde arabe," *L'Arche* 523 (September 2001): 83; see also Daniel Pipes, *The Hidden Hand: Middle East Fears of Conspiracy* (New York: St. Martin's Griffin, 1998), p. 311.

4. Robert S. Wistrich, *Muslim Anti-Semitism,* p. 4.

5. Interviews with David Bedein, Jerusalem, October 2002.

6. Quoted in Sean Salai, "Arabic News Bared," *Washington Times,* June 20, 2002, p. 2.

7. See www.saudiinstitute.org/hate.htm. The actual number of mosques in America—just as the number of Muslims—is a matter of dispute. Approximately 1,400 mosques are registered as nonprofit charitable institutions, but as many as 1,600 more are believed to exist. These are smaller prayer centers based in people's homes or hosted by a variety of local Islamic charities, according to Hedieh Mohahmadi, spokesperson for the Islamic Supreme Council of America, a group that has vigorously opposed the Saudi government domination of America's Islamic community. (Interview, October 1, 2002.)

8. Quoted in Lewis, *Semites and Anti-Semites,* p. 161.

9. The picture of Sadat in Jerusalem wearing his swastika tie adorns the cover of a forgotten paperback by Paul Eidelberg, *Sadat's Strategy* (Dollard des Ormeaux, Quebec: Dawn Publishing Company, 1979), ISBN 0-9690001-0-3.

10. "*Al-Ahram,* Egypt's Leading Government Daily: 'Israel—The Plague of Our Time and a Terrorist State,'" MEMRI Special Dispatch No. 238, July 9, 2001, translated from *Al Ahram,* June 23, 2001.

11. Although Karl Marx came from a distinguished line of rabbis, he was baptized a Lutheran and was, in fact, a notorious anti-Semite. His well-known anti-Semitic treatise, "On the Jewish Question," railed against Jewish emancipation. "What is the secular cult of the Jew? *Haggling.* What is his secular god? *Money.* Well then! Emancipation from *haggling* and *money,* from practical, real Judaism, would be the self-emancipation of our time. . . . Money is the jealous God of Israel, beside which no other God may stand." For more on Marx's anti-Semitism, see Prager and Telushkin, *Why the Jews?,* pp. 138–139.

12. *Al-Ahram* had earlier elaborated on this theme in a separate article on April 1, 2000. See also "Jews Are Destroying Russia: Anti-Semitic Article in the Leading Egyptian Daily," MEMRI Special Dispatch No. 86, April 12, 2000.

13. "Ramadan TV Special, *The Protocols of the Elders of Zion,*" MEMRI Special Dispatch No. 309, December 6, 2001, quoting from *Roz al-Youssuf* (Egypt), November 17, 2001.

14. Interviews with U.S. ambassador David Welch, Cairo, October 31, 2002, and with Egyptian Information Ministry officials.

15. Letter from President Hosni Mubarak to Congressman Henry Waxman and Benjamin Gilman, November 10, 2002, obtained by the author.

16. Interviews with an Ibrahim family member and with U.S. officials in the region, December 2002.

17. "Arab Press Debates Anti-Semitic Egyptian Series," part I, MEMRI, December 2002 (original source: *Akher Sa'a* [Egypt], November 20, 2002).

18. The Arabic-language edition was published in Damascus in 1984; Tlass's preface was dated April 1983. It was initially brought to the attention of the U.S. State Department in June 1986 by the Simon Wiesenthal Center. "US Probing Book on Jews Laid to Syria," *International Herald Tribune/The New York Times* Service, July 17, 1986. For a much more detailed account, which cites this and other original documents, see David Littman, "Syria's Blood Libel Revival at the UN, 1991–2000," from *Midstream* (New York), February–March 2000, available at mypage.bluewin.ch/ameland.libel.html.

19. Ibid.

20. Léon Poliakkov, *Histoire de l'antisemitism,* vol. III (Paris: Editions Calmann-Lévy); quoted by Waintrater, "La montée de l'antisémitisme dans le monde arabe," p. 69.

21. Littman, "Syria's Blood Libel Revival at the UN, 1991–2000."

22. Ibid. A summary of Ms. Chaalan's comments can be found in the minutes of the UNHRC meeting at E/CN.4/1991/SR.18, paragraphs 64–67.

23. Al-Jazeera, October 24, 2000, quoted in "Leading Egyptian Newspaper Raises Blood Libel," MEMRI Special Dispatch No. 150, November 6, 2000.

24. Charles Laurand, *The Murder of Father Toma and his Servant Ibrahim Amara* (Cairo, 1989), translated into Arabic by Dr. Youssef Nasrallah; MEMRI Special Dispatch No. 150, November 6, 2000. Hamooda's column appeared in *Al-Ahram* on October 28, 2000.

25. All quotes from "Leading Egyptian Newspaper Raises Blood Libel."

26. Confidential Egyptian source and Western diplomats, Cairo.

27. "The Arab Answer to 'Schindler's List,'" MEMRI Special Dispatch No. 190, March 1, 2001; translated from *Roz al-Yussuf* (Egypt), February 24, 2001.

28. MEMRI Special Dispatch No. 432, October 21, 2002 (original source: *Al-Hayat* [London], October 21, 2002).

29. "Saudi Government Daily: Jews Use Teenagers' Blood for 'Purim' pastries," *Al-Riyadh* (Saudi Arabia), March 10, 2002, MEMI Special Dispatch No. 354. All quotes are from this source.

30. "Editor of Saudi Government Daily *Al-Riyadh:* Statement on 'Purim' Blood Libel Articles," MEMRI Special Dispatch No. 357, March 21, 2002; Mr. al-Sudairi's statement appeared in *Al-Riyadh* on March 19, 2002.

31. Lowry was asked how he thought the United States should retaliate by targeting Mecca if Islamic terrorists detonated a nuclear device in an American city. Here is his reply in full: "This is a tough one, and I don't know quite what to think. Mecca seems extreme, of course, but then again few people would die and it would send a signal. Religions have suffered such catastrophic setbacks before. As for the Saudis, my only thought is that if we're going to hold them responsible for terrorism, we had better start doing it now, not after an even more catastrophic attack. And, as a general matter, the time for seriousness—including figuring out what we would do in retaliation, so maybe it can have some slight deterrent effect—is now rather than after thousands and thousands more American casualties." The exchange, which Lowry provided to me in full, was picked up by *The Washington Post* and the left-wing on-line journal *American Prospect,* both of which misreported Lowry's comments as actively urging the United States to bomb Mecca. The Saudi-backed Council on American Islamic Relations (CAIR) issued an "Action Alert" to its members on March 13, who launched a "spam" campaign against the *National Review* Web site, flooding it with abusive e-mail messages copied to the personal mailboxes of *NR* editors. The CAIR Action Alert came just as MEMRI published the original article on the blood libel by Dr. al-Jalahma.

32. "Egyptian Government Weekly Reproduces Nazi Propaganda Forgery," MEMRI Special Dispatch No. 339, January 31, 2002 (original source: Salah al-Din Hilmi, "The Jews Are Bloodsuckers and Will Yet Conquer America," *Akher Sa'a* [Egypt], January 9, 2002).

33. "Columnist for Saudi Daily *Al-Jazirah:* Jews Use Blood for Baked Goods," MEMRI Special Dispatch No. 421, September 19, 2002, quoting *Al-Jazirah* (Saudi Arabia), September 6, 2002.

34. Confidential sources of the author. Syria's very temporary drug eradication program was duly highlighted by the Drug Enforcement Agency and by the State Department's annual report on drug eradication programs for 1993.

35. SANA, May 5, 2001. I have compared the somewhat stilted English version of this text to the French, as published in *Revue L'Arche* 523 (September 2001): 65. When the English differs from my rendering of the French, I have put SANA's English in brackets.

36. Quoted by Fiamma Nirenstein, "How Suicide Bombers Are Made: Anti-Semitism in the Middle East," *Commentary,* September 1, 2001. Her shorter version of Assad's greeting accused the Jews of having "tried . . . to kill the principles of all religions with the same mentality with which they betrayed Jesus Christ" and in "the same way they tried to betray and kill the prophet Muhammad."

37. Amotz Asa-El, "The Sad Case of Bashar Assad," *Jerusalem Post,* May 17, 2001.

38. "President al-Assad interview," SANA, July 9, 2001.

39. *Le Figaro,* June 27, 2001.

40. "Today, the 15th of April, when we are celebrating Easter, the hostile actions of Sharon remind us of what his predecessors did to the Christ," Yasser Arafat's Fatah movement proclaimed in an editorial published on its Web site on April 15, 2001 (www.fateh.net). For hundreds of years, the Catholic Church promoted similar accusations against Jews.

41. "Egyptian Government–Sponsored Scientific Journal: On American and Israeli Bio-Warfare and Jews Spreading AIDS to Asia and Africa," MEMRI Special Dispatch No. 322, December 28, 2001.

42. Quoted in Waintrater, "La montée de l'antisémitisme dans le monde arabe," p. 66.

43. Robert S. Wistrich, *Muslim Anti-Semitism,* p. 8.

44. Waintrater, "La montée de l'antisémitisme dans le monde arabe," p. 63.

45. This speech was rebroadcast live to French Muslims via Radio-Orient in Paris. Translation cited in Meir Waintrater, "La montée de l'antisémitisme dans le monde arabe," p. 67.

46. The same hadith is regularly cited in mosques under the control of the Palestinian Authority in Gaza. See "Friday Sermon on PA TV: Blessings to Whoever Saved a Bullet to Stick It in a Jew's Head,'" MEMRI Special Dispatch No. 252, August 7, 2001.

47. Interview with Mufti Ikrama Sabri, Jerusalem, October 24, 2002.

48. "Qadhafi: The CIA and the Israeli Mossad Injected AIDS to Libyan children," *Al-Ahram* (Egypt), April 29, 2001, MEMRI Special Dispatch No. 214.

49. "Fears of Normalization with Israel in the Syrian Media," MEMRI Special Dispatch No. 67, January 6, 2000 (original source: "The Peace of Zion," *Al-'Usbu' al-Adabi* [Syria], January 1, 2000).

50. Raphael Israeli, "Poison: The Use of the Blood Libel in the War Against Israel," *Jerusalem Letter/Viewpoints,* April 15, 2002. Available on-line at www.jcpa.org/jl/vp476.htm.

51. These examples are cited in Waintrater, "La montée de l'antisémitisme dans le monde arabe," p. 73. Asked about these allegations, an IDF spokesman had just one word: "Ridiculous."

52. Examples cited by Wistrich, *Muslim Anti-Semitism,* p. 34 (original sources: *Al-Hayat al-Jadida,* May 15, 1997, and *Yediot Aharonot,* June 25, 1997).

53. *The Washington Post,* July 28, 1997. See also "Bush Administration Agrees to Finance Arafat Ministry that Circulates Anti-Israel Blood Libels," Zionist Organization of America report dated November 26, 2001.

54. Israeli, "Poison: The Use of the Blood Libel in the War Against Israel."

55. Deborah Camiel, "Arafat's Wife Has Surprise for Hillary," *Washington Times* (Reuters), November 11, 1999. See also "Suha Arafat: Israel Polluting Our Water," *Jerusalem Post,* November 12, 1999.

56. Wistrich, *Muslim Anti-Semitism,* p. 34 (original source: Nirenstein, "How Suicide Bombers Are Made," pp. 53–55).

57. Deborah Lipstadt, *Denying the Holocaust* (New York: Plume, 1993), p. 14.

58. Ibid. See also www.likud.nl/extr28.html.

59. Ahlmark initially formulated this statement as a resolution adopted at a 1990 conference in Oslo, "The Anatomy of Hate," which was signed by Czech president Václav Havel and Nobel laureates Nadime Gordimer and Elie Wiesel, among others.

60. Lipstadt, *Denying the Holocaust,* p. 14.

61. Article XXII of Oslo II (September 1995); reaffirmed in the Hebron Accord (January 1997), 2-b.

62. *Jerusalem Post,* January 26, 1995; "Holocaust Denial in the Middle East: The Latest Anti-Israel, Anti-Semitic Propaganda Theme," Anti-Defamation League, New York, 2002, available on-line at www.adl.org/holocaust/Denial_ME/hdme_origins.asp.

63. Interview with Mahmoud Abbas by Nahum Barnea and Ronny Shaked, senior correspondents, *Yediot Aharonot,* May 30, 2003.

64. Cited by www.likud.nl/extr28.html.

65. An erroneous reference to the Institute for Historical Review, based in Los Angeles, which announced in 1979 as a publicity stunt that it would pay $50,000 to anyone who "could prove that the Nazis operated gas-chambers to exterminate jews during World War II." For a full account, see Lipstadt, *Denying the Holocaust,* chap. 8, "The Institute for Historical Review."

66. Anti-Semitism in the Palestinian Media," MEMRI Special Dispatch No. 1, July 15, 1998 (original source: Seif 'Ali al-Jarwan, "Jewish Control of the World Media," *Al-Hayat al-Jadida,* July 2, 1998).

67. PA TV, interview with Ismail Elbakawi, discussing a book called *The Holocaust Industry.* Cf. Itamar Marcus, "Palestinians teach Holocaust denial again," Palestinian Media Watch, May 29, 2003, www.pmw.org.il.

68. "The Holocaust, Netanyahu and Me," *Al-Akhbar,* September 25, 1998. Cited in "Holocaust Denial in the Middle East."

69. "Anti-Semitism in the Egyptian Media; Part I: Holocaust Denial," *Al-Gumhuriya* (Egypt), March 4, 2000, MEMRI Special Dispatch No. 77. This was a far cry from Hannah Arendt's charge, in her 1963 account, *Eichmann in Jerusalem,* that Jewish community organizations set up by Hitler had provided lists of Jews, believing the Nazi authorities would use the lists to protect Jews and their property, when in reality they were used to round up Jews for extermination.

70. Ibid.

71. "The Egyptian Government Paper *Al-Akhbar* Once Again Defends Hitler," MEMRI Special Dispatch No. 231, June 20, 2001; translated from *Al-Akhbar,* May 27, 2001.

72. *Al-Hayat al-Jadida,* February 18, 1999, translated by *USA Today,* April 4, 2001.

73. Muhammad Kheir al-Wadi, "The Plague of the Third Millennium," *Teshreen,* January 31, 2000.

74. Reported by Agence France-Presse, May 14, 2000.

75. Cited by *Jerusalem Post,* April 25, 2001.

76. *Al-Shaab* (Egypt), March 3, 2000, cited in MEMRI Special Dispatch No. 77.

77. Interview with Sheikh Ikrima Sabri, Jerusalem, October 24, 2002.

78. "Zionism and Nazism: A Discussion on the TV Channel Al-Jazeera," MEMRI Special Dispatch No. 225, June 6, 2001.

79. Nirenstein, "How Suicide Bombers Are Made."

5: HITLER AND THE MUFTI

1. Lewis, *Semites and Anti-Semites,* p. 117. While detailing the extreme discrimination and occasional pogroms Jews suffered in Muslim lands throughout this period, Lewis argues that systematic anti-Semitism appeared in Islamic lands only in 1840 during the so-called Damascus Affair, the work of

Capuchin monks with active diplomatic support from the French consul (cf. p. 137). This view is disputed by Prager and Telushkin (see below).

2. CNN, January 7, 1998. The "enlightened Khatami" went on to describe the Israeli government as "a racist terrorist regime."

3. *Jumhuriya Islamiya,* January 8, 1998; quoted by Lewis, *Semites and Anti-Semites,* p. 265. Before the 1979 Islamic revolution, Iran's thriving Jewish population numbered well over eighty thousand. Today, a scant twenty thousand Jews remain. The arrest on espionage charges of dozens of Jews in the western Iranian city of Shiraz on Passover Eve in 1999 created panic among Jews remaining in Iran and their relatives overseas. The police roundup included three rabbis, the keeper of a Jewish cemetery, a sixteen-year-old student who was dragged from his classroom, Jewish studies teachers, ritual butchers, and circumcisers. The chief rabbi of the Sephardic community in Israel, Eliahu Bakhshi-Doron, alleged that "the Iranian government is apparently trying to get rid of the Jewish community." ("Special Report: Hardball over Iranian Jews," *Iran Brief,* July 6, 1999)

4. Lewis, *Semites and Anti-Semites,* p. 259.

5. *October* (Egypt), December 3, 2000, and December 10, 2000. Quoted in Meir Waintrater, "La montée de l'antisémitisme dans le monde arabe," p. 80.

6. Prager and Telushkin, *Why the Jews?,* p. 116.

7. Ibid., p. 117.

8. Cited in Meir Waintrater, "La montéee de l'antisémitisme dans le monde arabe," p. 66.

9. Prager and Telushkin, *Why the Jews?,* pp. 121–122.

10. Interviews with Dr. Rachal Suissa, Norway, July 20–21, 2002.

11. Daniel Pipes, *The Hidden Hand.*

12. Joseph B. Schechtman, *The Mufti and the Fuehrer* (New York: Thomas Yoseloff, 1965), p. 19.

13. Statement of British policy in Palestine issued by Mr. Churchill in June 1922, quoted in Walter Laqueur and Barry Rubin, eds., *The Israel-Arab Reader: A Documentary History of the Middle East Conflict* (New York: Penguin, 1987, paperback ed.), p. 46.

14. Schectman, *The Mufti and the Fuehrer,* p. 18.

15. Ibid.

16. See Alan Hart, *Arafat: Terrorist or Peacemaker?* (London: Sidgwick & Jackson, 1984), pp. 67–68.

17. Schechtman, *The Mufti and the Fuehrer,* p. 36.

18. Some crusaders believed the Mosque of Omar was the Templum Domini or part of the original Temple of Solomon, which was destroyed by the Babylonians when Nebuchadnezzar carried the Jews to captivity in what is today modern-day Iraq in 586 B.C. (See people.westminstercollege.edu/faculty/ mmarkowski/sscle/dome.html). The Dome of the Rock is not a mosque, nor was it built by the early Muslim caliph Omar, who built an earlier structure on the site that was torn down to build the present shrine. Muslim men pray instead at the Al-Aqsa Mosque located two hundred meters to the south on the Temple Mount. Muslims believe that this is the place where Abraham nearly sacrificed his son Isaac.

19. Interview, June 18, 2002.

20. Lewis, *Semites and Anti-Semites,* p. 147.

21. Ibid., p. 148.

22. Ibid., p. 140.

23. Cited in Lewis, *Semites and Anti-Semites,* p. 142.

24. Lukasz Hirszowicz, *The Third Reich and the Arab East* (London: Routledge & Kegan Paul, 1966), p. 34; Schectman, *The Mufti and the Fuehrer,* p. 77.

25. Hirszowicz, *The Third Reich and the Arab East,* p. 30; Lewis, *Semites and Anti-Semites,* p. 143.

26. Sami al-Jundi, *Al Bath* (Beirut, 1969), quoted in Lewis, *Semites and Anti-Semites,* p. 147.

27. Lewis, *Semites and Anti-Semites,* p. 150.

28. Kenneth R. Timmerman, *The Death Lobby: How the West Armed Iraq* (Boston: Houghton Mifflin, 1991), p. 1.

29. The June 1–2, 1941, pogrom in Baghdad is recounted in greater detail in Lewis, *Semites and Anti-Semites,* p. 158.

30. The Persians are of Aryan descent, racially distinct from the Arabs, a factor frequently overlooked in understanding the widespread mutual antipathy between Arabs and Persians.

31. Lewis, *Semites and Anti-Semites,* p. 150.

32. Daniel Carpi, "The Mufti of Jerusalem, Amin el-Huseini, and His Diplomatic Activity During World War II (October 1941–July 1943), in *Studies in Zionism,* 7 (spring 1983); quoted by Lewis, *Semites and Anti-Semites,* p. 151.

33. Quoted by Lewis, *Semites and Anti-Semites,* p. 151. The mufti published his memoires in Beirut in July 1970, four years before his death, in issue 122 of *Falastin,* the official PLO magazine.

34. Paul Longgrear and Raymond McNemar, "The Arab/Muslim Nazi Connection," *Canadian Friends,* International Christian Embassy, Jerusalem, www.cdn-friends-icej.ca/medigest/may00/arabnazi.html.

35. Lewis, *Semites and Anti-Semites,* p. 158. The German version of the memo was translated by the British after the war and published in *Documents on German Foreign Policy, 1918-1945,* series D, vol. X, London, 1964.

36. Lewis, *Semites and Anti-Semites,* p. 147.

37. "Record of the Conversation between the Führer and the Grand Mufti of Jerusalem on November 28, 1941, in the Presence of Reichs Foreign Minister and Minister Grobba in Berlin," *Documents on German Foreign Policy, 1918-1945,* series D, vol. XIII, London, 1964, quoted in Walter Laqueur, *The Israel-Arab Reader,* Harmondsworth, Middlesex, England: Penguin Books, Ltd., 1970, pp. 106–107.

38. Hitler's failure to seize the Middle East, where British forces in Palestine and Egypt were scantily defended, lost him the war, according to military historian Bevin Alexander. In *How Hitler Could Have Won World War II* (New York: Crown, 2000), Alexander argues that Germany could have easily reinforced Rommel's Afrika Corps as late as 1941 and evicted the British from the Middle East, then swung northward to Iran to sever the British-American arms supply line to Russia, while seizing desperately needed oil fields in Saudi Arabia and Iraq in the process. Instead, Alexander argues, Hitler's obsession with murdering Jews and Communists (whom he considered to be Jews and Jewish agents) totally blinded him as a military strategist and hurtled Germany to her destruction.

39. Hitler's often quoted last will and testament, written in his bunker in Berlin during the final days of the Allied advance, commanded the German people to complete his work in exterminating world Jewry. "Above all I charge the leaders of the nation and those under them to scrupulous observance of the laws of race and to the merciless opposition to the universal poisoner of all peoples, international Jewry." See Prager and Telushkin, *Why the Jews?,* p. 157.

40. Quoted in Wistrich, *Muslim Anti-Semitism,* p. 47, fn. 7.

41. Quoted in Prager and Telushkin, *Why the Jews?,* p. 124.

42. Quoted in Lewis, *Semites and Anti-Semites,* p. 155.

43. Quoted in Wistrich, *Muslim Anti-Semitism,* p. 2.

44. Longgear and McNemar, "The Arab/Muslim Nazi Connection."

45. Yigal Carmon, Jerusalem interview, October 24, 2002. Carmon wrote a book-length master's thesis on the mufti at Hebrew University in 1987–1988.

46. The accusation that the mufti visited Eichmann in Auschwitz was made by Dieter Wisliceny, one of Eichmann's deputies, during his trial in Nuremberg for war crimes right after the war. The mufti subsequently denied it. See Lewis, *Semites and Anti-Semites,* p. 156.

47. Longgear and McNemar, "The Arab/Muslim Nazi Connection."

48. Unpublished master's thesis, Yigal Carmon.

49. Lewis, *Semites and Anti-Semites,* p. 156.

50. As the recognized leader of the Palestinian Arabs, the mufti presided over a world Muslim conference in 1951 and in 1955 was a delegate to the Bandoeng conference of African and Asian countries. (Lewis, *Semites and Anti-Semites,* p. 160.)

51. Hannah Arendt, *Eichmann in Jerusalem* (New York: Bantam Books, 1977), p. 13.

52. Lewis, *Semites and Anti-Semites,* p. 157.

53. Source: Obituary of Faisal al-Husseini, Palestinian Academic Society for International Affairs (PASSIA), Special Bulletin on Jerusalem, May 2002, p. 12. Faisal al-Husseini was the son of Abdel Kader al-Husseini, a leader of the anti-Jewish riots in the 1930s who died fighting against Israel's independence in 1948. His grandfather was Musa Kasim al-Husseini, the effective mayor of Jerusalem during the British mandate. See also www.minfo.gov.ps/issues/faisal.htm and inic.utexas.edu/menic/oil/game/simulation/profiles/f1994/0018.html.

54. Interviews with Minister of Public Security Uzi Landau, Tel Aviv; Hebrew University scholar Michael Widlanski, who helped translate the documents; and other current and former Israeli officials, October 2002.

55. Suzanne Fields, "The Ghosts of Auschwitz," *Washington Times,* December 10, 2001.

56. Andrew Gower and Tony Walker *Behind the Myth: Yasser Arafat and the Palestinian Revolution* (New York: Olive Branch Press, 1991) p. 9; Said Aburish, in *Arafat: From Defender to Dictator* (London: Bloomsbury Press, 1998) p. 15.

57. Hart, *Arafat: Terrorist or Peacemaker?,* pp. 67–68.

58. Said Aburish, *Arafat: From Defender to Dictator,* p. 15.

59. Translated by Palestinian Media Watch, www.pmw.org.il.

60. "Netanyahu: 'I Promise I Will Expel Arafat,'" CNN, November 13, 2002.

6: THE HOUSE OF WAR

1. "The whole issue," Prince al-Waleed told *Okaz* daily, "is that I spoke about their position [on the Middle Est conflict] and they didn't like it because there are Jewish pressures and they were afraid of them." Quoted in the Saudi government daily *Ar-Riyadh,* October 13, 2001.

2. Information on IQRAA-TV's corporate status was provided to the author by Steven P. Stalinsky of the Middle East Media Research Institute and was drawn from the company's own Web site, www.art-tv.net/corporate/corporate.asp and from a related Web site, www.adduniverse.com/corporate/owners.asp.

3. Creditreform Swiss Companies (Geneva), 1999. Dar al-Maal al-Islami also shows up in Nassau, Bahamas, according to a German federal intelligence report (author's private collection).

4. Saleh Kamel hired Greenberg Traurig in his capacity as chairman of the General Council for Islamic Banks, an umbrella group established in 2001 that included the Faisal Islamic Bank, its subsidiary in Egypt, and four Al-Baraka subsidiaries. The Islamic Institute of Washington, D.C., which operates from the office suite of Republican lobbyist Grover Norquist at 1920 L Street NW, hosted a conference for the council in late September 2002 through its charitable wing, the Islamic Free Market Institute Foundation, according to the organization's own Web site (www.islamicinstitute.org). See also Eli Kintisch, "Top Lobbyist Demurs as Firm Is Hired by Islamic Banks," *Forward,* September 13, 2002, p. 8.

5. Confidential source. A Harvard University study conducted in May 2002 showed that the Internet Services Unit in Riyadh has banned 2,038 Internet sites, 250 of which were religious. (Julia Duin, "Daring Leaps of Faith," *Washington Times,* October 13, 2002.)

6. Robert Baer, "The Fall of the House of Saud," *Atlantic Monthly,* May 2003.

7. The telethon was broadcast by MBC. See Donna Abu-nasr, "Saudi Telethon Raises $56.7 Million for 'Martyrs,'" Associated Press, April 13, 2002. Money continued to flow into the telethon coffers for several more days, bringing the total raised to over $92 million and ultimately $109 million, according to subsequent reports.

8. Iraqi president Saddam Hussein offered a onetime grant of $25,000 to the family of a dead bomber, Saudi Arabia gave $5,300, the Palestinian Authority contributed $2,000, and the governments of the United Arab Emirates and Qatar kicked in an additional $500 each. The $33,000 total payment amounts to approximately six years the average Palestinian annual wage. See also Timmerman, "Documents Detail Saudi Terror Links."

9. Saudi Information Service, April 26, 2002.

10. Dinesh D'Souza, "Osama's Brain: Meet Sayyid Qutb," *Weekly Standard,* April 29, 2002.

11. Quoted in ibid.

12. Sayyid Kutb, *Islam: The Religion of the Future* (Beirut: Dar al-Qalam Press, 1971), pp. 75, 79.

13. Quoted in D'Souza, "Osama's Brain."

14. Ronald Nettler, *Past Trials and Present Tribulations: A Muslim Fundamentalist View of Jews* [English translation of *Our Struggles with the Jews*] (Oxford: Pergamon Press, 1987), p. 72.

15. Ibid., p. 83.

16. Ibid., p. 78.

17. Jews celebrate their deliverance by Xerxes in 480 B.C. (Esther 9:1–16), in the annual feast of Purim.

18. Amir Taheri, "Anti-West," in *American Foreign Policy Interests* 24, no. 2 (April 2002).

19. The Iranian regime dismissed him as an "agent of Savak" and trotted out documents shredded at the U.S. embassy in Tehran that were subsequently pieced together by revolutionaries that identified him as CIA source "SDULTIMATE/1." In fact, however, Rouhani never returned to Iran after 1972, because of his public opposition to the shah, and for many years he managed a publishing house in France called *La Pensée Chiite* (Shiite Thought), known for its moderate ecumenical views.

20. Author's notes. Another variant Rouhani used was "Hezballah" (Party of God) versus "Taghout" (Partisans of the Devil). "They [the Islamic Republic] believe it is their duty to eradicate the Taghout wherever they may be. "Senior Iranian Clerics Say 'Islamic' Republic Is Not Islamic," Foundation for Democracy in Iran, June 3, 1997)

21. Lubrani, who is Israel's "coordinator for Lebanon," was the unofficial Israeli ambassador to Tehran during the final years of the shah and the only foreign diplomat who accurately predicted the revolution.

22. The Islamic centers are funded through the Alavi Foundation in New York, a private foundation established by the shah in the mid-1970s that was taken over by Khomeini. After the revolution it was known as the Mostazafan Foundation, a branch of the Bonyad-e Mostazafan va Janbazan in Tehran. See Kenneth R. Timmerman, "Islamic Iran's American Base," *American Spectator* (December 1995).

23. Khamenei was elected "Supreme Guide of the Revolution" by the Council of Guardians in 1988, following Khomeini's death at the age of eighty-eight. Iranian opposition sources have long claimed that Khamenei, who along with Khomeini's own son Ahmad received military training at Palestinian camps in Lebanon in the 1970s, also received political indoctrination in East Germany in the 1960s as part of a long-term Soviet effort to penetrate the Iranian clergy. Several other revolutionary clerics, including the personal secretary to Khomeini himself, were alleged to be Soviet agents. I wrote about this extensively in *Fanning the Flames: Guns, Greed and Geopolitics in the Gulf War* (Zurich: Orell Fusli, 1987).

24. Cited by Amir Taheri, "Anti-West," p. 111.

25. In the February 2000 parliamentary elections, Iranian Jews replaced their quietest representative with Maurice Motamed, who openly criticized the regime for its persecution of Jews and traveled to the United States to meet with American and Iranian American Jewish leaders.

26. Farahanipour leads a broad-based nationalist movement that grew out of the 1999 student revolt called Marze-por Gohar and is now based in California. They maintain an English-language Web site at www.marzeporgohar.org.

27. Steve Martinovich, "Turning the Arab Street to Main St.," *Washington Times,* October 9, 2002.

28. A more detailed presentation of Iran's efforts to export the revolution was made by the author at an unclassified conference hosted by the Defense Intelligence Agency on April 30, 1998. The paper is available on-line at www.iran.org/tib/krt/krt_index.htm under the heading "Scholarly Articles and Monographs."

29. *Middle East Insight* (March–April 1988). Quoted by Wistrich, *Muslim Anti-Semitism,* p. 12.

30. Kenneth R. Timmerman, "Alliance in Terror," *Middle East Defense News* (*Mednews*), April 17, 1989.

31. "Iranian leaders Vow Death to Israel," Associated Press, March 11, 1994.

32. Tehran Radio, September 1, 1997.

33. Kenneth R. Timmerman, "Hamas Leader Visits Tehran," *Iran Brief,* May 4, 1998. See also "Iranian Leader Vows to Support Hamas," *Xinhua,* May 2, 1998.

34. Timmerman, "Hamas Leader Visits Tehran."

35. Interview with Israeli officials, Tel Aviv, October 1997. See also "Hezbollah Weapons," *Iran Brief,* October 6, 1997.

36. "Iran's Khatami Says End of Israel Needed for Peace," Reuters, October 2, 2000.

37. RFE/RL Iran Report, October 30, 2000, quoting domestic Iranian press reports.

38. As former U.S. hostages in Lebanon and family members of victims of the U.S. embassy bombing in Beirut in April 1983 also sued the government of Iran in U.S. courts, by June 2001 damage awards to the victims or their survivors in the United States topped $2 billion.

39. "The re-awakening of the Palestinian people, their freedom struggle inspired by Islamic slogans against Zionist usurpers, the awakening usurpers [*sic*], the awakening of the Muslim nations in Europe, the establishment of the Muslim Bosnia-Herzegovina . . . the coming to power of believers in the Islamic government in Turkey and Algeria through the usual channels of western democracy . . . the establishment of a government based on Islamic principles in the Sudan . . . are [all] tokens of the deep and increasing influence of the birth of an Islamic Republic in Iran throughout the Islamic world and Islamic ummah." *The Sunday Times* (London), April 8, 1998, paid advertisement issued on behalf of Ayatollah Ali Khamenei by Main Impact Ltd., London.

40. The five goals were (1) maintenance of the system of *velayat-e faghigh* (absolute clerical rule), (2) an aggressive expansion of Iran's influence in the Persian Gulf region, (3) an end to the U.S. military presence in the Persian Gulf, (4) active subversion of the Middle East peace process, and (5) determination to develop a broad spectrum of weapons of mass destruction, including nuclear weapons. An early version of this presentation, "Opportunities for Change in Iran," appeared in *Fighting Proliferation: New Concerns for the Nineties,* Henry Sokolski, ed. (Washington, D.C.: U.S. Department of Defense, Air University Press, September 1996). A longer version, presented to the U.S. Army War College, "A Competitive Strategies Approach to Iran," is available on-line at www.iran.org/tib/krt/krt_index.htm.

41. Sulaiman al-Hattlan, "In Saudi Arabia, an Extreme Problem," *The Washington Post,* May 8, 2002, p. A21.

42. Paul Barril, *Missions très spéciales* (Paris: Editions Presses de la Cité, 1984). Barril presents himself as something of a French Rambo, despite his quiet demeanor and short stature (he is only around five feet four, as I recall from meeting him in 1990). Barril's specialty these days is celebrity protection, especially for African heads of state. His Web site, www.barril.com, boasts that "during his ten years at the head of the GIGN he arrested 115 persons, participated in the surrender of 61 kidnappers, neutralized with his bare hands 17 armed individuals, and liberated more than 450 hostages."

43. "Mahdi" is a term used by Shiite Islam that translates roughly to "Savior." While rejected by Wahhabite Muslims, the notion appears in certain messianic Sunni sects and among the lower classes of society. Jouhayman appears to have played on these popular beliefs, not Wahhabite doctrine, in the hope of sparking a popular rebellion throughout the kingdom.

44. King Abdul Aziz, the founder of the al-Saud dynasty, had numerous wives, but since the assassination of King Faisal in 1975, Khaled's full brothers, known as the Sudairi seven, had become the dominant faction within a royal family that counted some six thousand princes. For more details, see Simon Henderson, *After King Fahd: Succession in Saudi Arabia* (Washington, D.C.: Washington Institute for Near East Policy, 1995).

45. Saeed Ismaeel, *The Difference Between the Shi'ites and the Majority of Muslim Scholars,* pamphlet printed and distributed in the United States by the World Assembly of Muslim Youth, a Saudi government–sponsored organization.

46. Author's notes of remarks by former U.S. ambassador to Saudi Arabia James Atkins, Christ Church, Kensington, Maryland, January 12, 2003. Atkins said a senior Saudi official made the comment during a conversation in Riyadh in November 2002.

47. Interview with Ali al-Ahmad, Washington, D.C., October 1, 2002.

48. Lowell Bergman and Martin Smith, "Hunting bin Laden," *PBS Frontline,* September 13, 2001; the full report is available on-line at www.pbs.org/wgbh/pages/frontline/shows/binladen/who/family.html.

49. Stephen Schwartz, *The Two Faces of Islam: The House of Sa'ud from Tradition to Terror* (New York: Doubleday, 2002), p. 118.

50. "Saudis Spread Hate Speech in U.S.," Saudi Institute, McLean, Virginia; available on-line at www.saudiinstitute.org. Established as a private venture by Saudi Shiite Ali al-Ahmad in September 2000, the institute receives a small grant for translating Saudi government propaganda from the Foundation for the Defense of Democracies, a private think tank in Washington, D.C.

51. The teachings of sect founder Muhammad ibn Abd al-Wahhab "came down to three points," writes Stephen Schwartz. "First, ritual is superior to intentions. Second, no reverence of the dead is permitted. Third, there can be no intercessory prayer." This led to a violent rejection of many long established Muslim practices, "including praying in favor of Muhammad and the recitation of blessings on the Prophet at the beginning of Friday congregational prayers." Abd al-Wahhab rejected all other schools of Islamic thought that did not accept his views "as idolators and apostates, and abused the prophets, scholars, saints, and other pious figures of the past," Schwartz writes. He urged that Muslims who had fallen into unbelief "should all be killed, their wives and daughters violated, and their possessions confiscated." (Schwartz, *The Two Faces of Islam,* pp. 69–71)

52. Bob Woodward, *Veil: The Secret Wars of the CIA, 1981–1987* (New York: Simon & Schuster, 1987), p. 130.

53. Author interviews and press conference by Sheikh Omar Bakri Mohammad, Abu Hamza al-Masri, and Mohammad al-Massari, London, September 11, 2002.

54. Schwartz, *The Two Faces of Islam,* p. 155.

55. The Treasury Department froze the assets of Muwafaq chairman Sheikh Yasin Abdallah al-Qadi, on October 12, 2001. Al-Qadi's lawyers in Britain said, "Our client is horrified and shocked that his name has been included in this [Treasury] list." (Press Trust of India, October 21, 2001)

56. Interview with Abdelbari Atwan, editor of *Al-Quds al-Arabi,* London, February 25, 1998.

57. Interview with Frank Anderson, Washington, D.C., March 18, 1998.

58. Edward Girardet, "A Brush with Laden on the Jihad Front Line," *Christian Science Monitor,* August 31, 1998, p. 19.

59. Interviews with former CIA officer Frank Anderson, who worked in Afghanistan in the 1980s; a member of the Saudi royal family; former ISI director general Hamid Gul; former ISI deputy director general Asad Durrani; and ISI director General Rana Chaudri, March 1998.

60. Kenneth R. Timmerman, "Orphans of the Cold War," *American Spectator* (May 1998).

61. Interview with Nabil Osman, Cairo, March 1998.

62. Private communication with the author, October 10, 2002.

63. Ibid., October 15, 2002. A nephew of the former shah of Iran, outcast by his own family because he remained in Iran for three years after the 1979 revolution, Patrick Ali Pahlavi was born a Catholic but converted to Islam in his twenties and studied in Paris with Ayatollah Mehdi Rouhani, among others.

64. The State Department publishes an annual report on religious freedom, which is available on-line at www.state.gov. State Department human rights reports, which also detail Saudi government abuses, are published regularly as well. Both were widely ignored by Congress and the press until September 11. Amazingly, given continued religious repression, the State Department removed Saudi Arabia from the 2002 report, released to Congress in early March 2003, apparently as part of the effort to win Saudi support to base U.S. troops and aircraft in the kingdom for the U.S.-led liberation of Iraq.

65. Executive Order 13224—Blocking Property and Prohibiting Transactions with Persons Who Commit, Threaten to Commit, or Support Terrorism. The list of blocked entities, commonly known as the "black list," is maintained by the U.S. Treasury Department and is regularly updated on-line.

66. Badr Almotawa, "U.S. Urged to Give Sound Proof in Julaidan Case," *Arab News,* September 9, 2002. Jalaidan was president of the Muslim Students Association while a student at the University of Arizona and headed the Islamic Center in Tuscson in 1983–1984 before traveling to Afghanistan to join Abdallah Azzam and bin Laden in 1985. His ties to bin Laden are detailed in Steve Fairanu and Alia Ibrahim, "Mysterious Trip to Flight 77 Cockpit: Suicide Pilot's Conversion to Radical Islam Remains Obscure," *The Washington Post,* September 10, 2002.

67. On the board of the Rabita Trust with Julaidan were Saudi prince Talal bin Abdul Aziz, the oldest living member of the al-Saud line, the secretary-generals of the Muslim World League and the International Islamic Relief Organization, and the president of the Council of the Saudi Chamber of Commerce. See also www.satp.org/satporgtp/countries/pakistan/terroristoutfits/Rabita_Trust.htm.

68. Sophie Landrin, "En tournee en France, le saoudien Abdullah Turki a ete fraichement acceuilli," *Le Monde,* October 10, 2002, p. 12. Author's translation.

69. Abdallah Turki's U.S. trip was announced by fax and carried on the league's U.S. Web site, www.mwla.org. I discuss ISASA propaganda below.

70. Communication with the author, January 31, 1998.

71. "Saudi Government Paper: 'Billions Spent by Saudi Royal Family to Spread Islam to Every Corner of the Earth,' " MEMRI Special Dispatch No. 360, March 27, 2002 (original source: *Ain al-Yaqeen* [Saudi government weekly in English], March 1, 2002).

72. The Holy Land Foundation for Relief and Development of Richardson, Texas, one of the largest Muslim "charities" in the United States, was blacklisted by the Treasury Department on December 4, 2001, after it was raided by the FBI as part of Operation Green Quest. Israeli officials had documented donations from the Holy Land Foundation to the military wings of Hamas and Islamic Jihad several years earlier, but the Clinton administration failed to act.

73. Op cit. *Ain al-Yaqueen* (see note 71).

74. The article lists the Dar al-Salam Institute, the Fresno Mosque in California, and Islamic Centers in Colombia, Missouri; East Lansing, Michigan; Los Angeles; New Brunswick, New Jersey; New York, NY; Tida, Maryland; Toledo, Ohio; Washington, D.C., and suburban Virginia. It also mentions the Islamic Cultural Center in Chicago, the King Fahd Mosque in Los Angeles, the Mosque of the Albanian Community in Chicago, the South-West Big Mosque off Chicago, and the Omar Ibn al-Khattab Mosque in Los Angeles.

75. Al-Haramain was blacklisted by the U.S. Treasury Department on March 11, 2002.

76. "Mufti Hits Out at Smear Campaign Against Charities," *Arab News* (Riyadh, in English), November 14, 2002.

77. FBIS report: Riyadh Kingdom of Saudi Arabia TV1 in Arabic, official television station of the Saudi government; Saudi Sheikh al-Sudais's Friday Sermon, May 31, 2002, at 0926 GMT, carries a live sermon from the Holy Mosque in Mecca.

78. FBIS report: Riyadh Kingdom of Saudi Arabia TV1 in Arabic, official television station of the Saudi government, June 21, 2002, at 0924 GMT, carries a live sermon from the Holy Mosque in Mecca.

79. FBIS report: Riyadh Kingdom of Saudi Arabia TV1 in Arabic, official television station of the Saudi government; broadcast of live sermon by Sheikh Usama bin Abdallah Khayyat from the Holy Mosque in Mecca, July 12, 2002; also available through Independent Media Review and Analysis, www.imra.org.il.

80. FBIS Report: Riyadh Kingdom of Saudi Arabia TV1 in Arabic, October 11, 2002, at 0915 GMT, live sermon from the Holy Mosque in Mecca.

81. This booklet was printed by the Ministry of Islamic Affairs and Endowments in Riyadh and paid for by the foundation of Ibrahim ibn Abdul Aziz al-Brahim, King Fahd's father-in-law, and distributed in the United States by the Institute for Islamic and Arabic Sciences. ("Saudis Spread Hate Speech in U.S.," Saudi Institute, September 9, 2002.)

82. Tim Maier's articles can be accessed on-line at findthekids.org/articles.html.

83. "Saudis Spread Hate Speech in U.S.," op cit.

84. ʿAtiyyah At-Tayyeb, "1.5 Million Pilgrims Invoke Allah's Curse on the Jews," *Makkah al-Mukarramah,* February 15, 2002.

85. Interview with the author, October 1, 2002, Washington, D.C.

86. Robert Fisk interview with bin Laden in Afghanistan's Nangarhar Province, *Independent* (London), July 10, 1996.

87. FBIS daily report, March 18, 1997, interview with Osama bin Laden by Hamid Mir; in *Pakistan* daily, translated from Urdu.

88. Jason Burke, "Bin Laden and Son: The Grooming of a Dynasty," *The Observer* (London), September 23, 2001.

89. "Al-Qaeda sur la route de la vengeance," *Libération* (Paris), October 15, 2002.

7: ARAFAT'S REIGN OF TERROR

1. Photographs of the June 23, 2001, ceremony taken from the Islamic Society Web site, translated by the Intelligence and Terrorism Information Center of Israel's Ministry of Defense. Dr. Reuven Ehrlich, ed., "Incitement and Propaganda Against Israel and Zionism," Information Bulletin No. 3, June 2002, pp. 39–47.

2. Ibid., p. 47.

3. Interviews with Robert Baer.

4. Interview with Itamar Marcus, Jerusalem, October 23, 2002.

5. The pledge to curb incitement in the schools was written into the follow-on Cairo agreement, signed on May 4, 1994. In Article XII, the two sides pledged "to foster mutual understanding and tolerance and . . . accordingly, [to] abstain from incitement, including hostile propaganda."

6. This commitment was reiterated in the Oslo II Interim Accord signed on September 28, 1995, where the Israeli government and the PLO reaffirmed "their mutual commitment to act, in accordance with this Agreement, immediately, efficiently and effectively against acts or threats of terrorism, violence or incitement, whether committed by Palestinians or Israelis." Although Palestinian officials frequently tell journalists that Israeli schoolbbooks contain the same kind of hate-filled material—and some journalists have simply printed this assertion without checking the facts—the UN-sponsored Center for Monitoring the Impact of Peace has examined the Israeli textbooks as well as those of the Palestinian Authority and has found the Israeli books free of hate speech, incitement, or derogatory comments about Arabs. Their reports are available on-line at www.edume.org.

7. Itamar Marcus, "The Palestinian Authority Schoolbooks," Center for Monitoring the Impact of Peace, Jerusalem, 1998; appendix 4, "The Palestinian Authority Educational System."

8. "Jews, Israel and Peace in Palestinian School Textbooks," Center for Monitoring the Impact of Peace, Jersaulem, 2001; available on-line from www.edume.org.

9. Ehrlich, ed., "Incitement and Propaganda Against Israel and Zionism," p. 8.

10. Ibid., p. 10.

11. I reviewed this and other examples in the original Arabic-language textbooks with Marcus.

12. *Al-Hayat al-Jadida,* August 13, 2002, translated by Palestinian Media Watch, www.pmw.org.il. The poll was conducted by Bir Zeit University in Ramallah.

13. MEMRI Special Dispatch No. 187, February 21, 2001, included as appendix B in a separate study of the new Palestinian curriculum by Goetz Nordbruch, "Narrating Palestinian Nationalism: A Study of the New Palestinian Textbooks," MEMRI, 2002.

14. Ibid.

15. Etgar Lefkovits, "Jerusalem Mufti Questioned on Suspicion of Incitement," *Jerusalem Post,* October 15, 2002.

16. Voice of Palestine radio, August 24, 2001. The 1997 quotes from Voice of Palestine Radio (July 11, 1997 and September 12, 1997) were translated by Palestinian Media Watch, www.pmw.org.il.

17. Interviews with Uzi Landau, Tel Aviv, October 23, 2002, and Sheikh Ikrima Sabri, Jerusalem, October 24, 2002.

18. "PA 'Mufti of Jerusalem and Palestine' Discusses the Intifada," MEMRI Special Dispatch No. 151, November 9, 2000 (original source: Egyptian weekly *Al-Ahram al-Arabi,* October 28, 2000).

19. The death notices appeared in the Palestinian newspapers *Al-Ayyam* (July 21, 2001) and *Al-Istiqlal* (October 4, 2001) and were translated by MEMRI Inquiry and Analysis Series No. 74, October 30, 2001, " '72 Black-Eyed Virgins': A Muslim Debate on the Rewards of Martyrs."

20. "The Highest Ranking Palestinian Authority Cleric: In Praise of Martyrdom Operations," MEMRI Special Dispatch No. 226, June 8, 2001 (original source: Voice of Palestine radio, May 25, 2001).

21. *Al-Ahram al-Arabi.*

22. Ehud Ya'ari, "Presentation to the Institute for Contemporary Affairs in Jerusalem," June 17, 2002, as printed in the *Australian Jewish Review* (August 2002): 10.

23. Michel Rocard, "Strengthening Palestinian Public Institutions," a Council on Foreign Relations task force report released on June 28, 1999. The report notes that donors pledged $4.2 billion for the 1994–1998 period, with an additional $3.3 billion pledged in 1999 for 2000–2004.

24. Interview with Tim Rothermel, Jerusalem, November 1, 1999.

25. The report, which I obtained, was put together by the general auditor, an official who works for Arafat's office. Despite this lack of independence, the report contained many precise allegations that fueled a subsequent Palestinian Legislative Council (PLC) investigation on corruption.

26. Interview with Dr. Mohammad Shtayyeh, director general of the Palestine Economic Council for Development and Reconstruction (PECDAR), November 1999.

27. Interview with former Israeli military intelligence officer, November 1999.

28. Ericsson mentioned the lunches with Dahlan at a dinner party at his official residence in East Jerusalem in November 1999.

29. Interview with former Israeli intelligence official, November 1999.

30. The dollar estimates of the lost revenue were provided to me by Hazmi Shaibi, chairman of the PLC Budget Committee, in an interview in Ramallah in November 1999.

31. The three companies that filed suit were Paz, Delek, and Sonol. Additional information on the case was provided to me by a former Israeli intelligence official who had access to internal reports on the subject. See also David Bedein, ed., "PA Accountability," *Israel Resource Review,* October 26, 1999. Ronen Bergman, an investigative reporter then working at the left-wing daily *Haaretz,* contributed heavily to this extensive report on PA corruption and broke many of these stories in *Haaretz.*

32. Former Israeli intelligence officer; interview with Arab affairs adviser to the mayor of Jerusalem; interview with former Israeli cabinet minister, November 1999, Israel.

33. Caroline B. Glick, "The Peres Center Scandal," *Jerusalem Post,* April 25, 2002.

34. *Financial Times,* December 2, 1998.

35. Interview in Ramallah, November 6, 1999.

36. Israeli Customs document showed transfers of roughly 1.2 billion New Israeli Shekels (NIS) through April 1998 (the shekel was worth close to $.32 from 1994 to 1998). An IMF official in Gaza showed me a recent Israeli Customs table, which showed transfers averaging around 35 million NIS ($8.75 million) per month into the account, for petroleum excise taxes alone. An aid to Israeli interior minister Nathan Sharansky also confirmed that figure. Through December 1999, that would bring the total transfers to over 2 billion NIS, or roughly $625 million. I also discussed this issue with officials at PECDAR and with Hazmi Shaibi, chairman of the Palestinian Legislative Council Budget Committee.

37. Source: Larry Garber, deputy director of the USAID mission to the West Bank and Gaza. Interview, Tel Aviv, November 5, 1999.

38. Interview with OPIC spokesman Larry Spinelli, Washington, D.C., October 14, 1999.

39. Glick, "The Peres Center Scandal."

40. Ibid.

41. When the Council on Foreign Relations issued its "Independent Task Force Report" on Palestinian institutions and Arafat's corruption on June 28, 1999, task force commissioners Michel Rocard of France and Henry Siegman of the United States—both of whom were political allies of Peres—

went out of their way to thank Terje Roed-Larsen for his assistance. While the report contained much useful information and made concrete recommendations for cleaning up the PA finances, it was largely ignored.

42. Bedein, ed., "PA Accountability." Ronen Bergman, an investigative reporter then working at the left-wing daily *Haaretz,* contributed to this extensive report on PA corruption.

43. Uri Dan, "Arafat Stole $8 Million per Month, Ex-Treasurer Says," *Jerusalem Post,* August 20, 2002. An Arafat spokesman, Yasser Abed Rabbo, claimed al-Russyan had been jailed for embezzlement.

44. Government Accounting Office, "PLO's Ability to Help Support Palestinian Authority Is Not Clear," report to Congressman Benjamin Gilman, chairman, Committee on International Relations, U.S. House of Representatives, November 28, 1995, GAO/NSIAD-96-23 Foreign Assistance, p. 5, note 6.

45. Yoram Ettinger, "Straight from the Jerusalem Cloakroom," 108, July 15, 2001. The declassified version of the report omitted these figures at the request of the CIA, which, "with certain minor exceptions," refused to allow the GAO to declassify its information on Arafat's finances. See "PLO's Ability" ibid, p. 1.

46. Interview with confidential source, May 26, 2003.

47. "Palestine Investment Fund: Initial Report on Valuation and Transparency," Democracy Council/Standard & Poor's, Los Angeles, CA, 2003, p. 83.

48. Interview with Bassam Eid, Jerusalem, November 1, 1999. These details were confirmed in separate interviews by Husham Kader, PLC member from Nablus; Khader Sheqirat, director of the human rights organization LAW in Beit Hanina; and others.

49. *Palestinian Human Rights Monitor* 6 (October 1998): 14.

50. Testimony taken by Bassam Eid, director of the Palestinian Human Rights Monitoring Group and published in the *Palestinian Human Rights Monitor* 5 (August 1998): 7. Eid related this and other cases to me.

51. Jon Dougherty, "Study Refutes Reporting of Intifada Casualties Says Nearly 80 Percent of Israelis Killed in Conflict are Non-Combatants," *WorldNetDaily,* July 10, 2002. The study by the International Policy Institute for Counter-Terrorism, an Israeli counterterrorism research group, found that "over 50 percent" of the 1,450 Palestinians killed since the second *intifada* began "were actively involved in the fighting," not including stone throwers or "unknowns." It also found that "Palestinians are directly responsible for the deaths of at least 185 of their own number."

52. Shlomo Shamir, "French Socialist Accuses PA of Using EU Funds for Terror," *Haaretz,* February 24, 2003.

8: THE BIG LIE

1. Interview with David Bedein, Jerusalem and Efrat, October 2002.

2. These maps appear on the PA Web site at www.pba-palestine.org and at www.fateh.org. Bedein makes this argument in detail in an article entitled "Why Would the PLO Attack a Left-Wing Kibbutz," published on his Web site, www.israelbehindthenews.com, on November 12, 2002, available at www.pmw.org.il.

3. Translation and video courtesy of Itamar Marcus, Palestinian Media Watch: "Ask for Death: The Indoctrination of Palestinian Children to Seek Death for Allah," November 2002, available at www.pmw.org.il.

4. The controversy over whose bullets actually killed Mohammad al-Dura remains. The Western media, led by the French News Agency and France 2 television, which owned the original footage, immediately claimed he was killed by Israelis. But a subsequent investigation by the Israeli army raised serious doubts, since Israeli soldiers would have had to fire around a corner to hit the position where Mohammad and his father had taken refuge. Further nourishing the controversy is the final frame before Mohammad is hit by bullets, when he turns away from the Israeli position and looks directly toward the camera with a look of horror. The PA police who were firing on the Israelis had taken up position along the same line as the French camera crew, who were Palestinian stringers. Did the PA police actually kill Mohammad al-Dura? To this day, no one knows for sure, since the boy's family refused to allow an autopsy. What is certain, however, is that his death on the third day of the *intifada* generated tremendous international sympathy for the Palestinians and almost universal condemnation of the Israelis.

5. Palestinian Media Watch, "Ask for Death."

6. Ibid., p. 2.

7. Eric Silver, "Frontline Jerusalem: The Children Who Dream of Dying," *Independent* (London), July 11, 2001, p. 13.

8. Cited in *Palestinian Media Watch,* "Ask for Death."

9. Approached by French intelligence chief Count Alexandre de Marenches in 1980 with a plan to kidnap Ayatollah Khomeini and hold him on a U.S. aircraft carrier until his supporters released U.S. hostages in Tehran, Carter replied in horror: "But he's a man of God!"

10. Palestinian Media Watch, Special Report No. 30, September 11, 2000 (original source: PA TV, July 28, 2000).

11. Ibid. (original source: Dr. Ahmed Yusuf Abu Halabiya, PA TV, October 13, 2000). For a complete translation of the sermon, preached in the Zayed bin Sultan al-Nahyan Mosque in Gaza, see "PA TV Broadcasts Call for Killing Jews and Americans," MEMRI Special Dispatch No. 138, October 14, 2000.

12. Sheikh Ibrahim Madhi, sermon at Sheikh 'Ijlin Mosque in Gaza, April 12, 2002. See appendix C, "Friday Sermon on Palestinian Authority TV," MEMRI Special Dispatch No. 370, April 17, 2002.

13. Dr. Ahmed Yusuf Abu Halabiya, PA TV, July 28, 2000, and August 11, 2000, translated by Palestinian Media Watch, Special Report No. 30, September 11, 2000.

14. Palestinian Media Watch, Special Report No. 30.

15. The French Press Agency was among the most notorious in overlooking the facts of these events in its coverage. For a critique, see Clément Weill-Raynal, "L'Agence France-presse: Le récit contre les faits," in "Les médias français sont-ils objectifs?," *L'Observatoire du monde juif* (June 2002).

16. Interview with Benny Morris, *New York Review of Books,* June 13, 2002. Sharon trounced Barak in the February 6, 2001, elections by a 22 percent margin, replacing him as prime minister.

17. *Al-Ayyam,* December 6, 2000; translation from the Israeli Ministry of Foreign Affairs Web site, www.mfa.gov.il, "Answers to Frequently Asked Questions (updated August 2002).

18. Clément Weill-Raynal, "L'Agence France Presse," p. 58.

19. Ibid. (original source: *Le nouvel observateur,* March 3, 2001).

20. Fox News, April 21, 2002; Fred Barnes, "Myths of the Intifada," *Weekly Standard,* April 25, 2002.

21. PA TV, September 1, 2000, quoted in "Palestinian Goal Is Destruction of Israel in Stages," Palestinian Media Watch, Special Report No. 31, updated May 2002. Hereafter "PMW Hudna report."

22. PMW Hudna report (original source: *Al-Ayyam,* May 30, 2000).

23. PMW Hudna report (original source: *Al-Hayat al-Jadida,* November 25, 1999).

24. PMW Hudna report (original source: *Al-Hayat al-Jadida,* April 14, 2000).

25. "Faysal al-Husseini in His Last Interview: The Oslo Accords Were a Trojan Horse," MEMRI Special Dispatch No. 236, July 2, 2001 (original source: Al-Arabi interview with reporter Shafiq Ahmad Ali, June 24, 2001).

26. "Palestinian Authority and P.L.O. Non-Compliance with Signed Agreements and Commitments: A Record of Bad Faith and Misconduct," Israeli government white paper, November 2000, released to the press by the Barak government on November 20, 2000. The May 4, 1994, Cairo Agreement was formally called the "Agreement on the Gaza Strip and the Jericho Area."

27. Ibid.

28. As reported by *Dagen* newspaper in Oslo. Arafat has never disputed the accuracy of this account of his remarks in Sweden. "The government of Israel already has, for example, full confirmation of the accuracy of the words Arafat has been quoted as saying in his meeting with Arab diplomats in Stockholm," respected Arab affairs commentor Ehud Ya׳ari wrote in the *Jerusalem Report* on April 4, 1996. "For reasons of momentary convenience, the [Peres] government chose not to challenge Arafat on his vision of the New Middle East. In the Israeli press, the item was pushed to the bottom of the inside pages."

29. The attacks: February 25, 1996: Twenty-six people were killed, eighty wounded, on bus number eighteen near the central bus station in Jerusalem; another person was killed outside Ashkelon. March 3, 1996: Nineteen people were killed, six wounded, in a repeat attack on bus number eighteen, this time on the Jaffa Road in Jerusalem. March 4, 1996: Twenty people were killed, seventy-five wounded, in a suicide attack on Ditzengoff Street in Tel Aviv.

30. *Jerusalem Post,* March 15, 1996; Barak white paper, "Palestinian Authority and P.L.O. Non-Compliance."

31. *Novoya Vremya,* May 25, 1997.

32. Barak white paper, "Palestinian Authority and P.L.O. Non-Compliance."

33. *Al-Sharq al-Awsat,* March 4, 2003. Translation courtesy of MEMRI, Special Report No. 15, "Abu Mazen: A Political Profile," April 29, 2003, note 24.

34. Letter from Bernice Wolf to the U.S. Consulate, Jerusalem, May 1, 2003, obtained by the author.

35. *Kul al-Arab,* August 25, 2000. Translation by MEMRI, Special Report 15, note 51, op cit.

36. *The New York Times,* March 31, 2003; *Haaretz,* March 31, 2003.

37. Interviews with Michael Widlanski, Jerusalem, October 2002. Some of these documents are available in the Arabic original, along with Widlanski's translations and commentaries, at www.medialine.org.

38. Report: "Arafat Linked to Attacks," Associated Press, May 2, 2002. Barghouti was put on trial in October 2002.

39. "The Palestinian Authority Employs Fatah Activists Involved in Terrorism and Suicide Attacks," Israel Defense Forces, April 15, 2002, TR2-280-02. Documents captured from the office of the commander of the "Special Forces," Colonel Bashir Nafa. This particular document set involves 150 Fatah/Tanzim/Al-Aqsa activists who were placed on the PA payroll. The Israelis have put several sets of captured documents on-line, in both the Arabic original and the English translation, on the IDF Web site, www.idf.il.

40. Kennneth R. Timmerman, "Proof That Saddam Bankrolls Terrorism," *Insight* magazine, November 13, 2002. See also "Documents Detail Saudi Terror Links." The Israelis have published several collections of these documents, which can be consulted freely by the public at the Ministry of Defense Center for Special Studies in the Tel Aviv suburb of Ramat Hasharon. Reporters seeking an appointment should call 03-548-2254.

41. Interview with Uzi Landau, Tel Aviv, October 23, 2002.

42. Ibid.

43. Arafat biographer Danny Rubinstein discusses these claims in *The Enigma of Yasser Arafat,* (South Royalton, Vt.: Steerforth Press, 1995), pp. 2–3 and 115.

44. Asher Arian, "Israeli Public Opinion on National Security 2002," Memorandum No. 61, July 2002, Jaffee Center for Strategic Studies, Tel Aviv University. Another 81 percent supported physical barriers ("separation") between Israelis and Palestinians, if it didn't involve the dismantling of Jewish settlements in the territories.

45. In an op-ed that appeared in the *International Herald Tribune* ("A 'Palestinian State,'" September 25, 2002), Council on Foreign Relations fellow Henry Siegman refers to Sharon's alleged "South African strategy" of creating Palestinian Bantustans, one of Arafat's favorite accusations in the 1980s. He also notes the bitter condemnation by Likud MK Benjamin Begin of the Transfer Party (Moledet). "The Transfer Party's joining the government is a profound political, moral, and social stain on Israel," he quotes the younger Begin as writing in February 1991. "Anyone who includes such a party in the coalition is in effect confirming UN resolutions that declare Zionism to be racism."

46. Mitch Potter, "Israeli Polls Find Fear and Confusion," *Toronto Star,* August 18, 2002, p. B01.

9: THE "NEW" ANTI-SEMITISM IN EUROPE

1. "ADL European Survey Findings: A Potent and Dangerous Mix," Anti-Defamation League, June 27, 2002.

2. "ADL Survey of Five European Countries Finds One in Five Hold Strong Anti-Semitic Sentiments," Anti-Defamation League, October 31, 2002. When the responses were tabulated across all ten European countries in the June and September polls, they gave the following results:

- Percentage of those who believe Jews are more loyal to Israel than their home country: Spain 72 percent, Italy 58 percent, Germany 55 percent, Austria 54 percent, Belgium 50 percent, Switzerland 49 percent, the Netherlands 48 percent, Denmark 45 percent, France 42 percent, U.K. 34 percent
- Percentage of those who believe Jews have too much power in the business world: Spain 63 percent, Belgium 44 percent, France 42 percent, Austria 40 percent, Switzerland 37 percent, Germany 32 percent, U.K. 21 percent, the Netherlands 20 percent, Denmark 13 percent
- Percentage of those who believe Jews still talk too much about the Holocaust: Germany 58 percent, Spain 57 percent, Austria 56 percent, Switzerland 52 percent, France 46 percent, Italy 43 percent, Belgium 38 percent, the Netherlands 35 percent, Denmark 30 percent, U.K. 23 percent

3. Examples cited by the Simon Wiesenthal Center, "Europe: An Intolerable Climate of Hate," *Response* (Summer 2002): 2–5. Both the Wiesenthal Center and the Anti-Defamation League have published chronologies of anti-Semitic attacks in Europe. See www.wiesenthal.com and www.adl.org.

4. The remark and many others like it are contained in a series of essays, *Les territoires perdus de la république,* Emmanuel Brenner, ed. (Paris, Les Milles et Une Nuits, 2002). See also Anna Topaloff, "Les territoires de la haine," *Le Figaro,* November 12, 2002.

5. Interview with a participant in the conference, January 8, 2003. Scharping also claimed that the U.S. census of 2000 was part of a plot to strengthen the control of Jews over American politics by increasing the number of House seats "controlled" by Jews.

6. Interview with a senior Israeli Foreign Ministry official, Washington, D.C., June 13, 2002.

7. Interview with Pierre Lellouche, in *Les Antifeujs: Le livre blanc des violences antisémites en France depuis septembre 2000* (Paris: Calmann-Lévy, 2002), pp. 168, 175.

8. Tom Gross inventories the invective against Barbara Amiel in "Prejudice and Abuse in Paris and London: Have the French and English Learned Nothing from the 20th Century?," *National Review,* January 10, 2002.

9. Deborah Orr, "I'm Fed Up Being Called an Anti-Semite," *Independent* (London), December 21, 2002.

10. Petronella Wyatt, "Poisonous Prejudice," *The Spectator,* December 8, 2001. See also Melanie Philipps, a columnist for the *Daily Mail,* in "British Polite Society Has Found a Not-So-New Target," *The Wall Street Journal Europe,* December 24, 2001

11. Yossi Klein Halevi, "Call It What It Is: A Global Surge of Anti-Semitism," *Los Angeles Times,* July 17, 2002. Halevi is the Israel correspondent for *The New Republic* and a senior writer for the *Jerusalem Report.*

12. "Europe: An Intolerable Climate of Hate," p. 4. For her comments on "rich Jews," see "ADL Calls on European Central Bank President to Publicly Condemn Wife's Anti-Semitic and Jewish Conspiracy Statements," Anti-Defamation League, May 30, 2002.

13. Anne Bayefsky, "What About Anti-Semitism?" *Washington Times,* May 10, 2002, p. A23.

14. Interview with the author, Stockholm, July 8, 2002.

15. Text of Raffarin's July 21, 2002, speech courtesy of the French Foreign Ministry.

16. Interview with a senior French Foreign Ministry official, Paris, July 2002.

17. SOS-Racisme, *Les Antifeujs.* In their Introduction, Patrick Klugman, president of the Union of Jewish Students in France, and Malek Boutih, president of SOS-Racisme, note that they felt compelled to jointly publish the "white book" despite their political differences because of their shared belief in French republican values. "Child of North Africa, grandson of Polish Jews, both of us French citizens under 30, our backgrounds lead us to question as much as to judge this racism that exists in the bosom of our generation." (p. 8)

18. "Europe: An Intolerable Climate of Hate," p. 2.

19. American Jewish Congress press release, July 31, 2002.

20. The first data on the explosion of anti-Semitic attacks in France was published by Shmuel Trigano, "Les juifs de France visés par l'intifada," *L'Observatoire du monde juif* 1 (November 2001). See also *Les Antifeujs,* a white paper published by SOS-Racisme (Paris: Calmann-Lévy, 2002), which contains an extensive list of anti-Semitic attacks in France current through January 31, 2002; and Shimon Samuels and Mark Knobel, "Antisemitism 2002 in France: 'Intifada' Import or Domestic Malaise?," Simon Wiesenthal Center, Paris, January 2002.

21. Interview with Michel and Adjedj Mimouni, Trappes, July 13, 2002.

22. Yvelines Panorama, October 18–24, 2000, p. 1. A front-page article, beneath the fold, described the synagogue burning, but without a picture.

23. *La lutte contre le racisme et la xenophobie: Rapport d'activitié* (Paris: Commission National Consultative des Droits de l'Homme, 2001), p. 29.

24. Eric Marty, "Un nouvel anti-semitism?," *Le Monde,* January 15, 2002.

25. I spoke to Rosen in Paris in mid-July 2002, in between his meetings with top French officials.

26. See SOS-Racisme, *Les Antifeujs,* and Commission National Consultative des Droits de l'Homme, *La lutte contre le racisme et la xenophobie.*

27. Interview with deputy director general of Israel's foreign ministry, Washington, D.C., June 13, 2002.

28. Interview with Moïse Cohen, Paris, July 10, 2002. The council, set up by Napoleon in the nineteenth century as the official voice of French Jewry, is known in French as the Consistoire.

29. Interview with Roger Cukierman, Paris, July 10, 2002

30. Ibid.

31. Pascal Boniface, "Lettre à un ami israélien," *Le Monde,* August 4, 2001.

32. Interview with Thierry Keller and Samuel Thomas, Paris, July 10, 2002. They are, respectively, treasurer and vice president of SOS-Racisme.

33. "Avant son proces: Un elu FN aurait réitèré ses propos négationnistes," *Le Dauphiné liberé,* February 9, 2001; the French Press Agency reported on the court decision against Theil on March 8, 2001.

34. Thierry Meyssan, *L'Effroyable imposture* (Chatou, France: Carnot, 2002), pp. 236–243.

35. On his Web site, Meyssan claims to have sold over two hundred thousand copies. For his own account of the press reaction to his thesis, see www.reseauvoltaire.net/article7709.html.

36. Meyssan was interviewed by Thierry Ardisson on French state television, *Tout le monde en parle,* France 2, March 16, 2002.

37. Guillaume Dasquié and Jean Guisnel, *L'Effroyable mensonge: Thèse et foutaises sur les attentats du 11 septembre* (Paris: Editions La Découverte, 2002); pp. 60–61. These authors and other French journalists pointed out the similarity in style and content between Meyssan's Réseau Voltaire and La Veille Taupe (the Old Mole), a formerly left-wing revolutionary publishing house that promoted the work of well-known Holocaust denier Robert Faurisson. See pp. 107–109.

38. Larouche was giving a live interview to K-TALK radio host Jack Stockwell in Salt Lake City, Utah, as the attacks unfolded in which he made those remarks. See www.larouchepub.com/pr_lar/2001/010911stockwell.html. See also Dasquié and Guisnel, *L'Effroyable mensonge,* pp. 96–99.

39. Meyssan, *L'Effroyable imposture,* p. 50.

40. Alain Finkelkraut interview, *Le Figaro,* April 23, 2002, cited in Dasquié and Guisnel, *L'Effroyable mensonge,* p. 109.

41. Presentation by Thierry Meyssan, "Who Was Behind the September Eleventh Attacks?," Abu Dhabi, April 8, 2002. Meyssan's surrealistic presentation is available at www.reseauvoltaire.net/actu/

ligue-arabe_en.htm and on the Zayed Center Web site at www.zccf.org.ae/LECTURES/E2_lectures/e201.htm.

42. Among the center's guests after Meyssan in 2002 was Jacques Cheminade, editor of the Larouche publication *Executive Intelligence Review* and "a French intellectual known for his pro-Arab and Muslim stances." See www.zccf.org.ae/e_publications.asp?year=2002.

43. Dasquié and Guisnel, *L'Effroyable mensonge,* pp. 95–103.

44. Interview with Victor Wagner, Vienna, July 5, 2002.

45. Jeff Barak, "I Don't Regret My Coalition with Haider," *Jerusalem Post,* November 28, 2000.

46. Interview with Dr. Ariel Muzicant, Vienna, July 5, 2002.

47. Ibid., July 4, 2002.

48. Tina Walzer and Stephan Templ, *Unser Wien: Arisierung auf Österreichisch* (Berlin: Aufbau-Verlag, 2001).

49. Walzer and Templ, *Unser Wien,* p. 143.

50. Ibid., p. 155.

51. "Austrian Rightist Haider Resigns as Party Leader," CNN, February 28, 2000.

52. Magali Perrault, "Trouble on the Island of the Blessed: The Implications of the Austrian Elections," *Central European Review,* October 11, 1999.

53. Interview with Peter Sichrovsky, Vienna, July 4, 2002.

54. See Yossi Klein Halevi and Vince Beiser, "Peter and the Wolves," *Jerusalem Report,* November 28, 1996; "Jewish Author Joins Austrian Far-Right Freedom Party," Jewish Telegraph Agency, November 1, 1996; "Joerg Haider: The Rise of an Austrian Extreme Rightist," Anti-Defamation League, 2001.

55. Paul Vallely, "The Iraq Conflict," *Independent,* April 11, 2003.

56. Interview with Fritz Edlinger, Vienna, July 4, 2002. Edlinger said his Austro-Arab Friendship Society had around five hundred members and raised around $1 million per year for "action" budgets in Iraq and Palestine.

57. Communication with Simon Wiesenthal, Vienna, June 28, 2002.

58. Telephone interview with Hanna Kvanmo, July 19, 2002.

59. Interview with Vebjørn Selbekk, Tomter, Norway, July 21, 2002. Selbekk tells the story of Norway's struggle with anti-Semitism in *Jødehbat på norsk: Fra eidsvollmennene til boot boys* [Hatred of Jews in Norway: From the founding fathers to the "boot boys"] (Norway: Hermon Forlag, 2001). The Boot Boys are neo-Nazi skinheads.

60. The first Norwegian Jew to be arrested was Benjamin Bild, who was picked up on March 1, 1941, on charges of sabotage and deported to Germany, where he died in a concentration camp on July 2, 1941, according to Selbekk's written account (*Jødehbat på norsk,* p. 68).

61. Both the majority and minority reports are available on-line at www.jd/norsk/publ/utredninger/NOU/012005-020017/index-indoo1-b-n-a.html. Most of the Jews who managed to escape were helped by members of the Norwegian Resistance, who organized a dramatic boat lift across the narrow fjord to Sweden. In some cases, they were aided by a young Swedish diplomat, Harald Edelstam, who hid Resistance fighters and Jews from the Gestapo in his official diplomatic residence in Oslo, according to an unpublished biography by his son, Erik Edelstam (communication with the author from Erik Edelstam).

62. *Aftonbladet,* April 21, 2002.

63. Interview with Israeli diplomat, Oslo, July 22, 2002; *Dagbladet,* April 7, 2002.

64. Copies of these and other anti-Semitic cartoons translated from Norwegian by Martin Bodd, Erez Uriely, and Christina Timmerman. Author's collection.

65. Tomm Kristiansen to Martin Bodd, e-mail correspondence dated April 3, 2002, provided to the author by Bodd.

66. Martin Bodd, communication with the author; interview Oslo, July 22, 2002; see also Kåre Hansen, "Det Mosaiske Trossamfund I Oslo er skremt etter skadeverk mot hjemmet til forstander Rolf Kirschner," *Aftenposten,* April 5, 2002.

67. Interview with Jason Rappoport, Oslo, July 23, 2002.

68. Interview with Jan Gregersen, Oslo, July 20, 2002.

69. Interviews with Nils Butenschoen and Kjell Bygstad, July 23, 2002.

70. Selbekk, *Jodehbat på norsk,* p. 137.

71. In 1976, Butenschoen says he and Bygstad split with the original Palestine Committee, which had become Maoist, and set up the Palestine Front, which continued to advocate PLO policies.

72. Selbekk, *Jodehbat på norsk,* pp. 130–131. Butenschoen and Bygstad were both evasive when I asked them about Larsen's involvement in the pro-PLO "solidarity" organizations in the 1970s.

73. Interview with Timor Goksul, Naqoura, Lebanon, February 24, 1992.

74. Yet another former Palestinian Front activist promoted by Brundtland's Labor Party was Jan Egeland, who became a state secretary of foreign affairs under Johan Jorgen Holst. Egeland had been a vice president of Amnesty International and today is president of the Norwegian Red Cross, a group that consistently sings in the pro-Arafat choir.

75. Aburish, *Arafat,* p. 247.

76. Ellis Shuman, "1999: A Lucrative Year for Mr. Larsen and His Wife," *Israel Insider.* Larsen was promoted to the top job at Fafo after his former boss, Gudmund Hernes, became a government minister in 1992.

77. The 1986–1992 grants, based on applications made by Larsen that "contained information that was directly misleading," were revealed in "FAFO Cover-up by Hernes," *Klassekampen,* November 29, 1996. In 1992, the payments were brought to the attention of Larsen's former boss, Gudmund Hernes, who was now the minister of education, research, and church affairs. He took no action.

78. "Roed-Larsen Scrambling for Cover," *Verdens Gang,* November 23, 1996.

79. "Millions Paid on the Side," *Arbeiderbladet,* November 18, 1996.

80. Halvor Tjønn, Ole Nygaard, Mariann Nordstrøm, and Klaus Børringbo, "Rød-Larsen Prize Shocks Norwegian Ministry of Foreign Affairs," *Aftenposten,* April 30, 2002.

81. "Norwegian Ambassador Reprimanded in Israeli Peace Prize Case," Associated Press, May 24, 2002.

82. Gunnar Johnsen and Hilde Harbo, "Juul Can Expect Punishment," *Aftenposten,* April 30, 2002.

83. David Bedein, communication with the author, December 10, 2002. Bedein's original article revealing the payments appeared in the Israeli weekend newspaper *Makor Rishon* on April 26, 2002. See also *Israel Resource Review,* April 29, 2002.

84. Tjønn, Nygaard, et al., "Rød-Larsen Prize Shocks Norwegian Ministry of Foreign Affairs."

85. Examples cited by Tom Gross, "Jeningrad: What the British Media Said," *National Review Online,* May 13, 2002. See www.nationalreview.com/comment/comment-gross051302.asp.

86. Caroline B. Glick, "The Peres Center Scandal," *Jerusalem Post,* April 25, 2002.

87. Shuman, "1999: A Lucrative Year for Mr. Larsen and His Wife."

88. Interview with Kåre Kristiansen, July 21, 2002. Willoch had been serving as Prime Minister from October 14, 1981, until June 6, 1983, in a Conservative Party government, but was forced to form a new government coalition on June 6 that included the Christian Democrats and the Center Party.

89. Doug Mellgren, "Norway's Largest Union Calls for Israel Boycott, While Parliament Members Activate Pro-Israel Group," Associated Press, April 28, 2002. By that point, only 23 of the Storting's 165 members remained.

90. The 1971 resolution called on the AUF to "support the forces which struggle for the national and social liberation of the Palestinian people. The qualification for lasting peace must be that Israel ceases to exist as a Jewish state."

91. "Conviction of Red Cross Nurses," from the Web site "New Sturmer," www.newsturmer.com/Norwegian%20uw2%20History/conviction_of_red_cross_nurses.htm.

92. Hanna Kvanmo, *Dommen* [The verdict] (Norway: Gyldendal Forlag, 1990), ISBN 82-05-19130-1. In the appendix, pp. 157–166, she reproduced the verdict of her trial.

93. Gilles William Goldnadel, *Le nouveau bréviaire de la haine* (Paris: Editions Ramsay, 2001), pp. 63, 111, 12–13.

94. Per Ahlmark, *Vänstern och tyranniet* (Stockholm: Timbro, 1994). The translation is from an English-language summary that was published in 1995 under the title *Tyranny and the Left: Is Democracy for Everybody?*, p. 9. I was in Lebanon at the time Palme made his remark, and the only persecution of Palestinian children in refugee camps was being carried out by Arafat's PLO guerrillas, who used the refugees as human shields to forestall Israeli attacks on PLO military positions. Dozens of Palestinian men were arrested and tortured by the PLO as they attempted to flee Beirut that summer; I met many of them in a secret Fatah detention center, where they told me their stories.

95. Per Ahlmark, "Combating Old/New Anti-Semitism," Speech at Yad Vashem, April 11, 2002, before an international conference, "The Legacy of Holocaust Survivors."

10: THE ISLAMIC REPUBLIC OF AMERICA

1. Laurie Zoloth, "Where Is the Outrage? Pogrom at SFSU," *San Francisco Bay,* May 20, 2002. Her account of the demonstration, and claims by pro-Palestinian demonstrators, is posted on the university Web site, userwww.sfsu.edu/~jewish/profz.html.

2. Ibid.

3. This particular graffiti, not mentioned by ADL, was witnessed by the author.

4. The Anti-Defamation League regularly tracks such incidents. For a more complete listing of campus hate, see www.adl.org/campus/campus_incidents.asp.

5. Daniel Pipes, "Extremists on Campus," *New York Post,* June 25, 2002. www.danielpipes.org/article/424.

6. Sean Gordon, "Montreal Riot Silences Netanyahu," *Ottawa Citizen,* September 10, 2002.

7. Joseph Farah, "Could It Happen Here?," *WorldNetDaily,* August 2, 2002.

8. Martin Kramer, "Ivory Towers on Sand: The Failure of Middle Eastern Studies in America," Washington Institute for Near East Policy, 2001.

9. See "Blaming the Jews," lead editorial, *The Washington Post,* March 12, 2003; and Spencer S. Hsu, "Moran Said Jews Are Pushing War," *The Washington Post,* March 11, 2003.

10. Zev Chafets, "Prof's Slip Is Showing—So's His Anti-Semitism," *New York Daily News,* February 19, 2003.

11. "Jihad: The Fight over Meaning," *Nightline* (ABC News), June 4, 2002.

12. Pat Collins, "Harvard's Islamic Embrace, and Cold Shoulder Towards ROTC," *Washington Times,* June 3, 2002.

13. Ruth Wisse, "How Harvard and MIT Professors Are Planting a Seed of Malevolence," *New York Sun,* May 20, 2002.

14. Lawrence H. Summers, Harvard University Prayer Service, September 17, 2002.

15. David Horowitz, "The Sick Mind of Noam Chomsky," *FrontPage* magazine, September 26, 2001.

16. Ibid.

17. Noam Chomsky, "On the Bombings," in *Lies of Our Times;* cited by Horowitz, "The Sick Mind of Noam Chomsky."

18. Werner Cohn, "The Hidden Alliances of Noam Chomsky," Americans for a Safe Israel, 1988.

19. Noam Chomsky, in *Lies of Our Times,* January 1, 1990.

20. Werner Cohn, "Partners in Hate: Noam Chomsky and the Holocaust Deniers," Preface to the 1994 edition of *The Hidden Alliances of Noam Chomsky, FrontPage* magazine, September 11, 2001.

21. Cohn found only two references linking Chomsky to neo-Nazi groups in *The New York Times* index. "The story is quite different in France, where *Le Monde* and other publications regularly refer to Chomsky's relationship to the French neo-Nazi propagandist Robert Faurisson," he wrote.

22. W. D. Rubinstein, "Chomsky and the Neo-Nazis," *Quadrant* (October 1981): 8–14. The reply by Chomsky and a rebuttal by Rubinstein are published in the April 1982 issue of *Quadrant* (Australia); cited by Cohn, "Partners in Hate."

Notes

23. *The Chomsky Reader,* James Peck, ed. (New York: Pantheon Books, 1987). Pantheon Books and the publisher of this book are both owned by Bertelsmann, a German publishing conglomerate.

24. Brad Whitsel, "The Turner Diaries and Cosmotheism: William Pierce's Theology of Revolution," *Nova Religio* 1, no. 2 (April 1998).

25. Steven Emerson, *American Jihad: The Terrorists Living Among Us* (New York: Free Press, 2002), pp. 18–19.

26. Kenneth R. Timmerman, *Shakedown: Exposing the Real Jesse Jackson* (Washington, D.C.: Regnery, 2002), p. 414.

27. Sheikh Mohammad Hisham Kabbani, "Islamic Extremism: A Viable Threat to U.S. National Security," Presentation at a U.S. State Department forum, Washington, D.C., January 7, 1999. Full text available at islamicsupremecouncil.org/radicalmovements/islamic_extremism.htm.

28. The signatories were American Muslim Political Coordination Council, American Muslim Alliance, American Muslim Council, Council on American Islamic Relations, Muslim Public Affairs Council, Islamic Circle of North America, Islamic Society of North America, and the Muslim Students Association of USA and Canada.

29. Dilshad Fakhroddin, "A Nation Divided: The State of the Muslim Community in America," *The Muslim Magazine,* Vol. 1, no. 4 (October 1998). Muzamil Siddiqi, an Indian-born Wahhabi imam who later became ISNA president, was proud of that funding. In a speech on August 23, 1992, he proudly told the board of the largest mosque in California of the Saudi money he had attracted. "Out of this $4,000 that the Islamic Society of Orange County gives to me, $2,020 are returned because we receive a check from Dar al-Ifta . . . a fatwa organization, a religious organization in Riyadh, Saudi Arabia."

30. Cited in Emerson, *American Jihad,* pp. 1–2. Emerson captured this and other pro-Hamas meetings on videotape. He first presented them to an American public television audience in an hour-long documentary, *Jihad in America,* on November 21, 1994. For his efforts, spokesmen for these groups regularly dismiss Emerson's work by calling him an "anti-Muslim bigot."

31. Ibid., p. 206.

32. Fakhroddin, "A Nation Divided," sidebar ("Pressured—By Whom?").

33. Ibid., p. 80.

34. Ibid., p. 80. The INS agent said his name was Shane Phelan.

35. Ibid, p. 81.

36. Dr. Robert Dickson Crane, "Addressing the Roots of Militant Extremism: The Wahhabi Threat," *The Muslim Magazine,* Vol. 2, no. 2 (spring 1999): 86.

37. Emerson, *American Jihad,* p. 2.

38. Ibid., p. 84.

39. Ziad Abu-Amr, *Islamic Fundamentalism in the West Bank and Gaza* (Bloomington, Ind.: Indiana University Press, 1994), p. 99; cited by Emerson, *American Jihad,* p. 110.

40. Emerson, *American Jihad,* pp. 111–112.

41. Ibid., p. 112.

42. "Attorney John Loftus Launches Lawsuit Exposing U.S. Federal Cover-Up of Saudi Florida Terror Ring," Complaint in the Circuit Court of Hillsborough County (Florida), May 16, 2002: Introduction.

43. Ibid., section 62.

44. Ibid., section 97.

45. Ibid., section 115–117.

46. Bin Laden's name continued to appear as president of the WAMY office in Annandale, Virginia, in official business listings, but all bin Laden family members left the United States shortly after 9/11.

47. "Members of the Palestinian Islamic Jihad Arrested, Charged with Racketeering and Conspiracy to Provide Support to Terrorists," Department of Justice press release, Washington, D.C., February 20, 2003.

48. "The Al-Arian Defense," *The Washington Post,* February 24, 2003.

49. *United States of America* vs. *Sami Amin al-Arian,* U.S. District Court, Middle District of Florida, federal indictment dated February 19, 2003 (unsealed February 20, 2003).

50. Oliver North with William Novak, *Under Fire: An American Story* (New York: HarperCollins, 1991).

51. Loftus complaint, section 119.

52. Interview with Fred Dutton, Washington, D.C., May 15, 2002. See also Timmerman, "Documents Detail Saudi Terror Links."

53. "Ihsan Elashyi Sentenced to 4 Years' Imprisonment," press release, U.S. Attorney for the Northern District of Texas, October 22, 2002.

54. Emerson, *American Jihad,* p. 84.

55. Ibid.

56. Marc Levin, "Records Show Ron Kirk Campaign Employed Anti-Israel Activist," *Houston Review* (Summer 2002), www.houstonreview.com/summer2002/kirkterrorism.html. Emerson, *American Jihad,* p. 133, notes that the Hamas Charter was printed and distributed from IAP's Tucson, Arizona, office.

57. Emerson, *American Jihad,* p. 85.

58. "Dallas Arrests, Suspects Linked to Hamas," Associated Press, December 18, 2002.

59. "Raid on Texas Business Is 'Anti-Muslim Witch Hunt,' say Muslim Leaders," Joint statement by the American Muslim Council, American Muslim Alliance, Council on American Islamic Relations, Islamic Society of North America, Islamic Circle of North America, Islamic Association for Palestine, Muslim Alliance in North America, Muslim Public Affairs Council, and Muslim Student Association of United States and Canada, September 6, 2001, available from www.islamicity.com.

60. Emerson, *American Jihad,* p. 198.

61. Nihad Awad, the PR director at IAP, became executive director of CAIR. Omar Ahmad, the original president of IAP, became CAIR board chairman.

62. Emerson, *American Jihad,* p. 202.

63. Levin, "Records Show Ron Kirk Campaign Employed Anti-Israel Activist."

64. U.S. Attorney General John Ashcroft, Press conference, December 4, 2001.

65. Eight organizations issued a joint statement condemning the administration action. The Council on American Islamic Relations, the American Muslim Council, the American Muslim Alliance, the Islamic Society of North America, the Islamic Circle of North America, the Muslim American Society, the Muslim Public Affairs Council, and the Muslim Student Association of the United States and Canada declared: "We ask that President Bush reconsider what we believe is an unjust and counterproductive move that can only damage America's credibility with Muslims in this country and around the world and could create the impression that there has been a shift from a war on terrorism to an attack on Islam. . . . No relief group anywhere in the world should be asked to question hungry orphans about their parents' religious beliefs, political affiliation, or legal status."

66. Action Memorandum from Dale L. Watson to R. Richard Newcomb, director, Office of Foreign Assets Control, Department of the Treasury, November 5, 2001, "Holy Land Foundation for Relief and Development/International Emergency Economic Powers Act."

67. Fact sheet on shutting down the terrorist financial network, the White House, December 4, 2001, www.whitehouse.gov/news/releases/2001/12/20011204-11.html.

68. John Berlau, "Bush Administration Targets Muslim Charities Aiding Terrorists: Nonprofits Raise Money for Terror Organizations," *Organization Trends* (newsletter of the Capital Research Center, Washington, D.C.), April 2002. Berlau is a reporter for *Insight* magazine.

69. Matthew A. Levitt, "Charitable and Humanitarian Organizations in the Network of International Terrorist Financing," Testimony Before the House Banking Subcommittee on International Trade and Finance, August 1, 2002. Levitt is a former FBI counterterrorism analyst.

70. *United States of America* v. *Benevolence International Foundation, Inc., and Enaam M. Arnaout, a/k/a "Abu Mahmoud," a/k/a "Abdel Samia,"* case no. 02 CR 892, Northern District of Illinois, Eastern Division, federal grand jury indictment, April 2002.

71. Patrick J. Fitzgerald, United States Attorney, "Government's Evidentiary Proffer Supporting the Admissibility of Coconspirator Statements," case no. 02 CR 892, filed under seal, February 2003, also known as the "Santiago proffer."

72. "The Islamic Fundamentalist/Extremist Movements in the Philippines and Their Links with International Terrorist Organizations," by Rodolfo Jazmines Garcia, police senior superintendent, National HQ Philippine National Police Intelligence Command, Special Investigation Group, Camp Crame, Quezon City, 1994.

73. "Affidavit of Robert Walker, in Support of Complaint Against Benevolence International Foundation, Inc., April 29, 2002, case no. 02 CR 414 (separate complaint on charges of perjury).

74. Search Warrant in Case Number 02-MG-114, presented before the United States District Court, Eastern District of Virginia, March 13, 2002. See also Judith Miller, "The Money Trail: Raids Seek Evidence of Money-Laundering," *The New York Times,* March 21, 2002.

75. Prosecution statement during the trial of the East Africa embassy bombers. See Miller, "The Money Trail."

76. Michael Isikoff and Mark Hosenball, "A Troubling Money Trail," *Newsweek* (Periscope), March 25, 2002.

77. Christopher H. Schmitt, Joshua Kurlantzick, and Philip Smucker, "When Charity Goes Awry," *U.S. News & World Report,* October 29, 2001; J. Michael Waller, " 'Wahhabi Lobby' Takes the Offensive," *Insight* magazine, July 29, 2002. For more on the raids, see Miller, "The Money Trail."

78. Schwartz, *The Two Faces of Islam,* p. 249.

79. Mark Hosenball, "Terror's Cash Flow," *Newsweek,* March 25, 2002.

80. For Arthur Hannah, see "Belated Accusations Against Al-Taqwa," *Intelligence Newsletter* no. 417, November 15–28, 2001.

81. Testimony of Juan C. Zarate, Deputy Assistant Secretary, Terrorism and Violent Crime, U.S. Department of the Treasury, House Financial Subcommittee Oversight and Investigations, February 12, 2002, p. 10.

82. The federal search warrant sought documents on a constellation of entities collectively referred to as "the Safa Group": African Muslim Agency, Aradi, Inc., FIQH Council, Grove Corporate, Inc., Graduate School of Islamic Social Sciences (formerly SISS), Heritage Education Trust, Humana Charitable Trust, International Institute of Islamic Thought, Mar-Jac Holdings, Inc., Mar-Jac Investments, Inc., Mar-Jac Poultry, Inc., Mena Corporation, Reston Investments, Inc., SAAR Foundation, SAAR International, Safa Trust, Sterling Charitable Gift Fund, Sterling Management Group, Inc., York Foundation, York International. Many of them were based at 555 Grove Street and headed by Jamal Barzinji.

83. Isikoff and Hosenball, "A Troubling Money Trail."

84. "News of Political Apocalypse Might Be Far-Fetched," reply by J. Michael Waller to Islamic Institute executive director Khaled Saffuri, *Insight* magazine, October 15–28, 2002.

85. Interview with Khaled Saffuri, February 20, 2003.

86. Schwartz, *The Two Faces of Islam,* p. 248.

87. Isikoff and Hosenball, "A Troubling Money Trail."

88. Doha Qatar Television Service in Arabic, official television station of the state of Qatar, on November 1, 2002, at 0849 GMT carries a fifty-five-minute live broadcast from Um Umar bin al-Khattab Mosque in Doha of Sheikh Yusuf al-Qaradawi (FBIS-U.S. government translation).

89. Kenneth R. Timmerman, "Al Gore's Arab Money Man," *American Spectator* (November 1997).

90. Franklin Foer, "Fevered Pitch, Grover Norquist's Strategic Alliance with Radical Islam," *The New Republic,* November 12, 2001.

91. " 'Big Dude' Gets Profiled," *Newsweek,* July 16, 2001, p. 24; Mike Allen and Richard Leiby, "Alleged Terrorist Met with Bush Advisor," *The Washington Post,* February 22, 2003, p. A10.

92. CAIR said it polled its members after the election and found that 72 percent had voted for Bush. However, CAIR has never released membership information or claimed to be a mass movement, but rather an association of a certain Muslim American elite.

93. For reasons that have never been explained, $1,000 contributions to the Bush for President campaign by al-Amoudi and al-Kebsi were refunded to them before the 2000 election.

94. The first quote is from Shawn Zeller, "Tough Sell," *National Journal,* December 14, 2002. The second comes from Eric Boehlert, "Betrayed by Bush," Salon.com, April 3, 2002.

95. Zeller, "Tough Sell."

96. Waller, " 'Wahhabi Lobby' Takes the Offensive."

97. Among the member organizations were the Ad Hoc Committee for Imad Hamad (Popular Front for the Liberation of Palestine), the Committee for Justice for Nasser Ahmed (al-Qaeda and Egyptian Jihad), a whole host of groups affiliated with the Provisional Irish Republican Army, the National Islamic Prison Foundation (Hamas, Hezbollah), Basque Congress for Peace (Basque Fatherland and Liberty-ETA), and many others.

98. "Dr. Mazen Al-Najjar to Be Released and Leave the Country," Tampa Bay Coalition for Justice and Peace, August 18, 2002.

99. J. Michael Waller, "Bush Challenges Terrorist Fronts," *Insight* magazine, May 20, 2002. After severe criticism, within ten days of 9/11 the groups pulled Web pages instructing members not to cooperate with the FBI and replaced them with press releases urging American Muslims to "volunteer" for paid positions as Arabic-language translators.

100. J. Michael Waller, "Supporters of Hamas and Hezbollah File Suit Against Bush," *Insight* magazine, July 27, 2002.

101. Schwartz, *The Two Faces of Islam,* p. 228.

102. David Keene, "Muslim Extremists Seeking to Foster One Islamic World," *The Hill,* February 20, 2003.

103. Michael Isatopf, "9/11 Hijackers: A Saudi Money Trail?" *Newsweek* Web exclusive, November 22, 2002.

104. Emerson, *American Jihad,* p. 205.

105. Five years later, when these comments were being widely quoted by prominent columnists, CAIR issued a press release claiming that Mr. Ahmad had been misquoted and that they were seeking a retraction from the California newspaper that originally carried his remarks. ("Readers of right-wing Web site threaten Muslims," April 29, 2003). CAIR claimed that "the alleged statement about the Koran by CAIR's board chairman was not in fact a quote." But the reporter stands by her story. As the story originally appeared, Mr. Ahmad was quoted directly as he spoke before a "packed crowd" of local Muslims. "If you choose to live here . . . you have a responsibility to deliver the message of Islam. Islam isn't in America to be equal to any other faith, but to become dominant. The Koran, the Muslim book of scripture, should be the highest authority in America, and Islam the only accepted religion on Earth." Lisa Gardiner, "American Muslim Leader Urges Faithful to Spread Word," *San Ramon Valley Herald,* July 4, 1998. The newspaper told a reporter from *WorldNetDaily* in May 2003 that CAIR had never approached them for a retraction. Ms. Gardiner is now a legislative aide for California Democratic Assemblyman John Dutra, and she told *WorldNetDaily* that the statements attributed to Mr. Ahmad were indeed accurate. See Art Moore, "Should Muslim Quran be USA's Top Authority?," *WorldNetDaily,* May 1, 2003.

106. Schwartz, *The Two Faces of Islam,* p. 237.

107. Ibid., p. 235.

108. Daniel Pipes, "CAIR: 'Moderate' Friends of Terror," *New York Post,* April 22, 2002.

109. Waller, " 'Wahhabi Lobby' Takes the Offensive."

110. The National Support Committee for Imam Jamil, www.thejusticefund.org. In support of H. Rap Brown, the group cited the Koran: "And they ill-treated them for no other reason than that they believed in Allah, Exalted in Power, Worthy of all Praise!" (85:8)

111. Transcript, "Making Sense with Alan Keyes," Fox News, June 18, 2002. Vickers resigned unexpectedly in February 2003.

112. Berlau, "Bush Administration Targets Muslim Charities Aiding Terrorists."

113. Khalid Duran, "How CAIR Put My Life in Peril," *Middle East Quarterly,* Winter 2002.

11: ISLAM ON THE MARCH: ON THE TRAIL OF OSAMA BIN LADEN

1. The fatwa was published in *Al-Quds al-Arabi* in London on February 23, 1998, and was translated by the CIA and circulated on Capitol Hill.

2. Later, when it came time for Osama to marry off one of his sons, just months before 9/11, several brothers and sisters made the arduous trip from Saudi Arabia to Kandahar, Afghanistan, to attend the ceremony.

3. Interview with Abdelbari Atwan, London, February 25, 1998.

4. Yigal Carmon, communication with the author, December 23, 2002.

5. Kenneth R. Timmerman, "Iraq Was Involved in Oklahoma City," *Insight* magazine, May 13, 2002, and "What They Knew, When They Knew It," *Insight* magazine, June 17, 2002.

6. Omar Bakri Mohammad, *Essential Fiqh* (London: Islamic Book Company, undated), p. 33.

7. Paul Harris, Burhan Wazir, and Kate Connolly, "Al-Qaeda's Bombers Used Britain to Plot Slaughter," *The Observer*, April 21, 2002.

8. "Moussaoui Making Use of Court-Appointed Defense Lawyers He Despises," CourtTV, August 23, 2002, www.courttv.com/trials/moussaoui/082302_ap.html.

9. The handwritten document is available at www.courttv.com/trials/moussaoui/docs/12302.html.

10. Al-Faysal was convicted on three counts of soliciting murder and three charges of racial incitement on February 24, 2003, crimes that carried a maximum penalty in Britain of life imprisonment. ("British Cleric Convicted of Soliciting Murder in Sermons," Fox News, February 24, 2003.)

11. Atatürk's September 22, 1924, speech was given at the the the Independence Trade School. The Turkish Ministry of Culture offers an excellent chronology of key events, see www.kultur.gov.tr/portal/tarih_en.asp?belgeno=5314.

12. Yehudit Barsky interview, June 12, 2002.

13. Amir Taheri, "Anti-West," *American Foreign Policy Interests* 24, no. 2, (April 2002): 111.

14. United States vs. Reid, January 30, 2003, sentencing hearing.

15. British police raided the Finsbury Park mosque on January 20, 2003, as part of an investigation involving an al-Qaeda cell in Britain found to be in possession of ricin, a deadly toxin made in military quantities by Iraq. A few days later, the Charity Commission, which oversees religious organizations, barred Abu Hamza from preaching and boarded up the mosque. On February 25, 2003, the British government announced it was tightening a law that would allow the Home Office to strip naturalized citizens, such as Abu Hamza, of British citizenship and deport them if they were wanted for sedition or on terrorism charges. MP Andrew Dismore told Parliament that Hamza was "spreading his message of hate against Jews, Hindus, the U.S. and the U.K." and had "seditiously abused the sanctity of the Finsbury Park mosque." Abu Hamza is wanted on terrorism charges in Yemen. See Bob Roberts, "Abu Hamza 'Will Be Deported in 6 Weeks,'" *Daily Mirror*, February 25, 2003.

16. James Q. Wilson, "The Reform Islam Needs," *The Wall Street Journal*, November 13, 2002.

17. See Kenneth R. Timmerman, "Top Egyptian Cleric Justifies Suicide Terrorism," *Insight* magazine, November 13, 2002.

18. Mordechai Arbell, "The Sefardim of the Island of Nevis," www.sefarad.org/publication/lm/035/15.html.

19. Samuel Kurinsky, "The Jews of St. Eustatius, Rescuers of the American Revolution," available via www.hebrewhistory.org.

20. John Hagee, "Exodus II," *JH Ministries* (Summer 2002): 22. The great seal of the United States was designed by three groups of consultants working in 1776, 1780, and 1782. The final design, set in 1782, configured the constellation of thirteen stars into the shape of a hexagram (Star of David). As Charles Thomson, secretary of the Continental Congress and the consultant who came up with the final design described it, "The Constellation denotes a new State taking its place and rank among other sovereign powers." For more, see www.greatseal.com; see also *The Great Seal of the United States,* U.S. Department of State, Bureau of Public Affairs, September 1996.

APPENDIX A: FRIDAY SERMON ON PALESTINIAN AUTHORITY TV

1. Sheikh Ibrahim Madhi is a Palestinian Authority employee.
2. Palestine Television (Palestinian Authority), April 12, 2002.

ACKNOWLEDGMENTS

The author wishes to give special thanks to David Steinmann and Joyce Press, for their tireless combing of on-line resources; to Shoshana and Steve Bryen, for constant inspiration and intellectual rigor; to Rabbi Abraham Cooper and Marvin Hier of the Simon Wiesenthal Center in Los Angeles, who first gave me the idea; and to Simon Wiesenthal, for his constant example.

In my travels I was helped by many people who gave me their time, offered their hospitality, and shared their memories and wisdom. Many friends in Gaza, the West Bank, Arab East Jerusalem, Cairo, Amman, Riyadh, Islamabad, and Peshawar I cannot name without putting them at risk; thank you again.

Those I can single out include Erez Uriely, Rachal Suissa, Jan Gregorsen, Kåre Kristiansen, Martin Bodd, Vebjørn Selbekk, and the late Leif Rossaak in Norway; Dov Weinstock (Dubak), Yigal Carmon, David and Sarah Bedein, Itamar Marcus, Yoram Ettinger, Michael Widlanski, Shalom Harari, Uzi Landau, Dr. Reuven Ehrlich, and Uri Lubrani in Israel; Hassan and Nelly Aghilipour, René Roudaut, General Michel Darmon, Thierry Keller, and Shimon Samuels in France; Dr. Hala Moustapha, David Welch, and Saad Eddin Ibrahim in Cairo; Georg Haber and Leon Zelman in Vienna; Per Ahlmark in Stockholm; John Fraser, Hedieh Mirahmadi, Ali al-Ahmad, J. Michael Waller, Steve Emerson, and Thor Ronay in Washington, D.C.

To Paul Rodriguez and Scott Stanley, my editors at *Insight* magazine, I owe a special debt of gratitude for their support during the months I spent overseas researching and writing this book. Portions of this book initially appeared, in somewhat different form, in the pages of *Insight*.

My publisher, Steve Ross, at Crown Publishing deserves tremendous credit for bucking the political currents. A special thanks to my agent, Suzanne Gluck of the William Morris Agency, who had the genius to hook us up, and to my inimitable editor, Doug Pepper, who got me back on track whenever I meandered too far down the byways of Middle East politics and culture. Erik and Anne Edelstam, gracious hosts and soul mates, reintroduced us to the south of France and were kind enough to allow us to use their home as our base so my family could be closer to me as I traveled, troubled, and wrote. Thank you again.

My wife, Christina, grew up in Sweden with a Holocaust survivor and knew this story long before I began to work on it. Our five children—Niclas, Julian, Clio, Diana, and Simon—inadvertently learned many things I wish they did not need to know.

Kensington, Maryland
Hjortsberg Gård, Sweden
Ste. Maxime, France

INDEX